ANIMAL MAN

Grant Morrison—writer
Chas Truog—penciller
(chapters 1–8)
Tom Grummett—penciller
(chapter 9)

Doug Hazlewood—inker
John Costanza—letterer
Tatjana Wood—colorist
Brian Bolland—covers

DC COMICS INC.

ANIMAL MAN
Published by DC Comics Inc. Copyright © 1991. All rights reserved.
Originally published in single magazine form by DC Comics Inc. as ANIMAL MAN #1-9.
Copyright © 1988, 1989 DC Comics Inc. All rights reserved.

All characters, their distinctive likenesses and related indicia featured in this
publication are trademarks of DC Comics Inc.

The stories, characters, and incidents featured in this publication are entirely
fictional.

Cover illustration by Brian Bolland

Publication design by Robbin Brosterman

Back cover quote by Mikal Gilmore from ROLLING STONE, #578, May 17, 1990.
By Straight Arrow Publishers, Inc. 1990
All Rights Reserved. Reprinted by Permission.

Back cover photograph courtesy of, and copyrighted © 1981 by, PCTA, People For The
Ethical Treatment Of Animals, P.O. Box 42516, Washington, DC 20015-0516

Special thanks to Leesuh Allen

DC Comics Inc., 1325 Avenue of the Americas, New York, NY 10019

A Warner Bros. Inc. Company
Printed in Canada. First Printing.

INTRO

Believe me, there are few things more
embarrassing than having to write the introduction to one's own book. Not for me
the dubious pleasure of an endorsement from
Stephen King or Clive Barker. Not for me the
glowing praise of my peers as they lie through
gritted teeth and wait for the check to arrive
by Federal Express. Not for me the detailed
analyses of technique, the backslapping bon-
homie, the hushed reverential tones. Instead,
I'm forced to take the stand and conduct my
own defense.

So what do I say?

'ANIMAL MAN was a fundamental milestone in the ongoing
development of graphic narrative and I consider myself
lucky, nay, privileged, nay, *blessed* to have known
Grant Morrison at this pivotal moment in his glittering
career...'

All too true, but comics readers value modesty and humil-
ity above all, so perhaps I'd do better to stick with world-
weary, self-deprecating cynicism.

'ANIMAL MAN? No big deal. It paid the rent, I suppose.'

Hmm, I could have a point there, but it still doesn't tell
the full story.

Better just to stick to the 'facts':

In 1987, at the height of the critical acclaim for
Alan Moore's work on SWAMP THING and WATCHMEN, DC Comics
dispatched a band of troubleshooters on what is quaintly
termed a 'headhunting mission' to the United Kingdom. The
brief was to turn up the stones and see if there weren't any
more cranky Brit authors who might be able to work wonders
with some of the dusty old characters languishing in DC's
back catalogue. As one of those who received the call that
year, I had no idea who I might dig up and revamp. On the
Glasgow to London train, however, my feverishly overstressed
brain at last lighted upon Animal Man. This minor character
from the pages of STRANGE ADVENTURES in the '60s had always,
for heaven only knows what murky reasons, fascinated me
and, as the train chugged through a picturesque landscape of
Tudor houses and smiling bobbies on bicycles, I began to put
together a scenario involving an out-of-work, married-with-

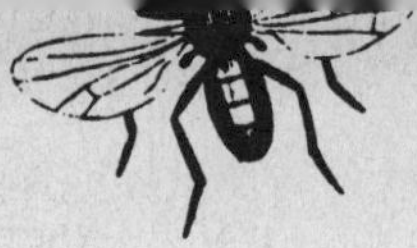
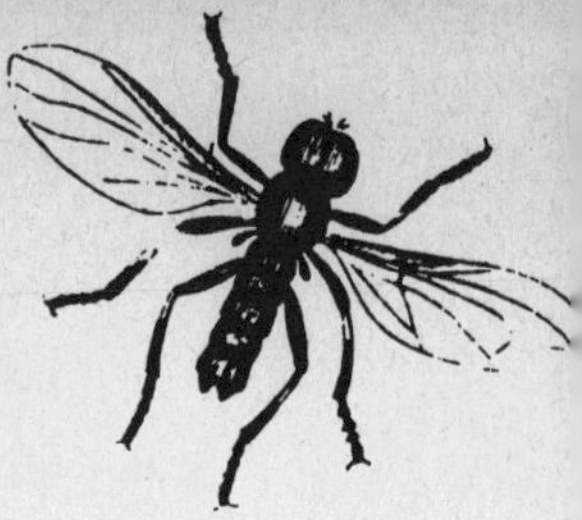

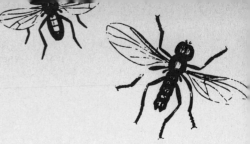

children, third-rate super-hero who becomes involved with animal rights issues and finds his true vocation in life.

Initially, ANIMAL MAN was conceived as a four-issue mini-series. My intention was to radicalize and realign the character of Buddy Baker and then leave him for someone else to pick up and develop. As it transpired, however, I was asked to continue the series into a regular monthly comic book and I suddenly found myself lost for ideas. Having no desire to produce yet another grittily realistic exploration of what it is to be superhuman and/or an urban vigilante with emotional problems, I cast desperately around for a new direction. What I finally came up with was *'The Coyote Gospel,'* which became the template for the further development of the entire series and which remains one of my own personal favorite stories. Hilariously enough, during the writing of *'The Coyote Gospel'* I was utterly convinced that what I was writing was absolute unreadable gibberish and that it would hammer the final nail into the coffin of my fledgling career as a writer of American super-hero comics. The success and popularity of the story took me entirely by surprise and encouraged me to go on to produce the entirely unreadable gibberish which has since become my stock-in-trade. At the same time, *'The Coyote Gospel'* initiated a plotline which was ultimately resolved in ANIMAL MAN #26, my final issue as writer. Hints as to the nature of this plotline were introduced as early as issue #8 and new readers should therefore not be too baffled by the appearance of a mysterious computer screen, a mysterious figure in the bushes, and an equally mysterious Native American physicist. These are simply teasing subplot elements and should not be allowed to affect your enjoyment, or otherwise, of the main story.

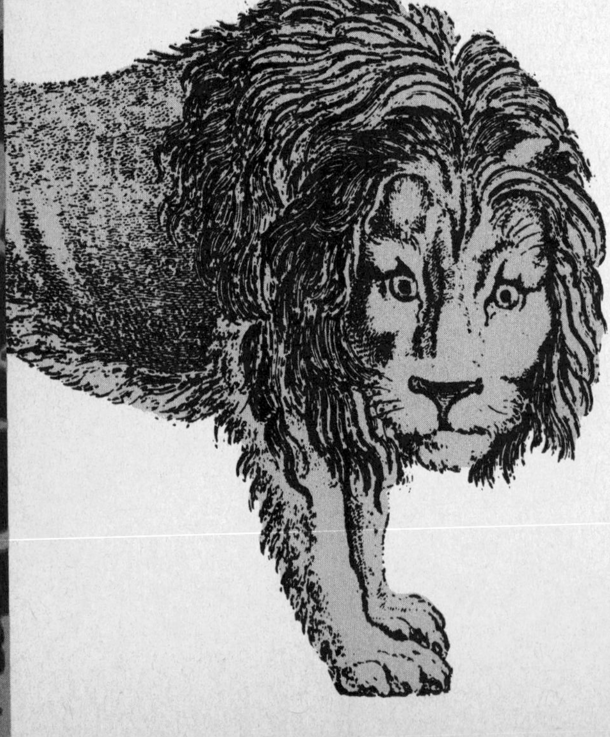

New readers may also find themselves mildly baffled by portentous references to an 'Invasion' in the stories *'Birds of Prey'* and *'The Death of the Red Mask.'* INVASION was, in fact, the name of a DC cross-

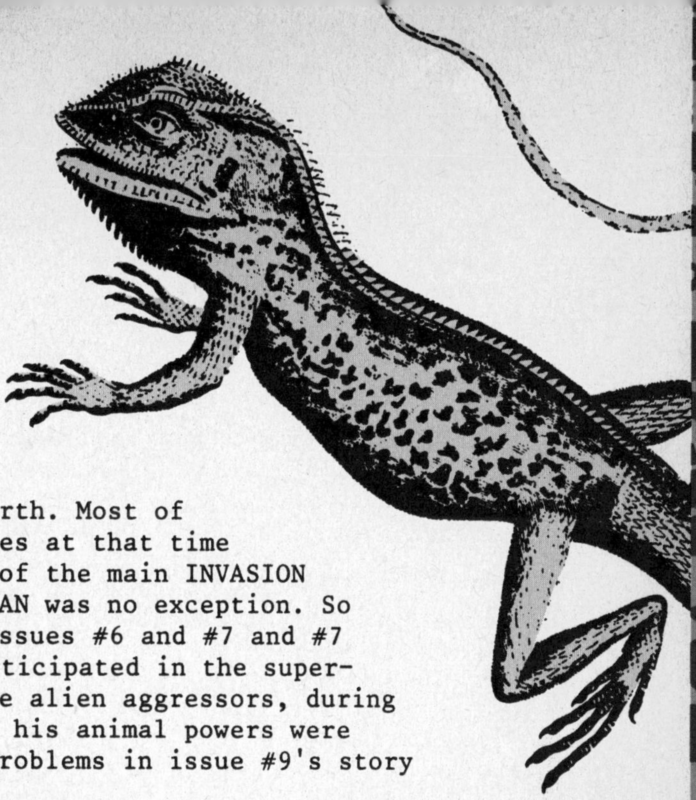

over series, in which a gang of unpleasant characters from outer space launched an entirely unprovoked assault on our own dear planet Earth. Most of the DC super-hero titles at that time were woven in and out of the main INVASION storyline and ANIMAL MAN was no exception. So it was that, between issues #6 and #7 and #7 and #8, Animal Man participated in the super-heroes' war against the alien aggressors, during which brief excitement his animal powers were scrambled, hence his problems in issue #9's story *'Home Improvements.'*

Confused? I know I am.

Now that I'm able to look back at ANIMAL MAN through the deluded soft focus of rose-colored spectacles, I see quite a lot that I actually like. I like the fact that most of the stories here are self-contained in twenty-four pages. I like the opportunity I was given to introduce a foul-mouthed Glaswegian version of DC's Mirror Master character and I like the at-home antics of the Baker family.

For me, the other important aspect of working on ANIMAL MAN was that not only did the comic provide a platform for my cranky and increasingly misanthropic views on the animal rights issue, it also encouraged me to put my money where my mouth was. So it was that shortly after beginning my work on ANIMAL MAN, I joined the Animal Liberation Front Supporters Group and I ate my last ever steak. Since then I've survived exclusively on water, grass, peanuts, and the kindness of strangers. It now seems to me that the subject of animal rights is probably too vast and complicated to be dealt with adequately in the pages of a super-hero comic book, but if ANIMAL MAN helped alert some readers to the pointless atrocities that are committed daily in the name of research, then it will have been worthwhile.

Which brings me to the bottom of the page. How *do* I write my own introduction without sounding either too smug and self-congratulatory or too fawningly humble?

'ANIMAL MAN was a comic written by Grant Morrison and drawn by Chas Truog and Doug Hazlewood and Tom Grummett, too. It had brilliant covers by Brian Bolland, was edited by Karen Berger and Art Young, colored by Tatjana Wood, and lettered by John Costanza. Some people liked it, some people didn't.'

Possibly.

Why not read on and judge for yourself?

—Grant Morrison

CHAPTER
ONE

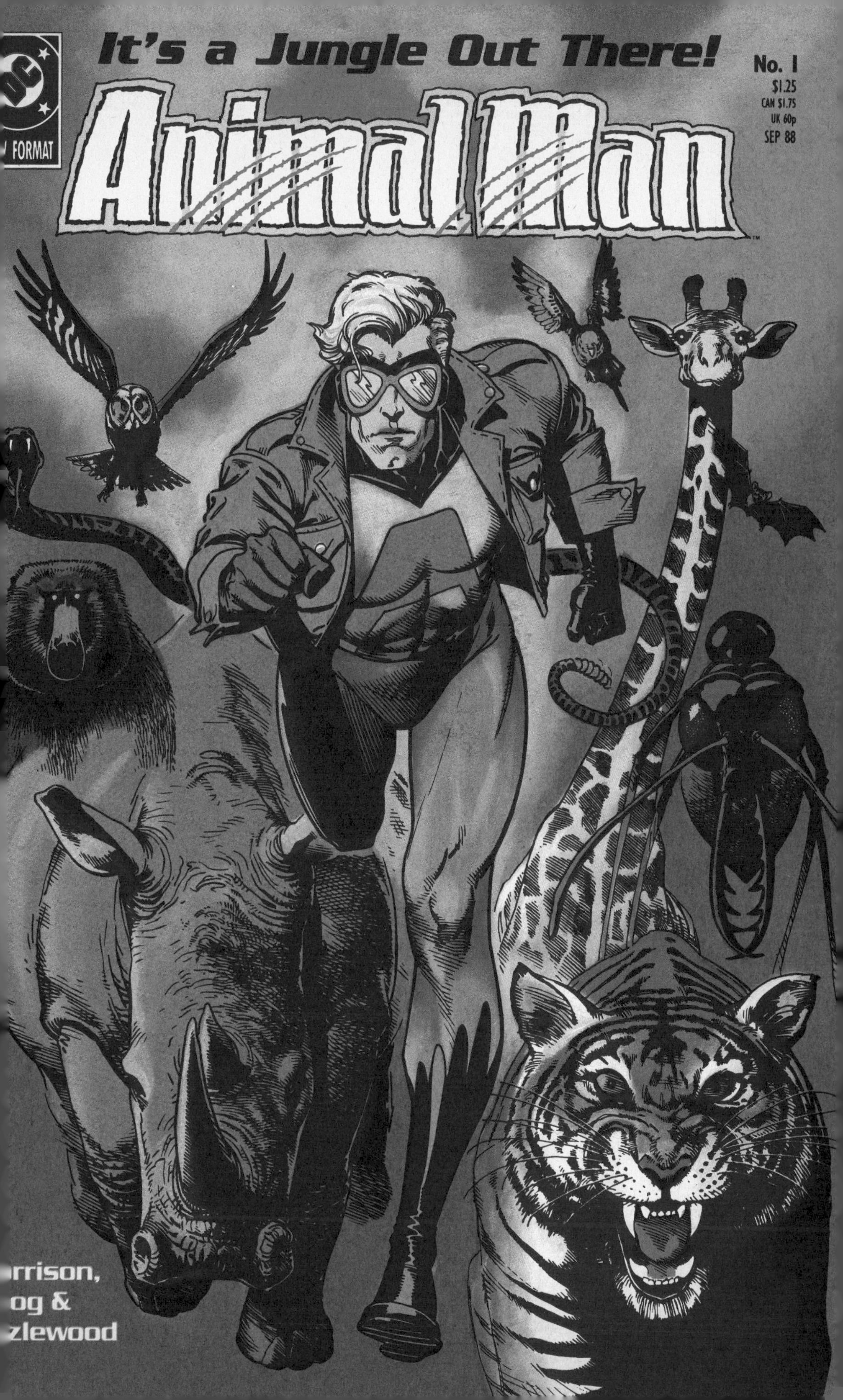
It's a Jungle Out There!
No. 1
$1.25
CAN $1.75
UK 60p
SEP 88
Animal Man
FORMAT
rrison,
og &
zlewood

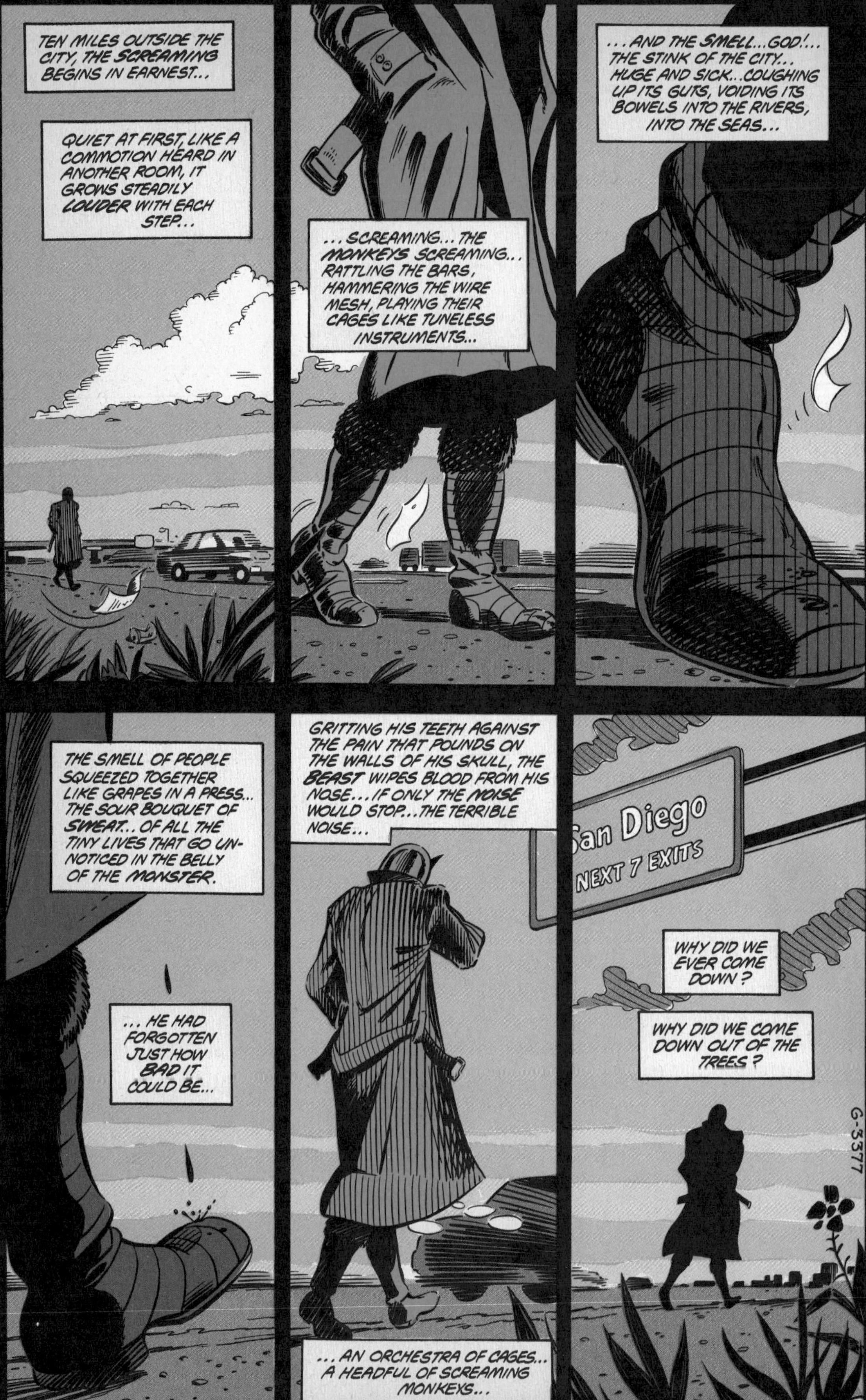

TEN MILES OUTSIDE THE CITY, THE SCREAMING BEGINS IN EARNEST...
QUIET AT FIRST, LIKE A COMMOTION HEARD IN ANOTHER ROOM, IT GROWS STEADILY LOUDER WITH EACH STEP...
...SCREAMING... THE MONKEYS SCREAMING... RATTLING THE BARS, HAMMERING THE WIRE MESH, PLAYING THEIR CAGES LIKE TUNELESS INSTRUMENTS...
...AND THE SMELL...GOD!... THE STINK OF THE CITY... HUGE AND SICK...COUGHING UP ITS GUTS, VOIDING ITS BOWELS INTO THE RIVERS, INTO THE SEAS...
THE SMELL OF PEOPLE SQUEEZED TOGETHER LIKE GRAPES IN A PRESS... THE SOUR BOUQUET OF SWEAT... OF ALL THE TINY LIVES THAT GO UN-NOTICED IN THE BELLY OF THE MONSTER.
...HE HAD FORGOTTEN JUST HOW BAD IT COULD BE...
GRITTING HIS TEETH AGAINST THE PAIN THAT POUNDS ON THE WALLS OF HIS SKULL, THE BEAST WIPES BLOOD FROM HIS NOSE... IF ONLY THE NOISE WOULD STOP...THE TERRIBLE NOISE...
...AN ORCHESTRA OF CAGES... A HEADFUL OF SCREAMING MONKEYS...
San Diego
NEXT 7 EXITS
WHY DID WE EVER COME DOWN?
WHY DID WE COME DOWN OUT OF THE TREES?
G-3377

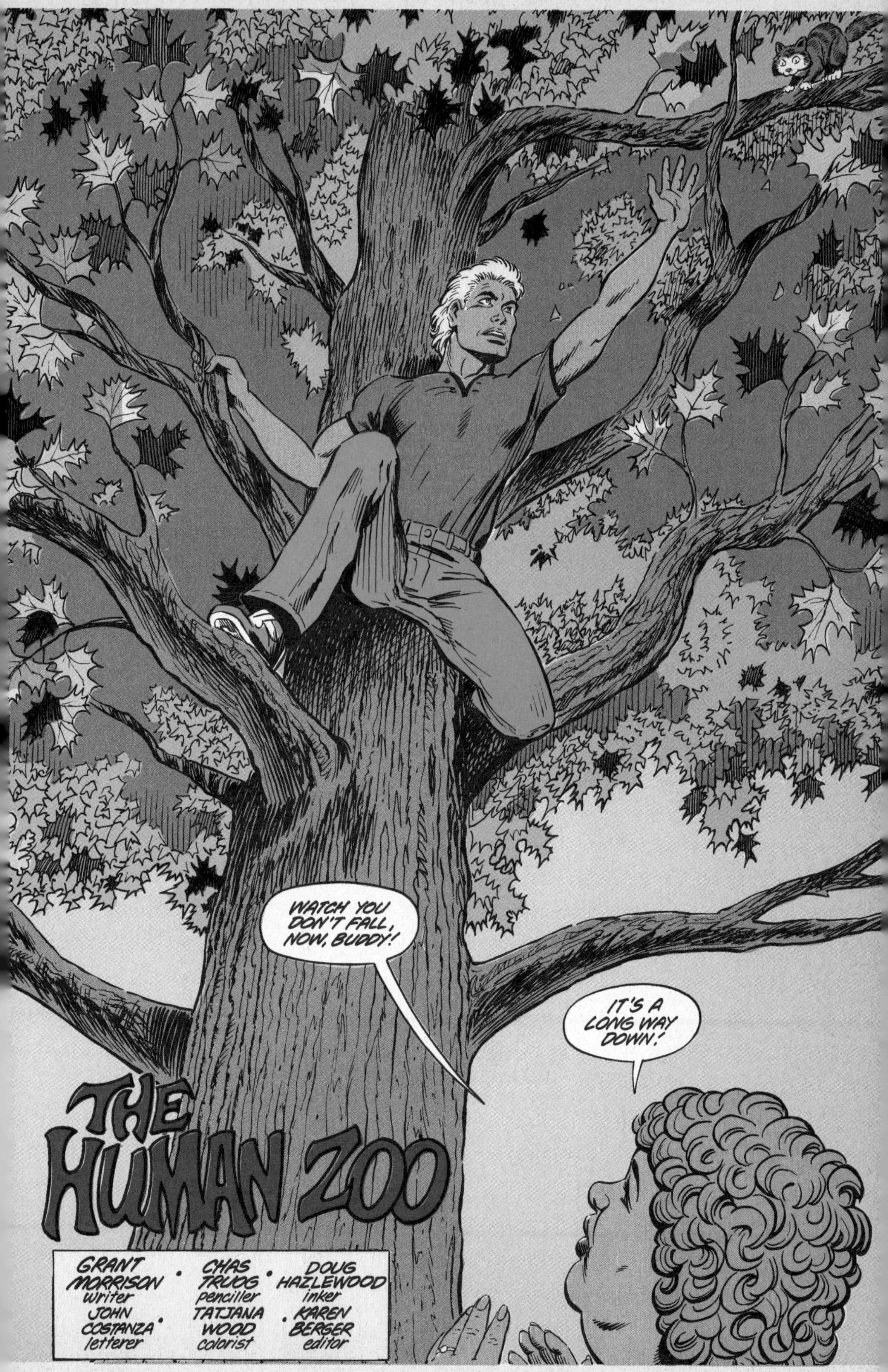
WATCH YOU DON'T FALL, NOW, BUDDY!
IT'S A LONG WAY DOWN!
THE HUMAN ZOO
GRANT MORRISON writer • CHAS TRUOG penciller • DOUG HAZLEWOOD inker
JOHN COSTANZA letterer • TATJANA WOOD colorist • KAREN BERGER editor

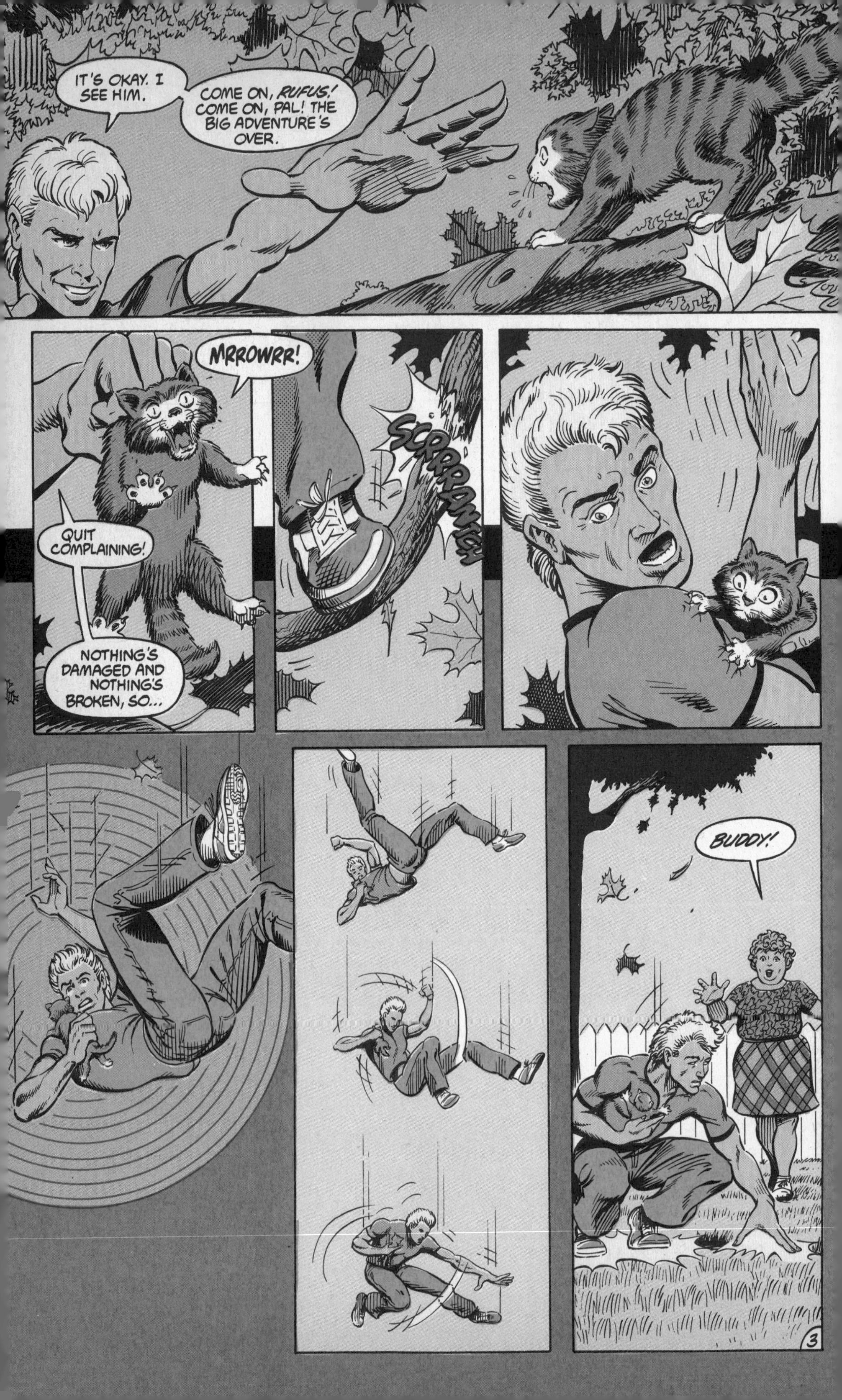
IT'S OKAY. I SEE HIM.
COME ON, RUFUS! COME ON, PAL! THE BIG ADVENTURE'S OVER.
MRROWRR!
QUIT COMPLAINING!
NOTHING'S DAMAGED AND NOTHING'S BROKEN, SO...
SCRRRANTCH
BUDDY!

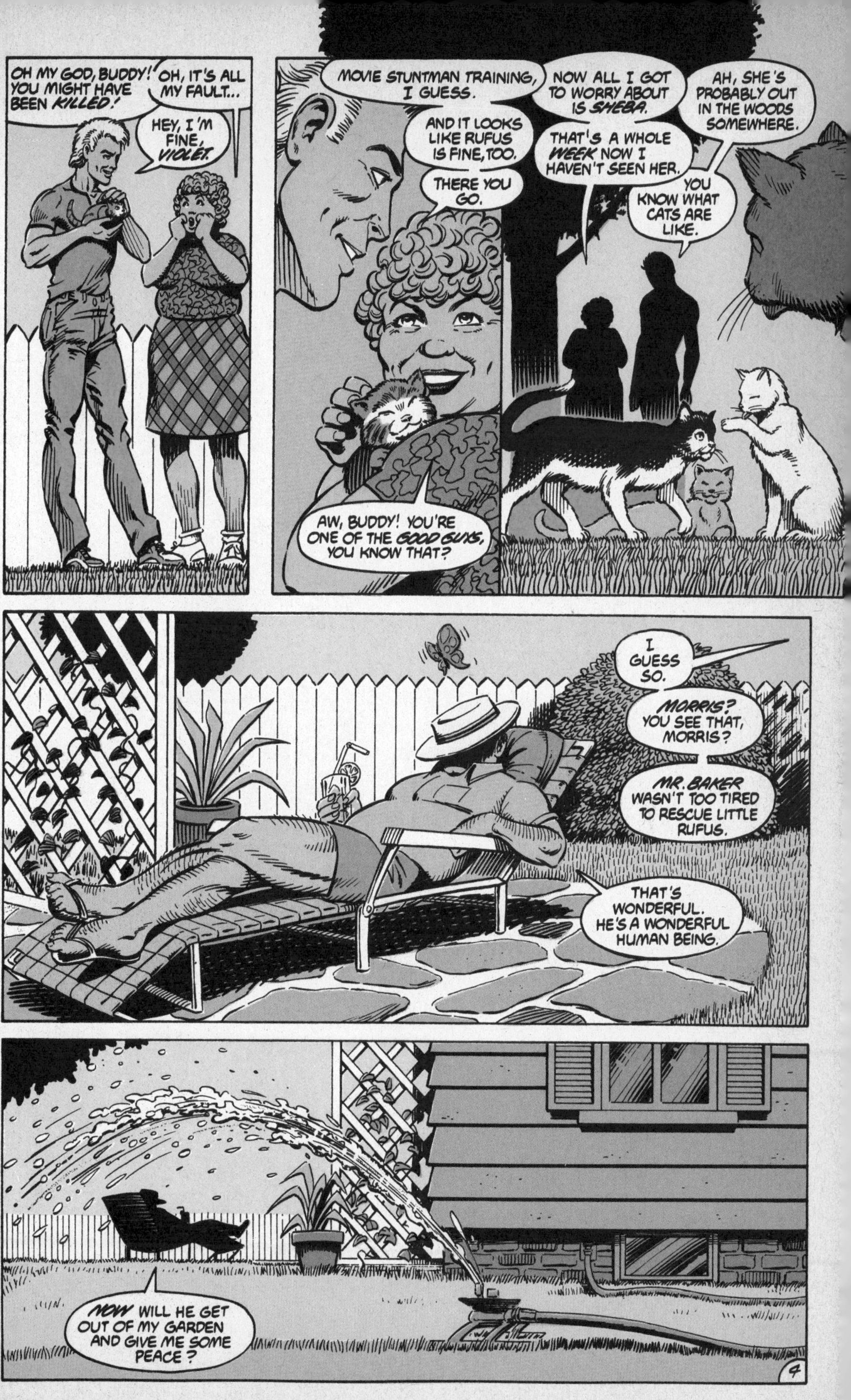
OH MY GOD, BUDDY! YOU MIGHT HAVE BEEN KILLED!
OH, IT'S ALL MY FAULT...
HEY, I'M FINE, VIOLET.
MOVIE STUNTMAN TRAINING, I GUESS.
AND IT LOOKS LIKE RUFUS IS FINE, TOO.
THERE YOU GO.
AW, BUDDY! YOU'RE ONE OF THE GOOD GUYS, YOU KNOW THAT?
NOW ALL I GOT TO WORRY ABOUT IS SHEBA.
THAT'S A WHOLE WEEK NOW I HAVEN'T SEEN HER.
AH, SHE'S PROBABLY OUT IN THE WOODS SOMEWHERE.
YOU KNOW WHAT CATS ARE LIKE.
I GUESS SO.
MORRIS? YOU SEE THAT, MORRIS?
MR. BAKER WASN'T TOO TIRED TO RESCUE LITTLE RUFUS.
THAT'S WONDERFUL. HE'S A WONDERFUL HUMAN BEING.
NOW WILL HE GET OUT OF MY GARDEN AND GIVE ME SOME PEACE?

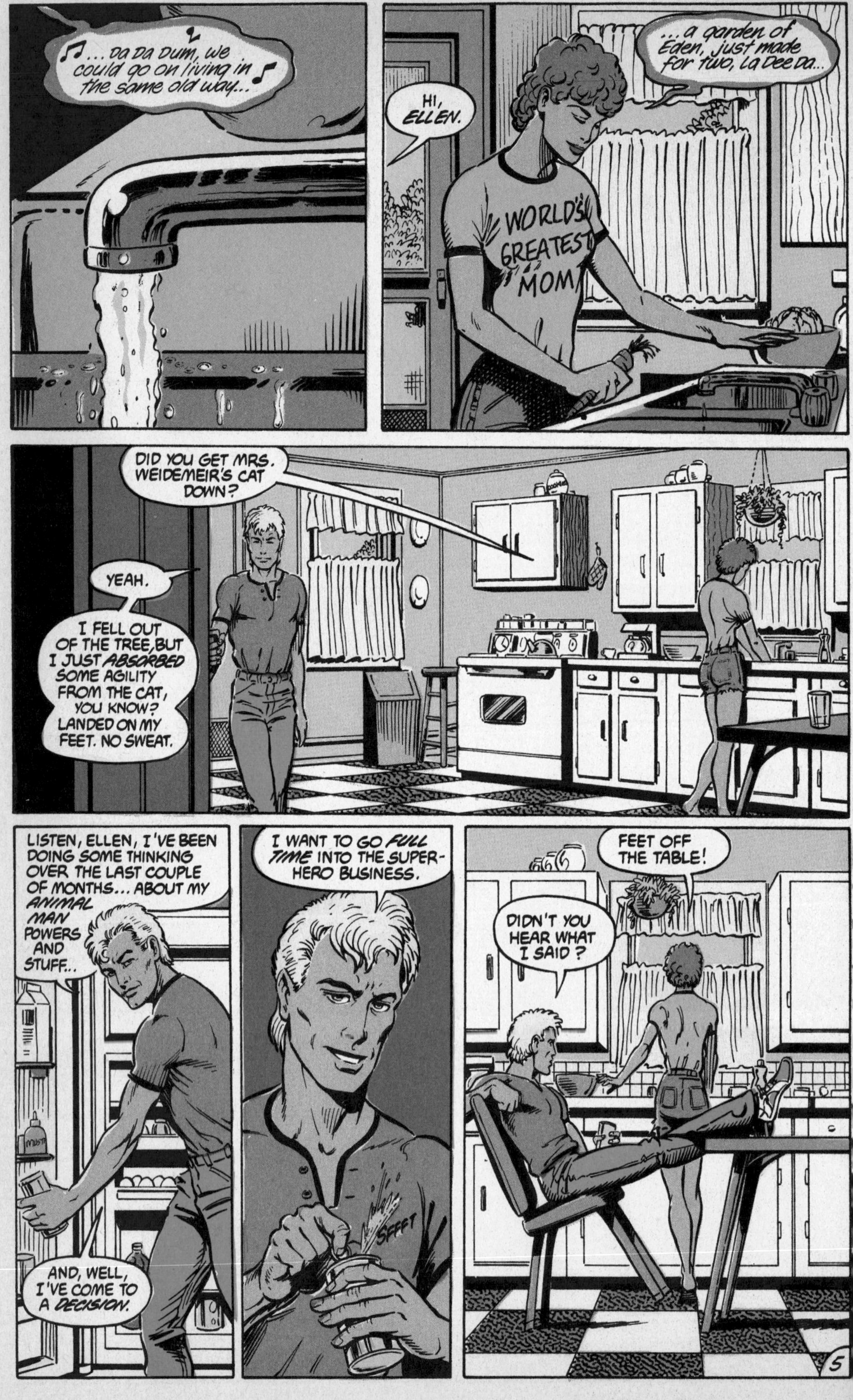

... Da Da Dum, we could go on living in the same old way...
Hi, Ellen.
... a garden of Eden, just made for two, La Dee Da...
WORLD'S GREATEST MOM
DID YOU GET MRS. WEIDEMEIR'S CAT DOWN?
YEAH.
I FELL OUT OF THE TREE, BUT I JUST ABSORBED SOME AGILITY FROM THE CAT, YOU KNOW? LANDED ON MY FEET. NO SWEAT.
LISTEN, ELLEN, I'VE BEEN DOING SOME THINKING OVER THE LAST COUPLE OF MONTHS... ABOUT MY ANIMAL MAN POWERS AND STUFF...
AND, WELL, I'VE COME TO A DECISION.
I WANT TO GO FULL TIME INTO THE SUPER-HERO BUSINESS.
SFFFT
FEET OFF THE TABLE!
DIDN'T YOU HEAR WHAT I SAID?

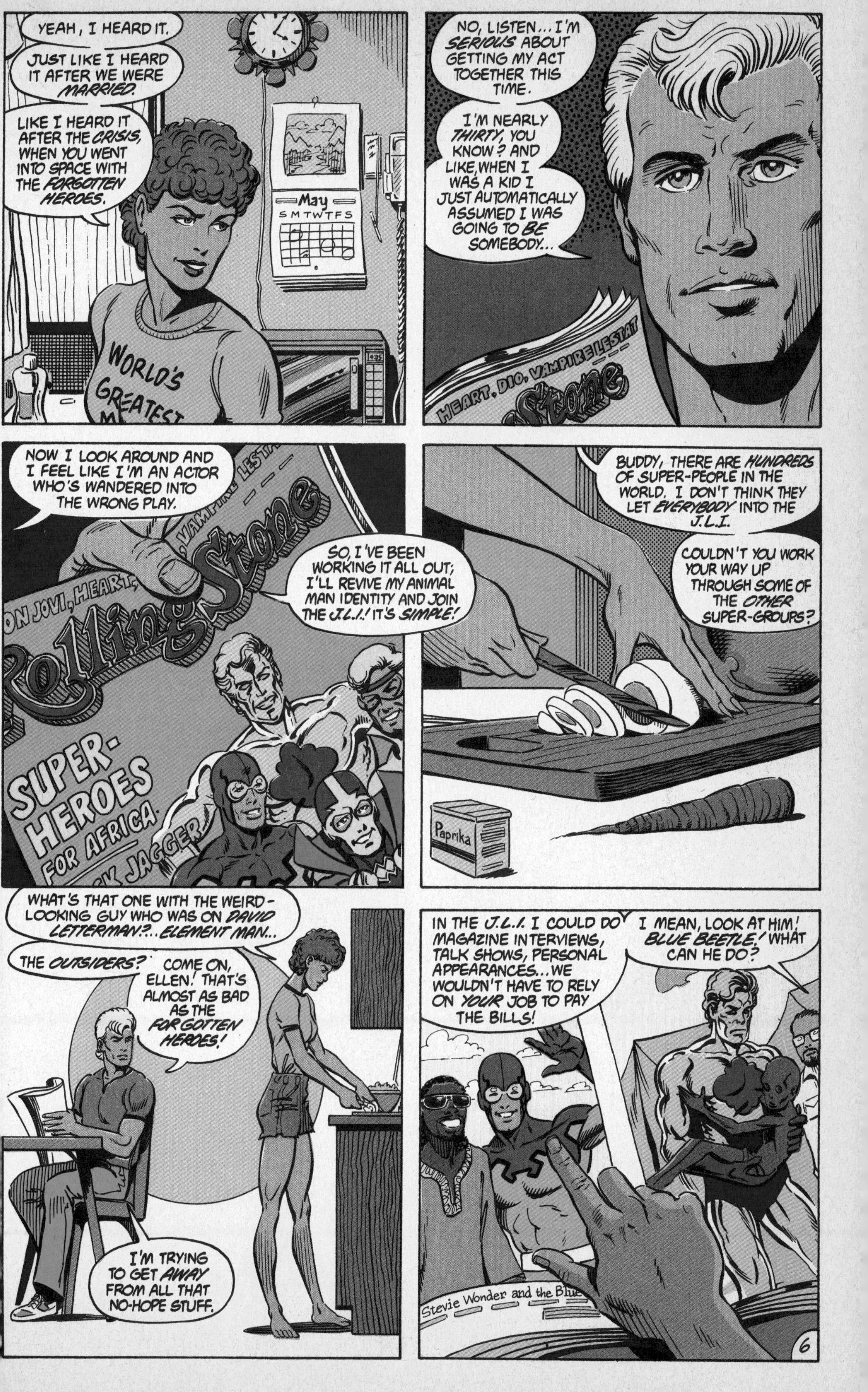

YEAH, I HEARD IT.
JUST LIKE I HEARD IT AFTER WE WERE MARRIED.
LIKE I HEARD IT AFTER THE CRISIS, WHEN YOU WENT INTO SPACE WITH THE FORGOTTEN HEROES.
May
S M T W T F S
WORLD'S GREATEST
NO, LISTEN... I'M SERIOUS ABOUT GETTING MY ACT TOGETHER THIS TIME.
I'M NEARLY THIRTY, YOU KNOW? AND LIKE, WHEN I WAS A KID I JUST AUTOMATICALLY ASSUMED I WAS GOING TO BE SOMEBODY...
HEART, DIO, VAMPIRE LESTAT
NOW I LOOK AROUND AND I FEEL LIKE I'M AN ACTOR WHO'S WANDERED INTO THE WRONG PLAY.
SO, I'VE BEEN WORKING IT ALL OUT; I'LL REVIVE MY ANIMAL MAN IDENTITY AND JOIN THE J.L.I.! IT'S SIMPLE!
ON JOVI, HEART,
VAMPIRE LESTA
Rolling Stone
SUPER-HEROES FOR AFRICA
CK JAGGER
BUDDY, THERE ARE HUNDREDS OF SUPER-PEOPLE IN THE WORLD. I DON'T THINK THEY LET EVERYBODY INTO THE J.L.I.
COULDN'T YOU WORK YOUR WAY UP THROUGH SOME OF THE OTHER SUPER-GROUPS?
Paprika
WHAT'S THAT ONE WITH THE WEIRD-LOOKING GUY WHO WAS ON DAVID LETTERMAN?... ELEMENT MAN...
THE OUTSIDERS?
COME ON, ELLEN! THAT'S ALMOST AS BAD AS THE FORGOTTEN HEROES!
I'M TRYING TO GET AWAY FROM ALL THAT NO-HOPE STUFF.
IN THE J.L.I. I COULD DO MAGAZINE INTERVIEWS, TALK SHOWS, PERSONAL APPEARANCES... WE WOULDN'T HAVE TO RELY ON YOUR JOB TO PAY THE BILLS!
I MEAN, LOOK AT HIM! BLUE BEETLE! WHAT CAN HE DO?
Stevie Wonder and the Blue
6

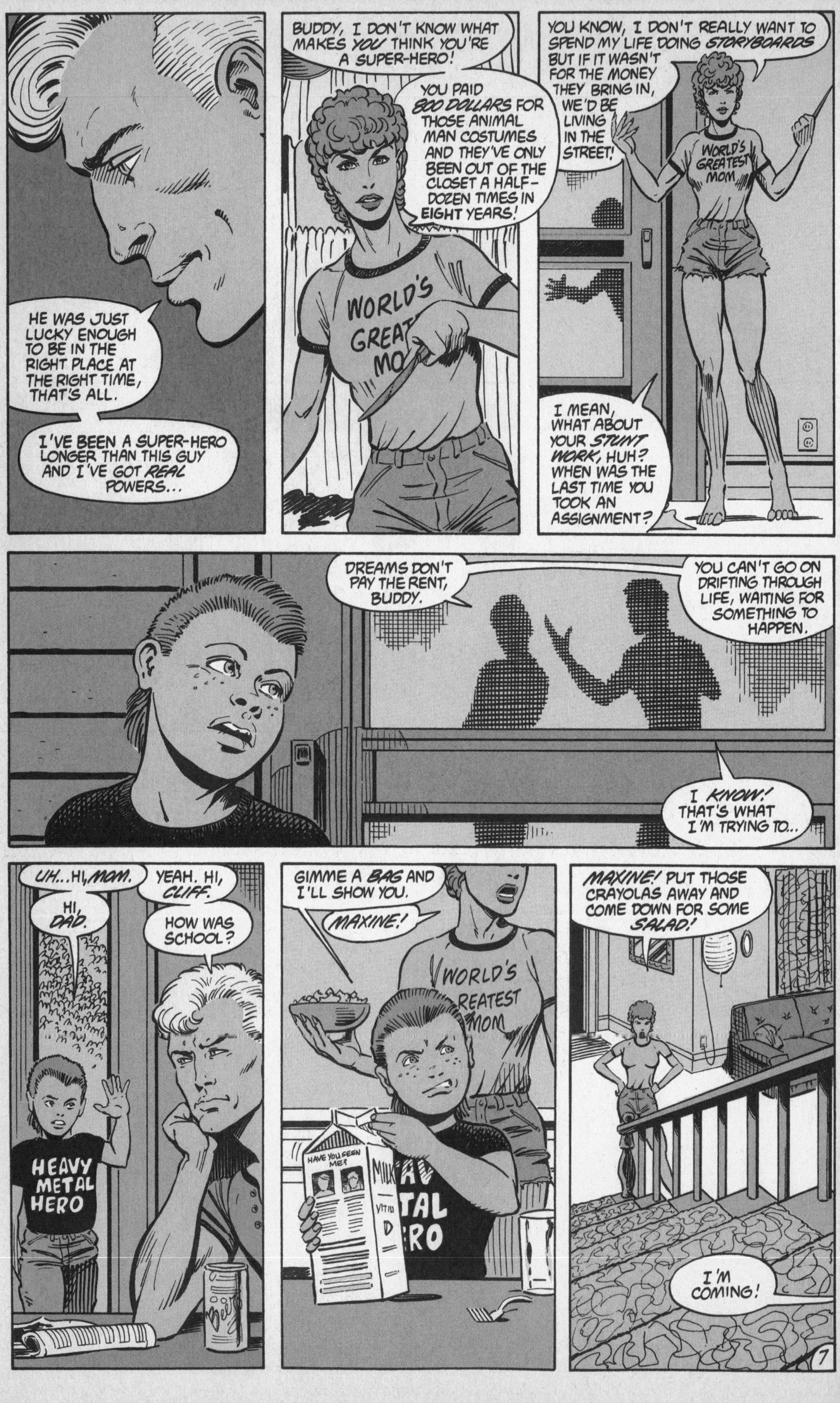
HE WAS JUST LUCKY ENOUGH TO BE IN THE RIGHT PLACE AT THE RIGHT TIME, THAT'S ALL.
I'VE BEEN A SUPER-HERO LONGER THAN THIS GUY AND I'VE GOT REAL POWERS...
BUDDY, I DON'T KNOW WHAT MAKES YOU THINK YOU'RE A SUPER-HERO!
YOU PAID 800 DOLLARS FOR THOSE ANIMAL MAN COSTUMES AND THEY'VE ONLY BEEN OUT OF THE CLOSET A HALF-DOZEN TIMES IN EIGHT YEARS!
WORLD'S GREAT MOM
YOU KNOW, I DON'T REALLY WANT TO SPEND MY LIFE DOING STORYBOARDS BUT IF IT WASN'T FOR THE MONEY THEY BRING IN, WE'D BE LIVING IN THE STREET!
WORLD'S GREATEST MOM
I MEAN, WHAT ABOUT YOUR STUNT WORK, HUH? WHEN WAS THE LAST TIME YOU TOOK AN ASSIGNMENT?
DREAMS DON'T PAY THE RENT, BUDDY.
YOU CAN'T GO ON DRIFTING THROUGH LIFE, WAITING FOR SOMETHING TO HAPPEN.
I KNOW! THAT'S WHAT I'M TRYING TO...
UH...HI, MOM.
HI, DAD.
YEAH. HI, CLIFF.
HOW WAS SCHOOL?
HEAVY METAL HERO
GIMME A BAG AND I'LL SHOW YOU.
MAXINE!
WORLD'S GREATEST MOM
HAVE YOU SEEN ME?
MILK
MAXINE! PUT THOSE CRAYOLAS AWAY AND COME DOWN FOR SOME SALAD!
I'M COMING!

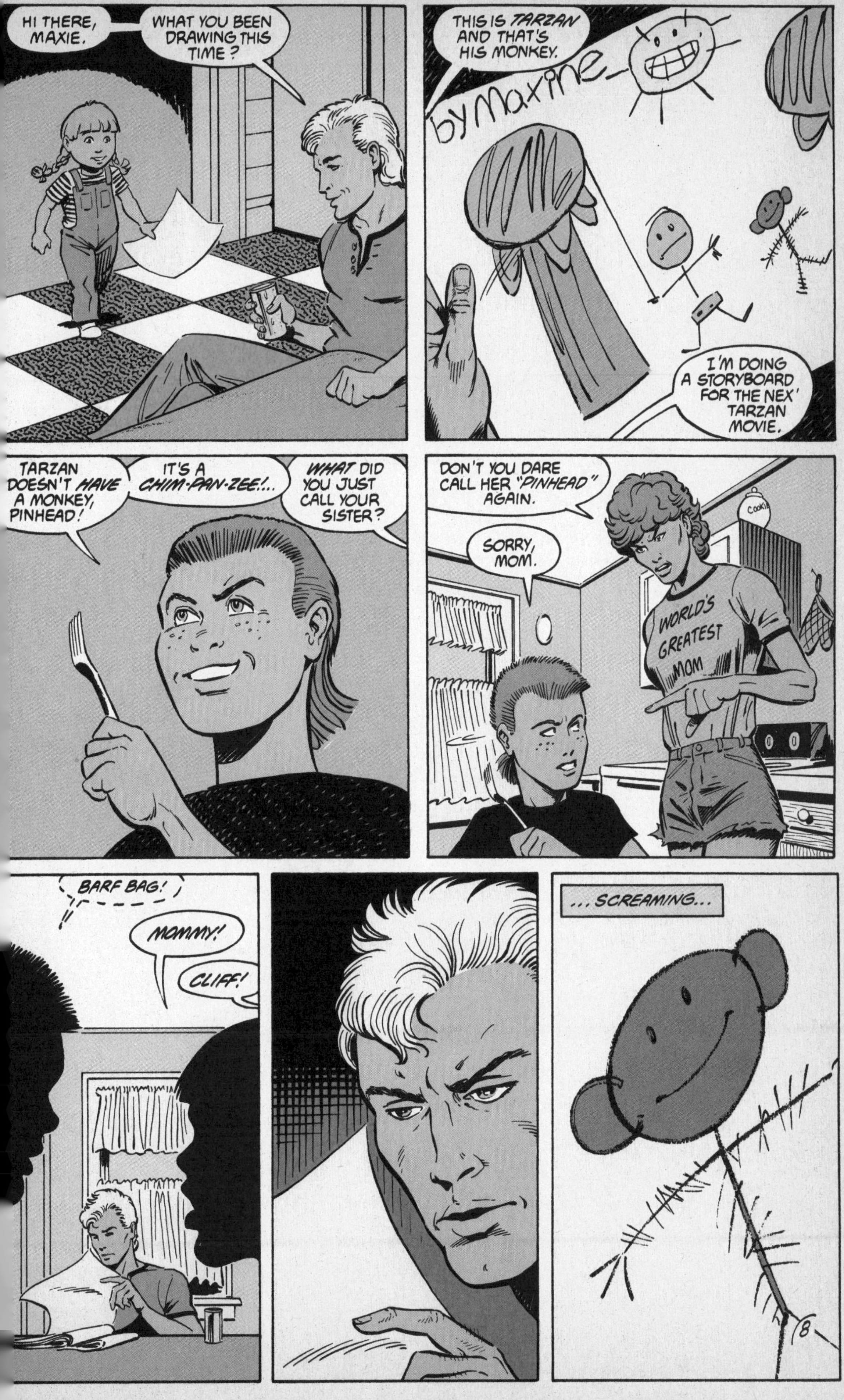
HI THERE, MAXIE.
WHAT YOU BEEN DRAWING THIS TIME?
THIS IS TARZAN AND THAT'S HIS MONKEY.
by Maxine
I'M DOING A STORYBOARD FOR THE NEX' TARZAN MOVIE.
TARZAN DOESN'T HAVE A MONKEY, PINHEAD!
IT'S A CHIM-PAN-ZEE!...
WHAT DID YOU JUST CALL YOUR SISTER?
DON'T YOU DARE CALL HER "PINHEAD" AGAIN.
SORRY, MOM.
COOKIE
WORLD'S GREATEST MOM
BARF BAG!
MOMMY!
CLIFF!
...SCREAMING...
8

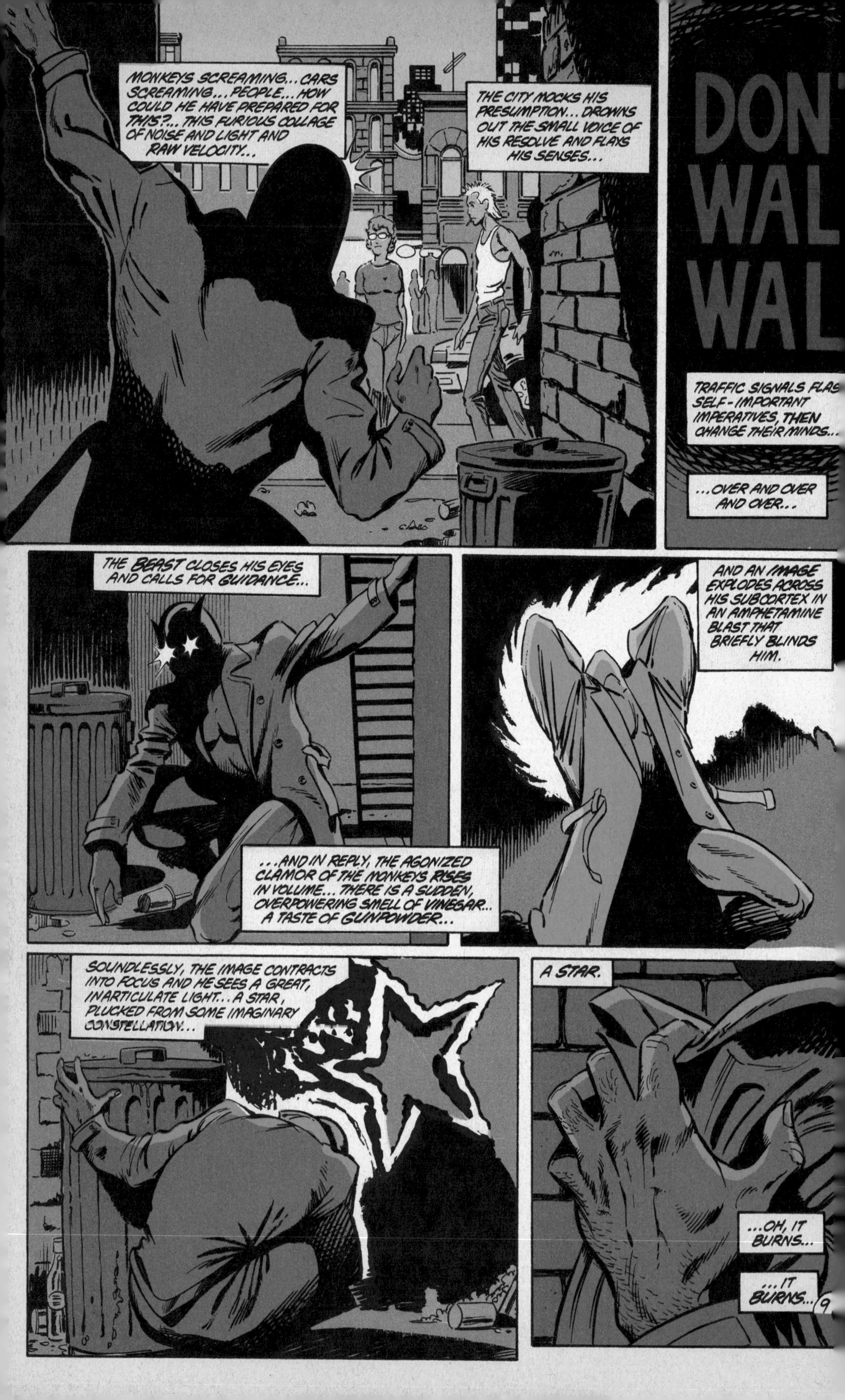
MONKEYS SCREAMING... CARS SCREAMING... PEOPLE... HOW COULD HE HAVE PREPARED FOR THIS?... THIS FURIOUS COLLAGE OF NOISE AND LIGHT AND RAW VELOCITY...
THE CITY MOCKS HIS PRESUMPTION... DROWNS OUT THE SMALL VOICE OF HIS RESOLVE AND FLAYS HIS SENSES...
DON'T WAL WAL WAL
TRAFFIC SIGNALS FLAS SELF-IMPORTANT IMPERATIVES, THEN CHANGE THEIR MINDS...
...OVER AND OVER AND OVER...
THE BEAST CLOSES HIS EYES AND CALLS FOR GUIDANCE...
...AND IN REPLY, THE AGONIZED CLAMOR OF THE MONKEYS RISES IN VOLUME... THERE IS A SUDDEN, OVERPOWERING SMELL OF VINEGAR... A TASTE OF GUNPOWDER...
AND AN IMAGE EXPLODES ACROSS HIS SUBCORTEX IN AN AMPHETAMINE BLAST THAT BRIEFLY BLINDS HIM.
SOUNDLESSLY, THE IMAGE CONTRACTS INTO FOCUS AND HE SEES A GREAT, INARTICULATE LIGHT... A STAR, PLUCKED FROM SOME IMAGINARY CONSTELLATION...
A STAR.
...OH, IT BURNS...
...IT BURNS...
9

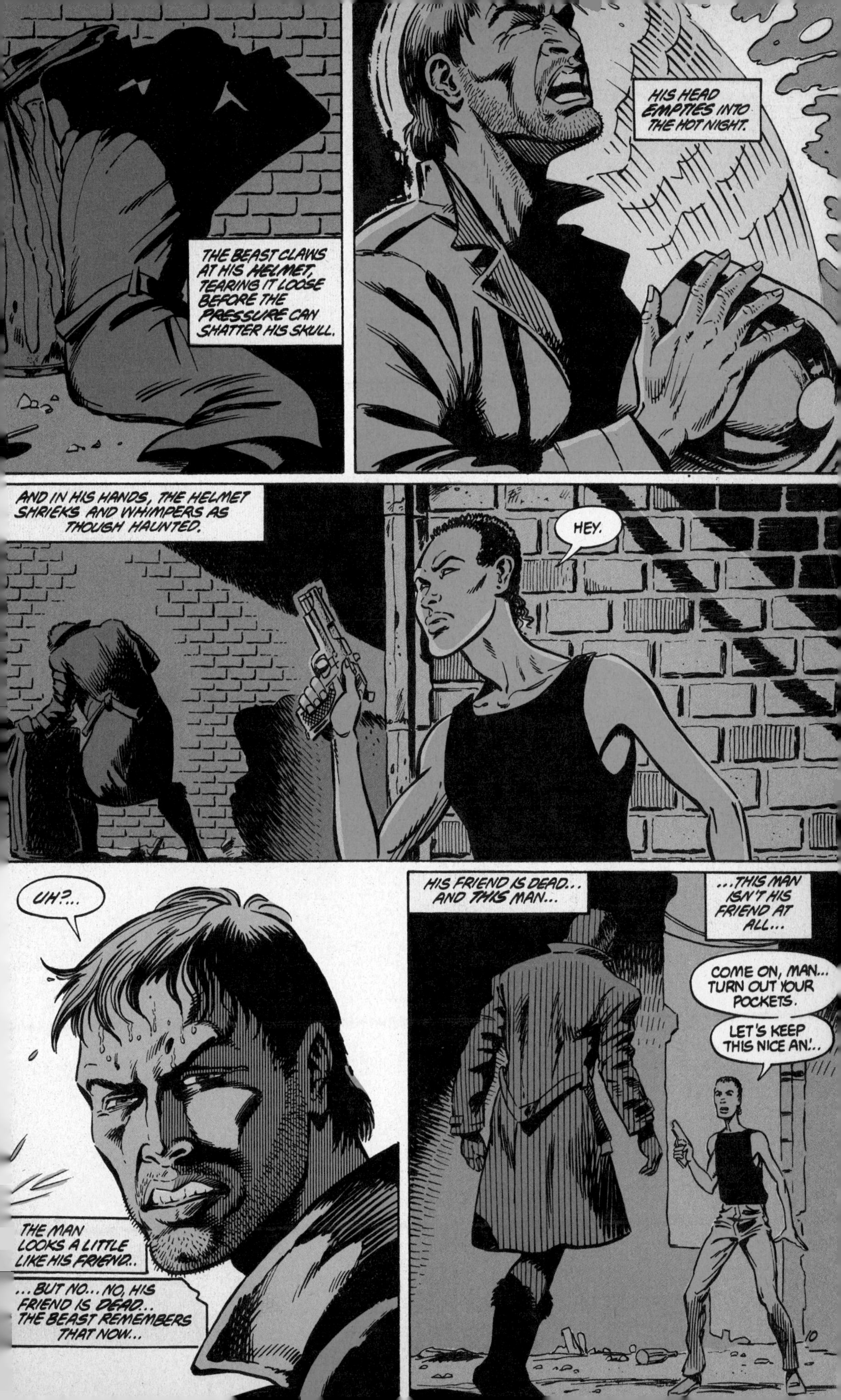
THE BEAST CLAWS AT HIS HELMET, TEARING IT LOOSE BEFORE THE PRESSURE CAN SHATTER HIS SKULL.
HIS HEAD EMPTIES INTO THE HOT NIGHT.
AND IN HIS HANDS, THE HELMET SHRIEKS AND WHIMPERS AS THOUGH HAUNTED.
HEY.
UH?...
THE MAN LOOKS A LITTLE LIKE HIS FRIEND..
...BUT NO... NO, HIS FRIEND IS DEAD... THE BEAST REMEMBERS THAT NOW...
HIS FRIEND IS DEAD... AND THIS MAN...
...THIS MAN ISN'T HIS FRIEND AT ALL...
COME ON, MAN... TURN OUT YOUR POCKETS.
LET'S KEEP THIS NICE AN'...
10

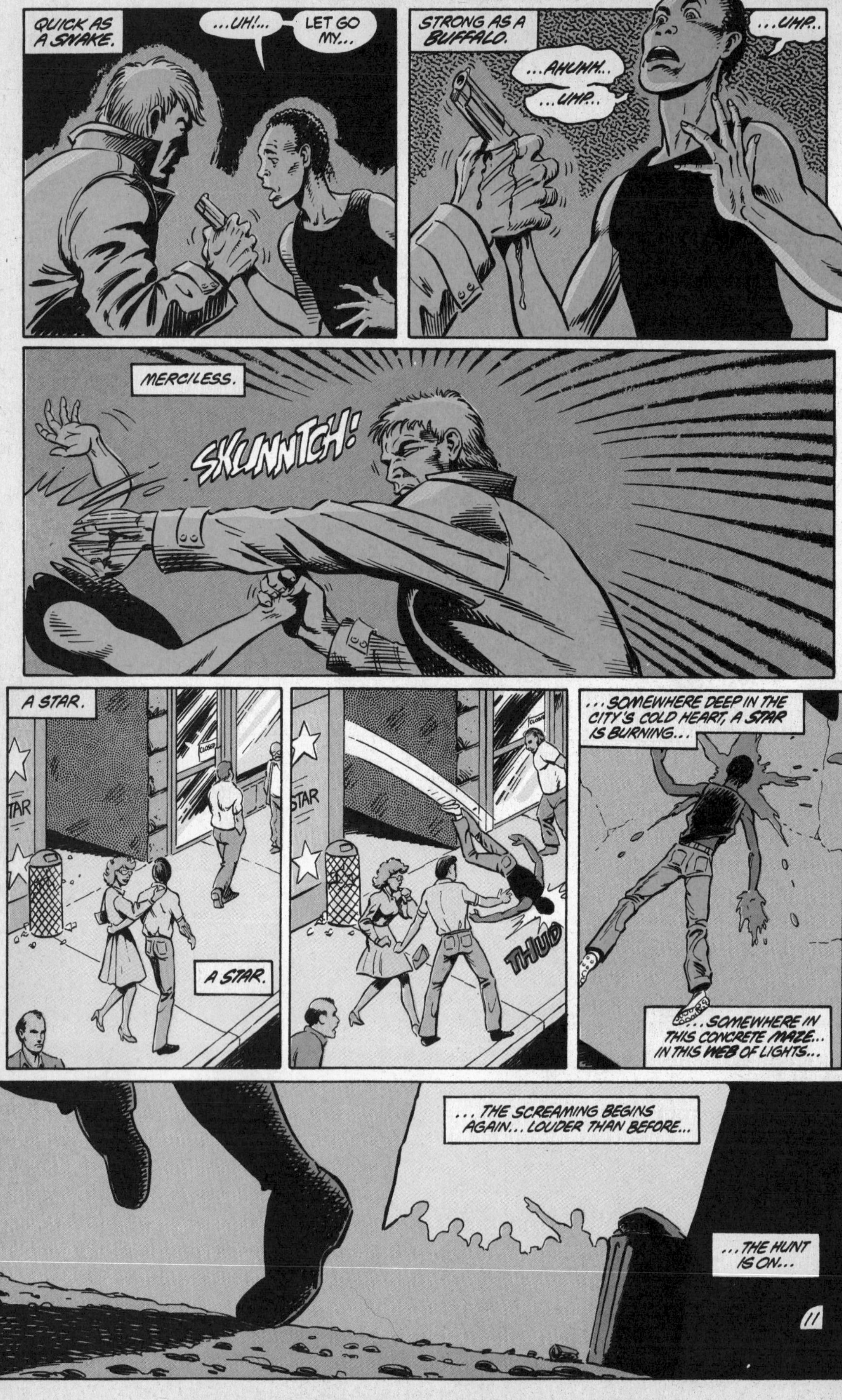
QUICK AS A SNAKE.
...UH!...
LET GO MY...
STRONG AS A BUFFALO.
...UHP...
...AHUNH...
...UHP...
MERCILESS.
SKUNNTCH!
A STAR.
STAR
CLOSED
A STAR.
STAR
THUD
...SOMEWHERE DEEP IN THE CITY'S COLD HEART, A STAR IS BURNING...
...SOMEWHERE IN THIS CONCRETE MAZE... IN THIS WEB OF LIGHTS...
...THE SCREAMING BEGINS AGAIN... LOUDER THAN BEFORE...
...THE HUNT IS ON...
11

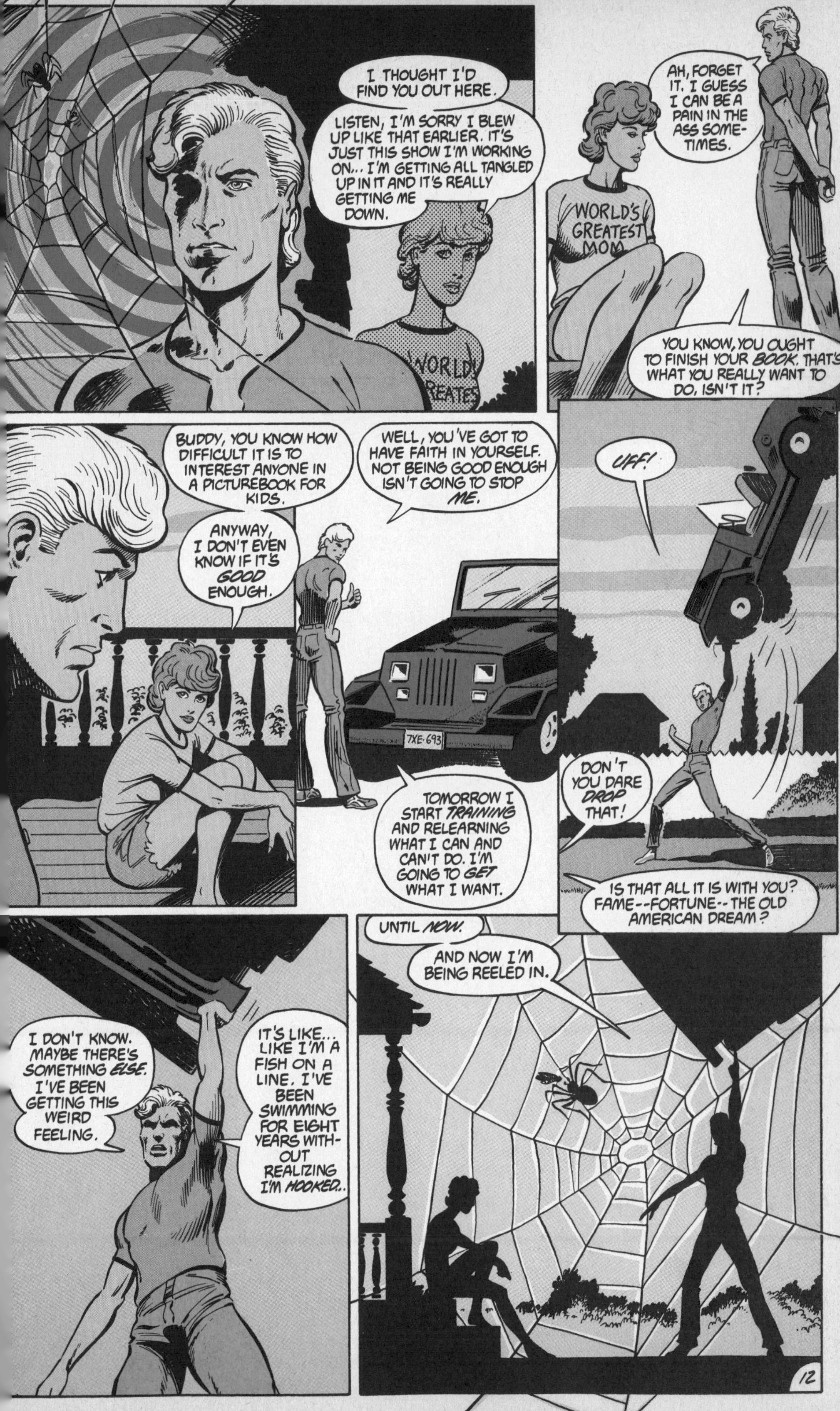

I THOUGHT I'D FIND YOU OUT HERE.
LISTEN, I'M SORRY I BLEW UP LIKE THAT EARLIER. IT'S JUST THIS SHOW I'M WORKING ON... I'M GETTING ALL TANGLED UP IN IT AND IT'S REALLY GETTING ME DOWN.
WORLD'S GREATEST MOM
AH, FORGET IT. I GUESS I CAN BE A PAIN IN THE ASS SOME-TIMES.
YOU KNOW, YOU OUGHT TO FINISH YOUR BOOK. THAT'S WHAT YOU REALLY WANT TO DO, ISN'T IT?
BUDDY, YOU KNOW HOW DIFFICULT IT IS TO INTEREST ANYONE IN A PICTUREBOOK FOR KIDS.
ANYWAY, I DON'T EVEN KNOW IF IT'S GOOD ENOUGH.
WELL, YOU'VE GOT TO HAVE FAITH IN YOURSELF. NOT BEING GOOD ENOUGH ISN'T GOING TO STOP ME.
7XE-693
TOMORROW I START TRAINING AND RELEARNING WHAT I CAN AND CAN'T DO. I'M GOING TO GET WHAT I WANT.
UFF!
DON'T YOU DARE DROP THAT!
IS THAT ALL IT IS WITH YOU? FAME--FORTUNE--THE OLD AMERICAN DREAM?
I DON'T KNOW. MAYBE THERE'S SOMETHING ELSE. I'VE BEEN GETTING THIS WEIRD FEELING.
IT'S LIKE... LIKE I'M A FISH ON A LINE. I'VE BEEN SWIMMING FOR EIGHT YEARS WITH-OUT REALIZING I'M HOOKED...
UNTIL NOW.
AND NOW I'M BEING REELED IN.

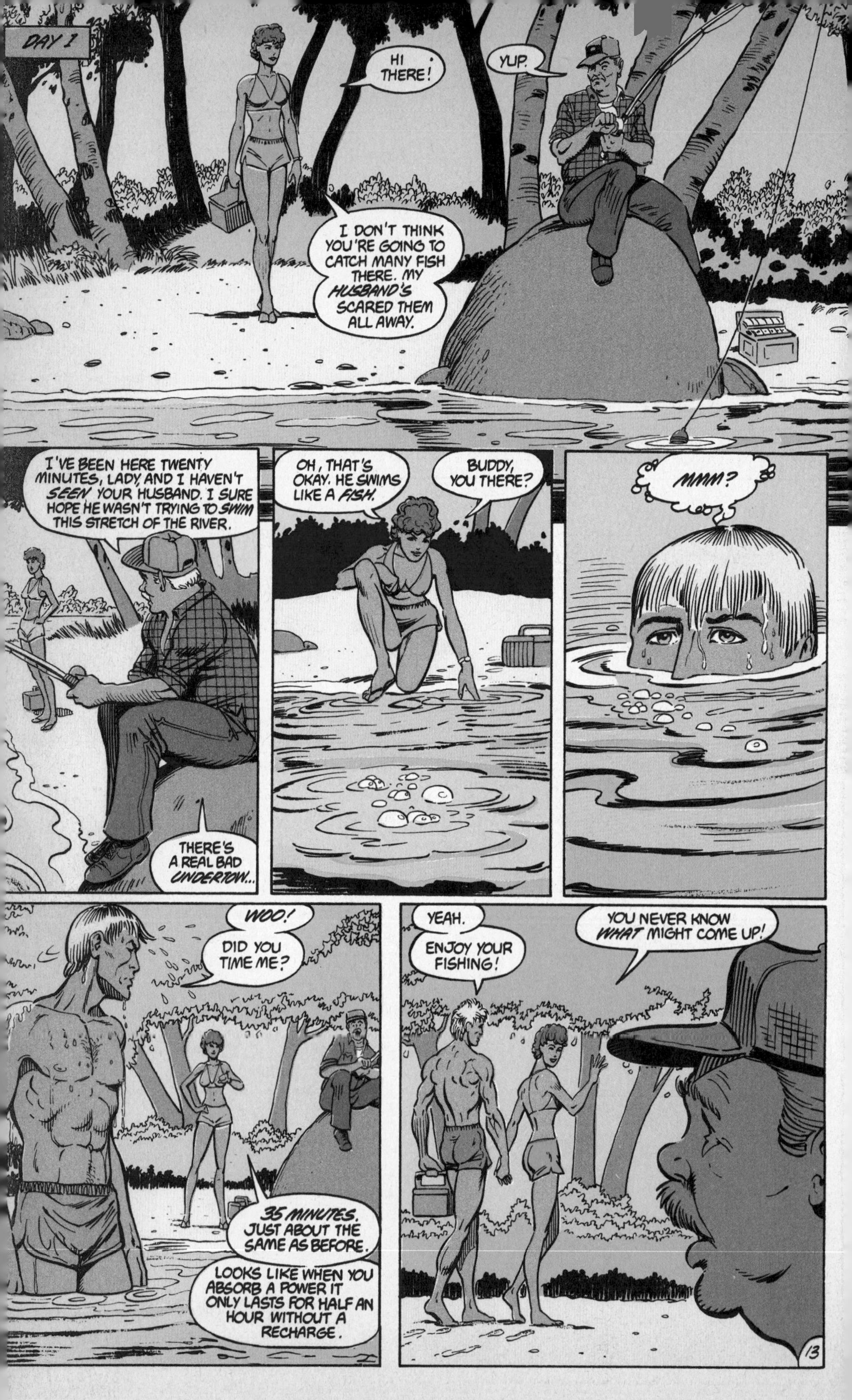
DAY 1
HI THERE!
YUP.
I DON'T THINK YOU'RE GOING TO CATCH MANY FISH THERE. MY HUSBAND'S SCARED THEM ALL AWAY.
I'VE BEEN HERE TWENTY MINUTES, LADY, AND I HAVEN'T SEEN YOUR HUSBAND. I SURE HOPE HE WASN'T TRYING TO SWIM THIS STRETCH OF THE RIVER.
THERE'S A REAL BAD UNDERTOW...
OH, THAT'S OKAY. HE SWIMS LIKE A FISH.
BUDDY, YOU THERE?
MMM?
WOO!
DID YOU TIME ME?
35 MINUTES. JUST ABOUT THE SAME AS BEFORE.
LOOKS LIKE WHEN YOU ABSORB A POWER IT ONLY LASTS FOR HALF AN HOUR WITHOUT A RECHARGE.
YEAH.
ENJOY YOUR FISHING!
YOU NEVER KNOW WHAT MIGHT COME UP!
13

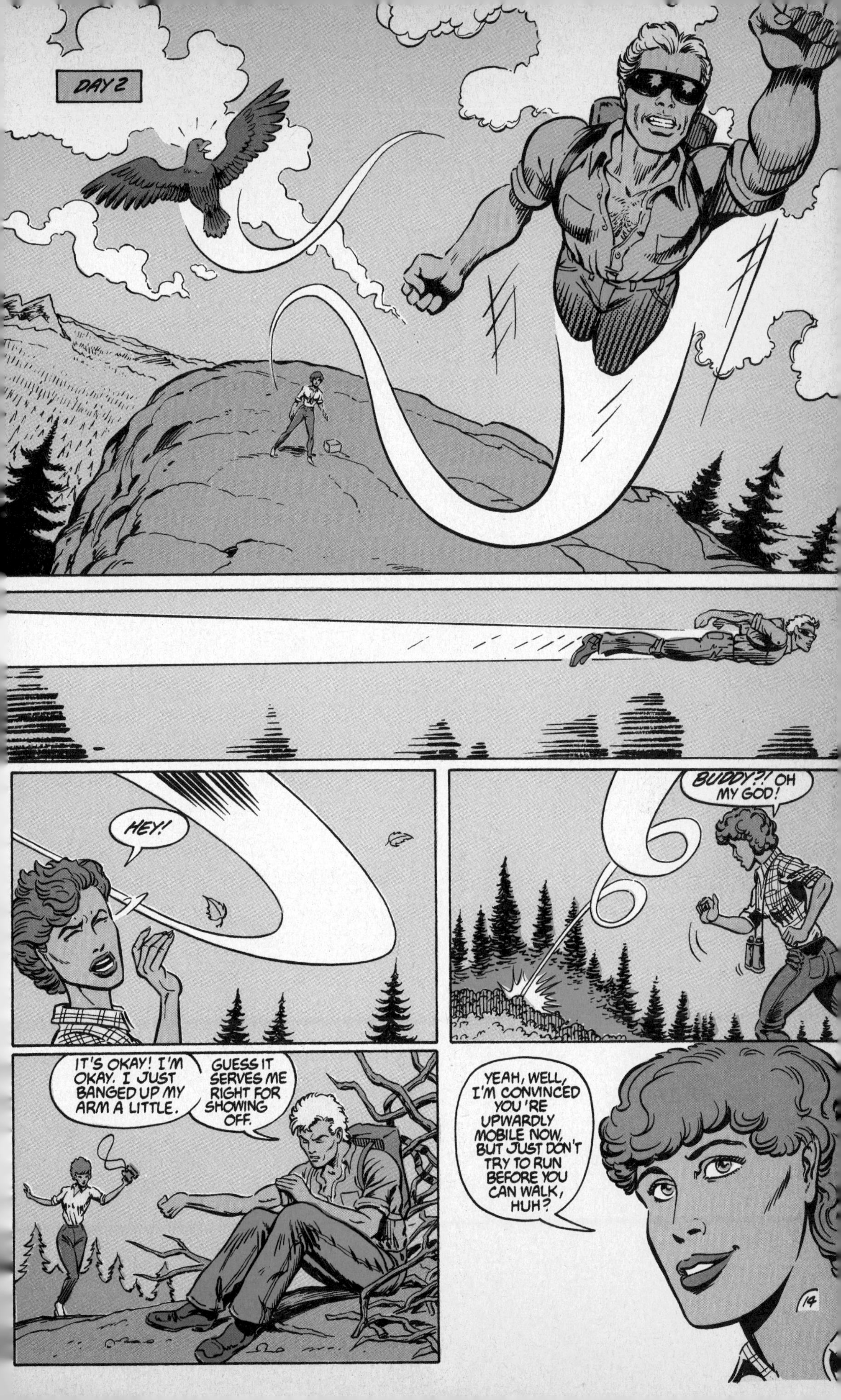
DAY 2
HEY!
BUDDY?! OH MY GOD!
IT'S OKAY! I'M OKAY. I JUST BANGED UP MY ARM A LITTLE.
GUESS IT SERVES ME RIGHT FOR SHOWING OFF.
YEAH, WELL, I'M CONVINCED YOU'RE UPWARDLY MOBILE NOW, BUT JUST DON'T TRY TO RUN BEFORE YOU CAN WALK, HUH?
14

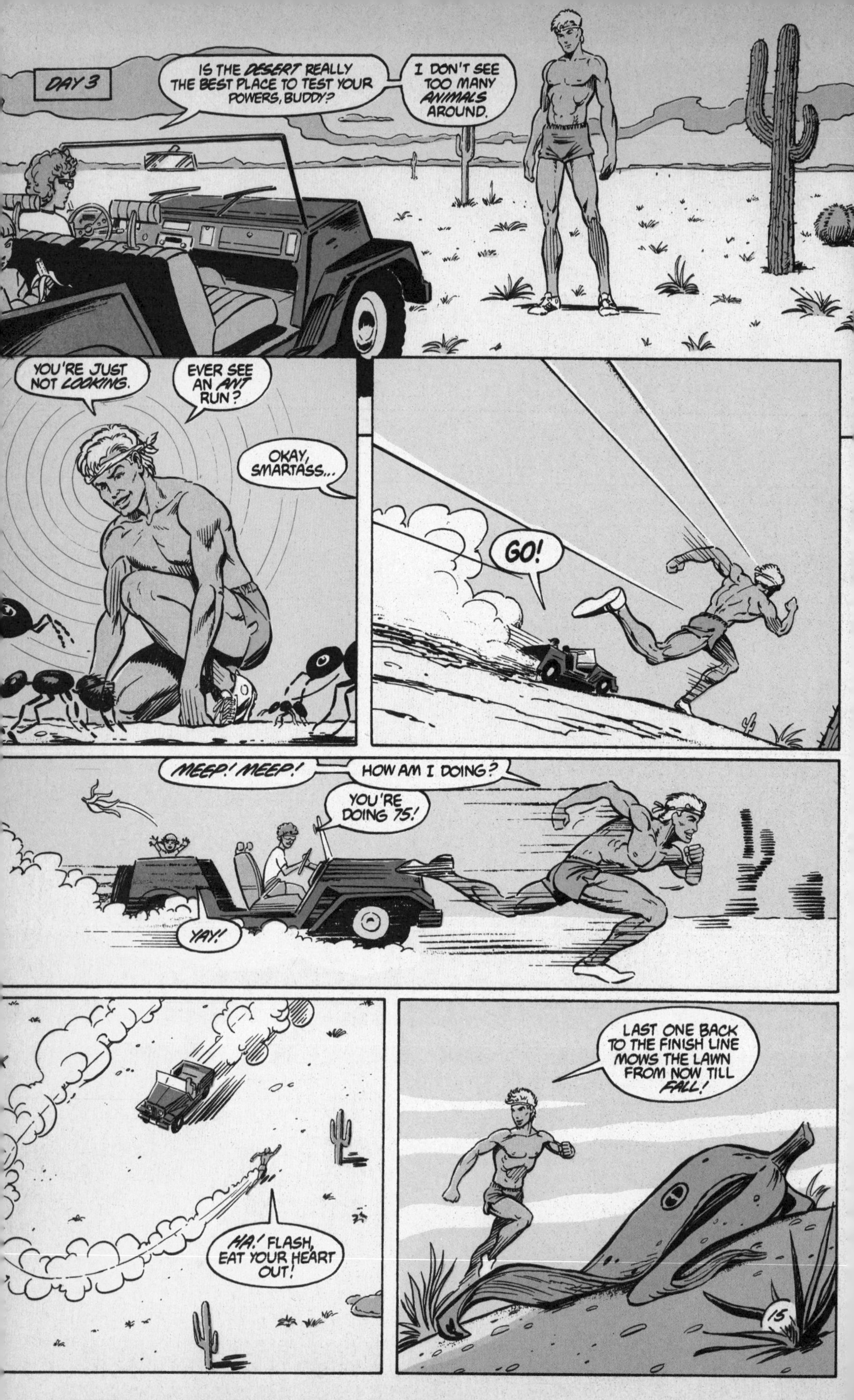
DAY 3
IS THE DESERT REALLY THE BEST PLACE TO TEST YOUR POWERS, BUDDY?
I DON'T SEE TOO MANY ANIMALS AROUND.
YOU'RE JUST NOT LOOKING.
EVER SEE AN ANT RUN?
OKAY, SMARTASS...
GO!
MEEP! MEEP!
HOW AM I DOING?
YOU'RE DOING 75!
YAY!
HA! FLASH, EAT YOUR HEART OUT!
LAST ONE BACK TO THE FINISH LINE MOWS THE LAWN FROM NOW TILL FALL!
15

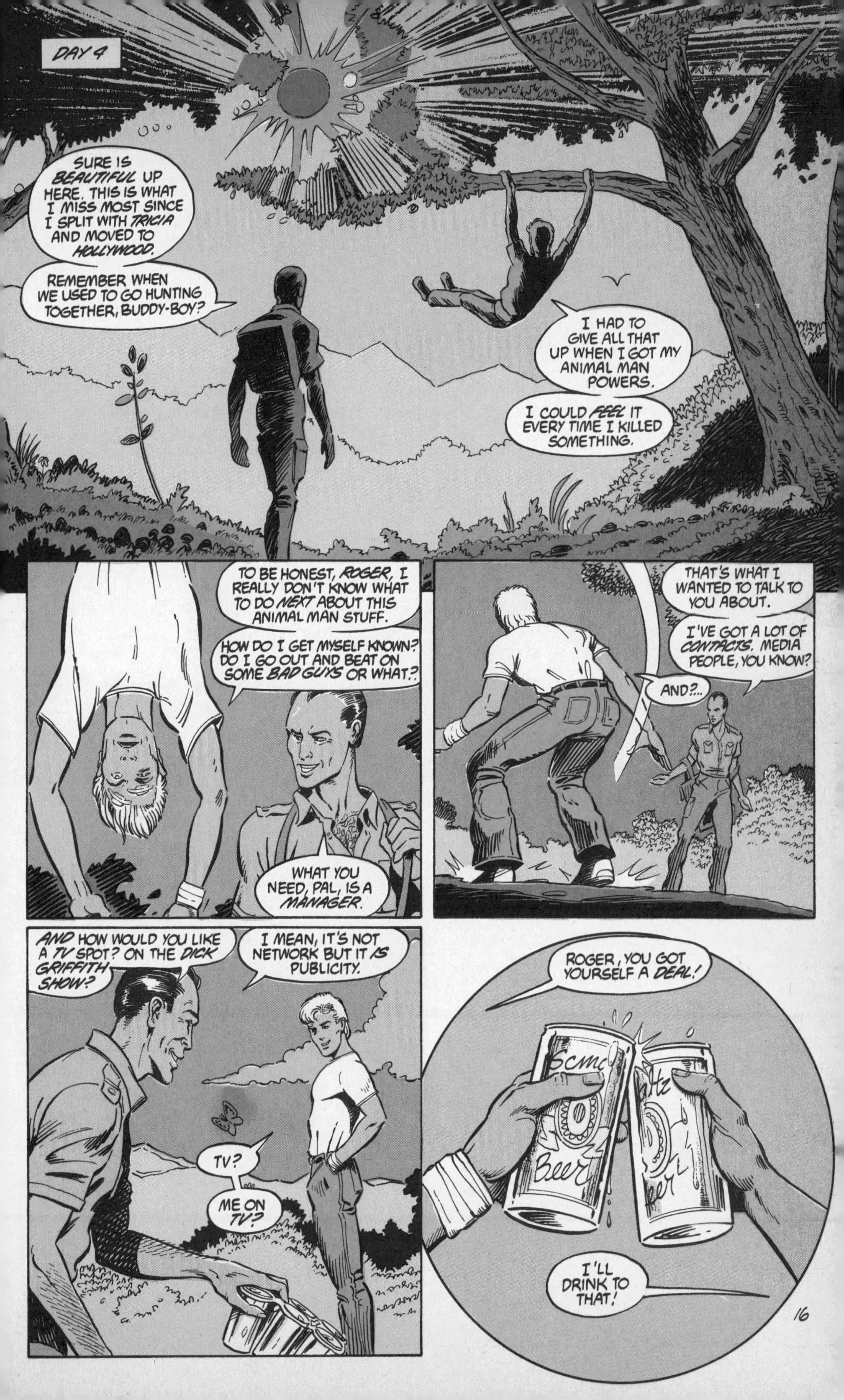
DAY 4
SURE IS BEAUTIFUL UP HERE. THIS IS WHAT I MISS MOST SINCE I SPLIT WITH TRICIA AND MOVED TO HOLLYWOOD.
REMEMBER WHEN WE USED TO GO HUNTING TOGETHER, BUDDY-BOY?
I HAD TO GIVE ALL THAT UP WHEN I GOT MY ANIMAL MAN POWERS.
I COULD FEEL IT EVERY TIME I KILLED SOMETHING.
TO BE HONEST, ROGER, I REALLY DON'T KNOW WHAT TO DO NEXT ABOUT THIS ANIMAL MAN STUFF.
HOW DO I GET MYSELF KNOWN? DO I GO OUT AND BEAT ON SOME BAD GUYS OR WHAT.?
WHAT YOU NEED, PAL, IS A MANAGER.
THAT'S WHAT I WANTED TO TALK TO YOU ABOUT.
I'VE GOT A LOT OF CONTACTS. MEDIA PEOPLE, YOU KNOW?
AND?..
AND HOW WOULD YOU LIKE A TV SPOT? ON THE DICK GRIFFITH SHOW?
I MEAN, IT'S NOT NETWORK BUT IT IS PUBLICITY.
TV?
ME ON TV?
ROGER, YOU GOT YOURSELF A DEAL!
Beer
I'LL DRINK TO THAT!

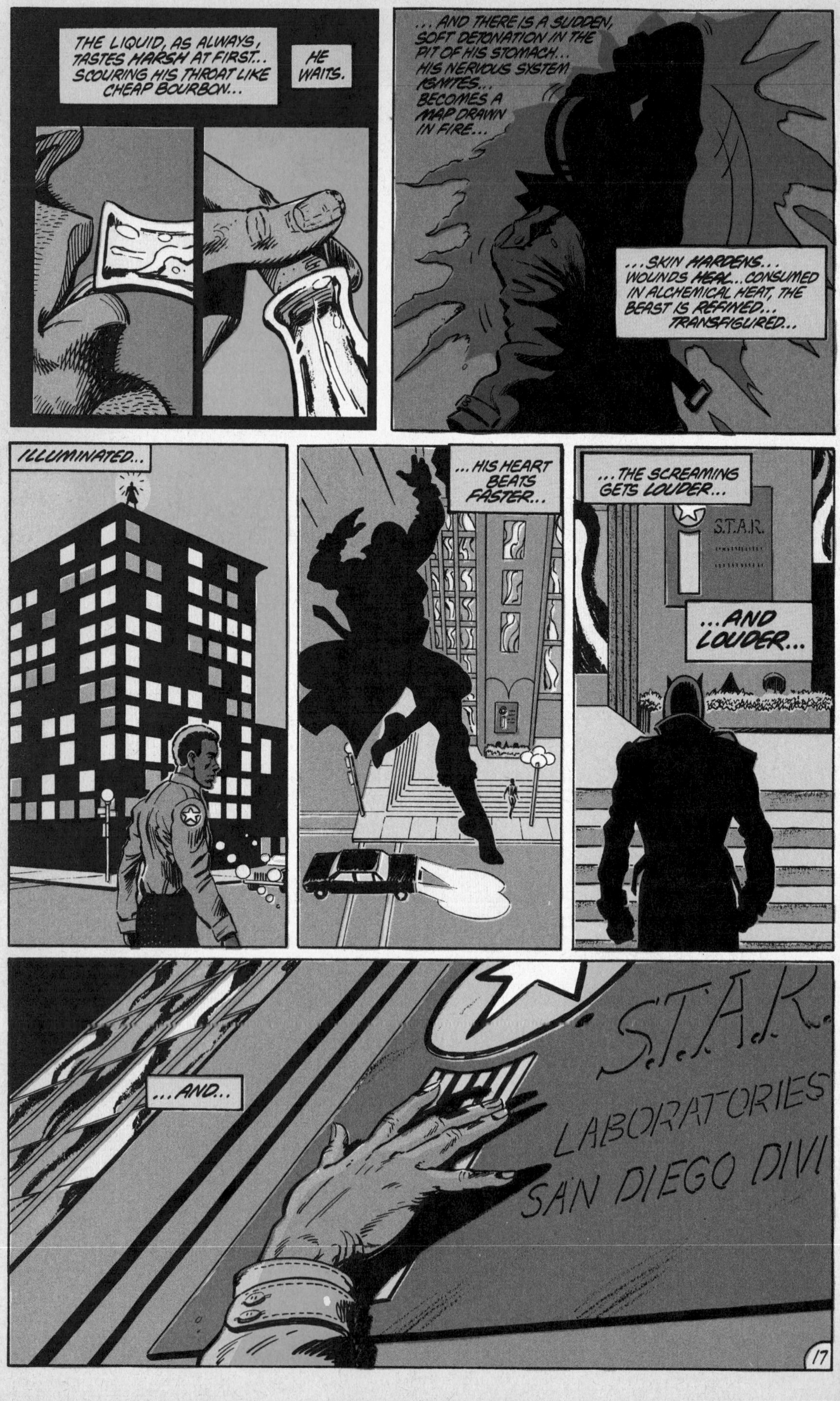
THE LIQUID, AS ALWAYS, TASTES HARSH AT FIRST... SCOURING HIS THROAT LIKE CHEAP BOURBON...
HE WAITS.
...AND THERE IS A SUDDEN, SOFT DETONATION IN THE PIT OF HIS STOMACH... HIS NERVOUS SYSTEM IGNITES... BECOMES A MAP DRAWN IN FIRE...
...SKIN HARDENS... WOUNDS HEAL... CONSUMED IN ALCHEMICAL HEAT, THE BEAST IS REFINED... TRANSFIGURED...
ILLUMINATED...
...HIS HEART BEATS FASTER...
...THE SCREAMING GETS LOUDER...
S.T.A.R.
...AND LOUDER...
...AND...
S.T.A.R.
LABORATORIES
SAN DIEGO DIVI

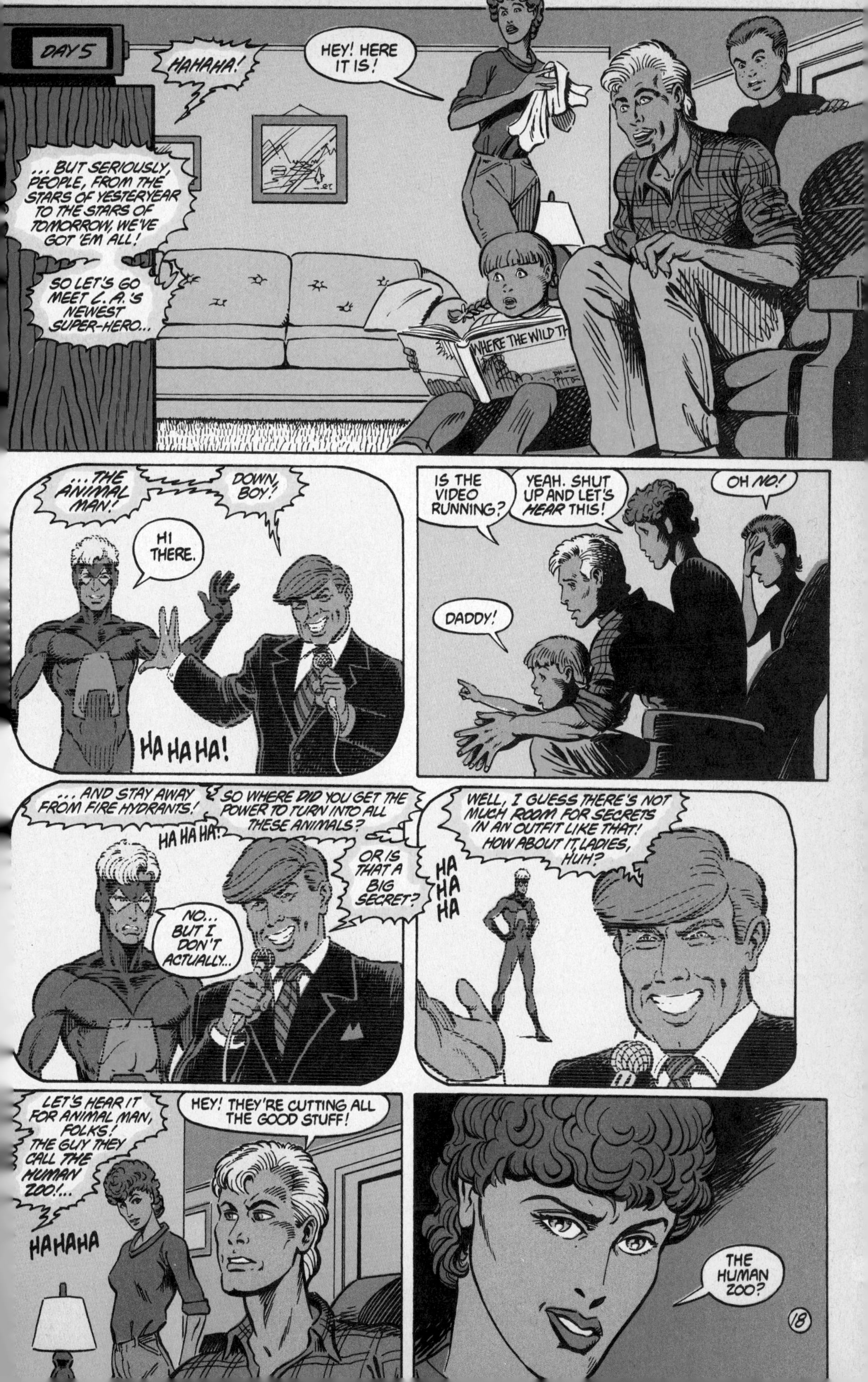
DAY 5
HAHAHA!
HEY! HERE IT IS!
... BUT SERIOUSLY, PEOPLE, FROM THE STARS OF YESTERYEAR TO THE STARS OF TOMORROW, WE'VE GOT 'EM ALL!
SO LET'S GO MEET L.A.'S NEWEST SUPER-HERO...
WHERE THE WILD TH
...THE ANIMAL MAN!
DOWN, BOY!
HI THERE.
HA HA HA!
IS THE VIDEO RUNNING?
YEAH. SHUT UP AND LET'S HEAR THIS!
OH NO!
DADDY!
... AND STAY AWAY FROM FIRE HYDRANTS!
HA HA HA!
SO WHERE DID YOU GET THE POWER TO TURN INTO ALL THESE ANIMALS?
OR IS THAT A BIG SECRET?
NO... BUT I DON'T ACTUALLY...
WELL, I GUESS THERE'S NOT MUCH ROOM FOR SECRETS IN AN OUTFIT LIKE THAT! HOW ABOUT IT, LADIES, HUH?
HA HA HA
LET'S HEAR IT FOR ANIMAL MAN, FOLKS! THE GUY THEY CALL THE HUMAN ZOO!...
HAHAHA
HEY! THEY'RE CUTTING ALL THE GOOD STUFF!
THE HUMAN ZOO?
18

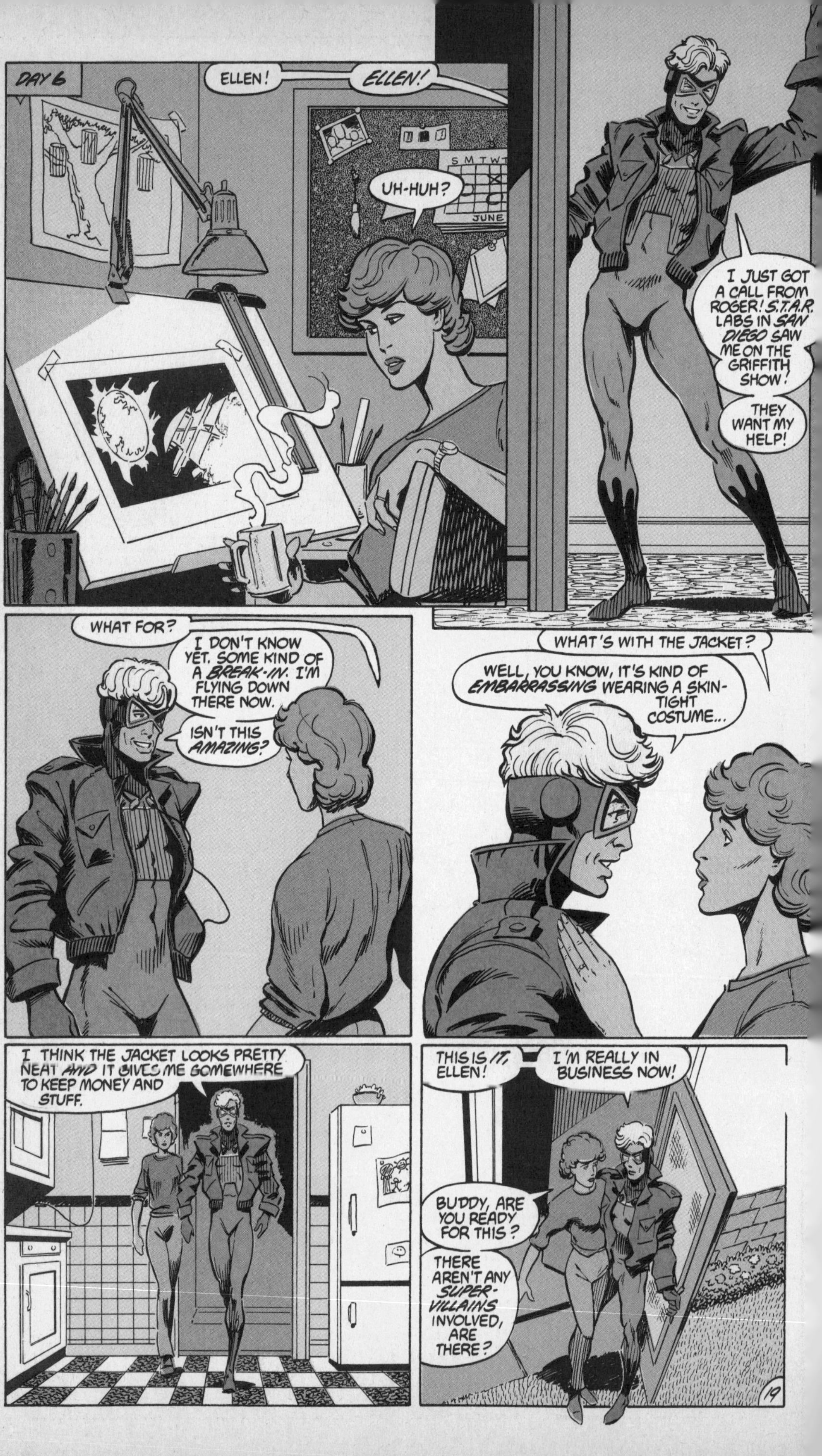
DAY 6
ELLEN!
ELLEN!
UH-HUH?
JUNE
S M T W T
I JUST GOT A CALL FROM ROGER! S.T.A.R. LABS IN SAN DIEGO SAW ME ON THE GRIFFITH SHOW!
THEY WANT MY HELP!
WHAT FOR?
I DON'T KNOW YET. SOME KIND OF A BREAK-IN. I'M FLYING DOWN THERE NOW.
ISN'T THIS AMAZING?
WHAT'S WITH THE JACKET?
WELL, YOU KNOW, IT'S KIND OF EMBARRASSING WEARING A SKIN-TIGHT COSTUME...
I THINK THE JACKET LOOKS PRETTY NEAT AND IT GIVES ME SOMEWHERE TO KEEP MONEY AND STUFF.
THIS IS IT, ELLEN!
I'M REALLY IN BUSINESS NOW!
BUDDY, ARE YOU READY FOR THIS?
THERE AREN'T ANY SUPER-VILLAINS INVOLVED, ARE THERE?
19

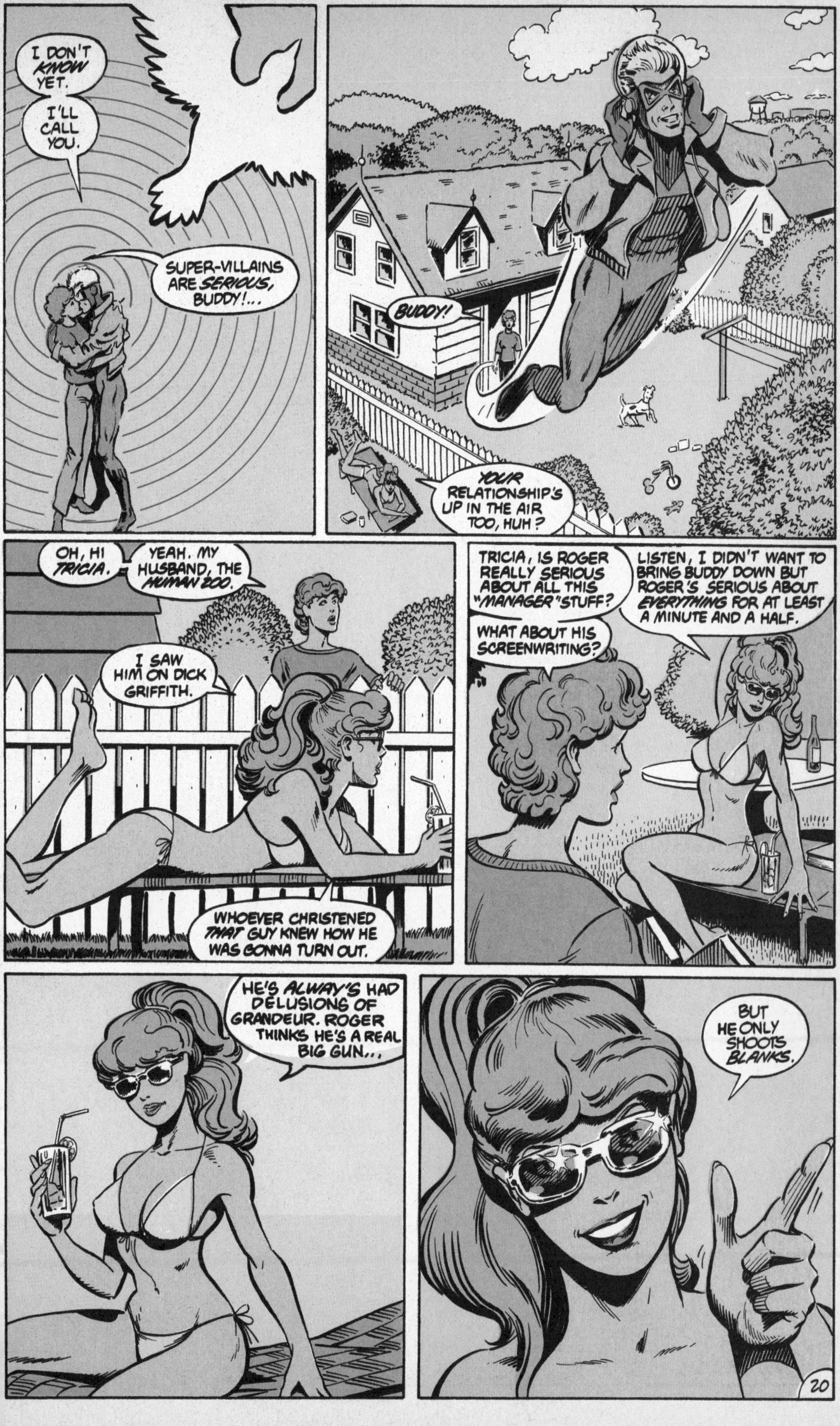

I DON'T KNOW YET.
I'LL CALL YOU.
SUPER-VILLAINS ARE SERIOUS, BUDDY!...
BUDDY!
YOUR RELATIONSHIP'S UP IN THE AIR TOO, HUH?
OH, HI TRICIA.
YEAH. MY HUSBAND, THE HUMAN ZOO.
I SAW HIM ON DICK GRIFFITH.
WHOEVER CHRISTENED THAT GUY KNEW HOW HE WAS GONNA TURN OUT.
TRICIA, IS ROGER REALLY SERIOUS ABOUT ALL THIS "MANAGER" STUFF?
WHAT ABOUT HIS SCREENWRITING?
LISTEN, I DIDN'T WANT TO BRING BUDDY DOWN BUT ROGER'S SERIOUS ABOUT EVERYTHING FOR AT LEAST A MINUTE AND A HALF.
HE'S ALWAY'S HAD DELUSIONS OF GRANDEUR. ROGER THINKS HE'S A REAL BIG GUN...
BUT HE ONLY SHOOTS BLANKS.

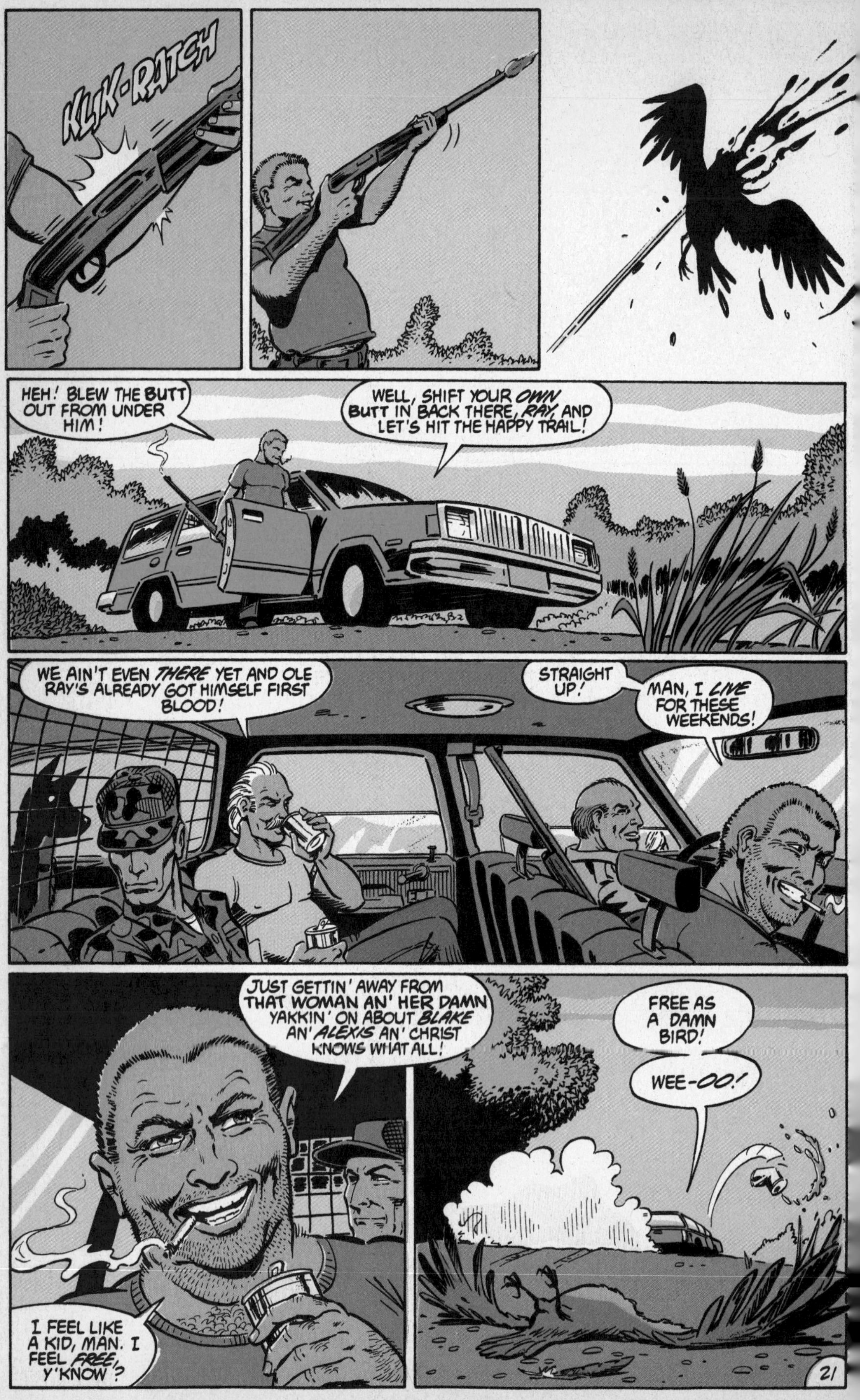
KLIK-RATCH
HEH! BLEW THE BUTT OUT FROM UNDER HIM!
WELL, SHIFT YOUR OWN BUTT IN BACK THERE, RAY, AND LET'S HIT THE HAPPY TRAIL!
WE AIN'T EVEN THERE YET AND OLE RAY'S ALREADY GOT HIMSELF FIRST BLOOD!
STRAIGHT UP!
MAN, I LIVE FOR THESE WEEKENDS!
JUST GETTIN' AWAY FROM THAT WOMAN AN' HER DAMN YAKKIN' ON ABOUT BLAKE AN' ALEXIS AN' CHRIST KNOWS WHAT ALL!
I FEEL LIKE A KID, MAN. I FEEL FREE, Y'KNOW?
FREE AS A DAMN BIRD!
WEE-OO!

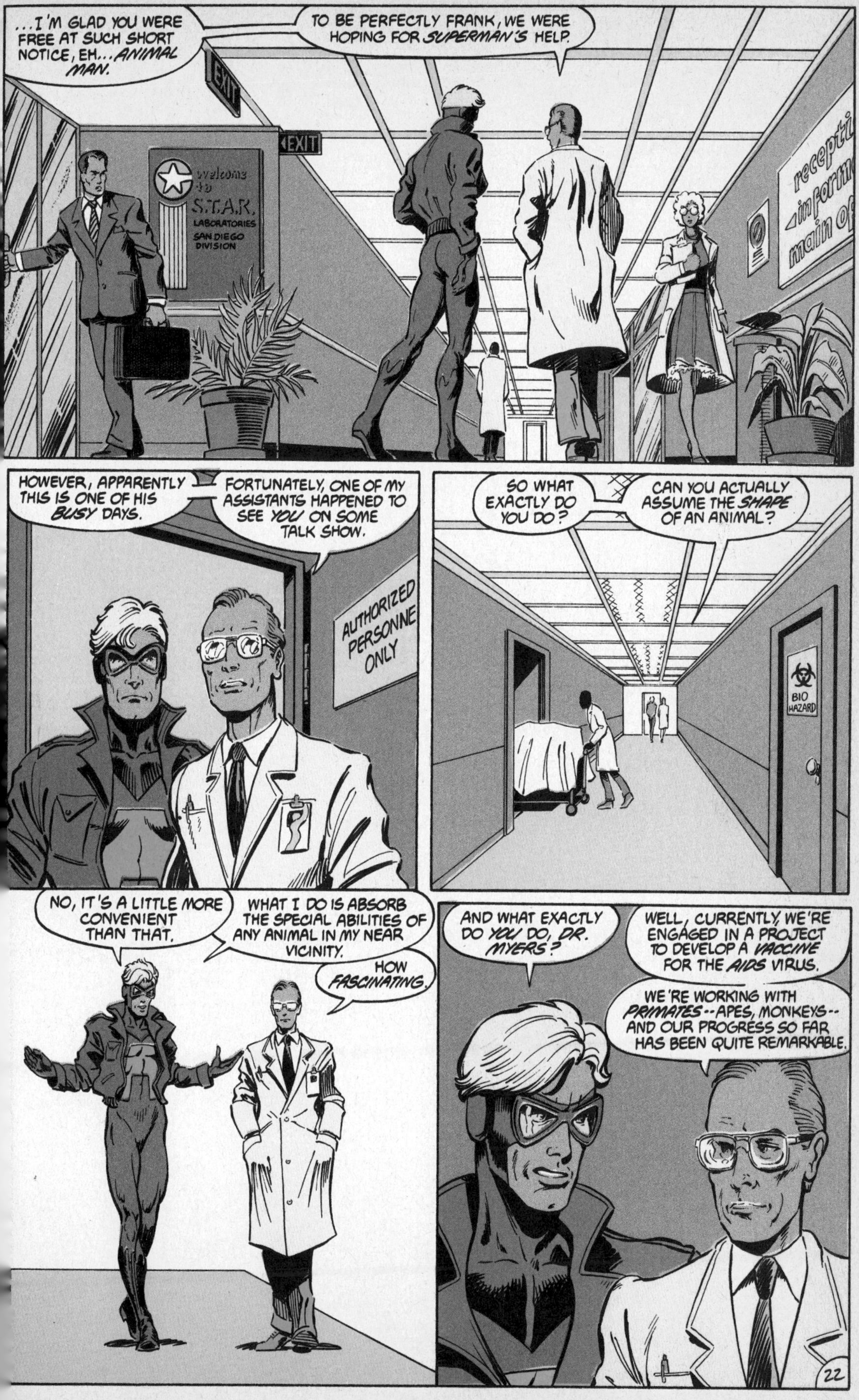
...I'M GLAD YOU WERE FREE AT SUCH SHORT NOTICE, EH... ANIMAL MAN.
TO BE PERFECTLY FRANK, WE WERE HOPING FOR SUPERMAN'S HELP.
EXIT
EXIT
welcome to S.T.A.R. LABORATORIES SAN DIEGO DIVISION
HOWEVER, APPARENTLY THIS IS ONE OF HIS BUSY DAYS.
FORTUNATELY, ONE OF MY ASSISTANTS HAPPENED TO SEE YOU ON SOME TALK SHOW.
AUTHORIZED PERSONNE ONLY
SO WHAT EXACTLY DO YOU DO?
CAN YOU ACTUALLY ASSUME THE SHAPE OF AN ANIMAL?
BIO HAZARD
NO, IT'S A LITTLE MORE CONVENIENT THAN THAT.
WHAT I DO IS ABSORB THE SPECIAL ABILITIES OF ANY ANIMAL IN MY NEAR VICINITY.
HOW FASCINATING.
AND WHAT EXACTLY DO YOU DO, DR. MYERS?
WELL, CURRENTLY, WE'RE ENGAGED IN A PROJECT TO DEVELOP A VACCINE FOR THE AIDS VIRUS.
WE'RE WORKING WITH PRIMATES--APES, MONKEYS--AND OUR PROGRESS SO FAR HAS BEEN QUITE REMARKABLE.

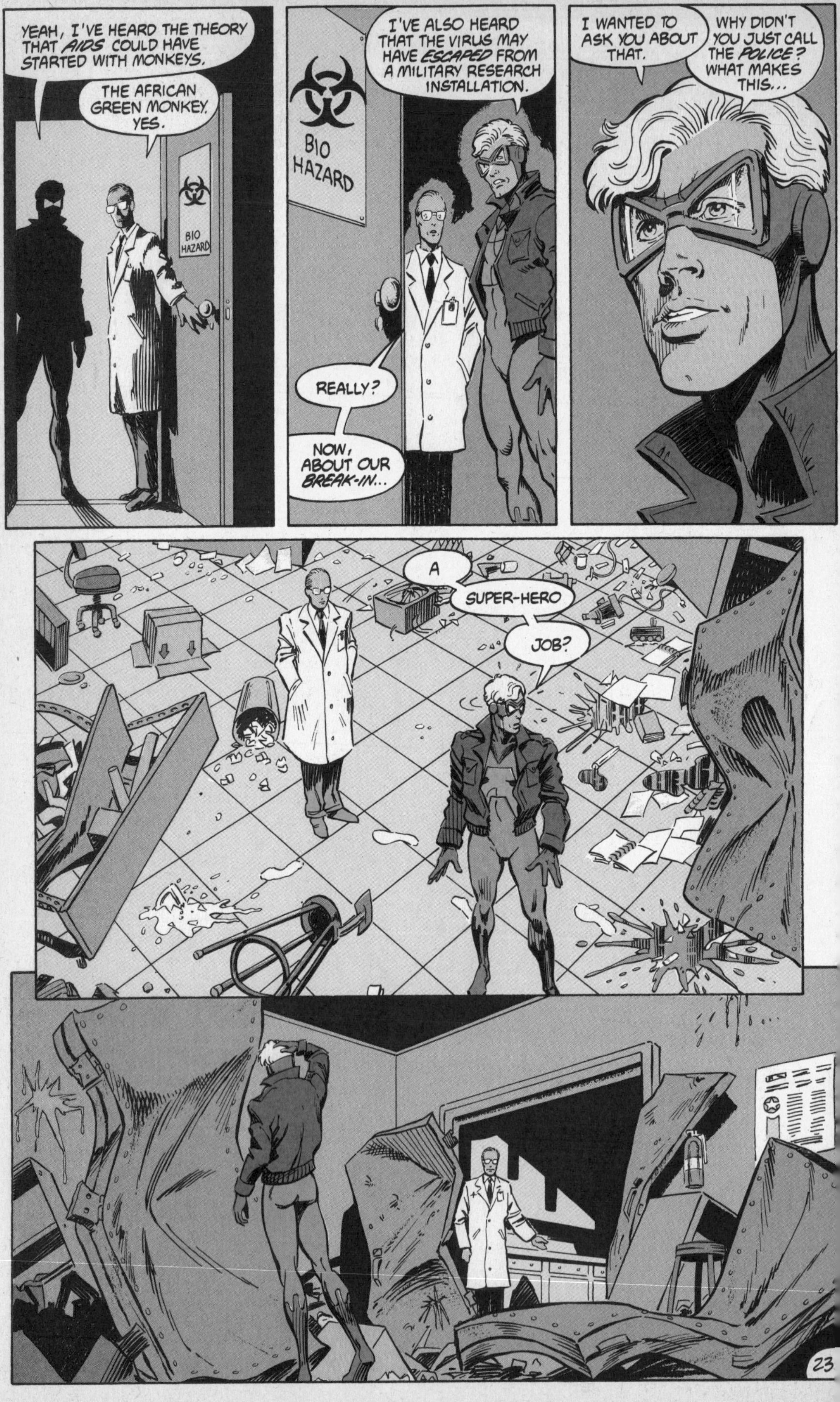
YEAH, I'VE HEARD THE THEORY THAT *AIDS* COULD HAVE STARTED WITH MONKEYS.
THE AFRICAN GREEN MONKEY. YES.
BIO HAZARD
I'VE ALSO HEARD THAT THE VIRUS MAY HAVE *ESCAPED* FROM A MILITARY RESEARCH INSTALLATION.
BIO HAZARD
REALLY?
NOW, ABOUT OUR *BREAK-IN*...
I WANTED TO ASK YOU ABOUT THAT.
WHY DIDN'T YOU JUST CALL THE *POLICE*? WHAT MAKES THIS...
A
SUPER-HERO
JOB?

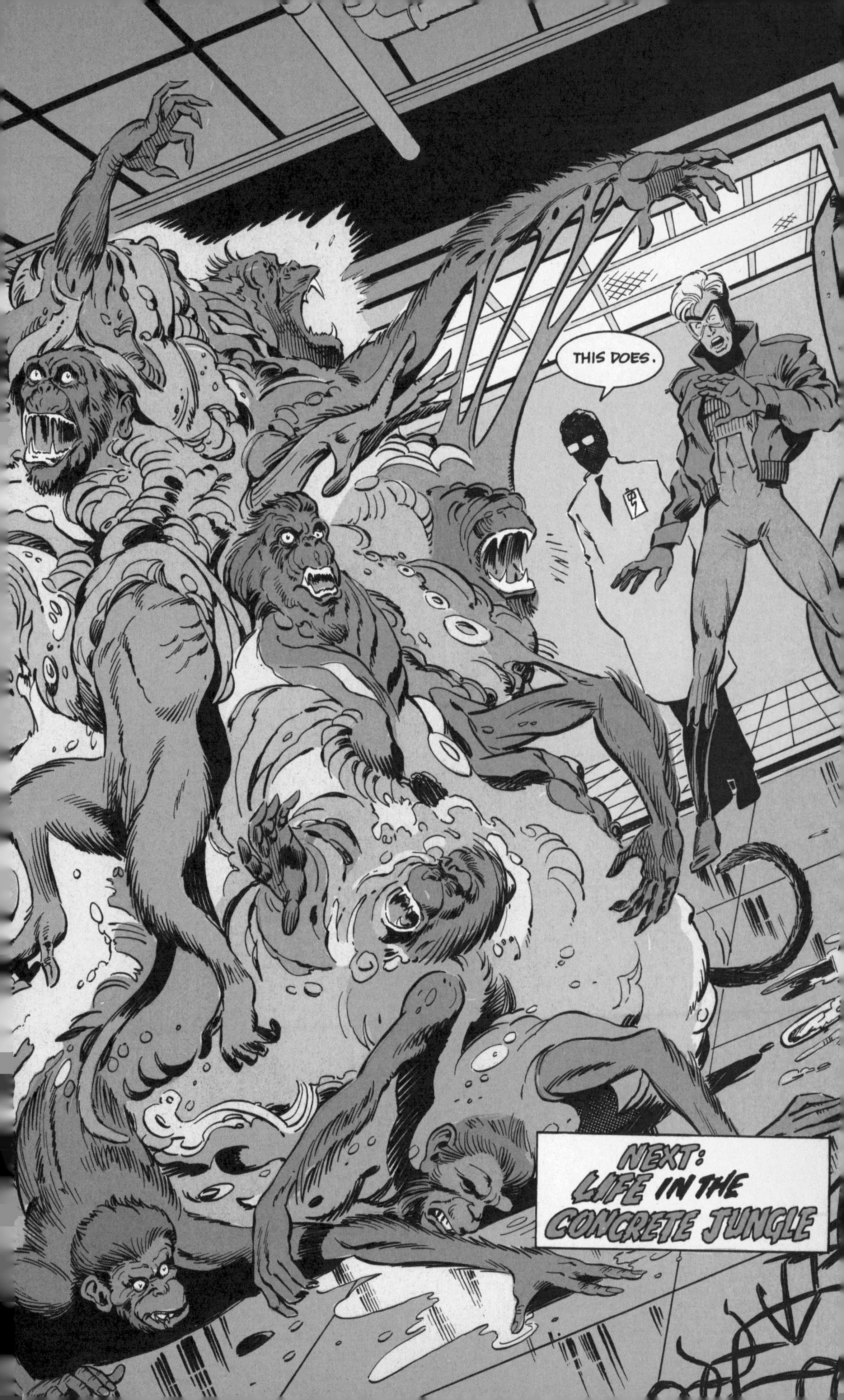
THIS DOES.
NEXT: LIFE IN THE CONCRETE JUNGLE

CHAPTER
TWO

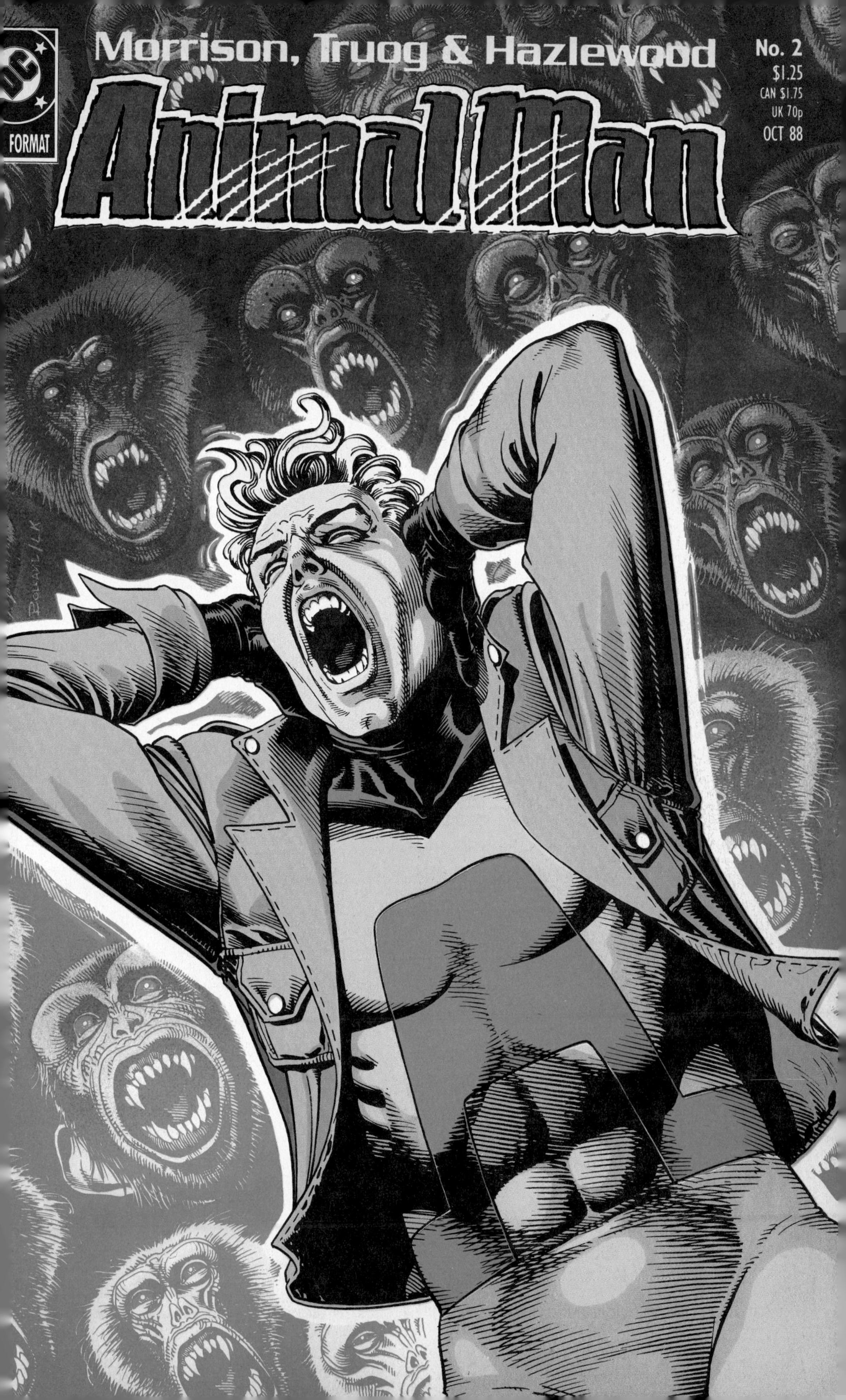
DC
FORMAT
Morrison, Truog & Hazlewood
Animal Man
No. 2
$1.25
CAN $1.75
UK 70p
OCT 88

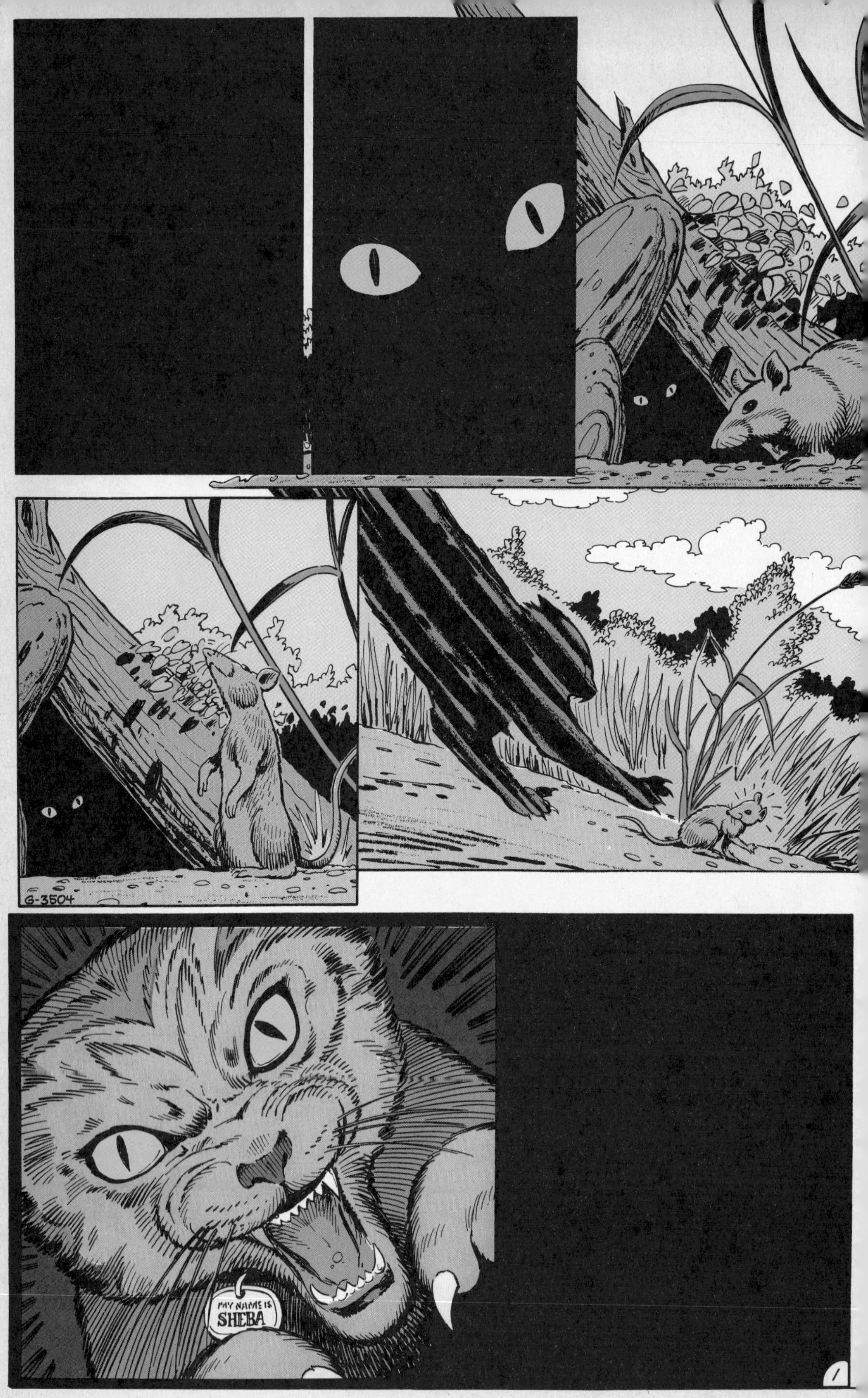
G-3504
MY NAME IS
SHEBA

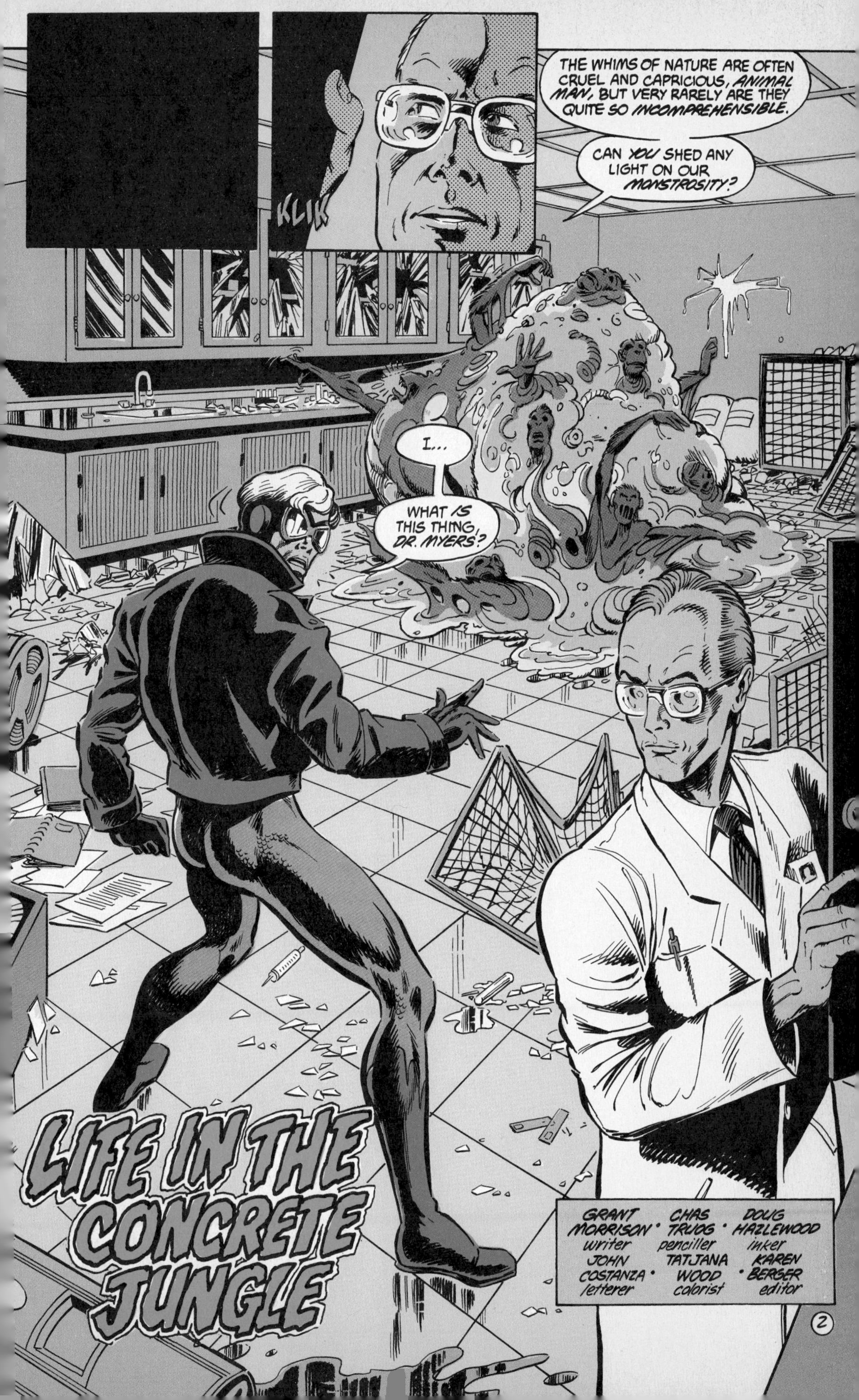
KLIK
THE WHIMS OF NATURE ARE OFTEN CRUEL AND CAPRICIOUS, ANIMAL MAN, BUT VERY RARELY ARE THEY QUITE SO INCOMPREHENSIBLE.
CAN YOU SHED ANY LIGHT ON OUR MONSTROSITY?
I...
WHAT IS THIS THING, DR. MYERS?
LIFE IN THE CONCRETE JUNGLE
GRANT MORRISON • writer
CHAS TRUOG • penciller
DOUG HAZLEWOOD • inker
JOHN COSTANZA • letterer
TATJANA WOOD • colorist
KAREN BERGER • editor
2

IT'S A *MONKEY.*

MORE SPECIFICALLY, IT'S SEVERAL OF OUR LAB MONKEYS, APPARENTLY FUSED TOGETHER INTO ONE UNWORKABLE ORGANISM.

UNTIL WE DO SOME *PROPER* TESTS, THAT'S *ALL* WE CAN SAFELY SPECULATE.

FASCINATING, ISN'T IT?

LOOK AT THEIR *EYES.* THEY SIMPLY CAN'T COMPREHEND WHAT IT IS THEY'VE BECOME.

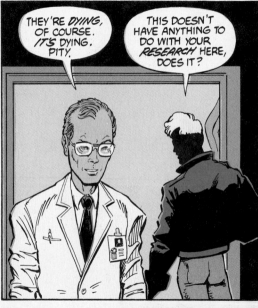

THEY'RE *DYING,* OF COURSE. *IT'S* DYING. PITY.

THIS DOESN'T HAVE ANYTHING TO DO WITH YOUR *RESEARCH* HERE, DOES IT?

WE'RE TRYING TO DEVELOP AN *AIDS* VACCINE HERE AT *S.T.A.R.,* ANIMAL MAN, NOT FRANKEN-STEIN'S MONSTERS.

AND ALL THIS *DAMAGE?*

THE...UH...MONKEYS DIDN'T CAUSE *THIS,* DID THEY?

NO, SOMETHING QUITE DIFFERENT WAS RESPONSIBLE FOR THIS.

IT HAPPENED EARLY THIS MORNING.

3

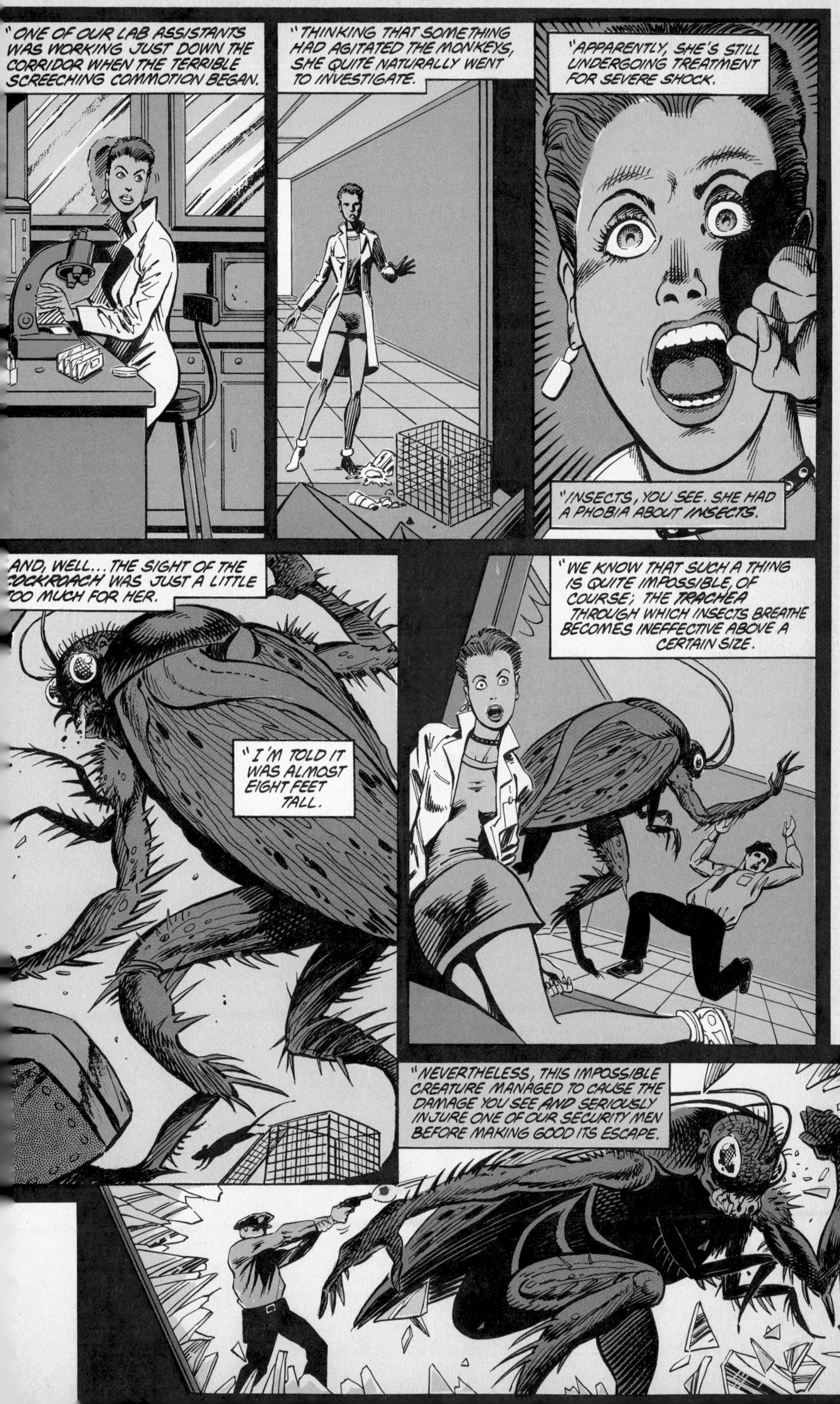
"ONE OF OUR LAB ASSISTANTS WAS WORKING JUST DOWN THE CORRIDOR WHEN THE TERRIBLE SCREECHING COMMOTION BEGAN.
"THINKING THAT SOMETHING HAD AGITATED THE MONKEYS, SHE QUITE NATURALLY WENT TO INVESTIGATE.
"APPARENTLY, SHE'S STILL UNDERGOING TREATMENT FOR SEVERE SHOCK.
"INSECTS, YOU SEE. SHE HAD A PHOBIA ABOUT INSECTS.
AND, WELL... THE SIGHT OF THE COCKROACH WAS JUST A LITTLE TOO MUCH FOR HER.
"I'M TOLD IT WAS ALMOST EIGHT FEET TALL.
"WE KNOW THAT SUCH A THING IS QUITE IMPOSSIBLE, OF COURSE; THE TRACHEA THROUGH WHICH INSECTS BREATHE BECOMES INEFFECTIVE ABOVE A CERTAIN SIZE.
"NEVERTHELESS, THIS IMPOSSIBLE CREATURE MANAGED TO CAUSE THE DAMAGE YOU SEE AND SERIOUSLY INJURE ONE OF OUR SECURITY MEN BEFORE MAKING GOOD ITS ESCAPE.

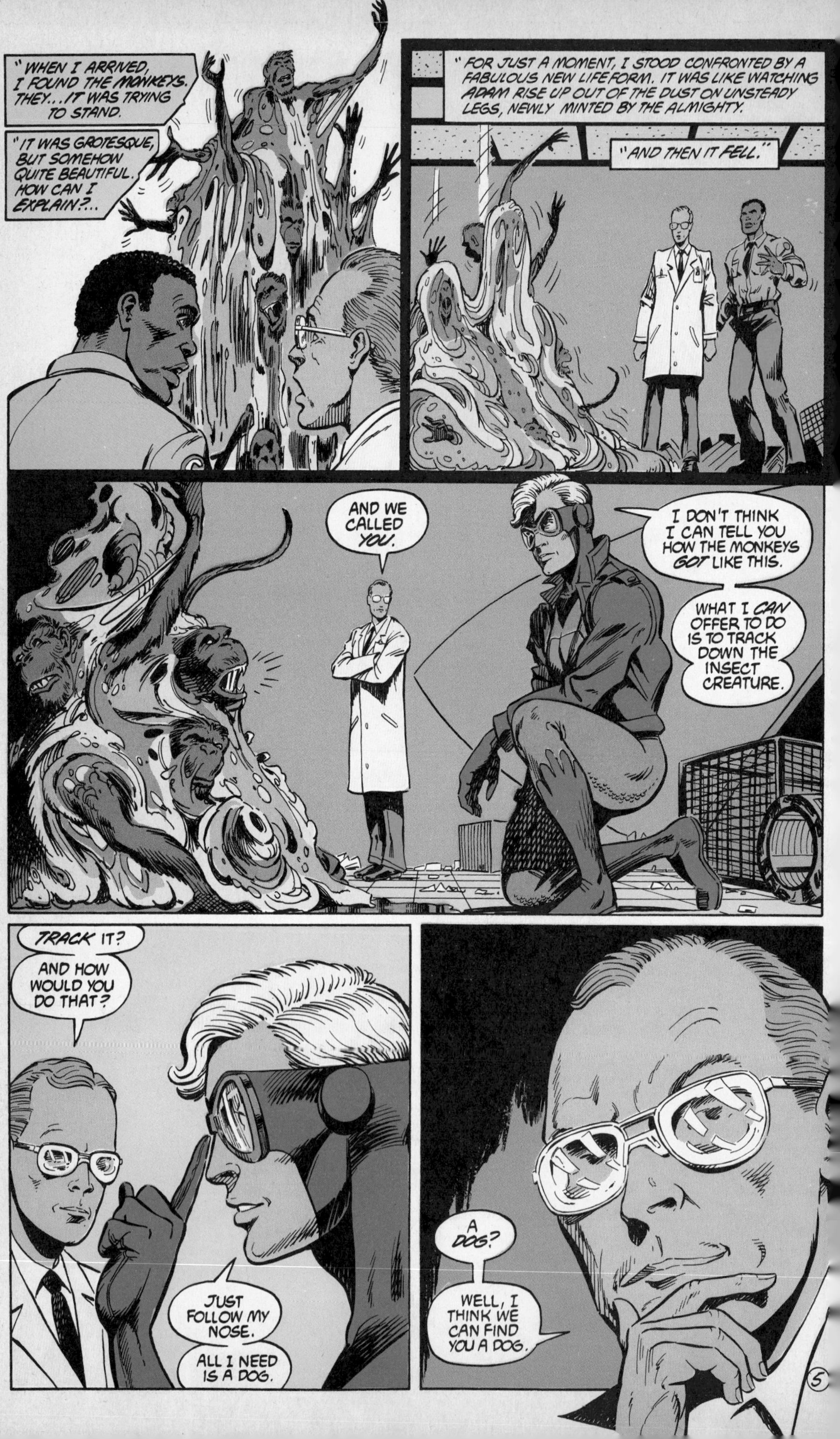
"WHEN I ARRIVED, I FOUND THE MONKEYS. THEY... IT WAS TRYING TO STAND.
"IT WAS GROTESQUE, BUT SOMEHOW QUITE BEAUTIFUL. HOW CAN I EXPLAIN?...
"FOR JUST A MOMENT, I STOOD CONFRONTED BY A FABULOUS NEW LIFE FORM. IT WAS LIKE WATCHING ADAM RISE UP OUT OF THE DUST ON UNSTEADY LEGS, NEWLY MINTED BY THE ALMIGHTY.
"AND THEN IT FELL."
AND WE CALLED YOU.
I DON'T THINK I CAN TELL YOU HOW THE MONKEYS GOT LIKE THIS.
WHAT I CAN OFFER TO DO IS TO TRACK DOWN THE INSECT CREATURE.
TRACK IT?
AND HOW WOULD YOU DO THAT?
JUST FOLLOW MY NOSE.
ALL I NEED IS A DOG.
A DOG?
WELL, I THINK WE CAN FIND YOU A DOG.
5

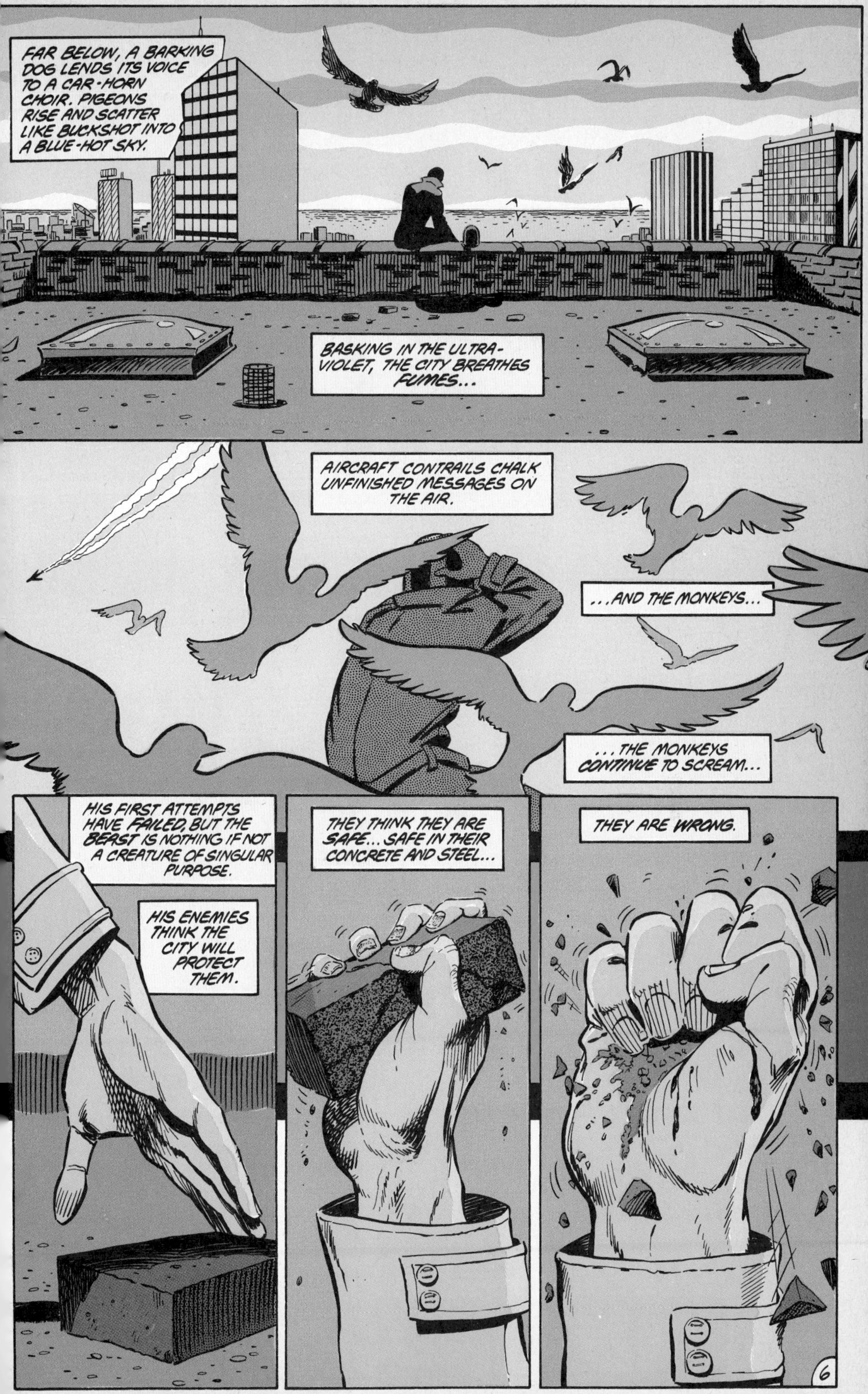
FAR BELOW, A BARKING DOG LENDS ITS VOICE TO A CAR-HORN CHOIR. PIGEONS RISE AND SCATTER LIKE BUCKSHOT INTO A BLUE-HOT SKY.
BASKING IN THE ULTRA-VIOLET, THE CITY BREATHES FUMES...
AIRCRAFT CONTRAILS CHALK UNFINISHED MESSAGES ON THE AIR.
...AND THE MONKEYS...
...THE MONKEYS CONTINUE TO SCREAM...
HIS FIRST ATTEMPTS HAVE FAILED, BUT THE BEAST IS NOTHING IF NOT A CREATURE OF SINGULAR PURPOSE.
HIS ENEMIES THINK THE CITY WILL PROTECT THEM.
THEY THINK THEY ARE SAFE... SAFE IN THEIR CONCRETE AND STEEL...
THEY ARE WRONG.
6

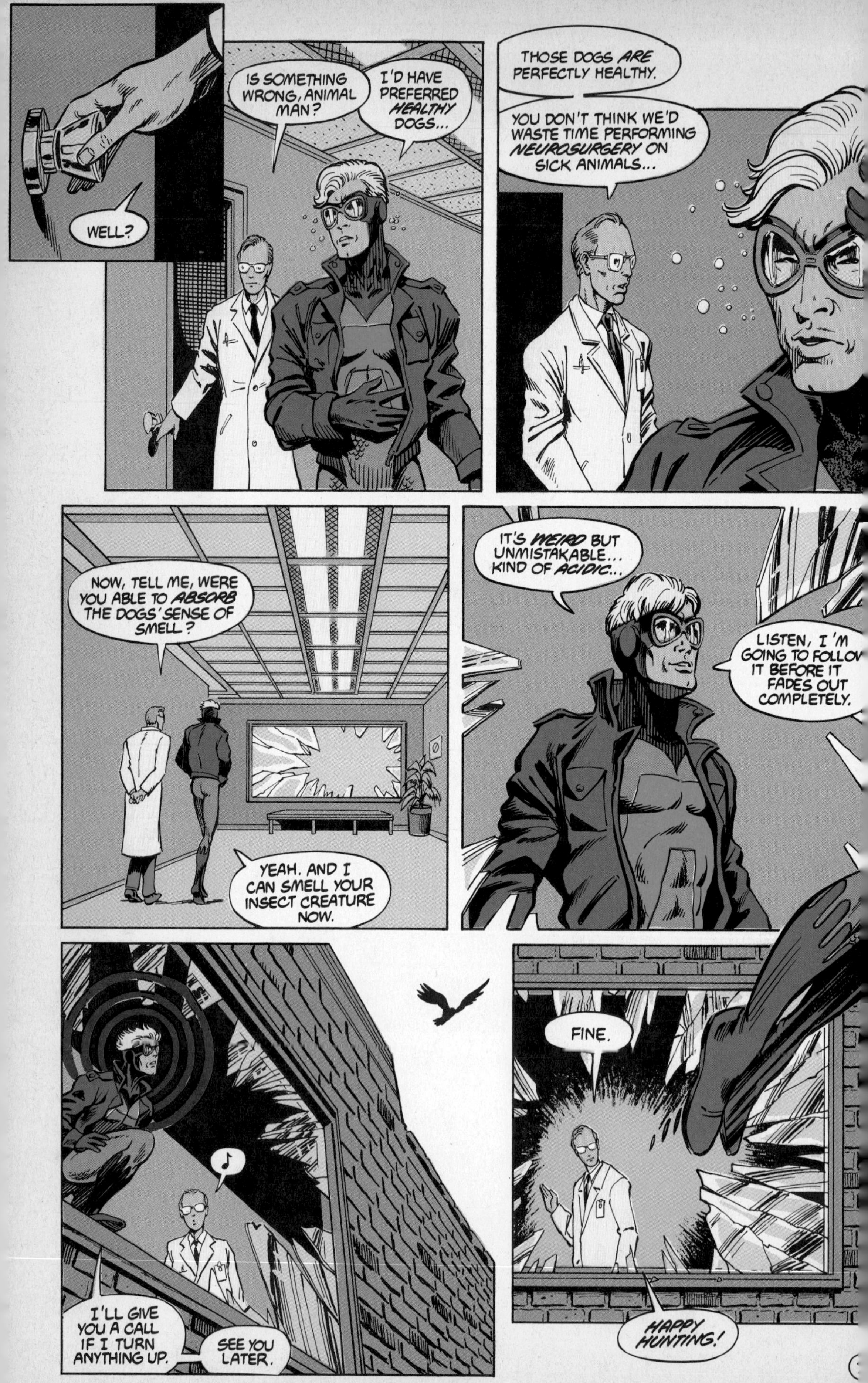
WELL?
IS SOMETHING WRONG, ANIMAL MAN?
I'D HAVE PREFERRED HEALTHY DOGS...
THOSE DOGS ARE PERFECTLY HEALTHY.
YOU DON'T THINK WE'D WASTE TIME PERFORMING NEUROSURGERY ON SICK ANIMALS...
NOW, TELL ME, WERE YOU ABLE TO ABSORB THE DOGS' SENSE OF SMELL?
YEAH. AND I CAN SMELL YOUR INSECT CREATURE NOW.
IT'S WEIRD BUT UNMISTAKABLE... KIND OF ACIDIC...
LISTEN, I'M GOING TO FOLLOW IT BEFORE IT FADES OUT COMPLETELY.
FINE.
HAPPY HUNTING!
I'LL GIVE YOU A CALL IF I TURN ANYTHING UP.
SEE YOU LATER.

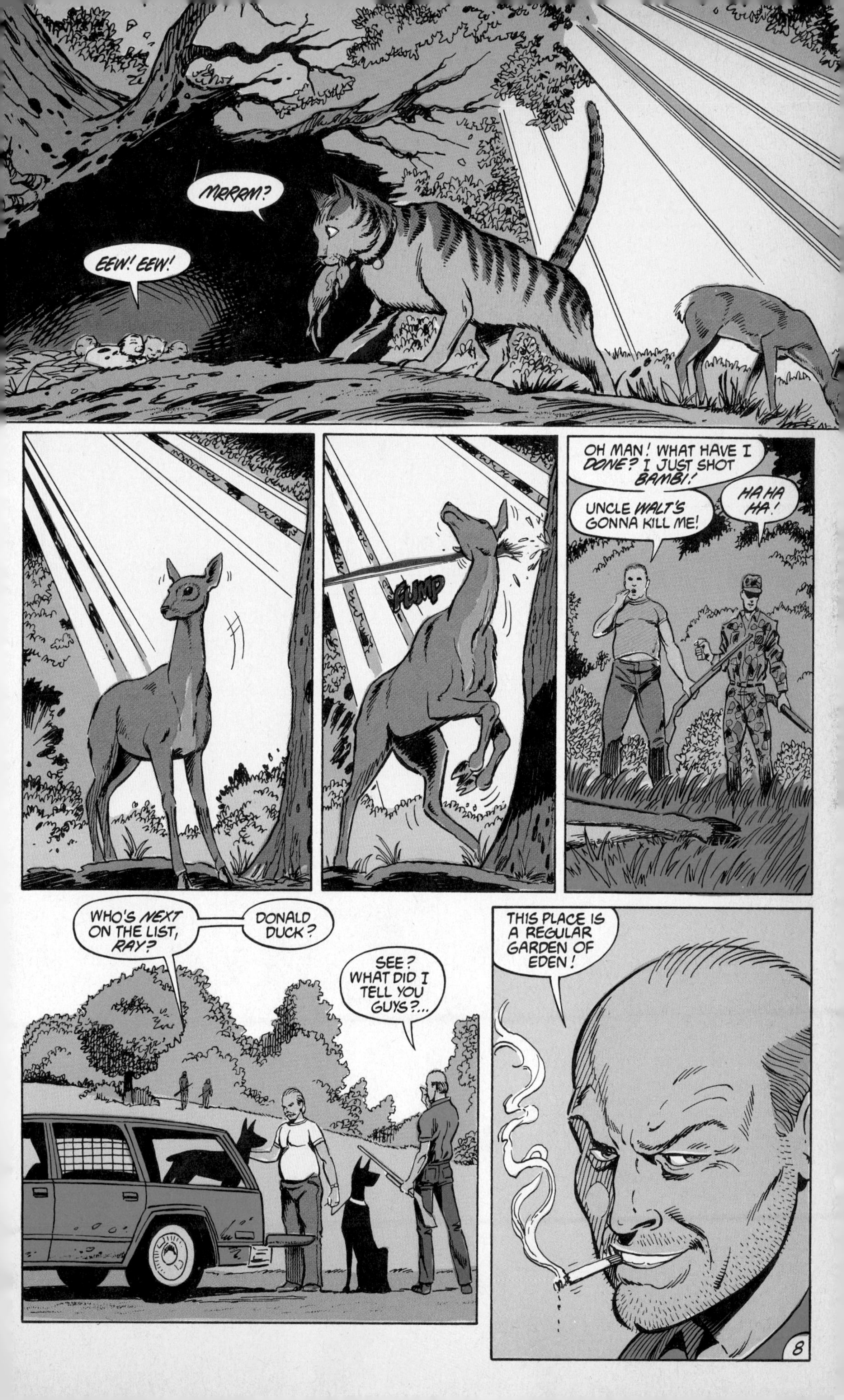
MRRRM?
EEW! EEW!
FUMP
OH MAN! WHAT HAVE I DONE? I JUST SHOT BAMBI!
UNCLE WALT'S GONNA KILL ME!
HA HA HA!
WHO'S NEXT ON THE LIST, RAY?
DONALD DUCK?
SEE? WHAT DID I TELL YOU GUYS?...
THIS PLACE IS A REGULAR GARDEN OF EDEN!
8

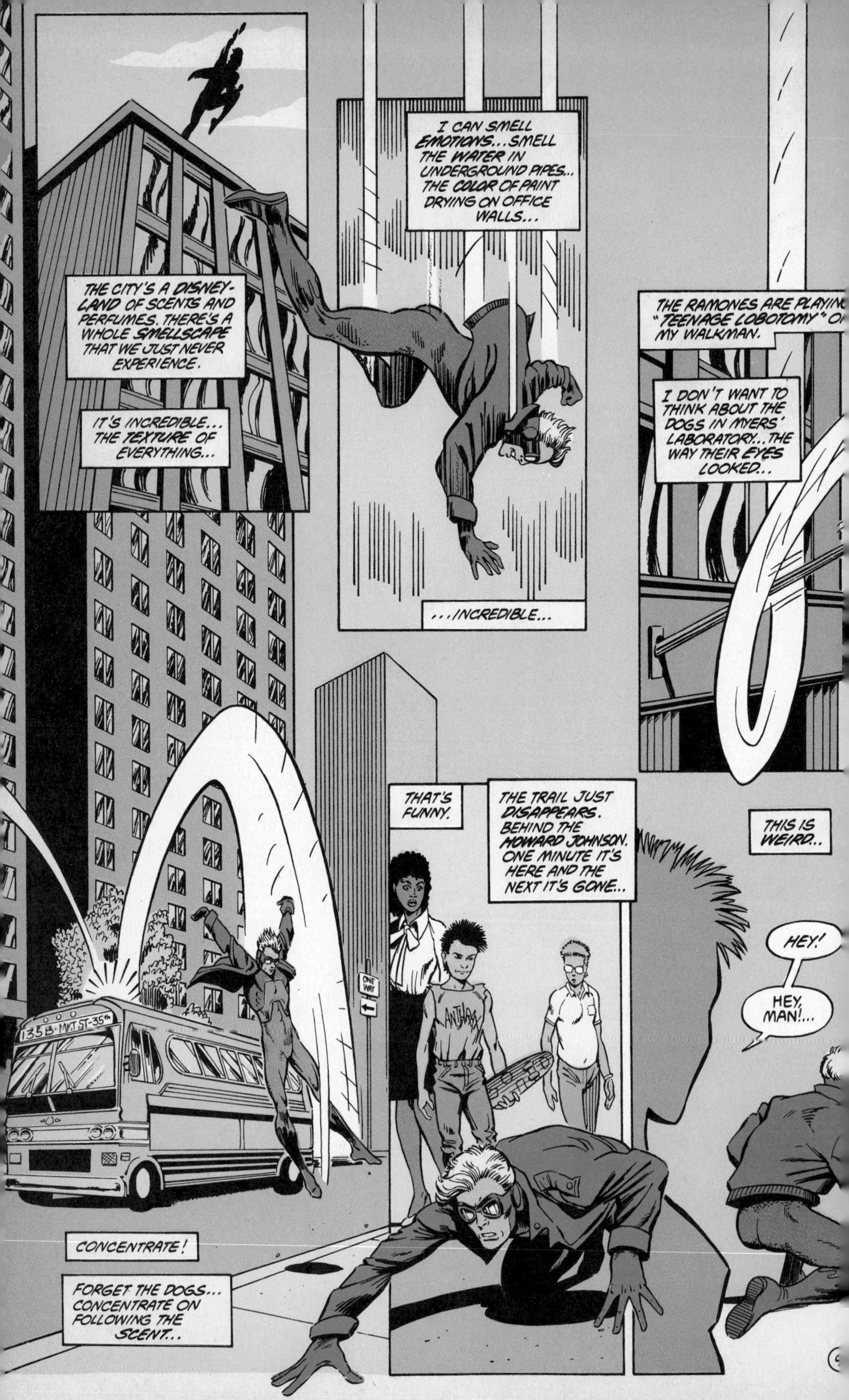
THE CITY'S A DISNEY-LAND OF SCENTS AND PERFUMES. THERE'S A WHOLE SMELLSCAPE THAT WE JUST NEVER EXPERIENCE.
IT'S INCREDIBLE... THE TEXTURE OF EVERYTHING...
I CAN SMELL EMOTIONS... SMELL THE WATER IN UNDERGROUND PIPES... THE COLOR OF PAINT DRYING ON OFFICE WALLS...
...INCREDIBLE...
THE RAMONES ARE PLAYING "TEENAGE LOBOTOMY" ON MY WALKMAN.
I DON'T WANT TO THINK ABOUT THE DOGS IN MYERS' LABORATORY... THE WAY THEIR EYES LOOKED...
135B-MKT.ST-35th
ONE WAY
ANTHRAX
CONCENTRATE!
FORGET THE DOGS... CONCENTRATE ON FOLLOWING THE SCENT...
THAT'S FUNNY.
THE TRAIL JUST DISAPPEARS. BEHIND THE HOWARD JOHNSON. ONE MINUTE IT'S HERE AND THE NEXT IT'S GONE...
THIS IS WEIRD...
HEY!
HEY, MAN!...

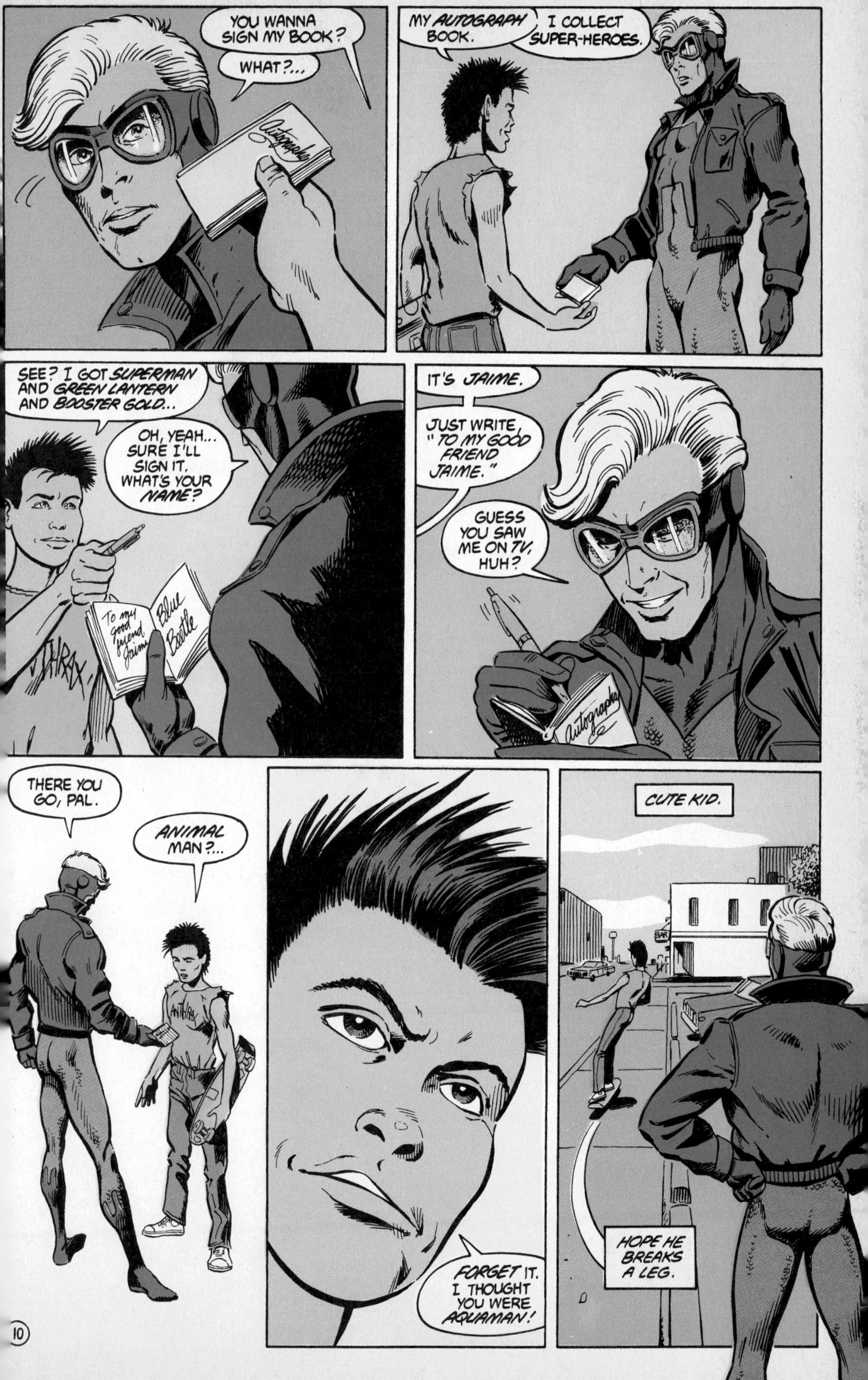
YOU WANNA SIGN MY BOOK?
WHAT?...
MY AUTOGRAPH BOOK.
I COLLECT SUPER-HEROES.
SEE? I GOT SUPERMAN AND GREEN LANTERN AND BOOSTER GOLD...
OH, YEAH... SURE I'LL SIGN IT. WHAT'S YOUR NAME?
To my good friend Jaime
Blue Beetle
IT'S JAIME.
JUST WRITE, "TO MY GOOD FRIEND JAIME."
GUESS YOU SAW ME ON TV, HUH?
Autographs
THERE YOU GO, PAL.
ANIMAL MAN?...
FORGET IT. I THOUGHT YOU WERE AQUAMAN!
CUTE KID.
BAR
HOPE HE BREAKS A LEG.

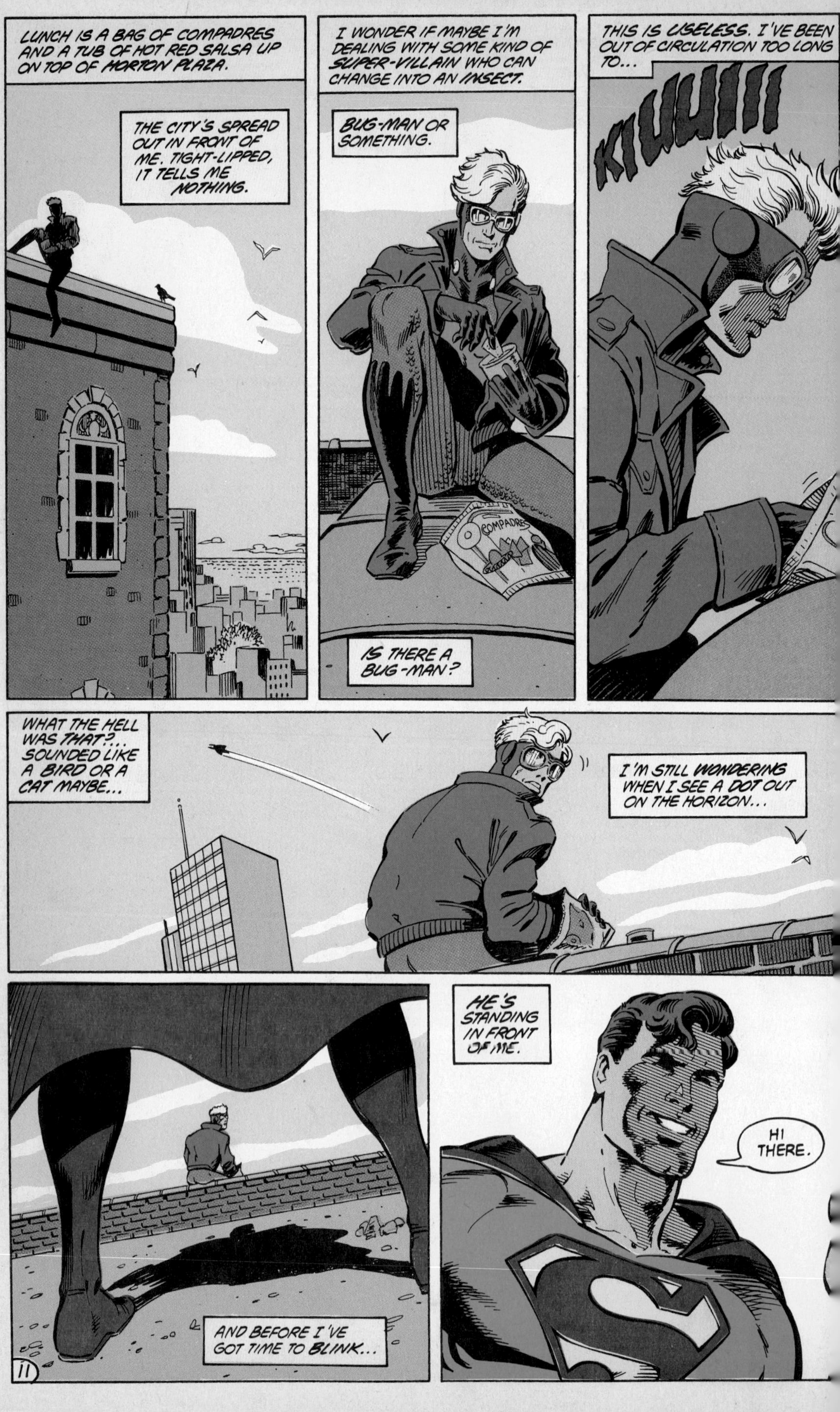
LUNCH IS A BAG OF COMPADRES AND A TUB OF HOT RED SALSA UP ON TOP OF HORTON PLAZA.
THE CITY'S SPREAD OUT IN FRONT OF ME. TIGHT-LIPPED, IT TELLS ME NOTHING.
I WONDER IF MAYBE I'M DEALING WITH SOME KIND OF SUPER-VILLAIN WHO CAN CHANGE INTO AN INSECT.
BUG-MAN OR SOMETHING.
COMPADRES
IS THERE A BUG-MAN?
THIS IS USELESS. I'VE BEEN OUT OF CIRCULATION TOO LONG TO...
KIUUIII
WHAT THE HELL WAS THAT?... SOUNDED LIKE A BIRD OR A CAT MAYBE...
I'M STILL WONDERING WHEN I SEE A DOT OUT ON THE HORIZON...
AND BEFORE I'VE GOT TIME TO BLINK...
HE'S STANDING IN FRONT OF ME.
HI THERE.
11

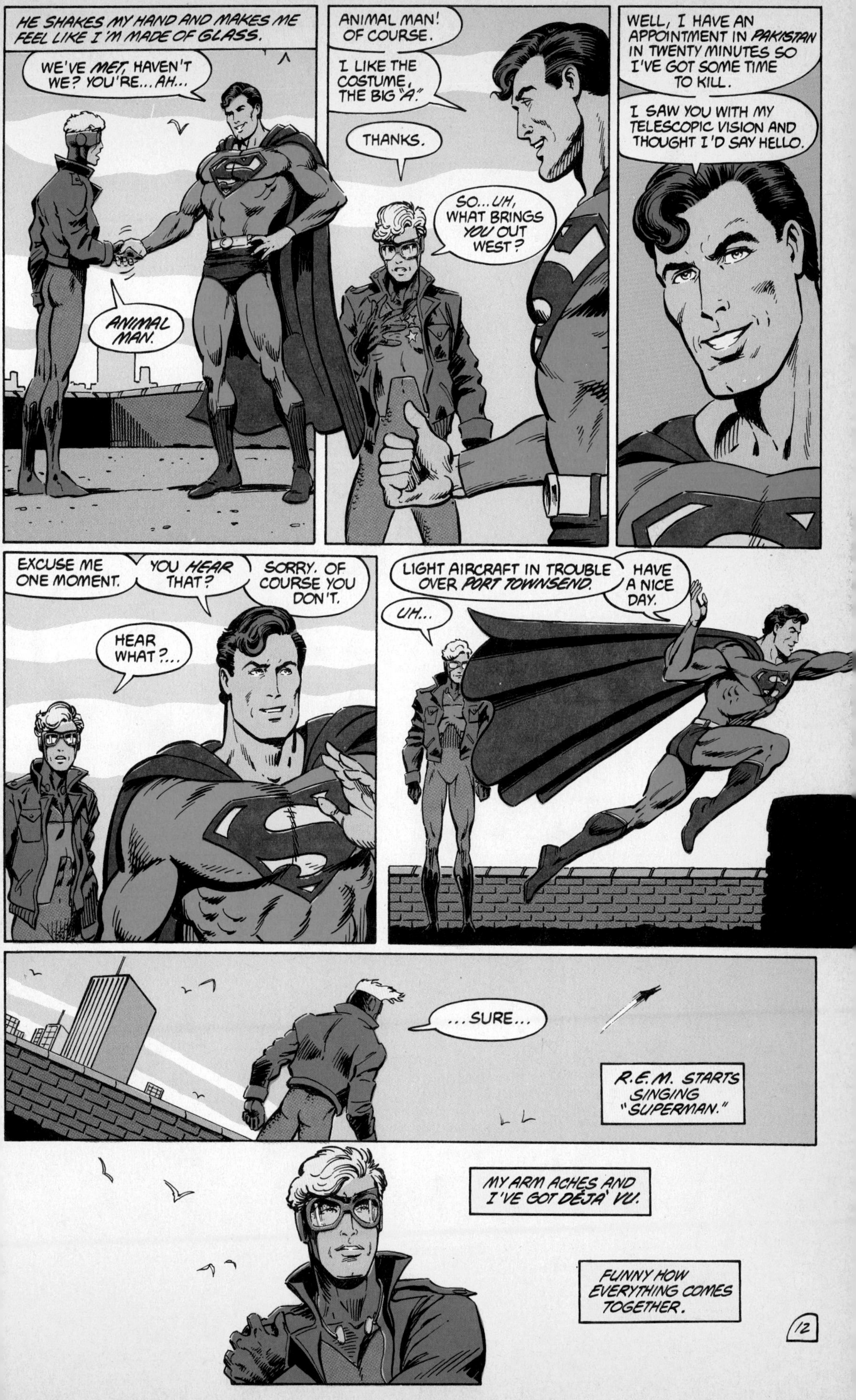
HE SHAKES MY HAND AND MAKES ME FEEL LIKE I'M MADE OF GLASS.
WE'VE MET, HAVEN'T WE? YOU'RE... AH...
ANIMAL MAN.
ANIMAL MAN! OF COURSE.
I LIKE THE COSTUME, THE BIG "A."
THANKS.
SO... UH, WHAT BRINGS YOU OUT WEST?
WELL, I HAVE AN APPOINTMENT IN PAKISTAN IN TWENTY MINUTES SO I'VE GOT SOME TIME TO KILL.
I SAW YOU WITH MY TELESCOPIC VISION AND THOUGHT I'D SAY HELLO.
EXCUSE ME ONE MOMENT.
YOU HEAR THAT?
SORRY. OF COURSE YOU DON'T.
HEAR WHAT?...
LIGHT AIRCRAFT IN TROUBLE OVER PORT TOWNSEND.
HAVE A NICE DAY.
UH...
...SURE...
R.E.M. STARTS SINGING "SUPERMAN."
MY ARM ACHES AND I'VE GOT DÉJÀ VU.
FUNNY HOW EVERYTHING COMES TOGETHER.
12

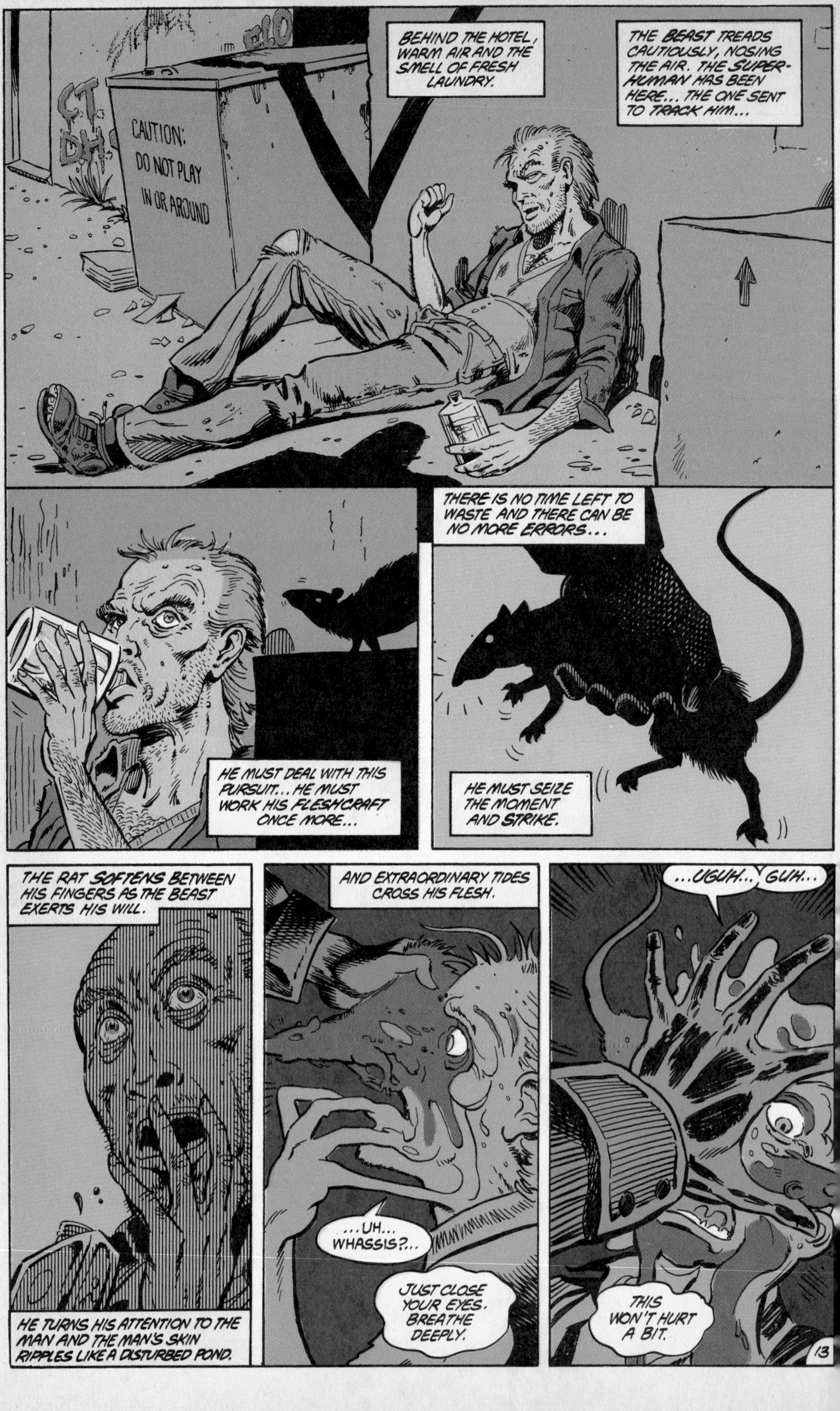

STEFFEN
ELO
C.T.
DH
CAUTION:
DO NOT PLAY
IN OR AROUND
BEHIND THE HOTEL, WARM AIR AND THE SMELL OF FRESH LAUNDRY.
THE BEAST TREADS CAUTIOUSLY, NOSING THE AIR. THE SUPER-HUMAN HAS BEEN HERE... THE ONE SENT TO TRACK HIM...
HE MUST DEAL WITH THIS PURSUIT... HE MUST WORK HIS FLESHCRAFT ONCE MORE...
THERE IS NO TIME LEFT TO WASTE AND THERE CAN BE NO MORE ERRORS...
HE MUST SEIZE THE MOMENT AND STRIKE.
THE RAT SOFTENS BETWEEN HIS FINGERS AS THE BEAST EXERTS HIS WILL.
HE TURNS HIS ATTENTION TO THE MAN AND THE MAN'S SKIN RIPPLES LIKE A DISTURBED POND.
AND EXTRAORDINARY TIDES CROSS HIS FLESH.
...UH... WHASSIS?...
JUST CLOSE YOUR EYES. BREATHE DEEPLY.
...UGUH... GUH...
THIS WON'T HURT A BIT.

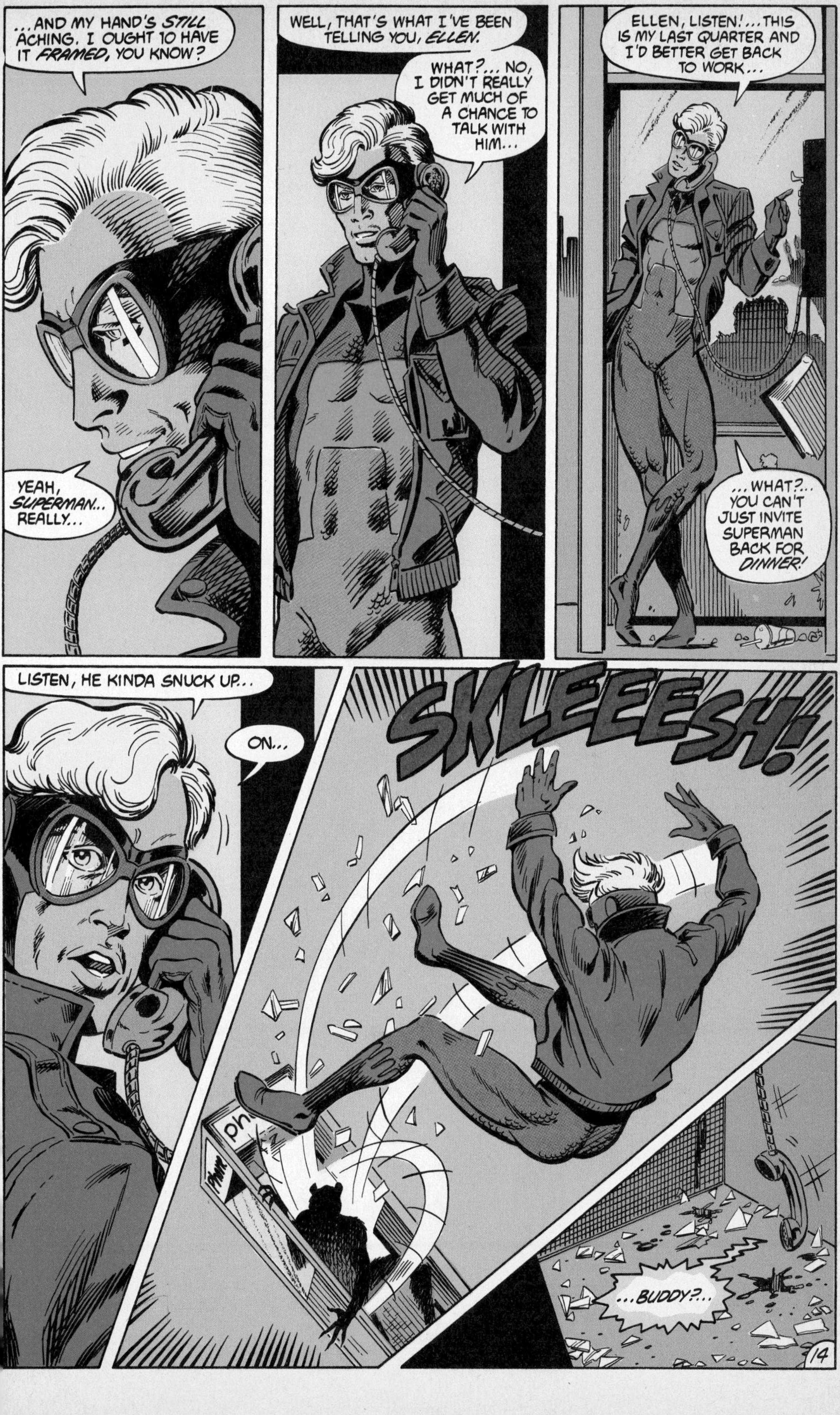

...AND MY HAND'S STILL ACHING. I OUGHT TO HAVE IT FRAMED, YOU KNOW?
YEAH, SUPERMAN... REALLY...
WELL, THAT'S WHAT I'VE BEEN TELLING YOU, ELLEN.
WHAT?... NO, I DIDN'T REALLY GET MUCH OF A CHANCE TO TALK WITH HIM...
ELLEN, LISTEN!...THIS IS MY LAST QUARTER AND I'D BETTER GET BACK TO WORK...
...WHAT?... YOU CAN'T JUST INVITE SUPERMAN BACK FOR DINNER!
LISTEN, HE KINDA SNUCK UP...
ON...
SKLEEESH!
...BUDDY?...

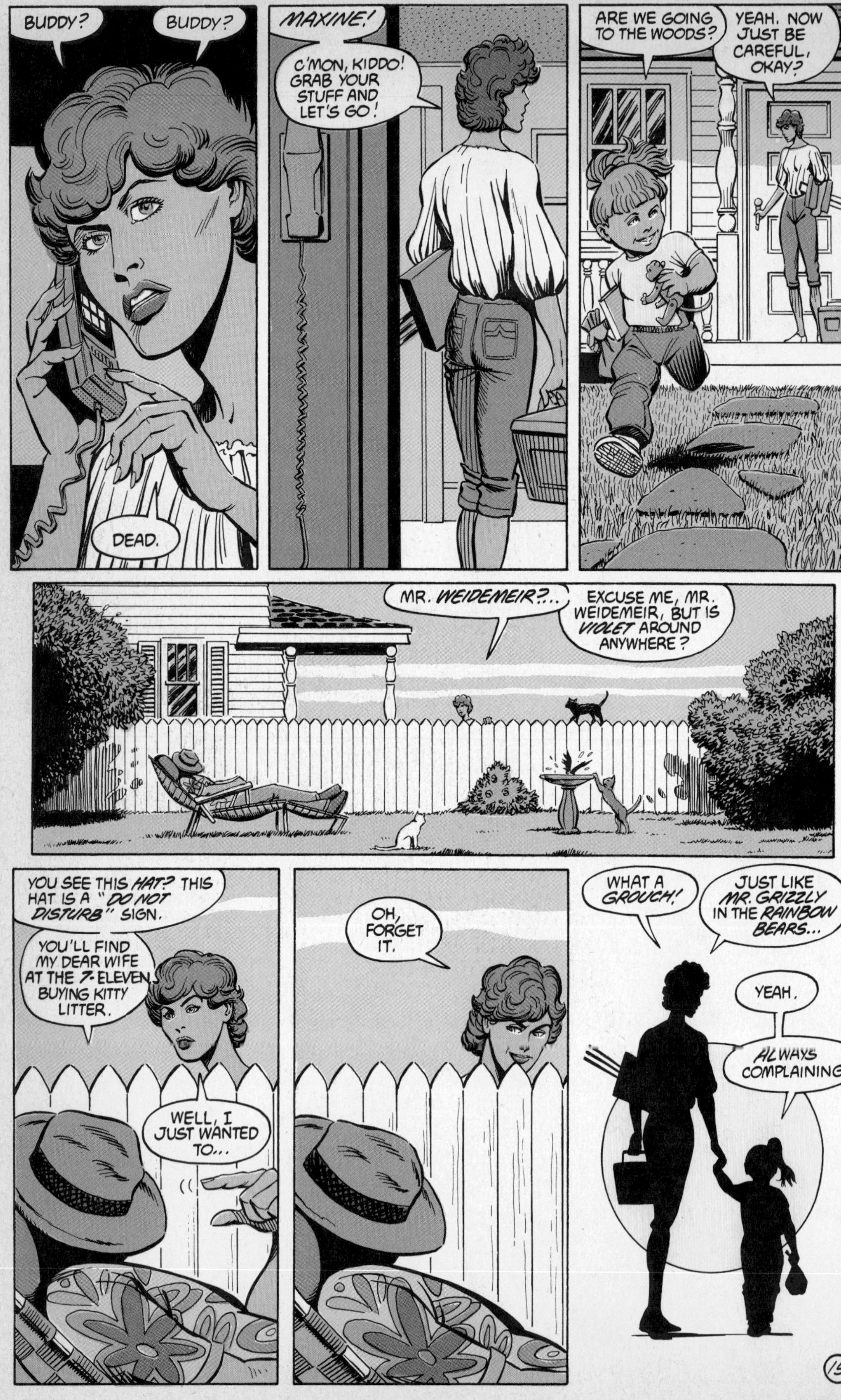
BUDDY?
BUDDY?
DEAD.
MAXINE!
C'MON, KIDDO! GRAB YOUR STUFF AND LET'S GO!
ARE WE GOING TO THE WOODS?
YEAH. NOW JUST BE CAREFUL, OKAY?
MR. WEIDEMEIR?...
EXCUSE ME, MR. WEIDEMEIR, BUT IS VIOLET AROUND ANYWHERE?
YOU SEE THIS HAT? THIS HAT IS A "DO NOT DISTURB" SIGN.
YOU'LL FIND MY DEAR WIFE AT THE 7-ELEVEN BUYING KITTY LITTER.
WELL, I JUST WANTED TO...
OH, FORGET IT.
WHAT A GROUCH!
JUST LIKE MR. GRIZZLY IN THE RAINBOW BEARS...
YEAH.
ALWAYS COMPLAINING!

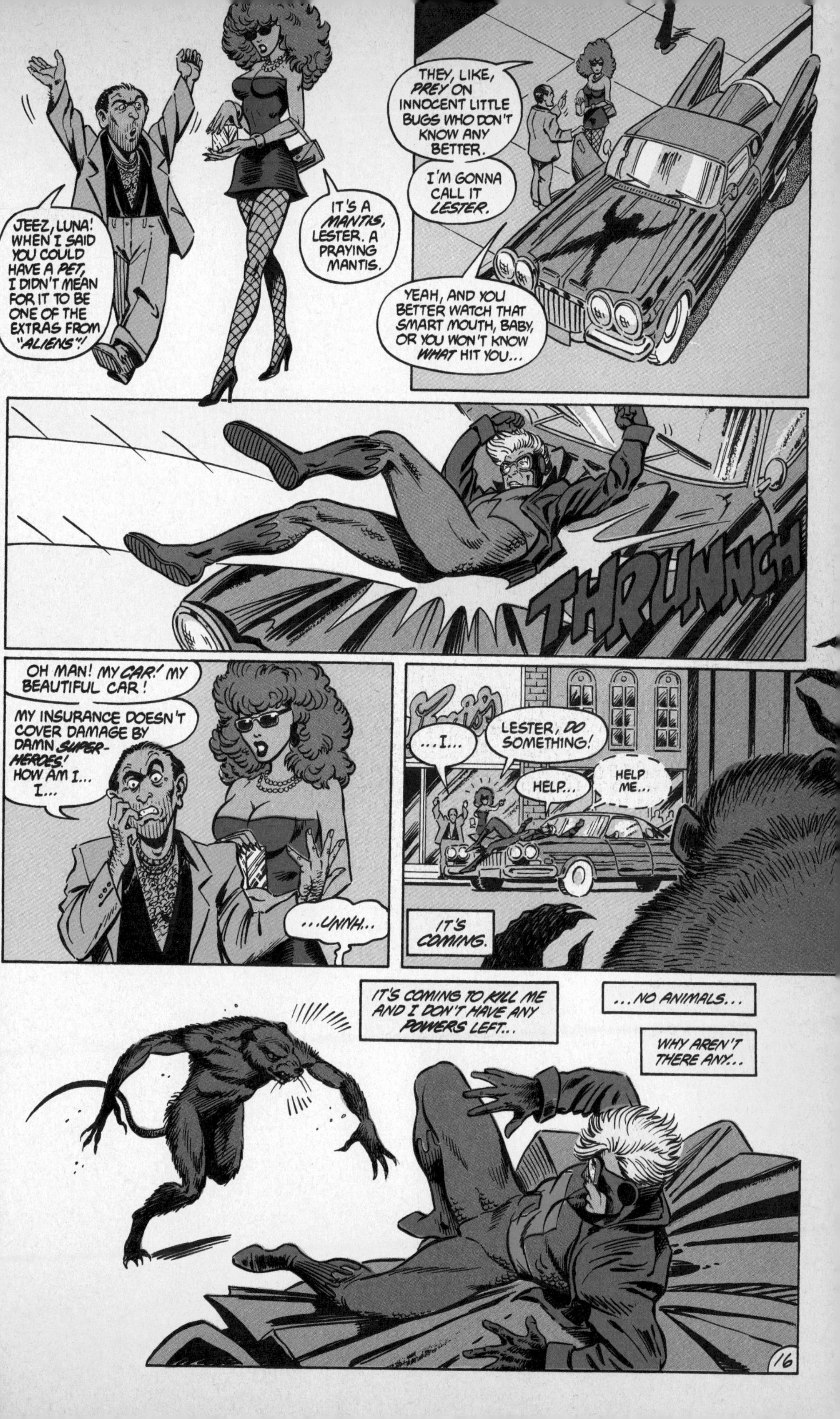

JEEZ, LUNA! WHEN I SAID YOU COULD HAVE A PET, I DIDN'T MEAN FOR IT TO BE ONE OF THE EXTRAS FROM "ALIENS"!
IT'S A MANTIS, LESTER. A PRAYING MANTIS.
THEY, LIKE, PREY ON INNOCENT LITTLE BUGS WHO DON'T KNOW ANY BETTER.
I'M GONNA CALL IT LESTER.
YEAH, AND YOU BETTER WATCH THAT SMART MOUTH, BABY, OR YOU WON'T KNOW WHAT HIT YOU...
THRUNNCH
OH MAN! MY CAR! MY BEAUTIFUL CAR!
MY INSURANCE DOESN'T COVER DAMAGE BY DAMN SUPER-HEROES! HOW AM I... I...
...UNNH...
...I...
LESTER, DO SOMETHING!
HELP...
HELP ME...
IT'S COMING.
IT'S COMING TO KILL ME AND I DON'T HAVE ANY POWERS LEFT...
...NO ANIMALS...
WHY AREN'T THERE ANY...

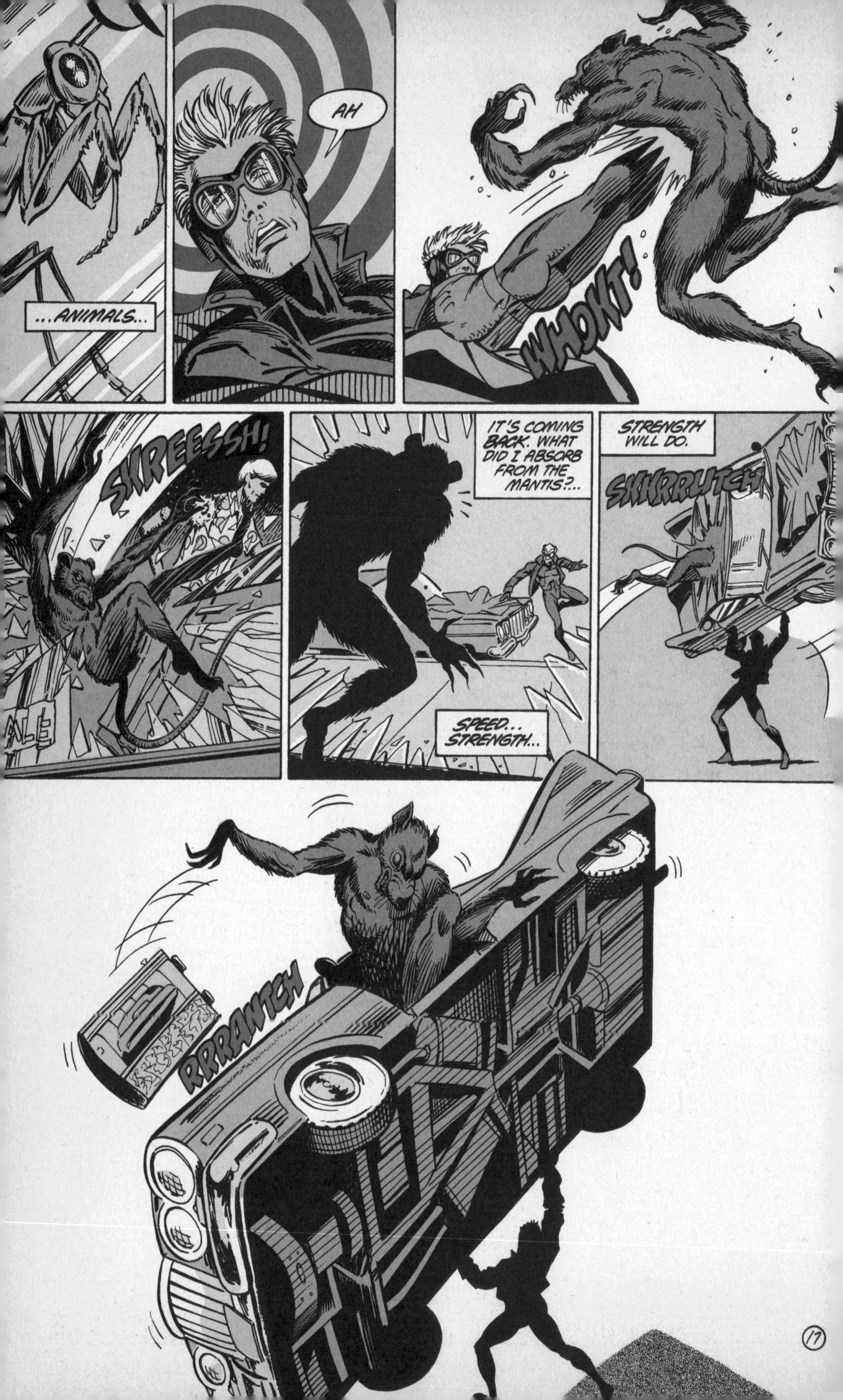
...ANIMALS...
AH
WHOKT!
SKREESSH!
IT'S COMING BACK. WHAT DID I ABSORB FROM THE MANTIS?...
SPEED... STRENGTH...
STRENGTH WILL DO.
SKHRRUTCH
RRRANTCH

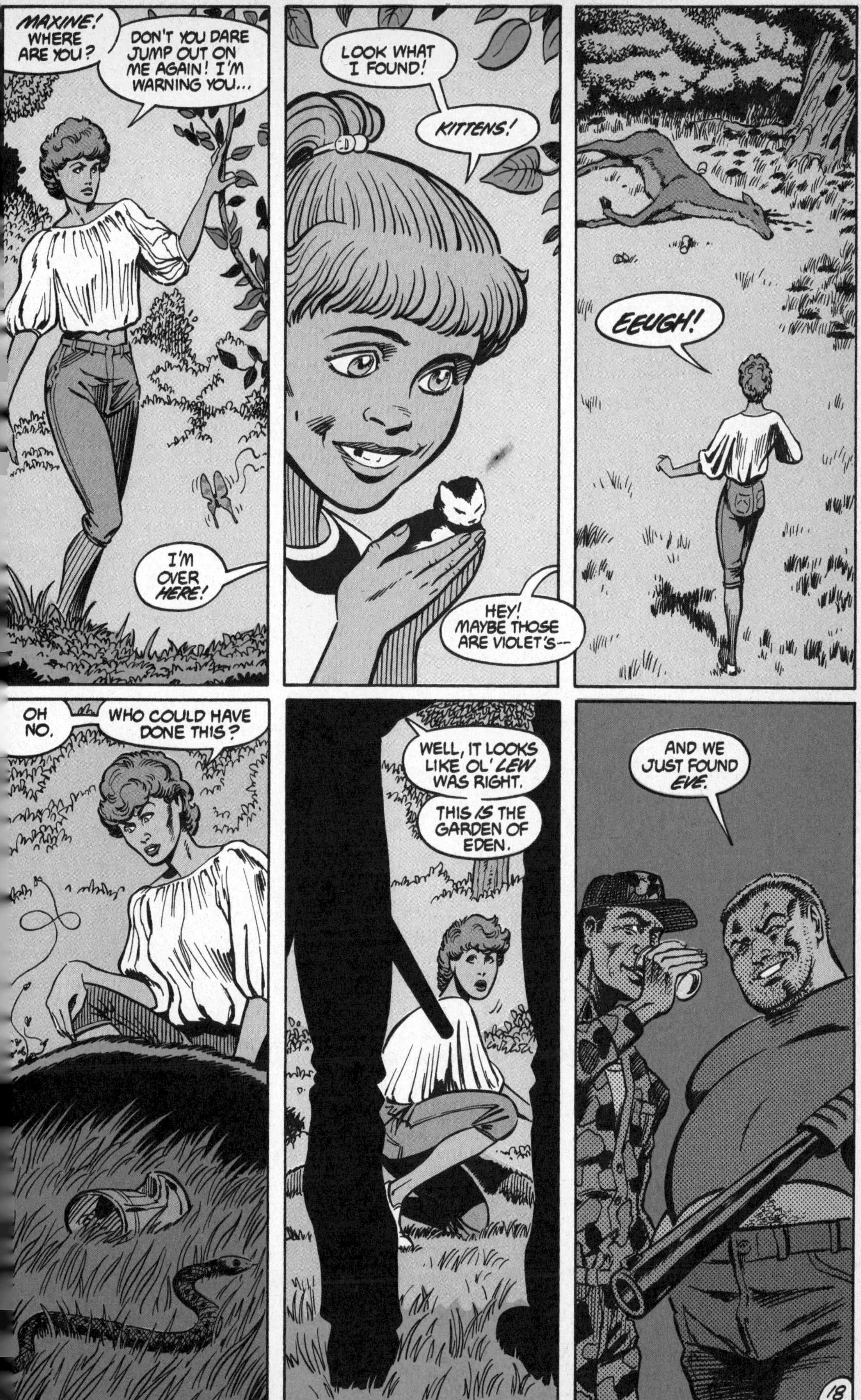
MAXINE! WHERE ARE YOU?
DON'T YOU DARE JUMP OUT ON ME AGAIN! I'M WARNING YOU...
I'M OVER HERE!
LOOK WHAT I FOUND!
KITTENS!
HEY! MAYBE THOSE ARE VIOLET'S--
EEUGH!
OH NO.
WHO COULD HAVE DONE THIS?
WELL, IT LOOKS LIKE OL' LEW WAS RIGHT.
THIS IS THE GARDEN OF EDEN.
AND WE JUST FOUND EVE.
18

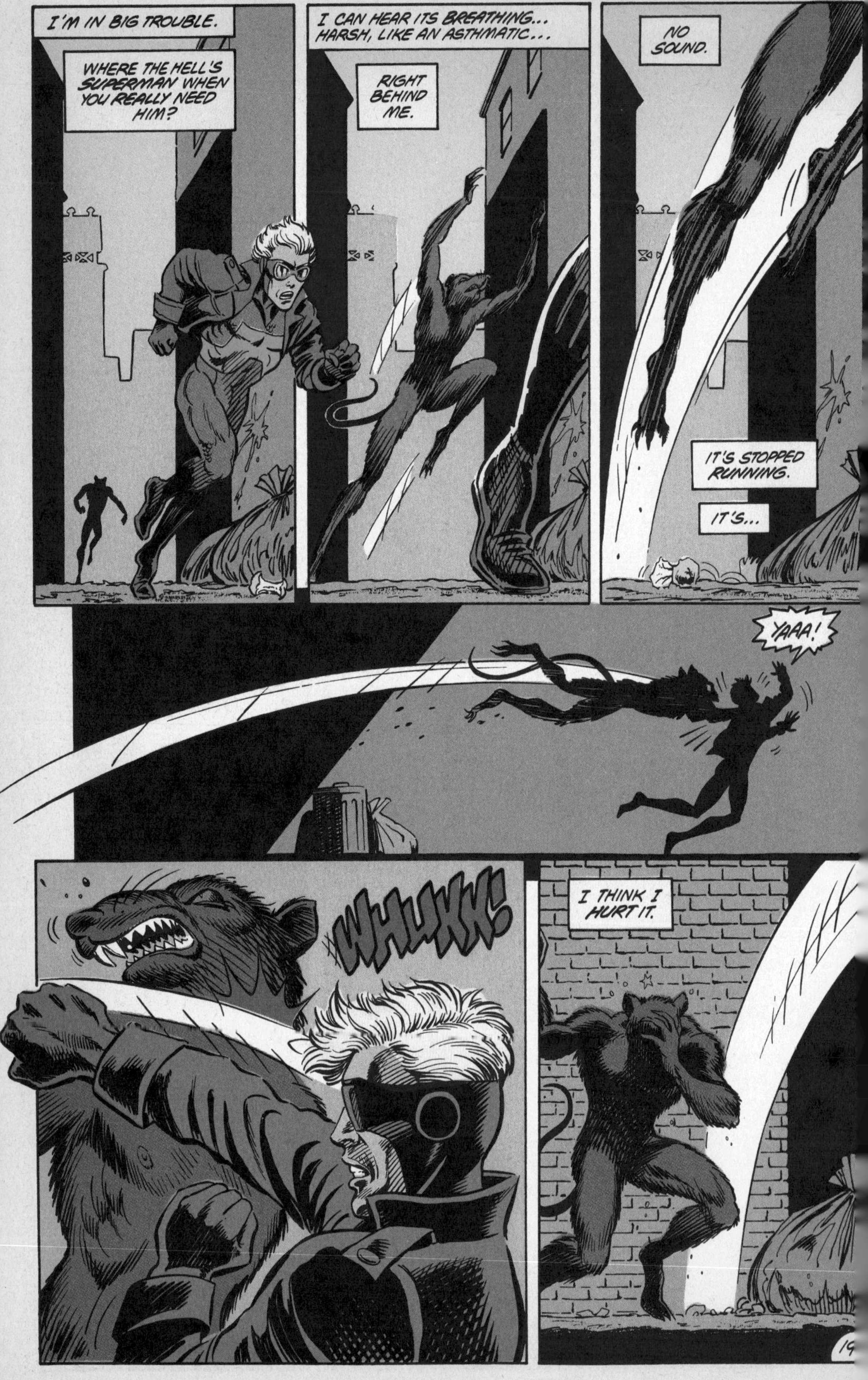
I'M IN BIG TROUBLE.
WHERE THE HELL'S SUPERMAN WHEN YOU REALLY NEED HIM?
I CAN HEAR ITS BREATHING... HARSH, LIKE AN ASTHMATIC...
RIGHT BEHIND ME.
NO SOUND.
IT'S STOPPED RUNNING.
IT'S...
YAAA!
WHUKK!
I THINK I HURT IT.

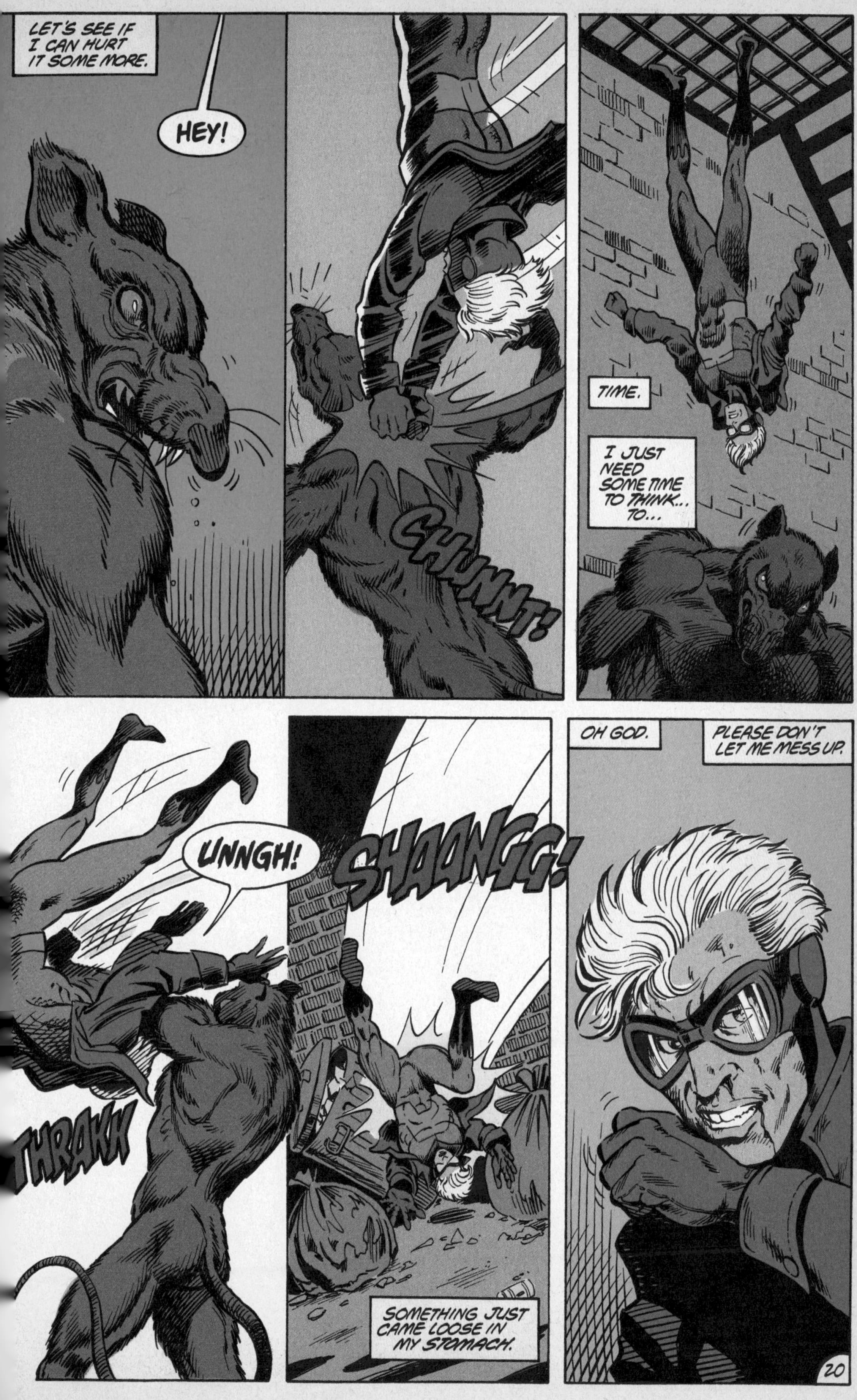
LET'S SEE IF I CAN HURT IT SOME MORE.
HEY!
CHUNNT!
TIME.
I JUST NEED SOME TIME TO THINK... TO...
UNNGH!
THRAKK
SHAANGG!
SOMETHING JUST CAME LOOSE IN MY STOMACH.
OH GOD.
PLEASE DON'T LET ME MESS UP.

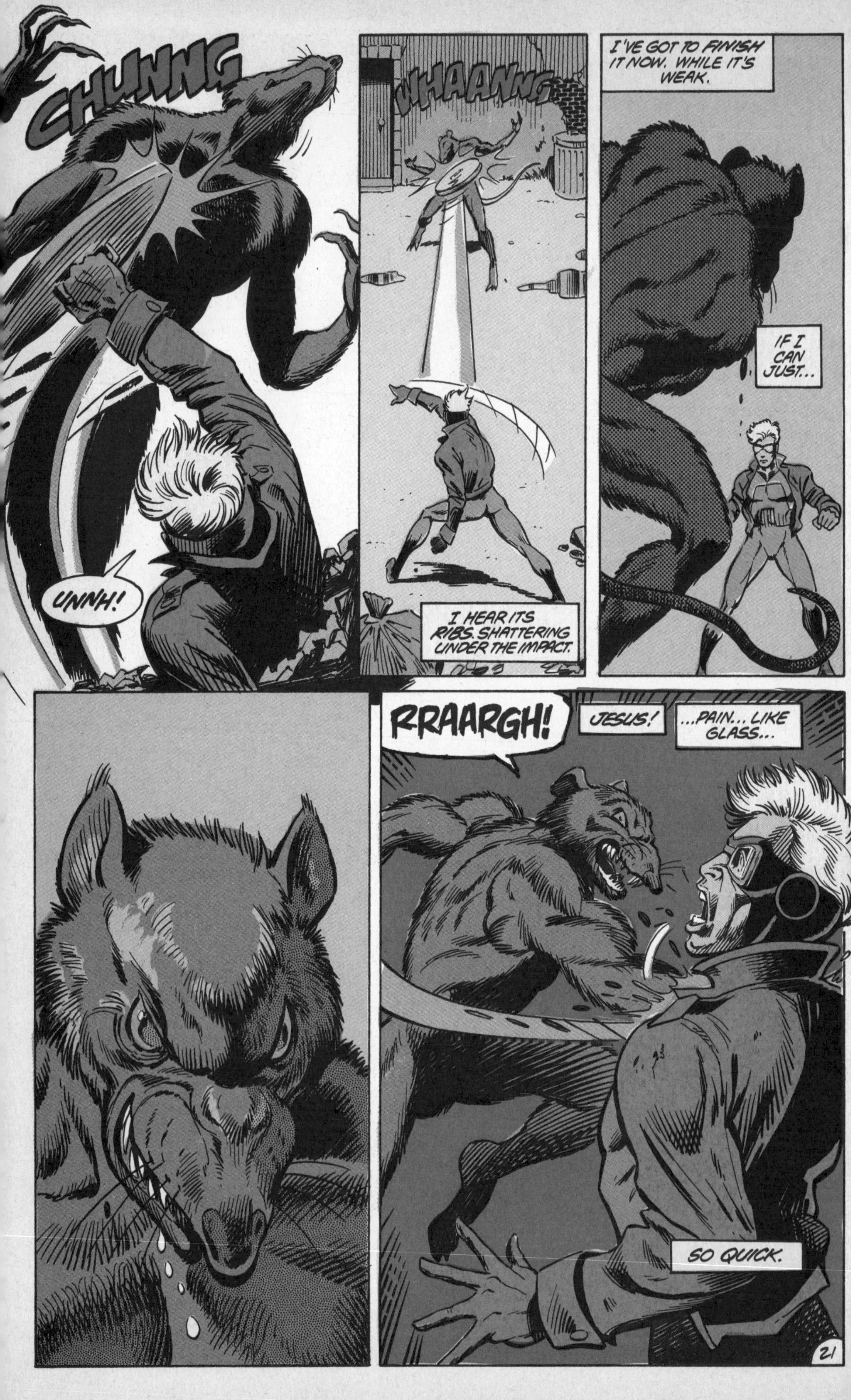
CHUNNG
UNNH!
WHAANNG
I HEAR ITS RIBS. SHATTERING UNDER THE IMPACT.
I'VE GOT TO FINISH IT NOW. WHILE IT'S WEAK.
IF I CAN JUST...
RRAARGH!
JESUS!
...PAIN... LIKE GLASS...
SO QUICK.

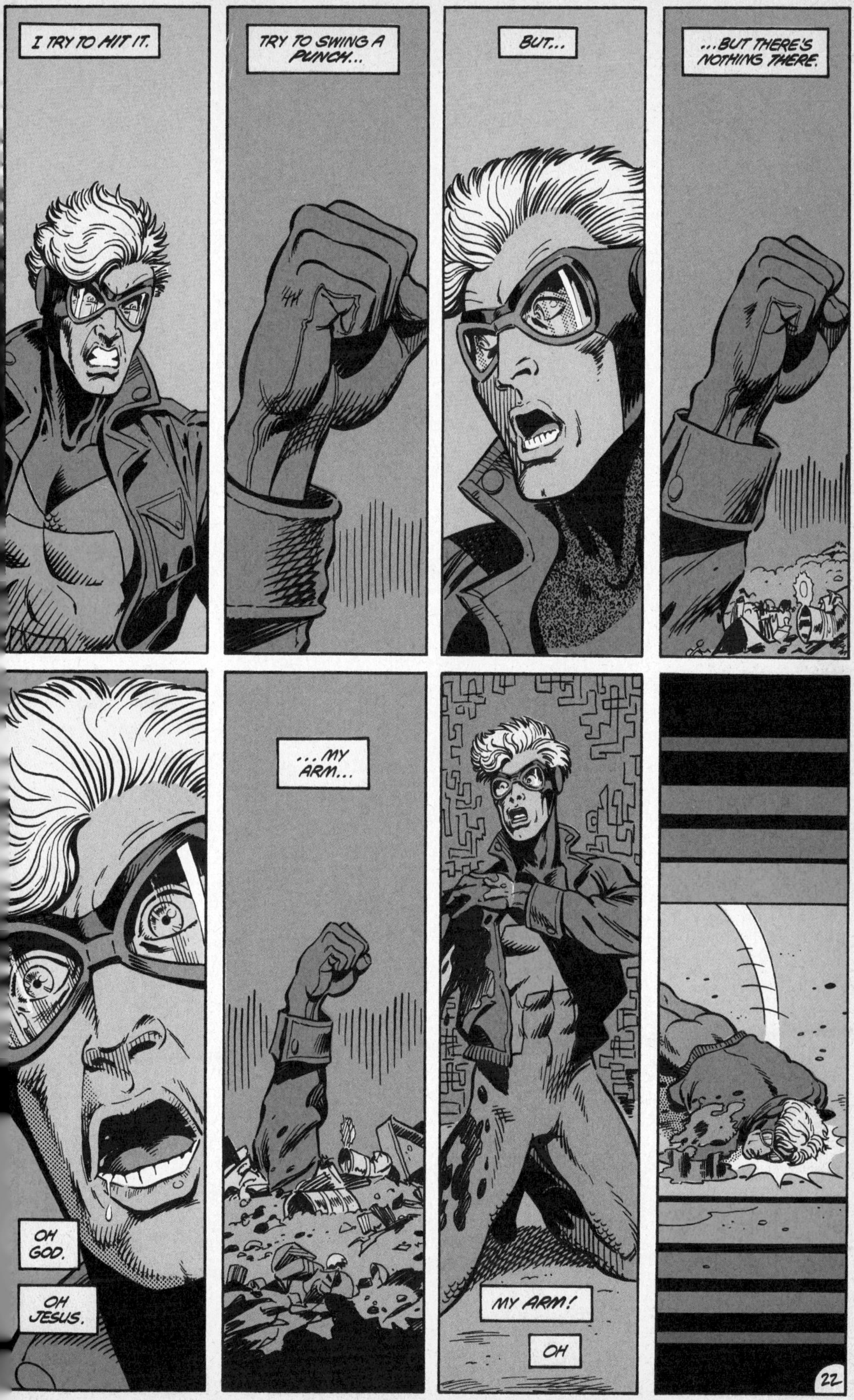
I TRY TO HIT IT.
TRY TO SWING A PUNCH...
BUT...
...BUT THERE'S NOTHING THERE.
OH GOD.
OH JESUS.
...MY ARM...
MY ARM!
OH

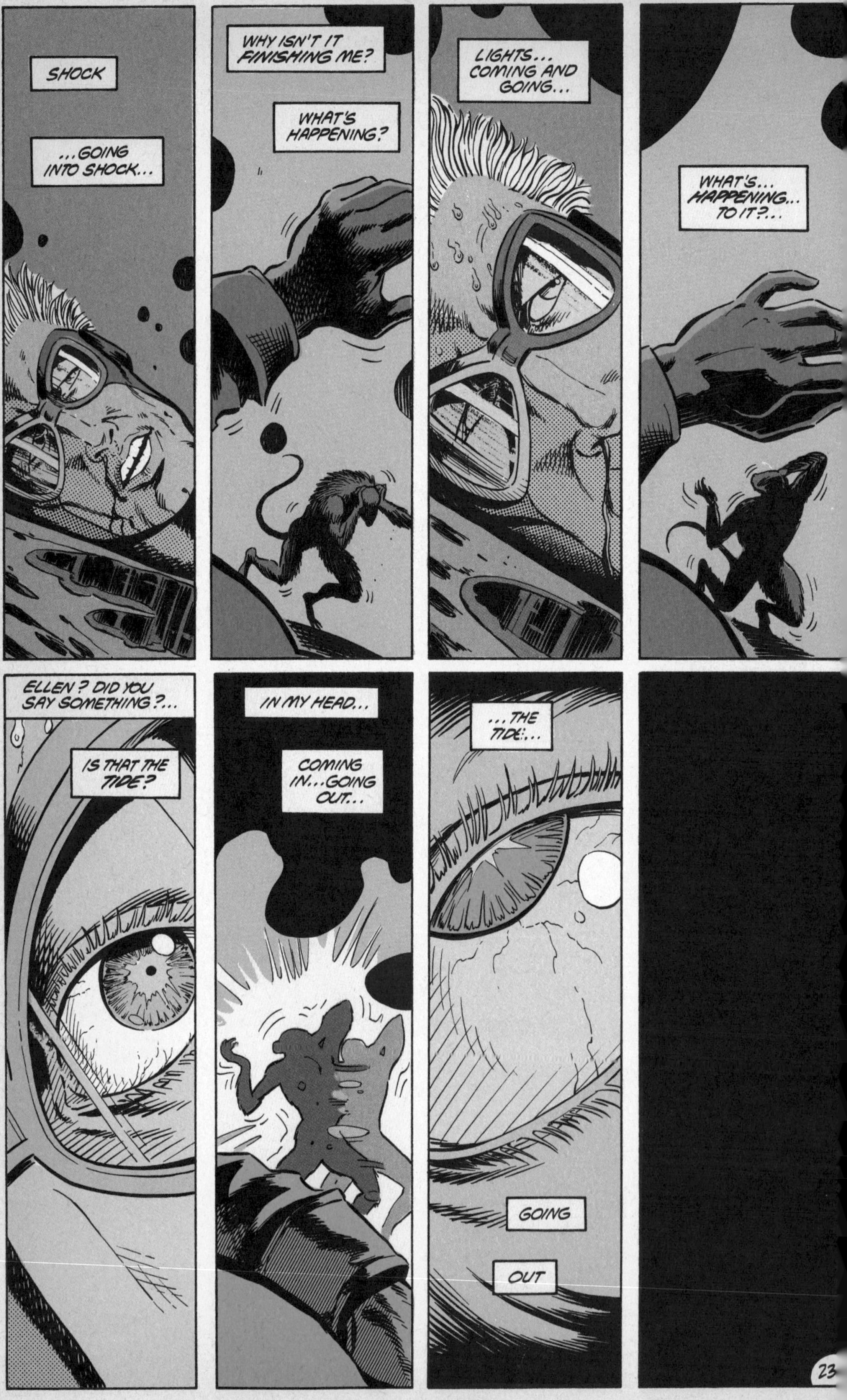
SHOCK
...GOING INTO SHOCK...
WHY ISN'T IT FINISHING ME?
WHAT'S HAPPENING?
LIGHTS... COMING AND GOING...
WHAT'S... HAPPENING... TO IT?...
ELLEN? DID YOU SAY SOMETHING?...
IS THAT THE TIDE?
IN MY HEAD...
COMING IN...GOING OUT...
...THE TIDE...
GOING
OUT

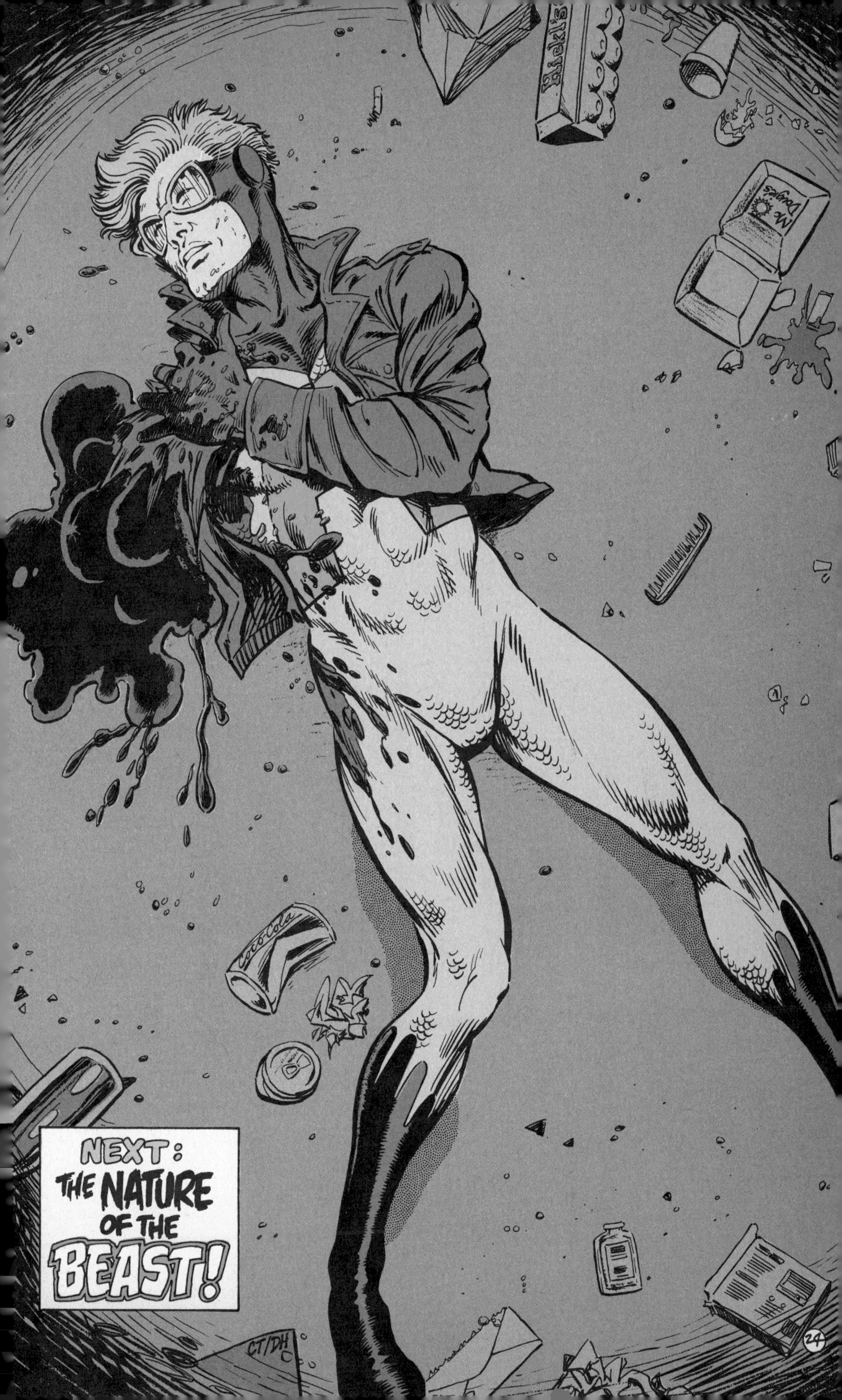
NEXT:
THE NATURE OF THE BEAST!
CT/DH

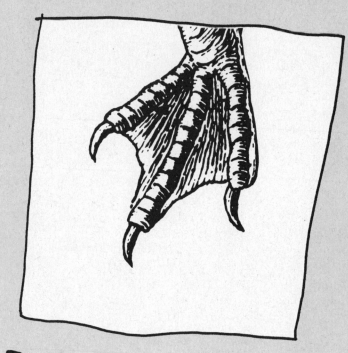

CHAPTER
THREE

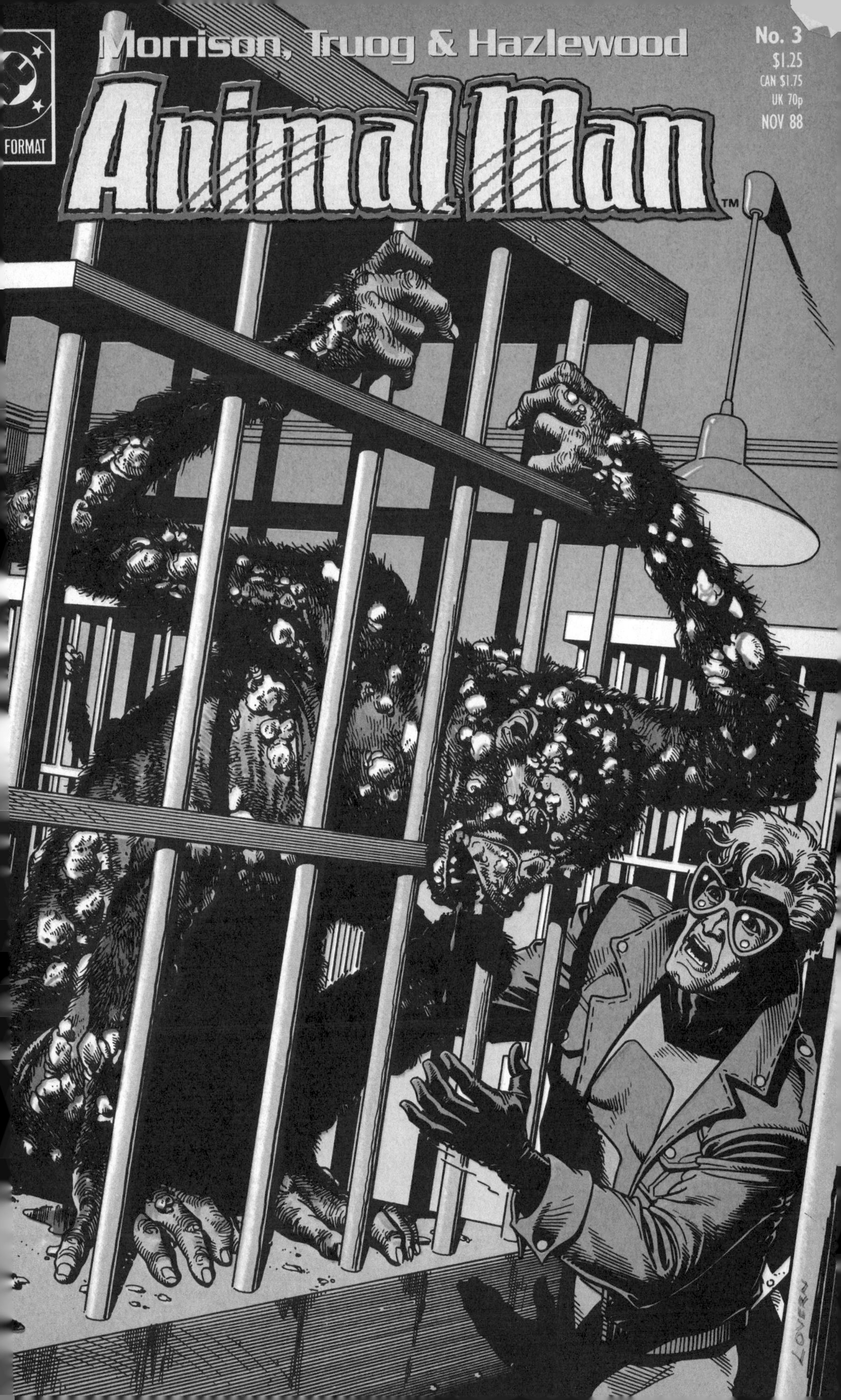

FORMAT
Morrison, Truog & Hazlewood
Animal Man
No. 3
$1.25
CAN $1.75
UK 70p
NOV 88

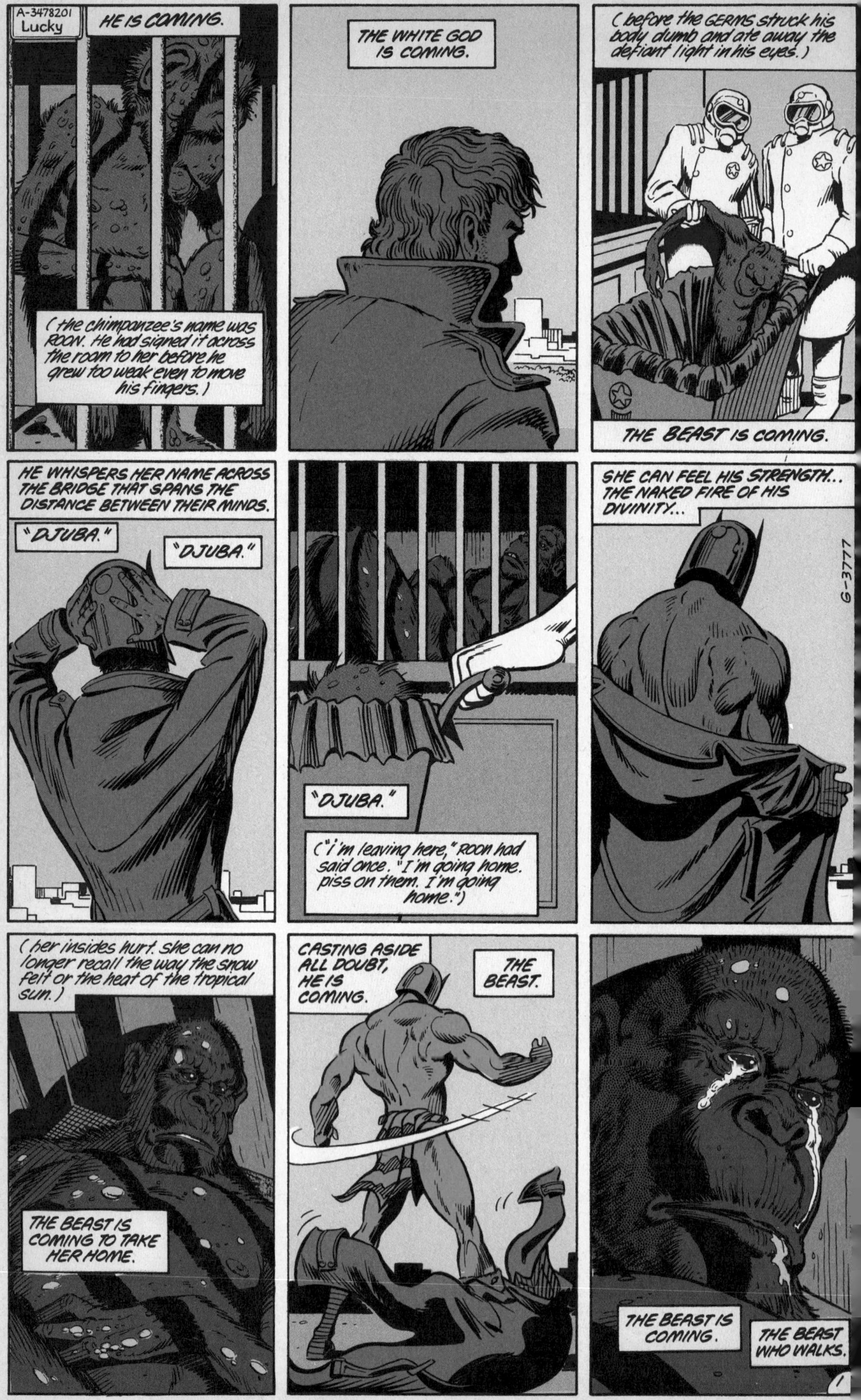
A-3478201
Lucky
HE IS COMING.
(the chimpanzee's name was ROON. He had signed it across the room to her before he grew too weak even to move his fingers.)
THE WHITE GOD IS COMING.
(before the GERMS struck his body dumb and ate away the defiant light in his eyes.)
THE BEAST IS COMING.
HE WHISPERS HER NAME ACROSS THE BRIDGE THAT SPANS THE DISTANCE BETWEEN THEIR MINDS.
"DJUBA."
"DJUBA."
"DJUBA."
("I'm leaving here," Roon had said once. "I'm going home. piss on them. I'm going home.")
SHE CAN FEEL HIS STRENGTH... THE NAKED FIRE OF HIS DIVINITY...
G-3777
(her insides hurt. She can no longer recall the way the snow felt or the heat of the tropical sun.)
THE BEAST IS COMING TO TAKE HER HOME.
CASTING ASIDE ALL DOUBT, HE IS COMING.
THE BEAST.
THE BEAST IS COMING.
THE BEAST WHO WALKS.
1

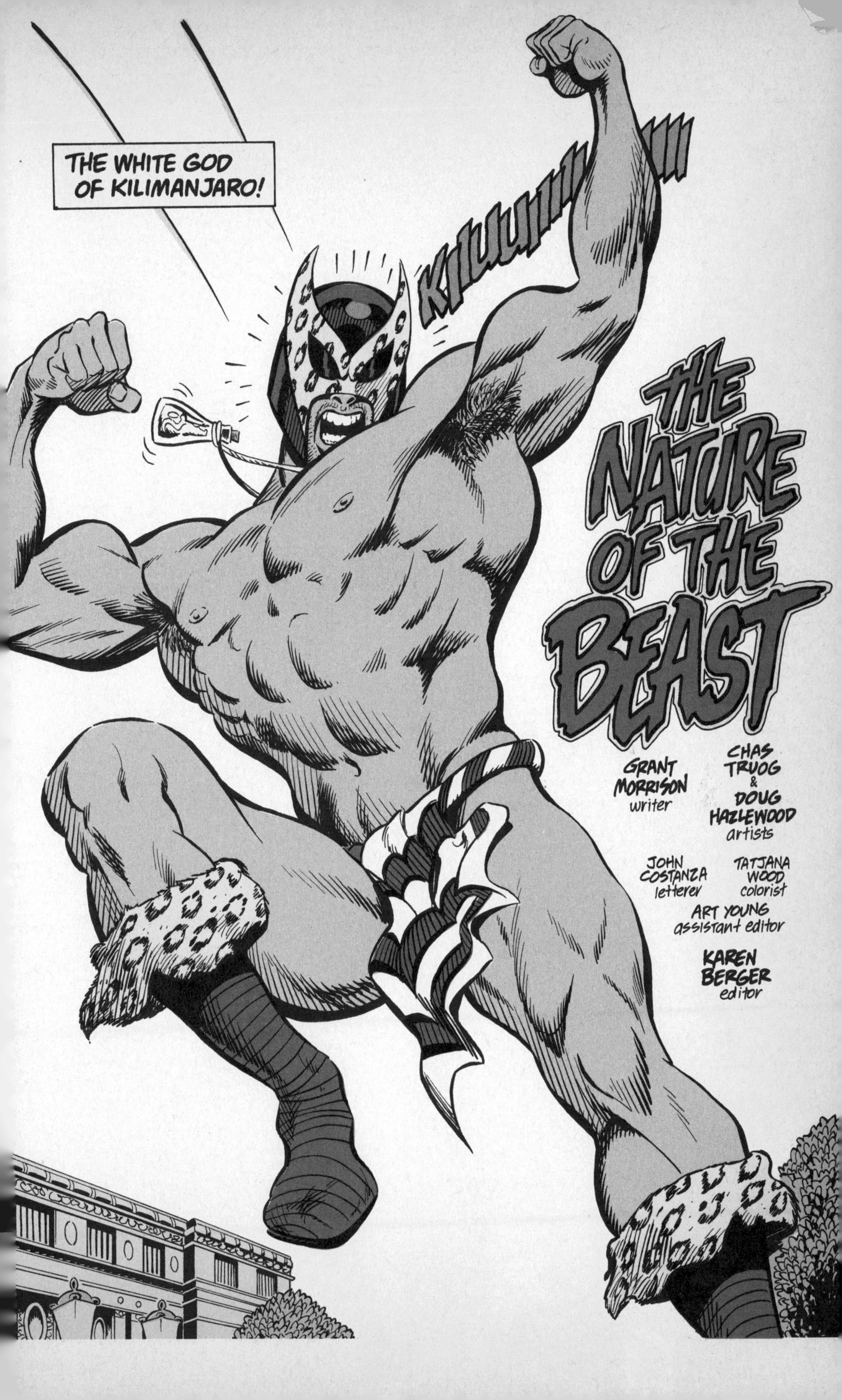
THE WHITE GOD OF KILIMANJARO!
KIIUUU!!!!!!!!
THE NATURE OF THE BEAST
GRANT MORRISON writer
CHAS TRUOG & DOUG HAZLEWOOD artists
JOHN COSTANZA letterer
TATJANA WOOD colorist
ART YOUNG assistant editor
KAREN BERGER editor

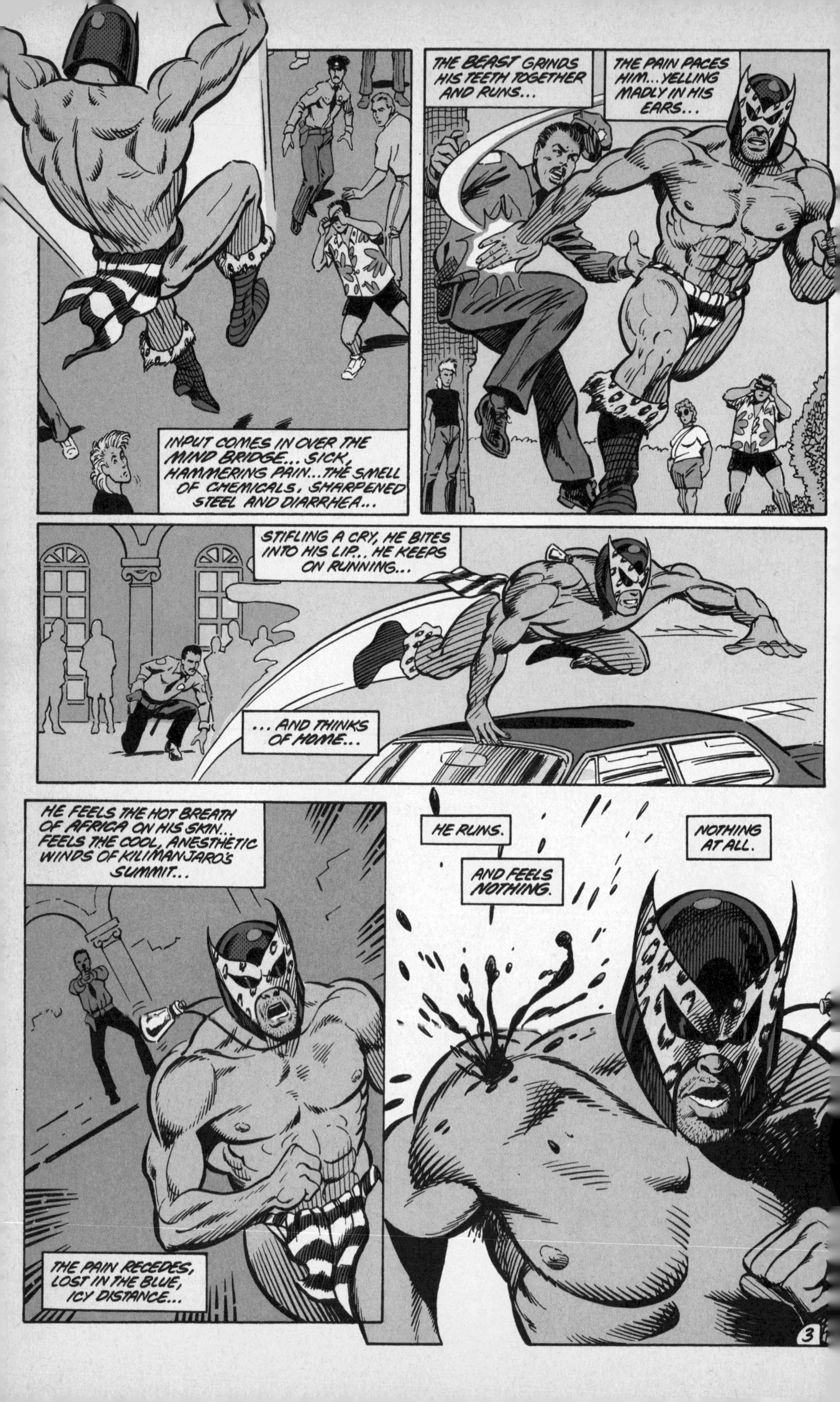
INPUT COMES IN OVER THE MIND BRIDGE... SICK, HAMMERING PAIN...THE SMELL OF CHEMICALS, SHARPENED STEEL AND DIARRHEA...
THE BEAST GRINDS HIS TEETH TOGETHER AND RUNS...
THE PAIN PACES HIM...YELLING MADLY IN HIS EARS...
STIFLING A CRY, HE BITES INTO HIS LIP... HE KEEPS ON RUNNING...
...AND THINKS OF HOME...
HE FEELS THE HOT BREATH OF AFRICA ON HIS SKIN... FEELS THE COOL, ANESTHETIC WINDS OF KILIMANJARO'S SUMMIT...
THE PAIN RECEDES, LOST IN THE BLUE, ICY DISTANCE...
HE RUNS.
AND FEELS NOTHING.
NOTHING AT ALL.

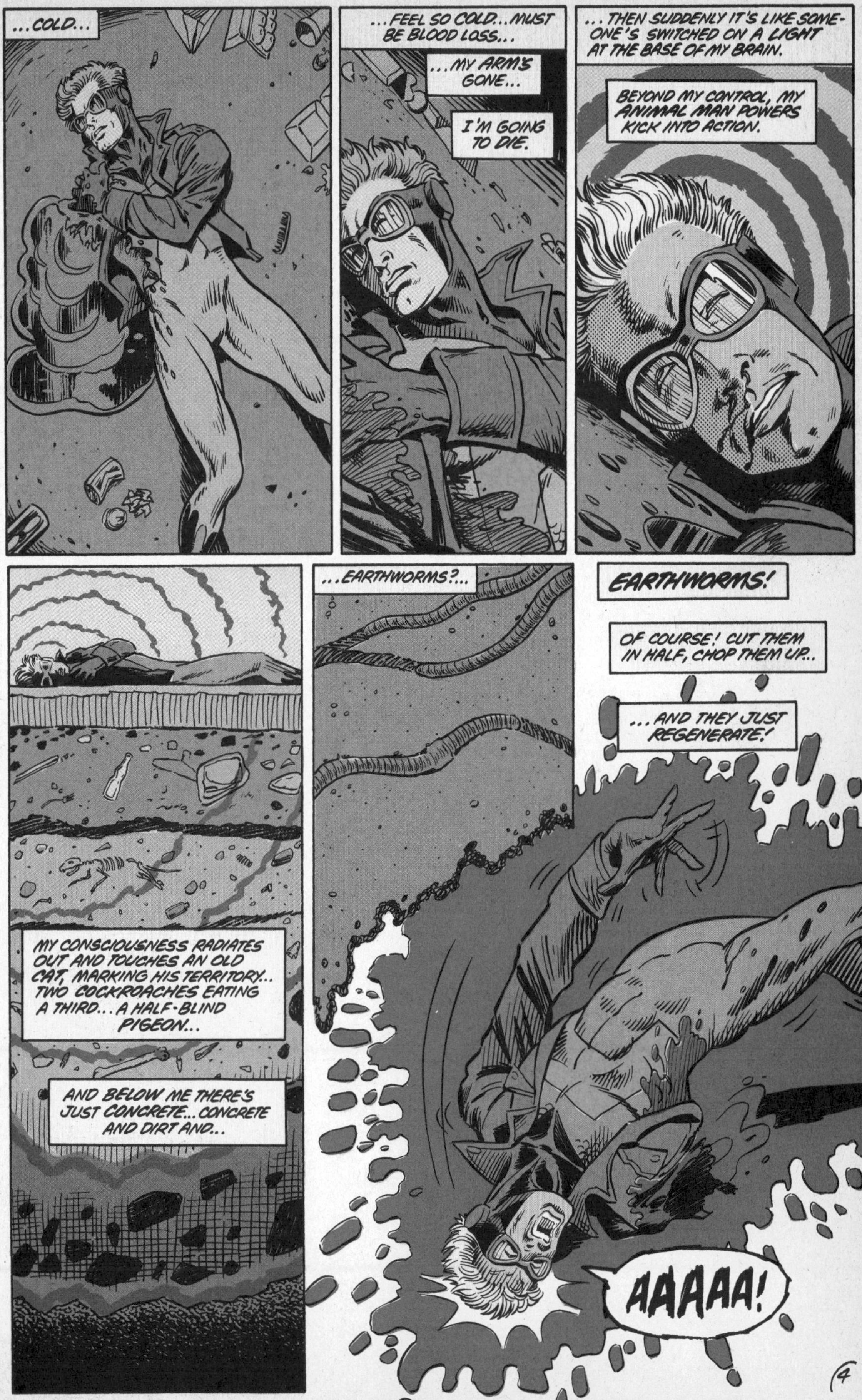
...COLD...
...FEEL SO COLD...MUST BE BLOOD LOSS...
...MY ARM'S GONE...
I'M GOING TO DIE.
...THEN SUDDENLY IT'S LIKE SOME-ONE'S SWITCHED ON A LIGHT AT THE BASE OF MY BRAIN.
BEYOND MY CONTROL, MY ANIMAL MAN POWERS KICK INTO ACTION.
MY CONSCIOUSNESS RADIATES OUT AND TOUCHES AN OLD CAT, MARKING HIS TERRITORY... TWO COCKROACHES EATING A THIRD... A HALF-BLIND PIGEON...
AND BELOW ME THERE'S JUST CONCRETE... CONCRETE AND DIRT AND...
...EARTHWORMS?...
EARTHWORMS!
OF COURSE! CUT THEM IN HALF, CHOP THEM UP...
...AND THEY JUST REGENERATE!
AAAAA!
4

MY SHOULDER CLENCHES, LIKE A FIST.

MY HEART RATE INCREASES... BLOOD PRESSURE RISES...

PAIN SLAMS DOWN MY RIGHT SIDE AND I START TO HYPER-VENTILATE.

I DIDN'T EXPECT IT TO FEEL SO WEIRD.

BONES EXTEND WITH A DRY, SPLINTERING SOUND ...MUSCLES LOCK INTO PLACE...NERVES TWIST INTO INTRICATE TANGLES...

I TRY TO STAND.

...SWEATING...DIZZY...I WANT TO LAUGH...I WANT TO THROW UP...I WISH IT WOULD STOP. I WISH IT WOULD JUST...

...STOP...

THE SCAR'S GONE. THE ONE I GOT FROM MY BIKE, WHEN I WAS TEN... AND MY FINGER-NAILS...UNBITTEN...

OH GOD.

I JUST GREW A NEW ARM.

...UNNH...

NOW WHAT?...

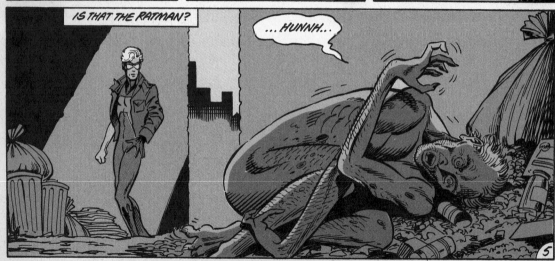

IS THAT THE RATMAN?

...HUNNH...

5

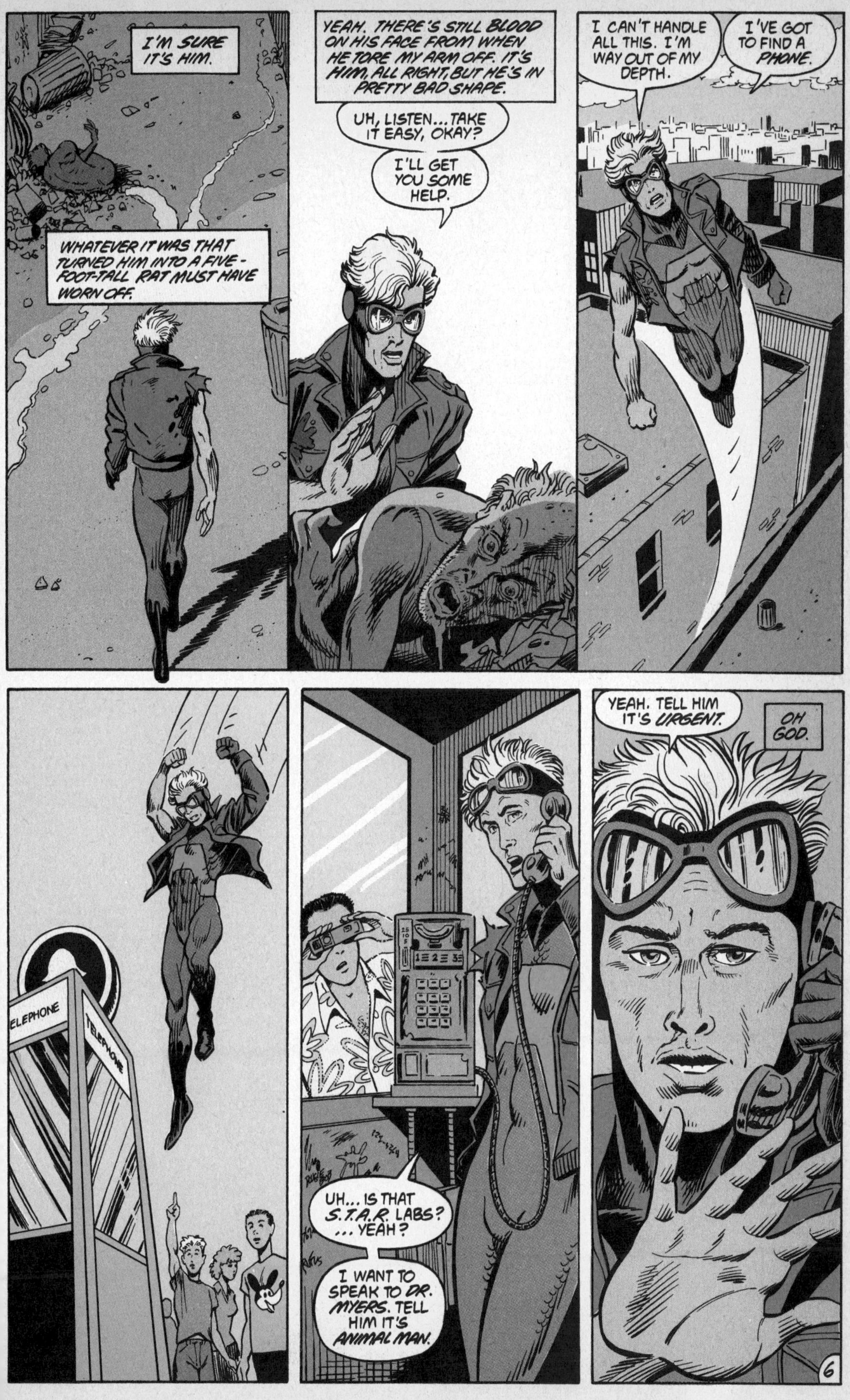
I'M SURE IT'S HIM.
WHATEVER IT WAS THAT TURNED HIM INTO A FIVE-FOOT-TALL RAT MUST HAVE WORN OFF.
YEAH. THERE'S STILL BLOOD ON HIS FACE FROM WHEN HE TORE MY ARM OFF. IT'S HIM, ALL RIGHT, BUT HE'S IN PRETTY BAD SHAPE.
UH, LISTEN... TAKE IT EASY, OKAY?
I'LL GET YOU SOME HELP.
I CAN'T HANDLE ALL THIS. I'M WAY OUT OF MY DEPTH.
I'VE GOT TO FIND A PHONE.
TELEPHONE
TELEPHONE
UH... IS THAT S.T.A.R. LABS? ...YEAH?
I WANT TO SPEAK TO DR. MYERS. TELL HIM IT'S ANIMAL MAN.
YEAH. TELL HIM IT'S URGENT.
OH GOD.
6

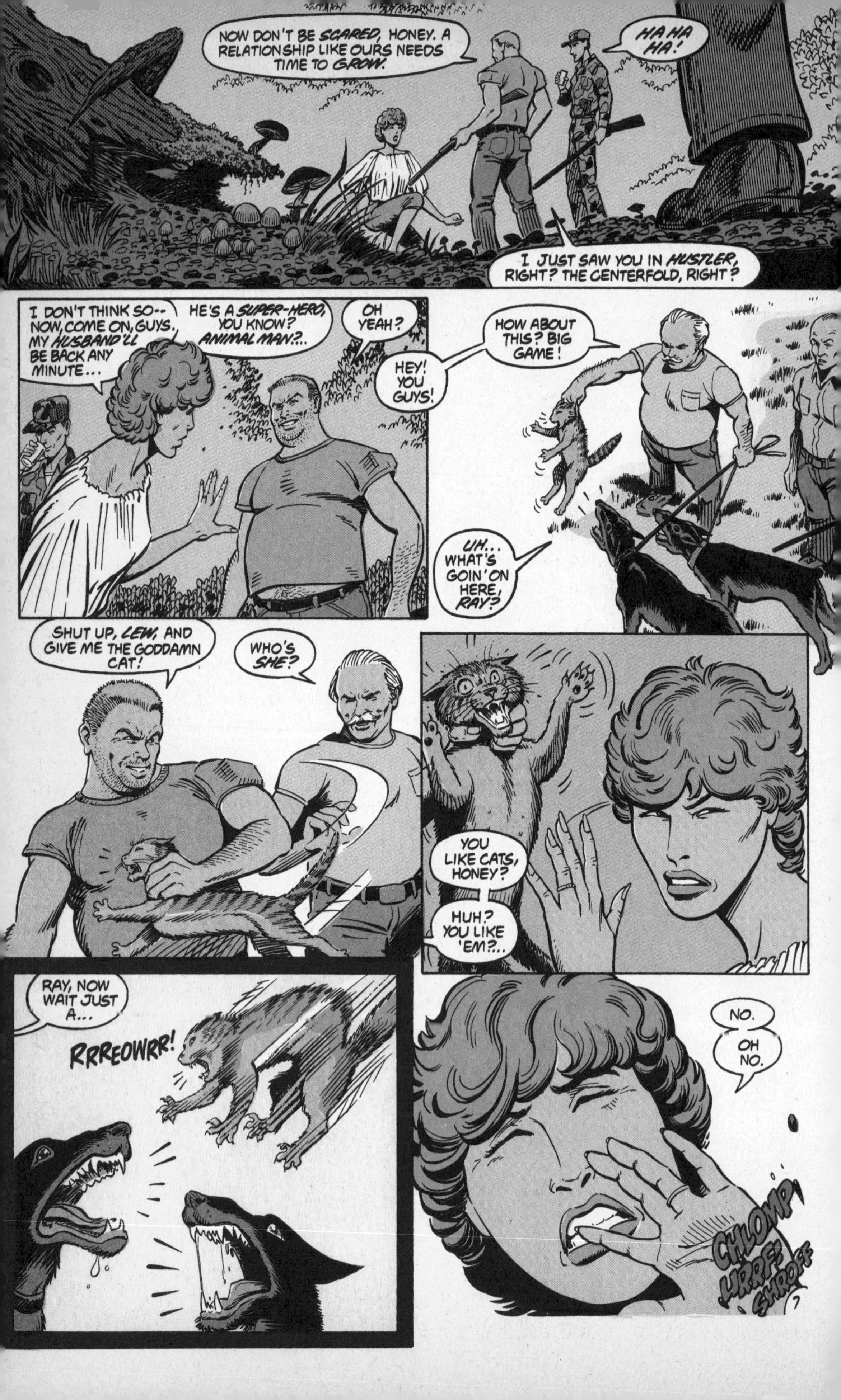
NOW DON'T BE SCARED, HONEY. A RELATIONSHIP LIKE OURS NEEDS TIME TO GROW.
HA HA HA!
I JUST SAW YOU IN HUSTLER, RIGHT? THE CENTERFOLD, RIGHT?
I DON'T THINK SO-- NOW, COME ON, GUYS. MY HUSBAND'LL BE BACK ANY MINUTE...
HE'S A SUPER-HERO, YOU KNOW? ANIMAL MAN?...
OH YEAH?
HEY! YOU GUYS!
HOW ABOUT THIS? BIG GAME!
UH... WHAT'S GOIN' ON HERE, RAY?
SHUT UP, LEW, AND GIVE ME THE GODDAMN CAT!
WHO'S SHE?
YOU LIKE CATS, HONEY?
HUH? YOU LIKE 'EM?...
RAY, NOW WAIT JUST A...
RRREOWRR!
NO.
OH NO.
CHLOMP
URRF
SHROFF
7

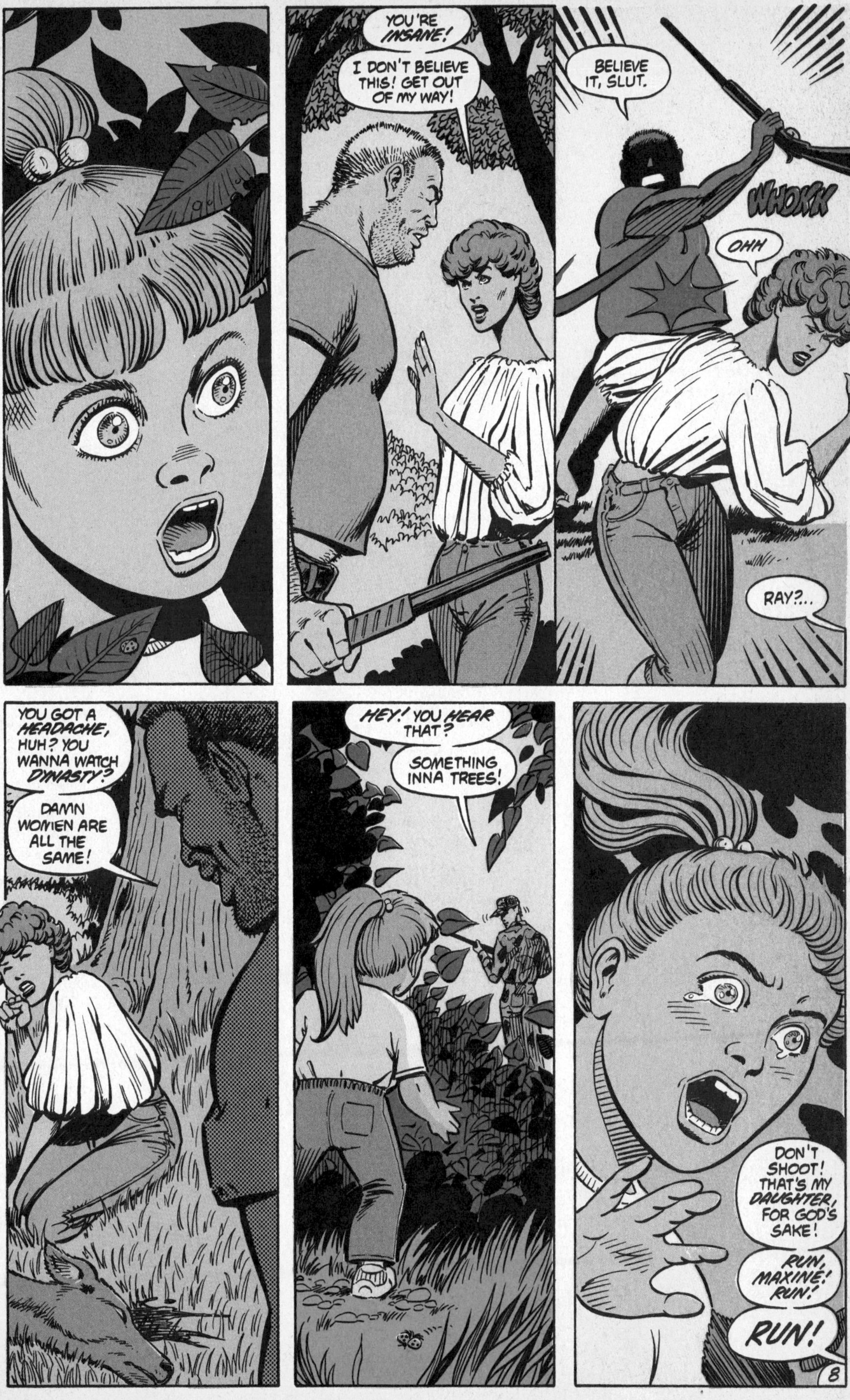

YOU'RE INSANE!
I DON'T BELIEVE THIS! GET OUT OF MY WAY!
BELIEVE IT, SLUT.
WHOKK
OHH
RAY?...
YOU GOT A HEADACHE, HUH? YOU WANNA WATCH DYNASTY?
DAMN WOMEN ARE ALL THE SAME!
HEY! YOU HEAR THAT?
SOMETHING INNA TREES!
DON'T SHOOT! THAT'S MY DAUGHTER, FOR GOD'S SAKE!
RUN, MAXINE! RUN!
RUN!

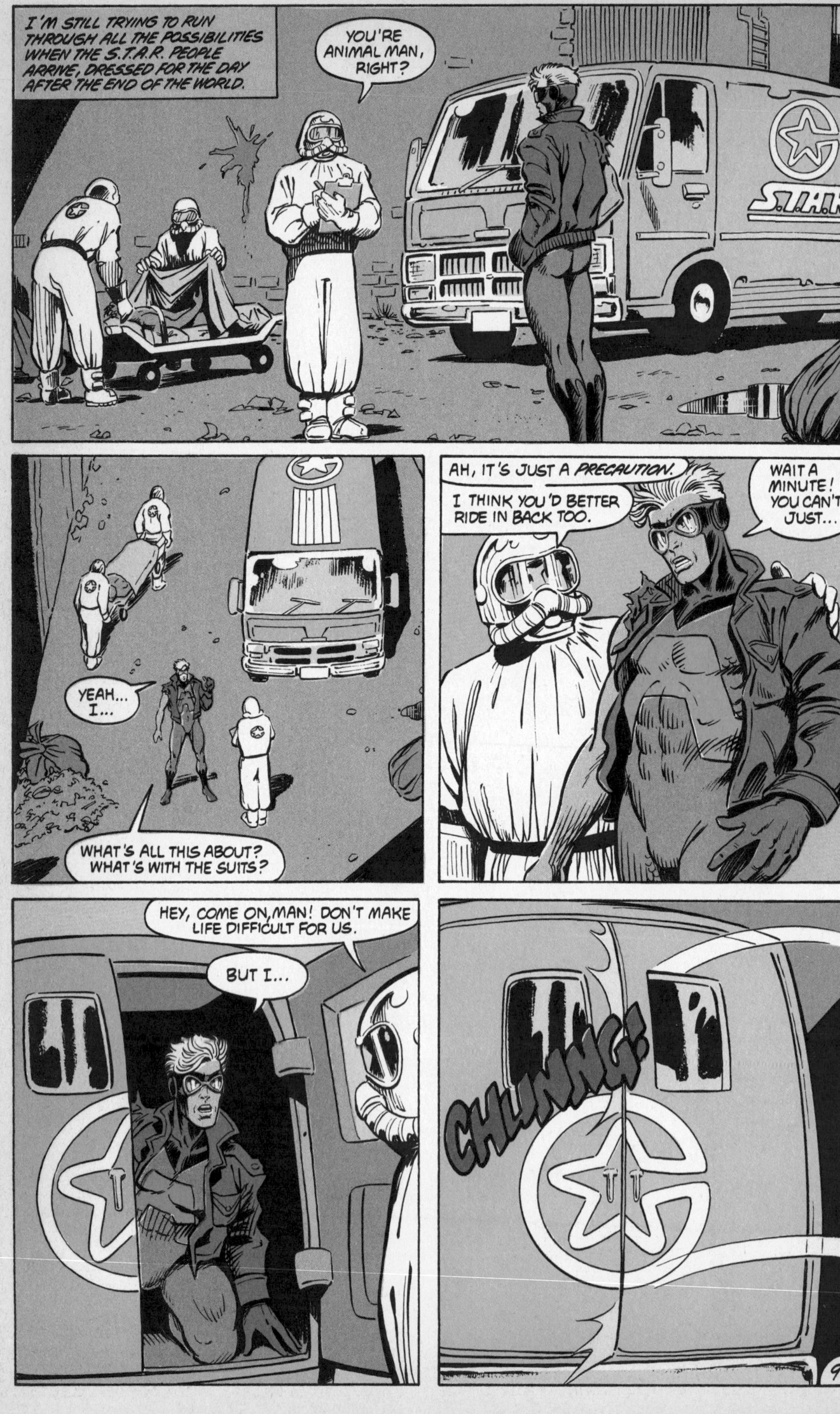
I'M STILL TRYING TO RUN THROUGH ALL THE POSSIBILITIES WHEN THE S.T.A.R. PEOPLE ARRIVE, DRESSED FOR THE DAY AFTER THE END OF THE WORLD.
YOU'RE ANIMAL MAN, RIGHT?
S.T.A.R.
YEAH... I...
WHAT'S ALL THIS ABOUT? WHAT'S WITH THE SUITS?
AH, IT'S JUST A PRECAUTION.
I THINK YOU'D BETTER RIDE IN BACK TOO.
WAIT A MINUTE! YOU CAN'T JUST...
HEY, COME ON, MAN! DON'T MAKE LIFE DIFFICULT FOR US.
BUT I...
CHUNNG!

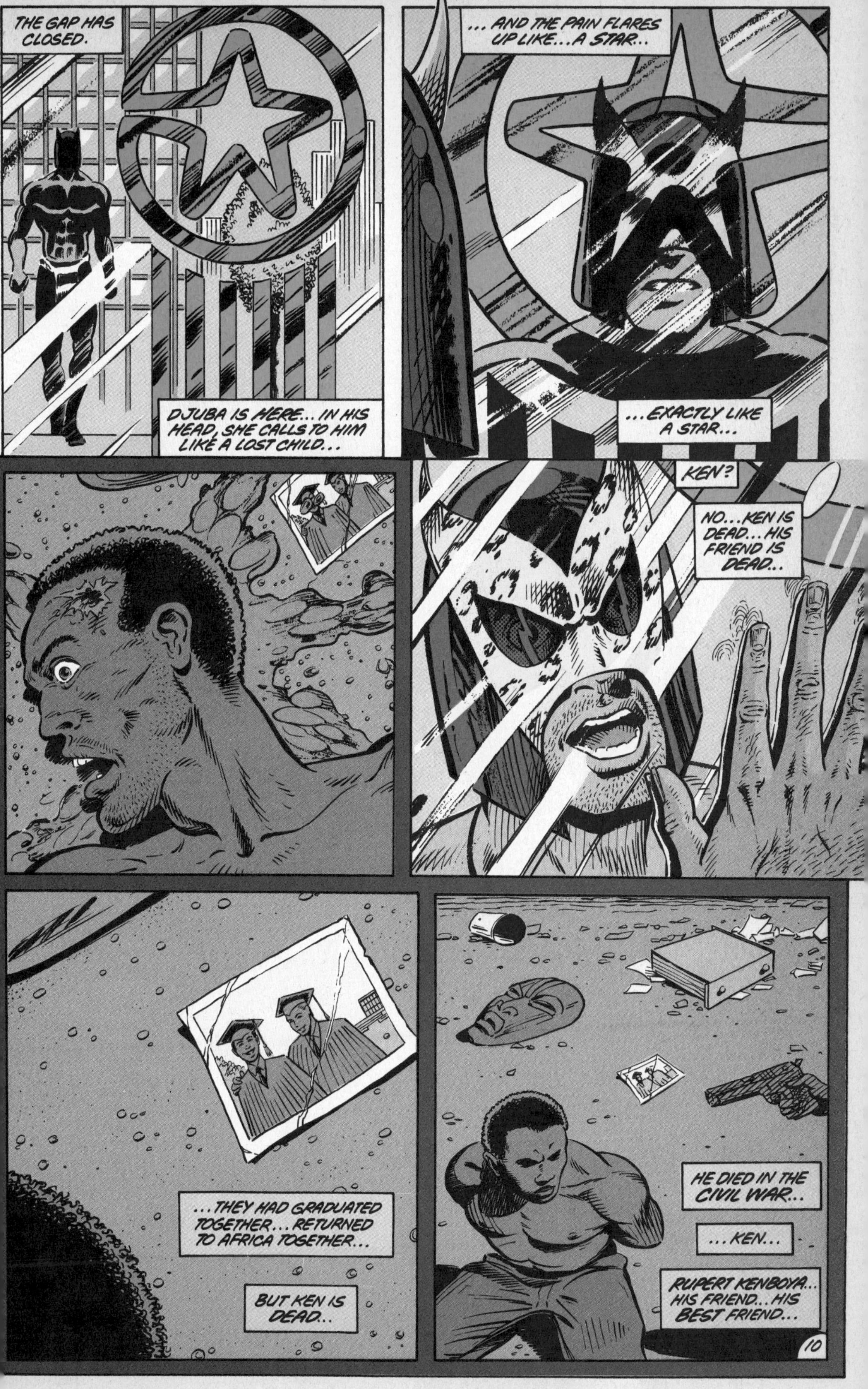
THE GAP HAS CLOSED.
DJUBA IS HERE... IN HIS HEAD, SHE CALLS TO HIM LIKE A LOST CHILD...
... AND THE PAIN FLARES UP LIKE... A STAR...
... EXACTLY LIKE A STAR...
KEN?
NO... KEN IS DEAD... HIS FRIEND IS DEAD...
... THEY HAD GRADUATED TOGETHER... RETURNED TO AFRICA TOGETHER...
BUT KEN IS DEAD...
HE DIED IN THE CIVIL WAR...
... KEN...
RUPERT KENBOYA... HIS FRIEND... HIS BEST FRIEND...
10

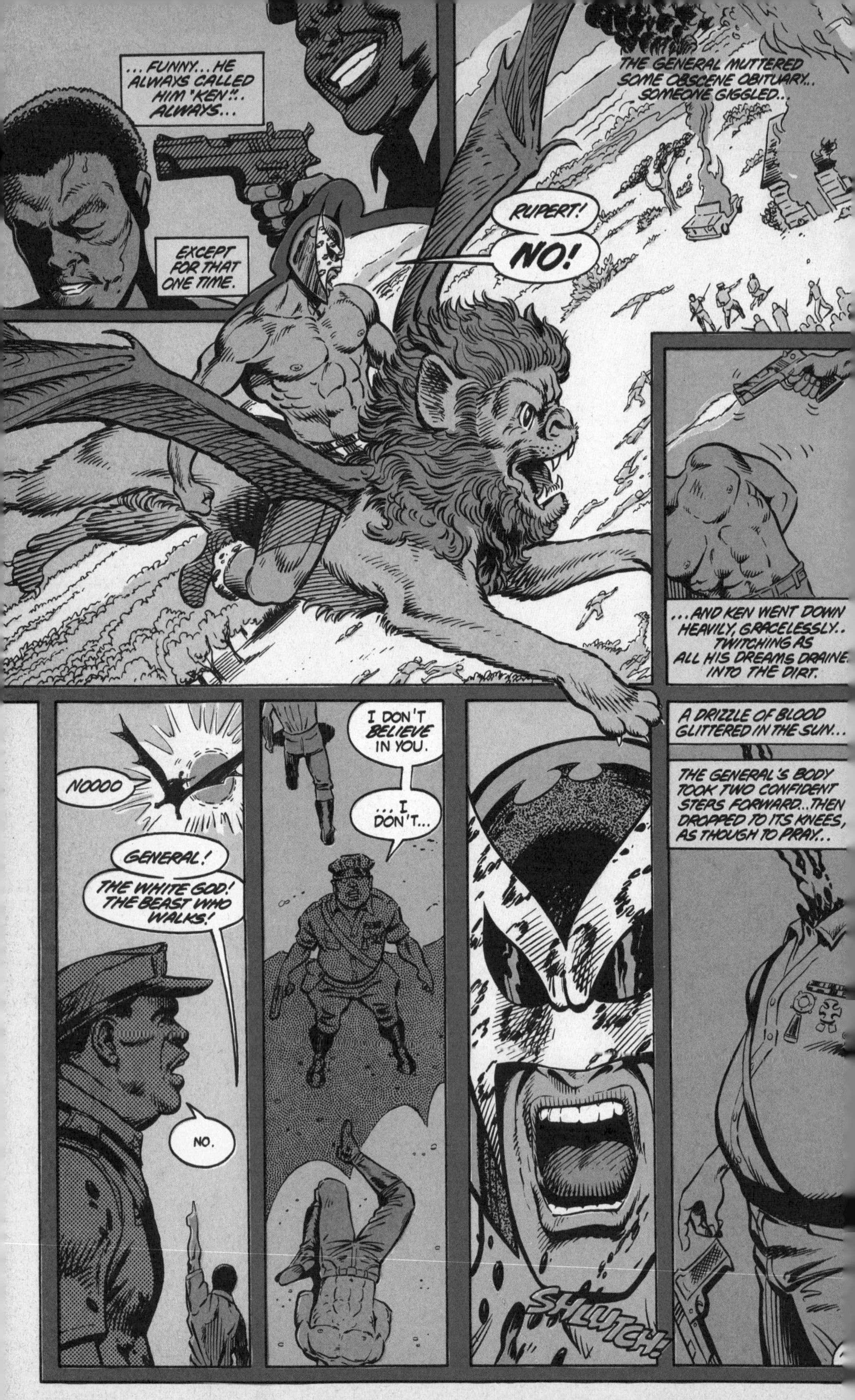
...FUNNY...HE ALWAYS CALLED HIM "KEN"... ALWAYS...
EXCEPT FOR THAT ONE TIME.
THE GENERAL MUTTERED SOME OBSCENE OBITUARY... SOMEONE GIGGLED...
RUPERT!
NO!
...AND KEN WENT DOWN HEAVILY, GRACELESSLY... TWITCHING AS ALL HIS DREAMS DRAINE INTO THE DIRT.
NOOOO
GENERAL!
THE WHITE GOD! THE BEAST WHO WALKS!
NO.
I DON'T BELIEVE IN YOU.
...I DON'T...
SHLUTCH!
A DRIZZLE OF BLOOD GLITTERED IN THE SUN...
THE GENERAL'S BODY TOOK TWO CONFIDENT STEPS FORWARD...THEN DROPPED TO ITS KNEES, AS THOUGH TO PRAY...

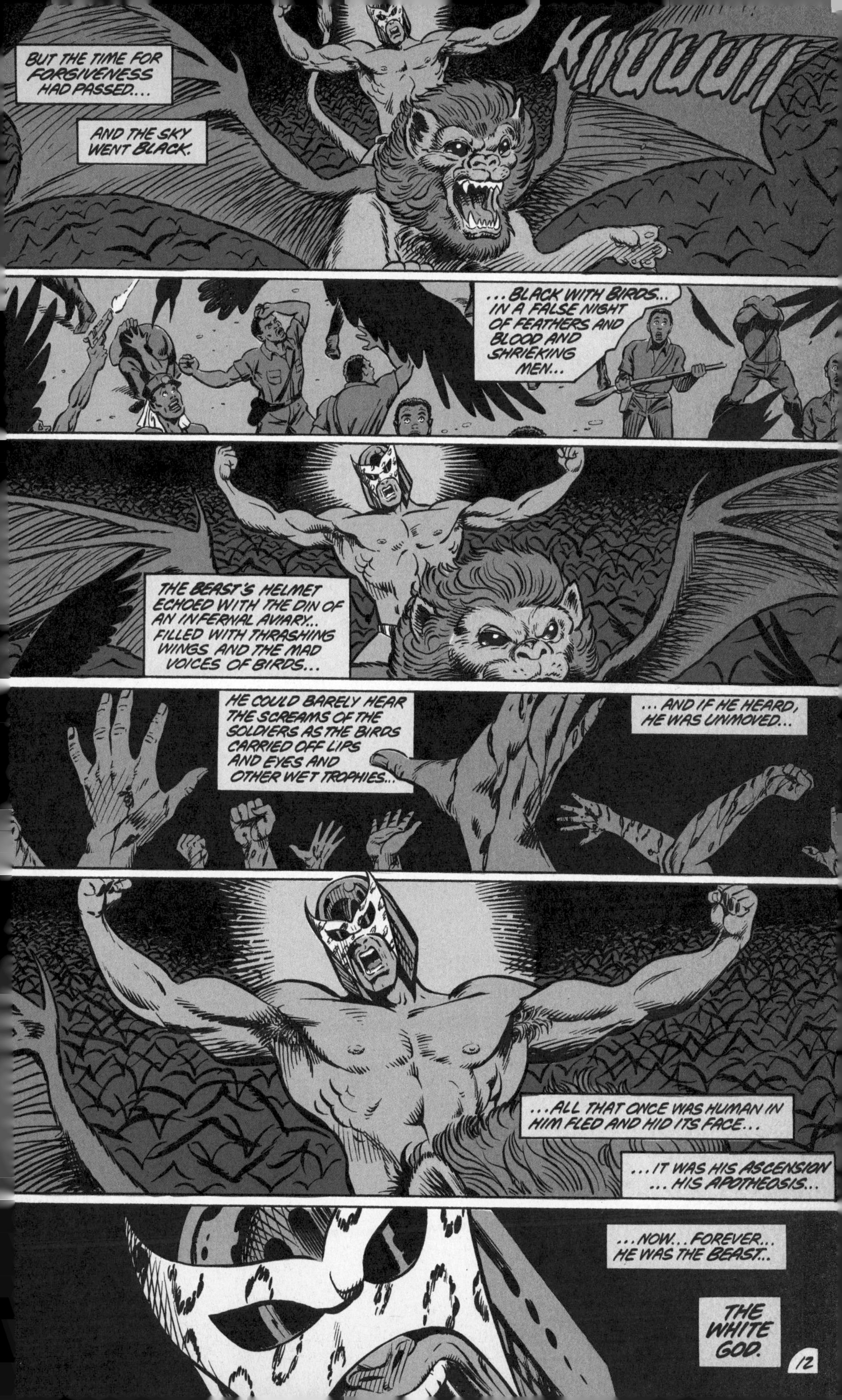

BUT THE TIME FOR FORGIVENESS HAD PASSED....
AND THE SKY WENT BLACK.
...BLACK WITH BIRDS... IN A FALSE NIGHT OF FEATHERS AND BLOOD AND SHRIEKING MEN...
THE BEAST'S HELMET ECHOED WITH THE DIN OF AN INFERNAL AVIARY... FILLED WITH THRASHING WINGS AND THE MAD VOICES OF BIRDS...
HE COULD BARELY HEAR THE SCREAMS OF THE SOLDIERS AS THE BIRDS CARRIED OFF LIPS AND EYES AND OTHER WET TROPHIES...
...AND IF HE HEARD, HE WAS UNMOVED...
...ALL THAT ONCE WAS HUMAN IN HIM FLED AND HID ITS FACE...
...IT WAS HIS ASCENSION ...HIS APOTHEOSIS...
...NOW...FOREVER... HE WAS THE BEAST...
THE WHITE GOD.
12

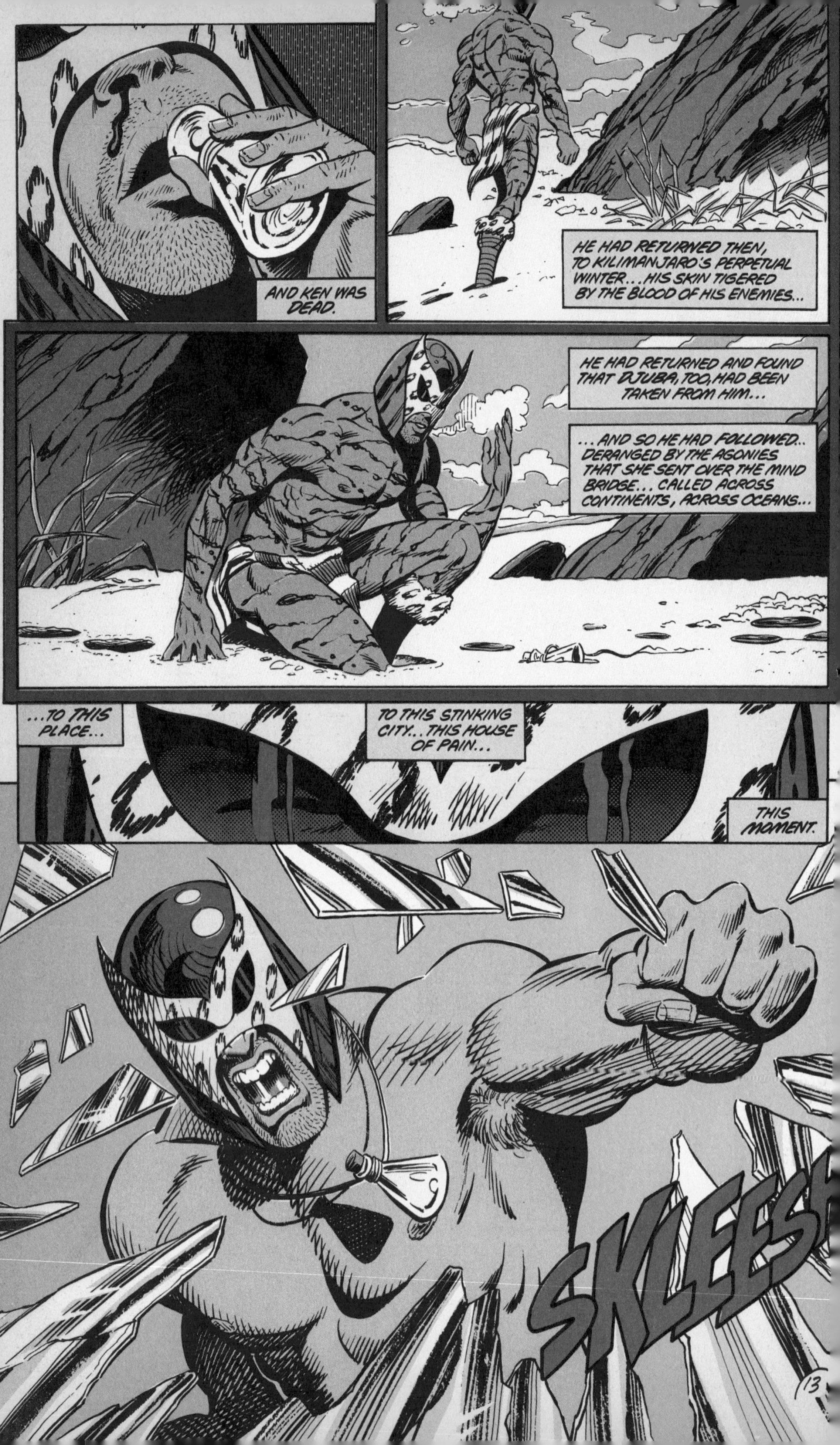
AND KEN WAS DEAD.
HE HAD RETURNED THEN, TO KILIMANJARO'S PERPETUAL WINTER... HIS SKIN TIGERED BY THE BLOOD OF HIS ENEMIES...
HE HAD RETURNED AND FOUND THAT DJUBA, TOO, HAD BEEN TAKEN FROM HIM...
...AND SO HE HAD FOLLOWED... DERANGED BY THE AGONIES THAT SHE SENT OVER THE MIND BRIDGE... CALLED ACROSS CONTINENTS, ACROSS OCEANS...
...TO THIS PLACE...
TO THIS STINKING CITY...THIS HOUSE OF PAIN...
THIS MOMENT.
SKLEESH

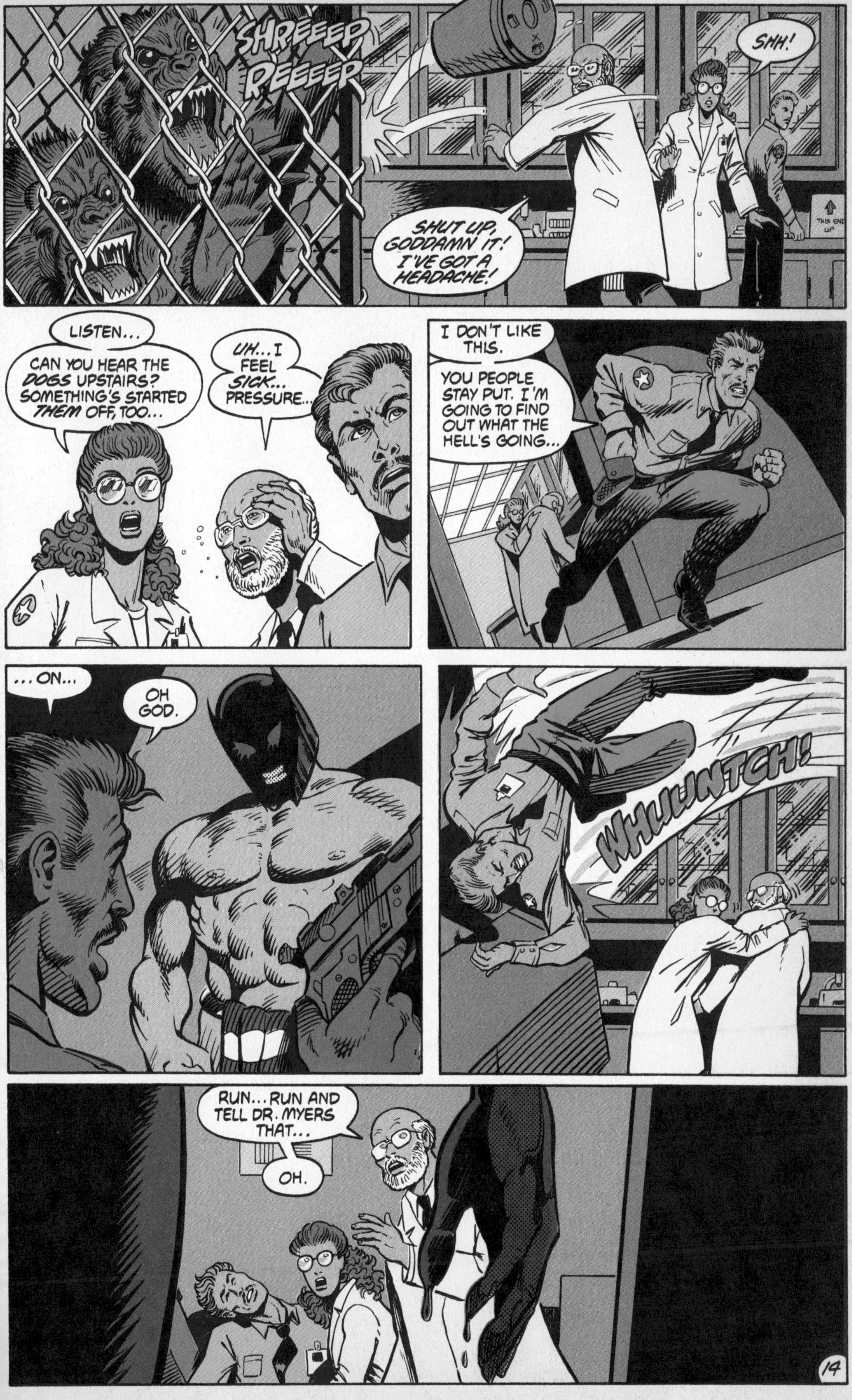
SHREEEP
REEEEP
SMH!
SHUT UP, GODDAMN IT! I'VE GOT A HEADACHE!
THIS END UP
LISTEN...
CAN YOU HEAR THE DOGS UPSTAIRS? SOMETHING'S STARTED THEM OFF, TOO...
UH... I FEEL SICK... PRESSURE...
I DON'T LIKE THIS.
YOU PEOPLE STAY PUT. I'M GOING TO FIND OUT WHAT THE HELL'S GOING...
...ON...
OH GOD.
WHUUNTCH!
RUN... RUN AND TELL DR. MYERS THAT...
OH.
14

MR. WEIDEMEIR?

MY MOMMY'S UP IN THE WOODS AND SHE'S CRYING AND THE MEN HAVE GOT GUNS AND THEY'RE GOING TO MAKE THE DOGS EAT THE LITTLE KITTENS.

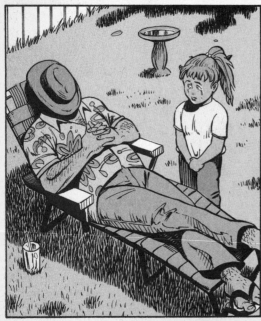

YOUR MOMMY'S *WHERE?*

15

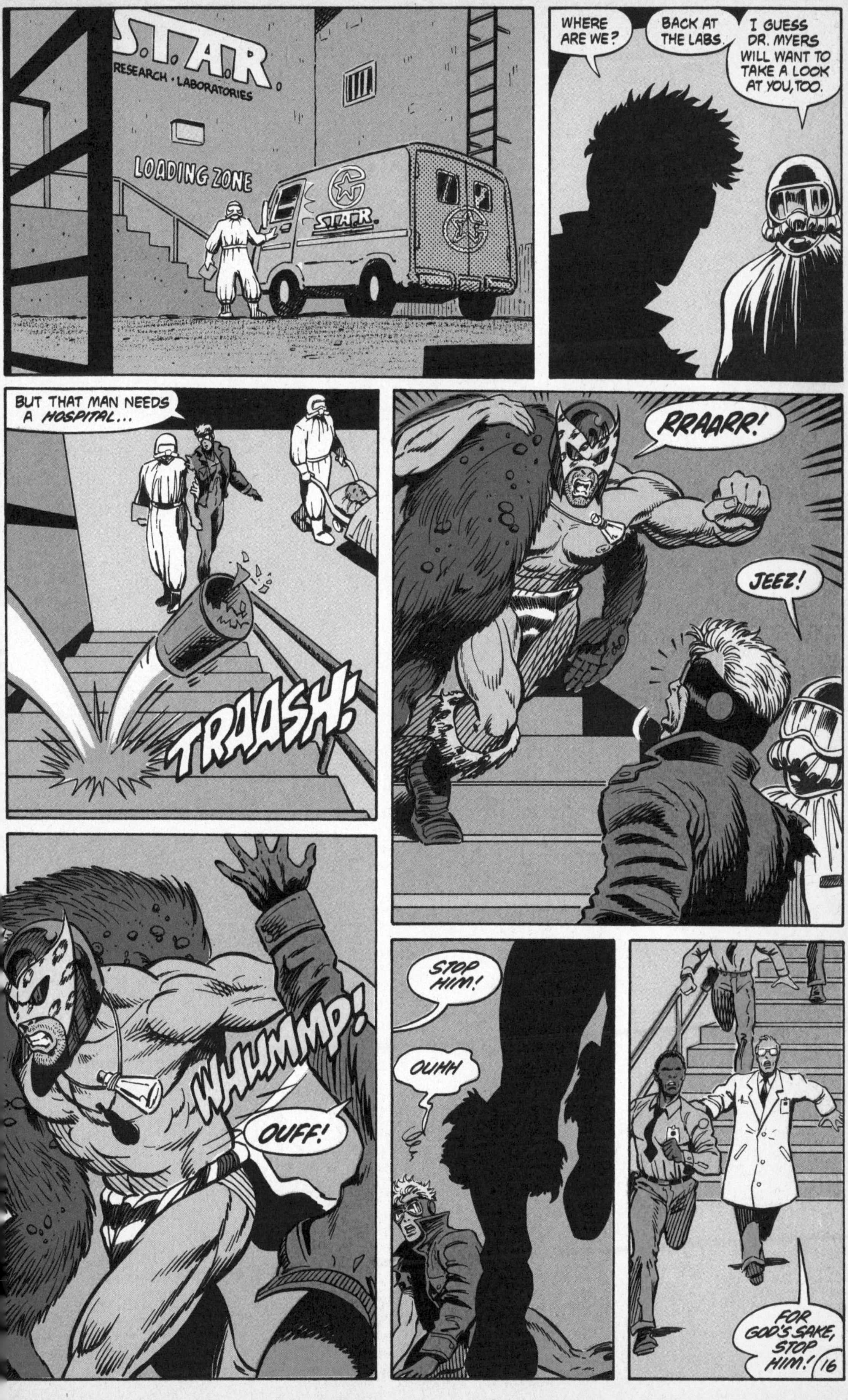
S.T.A.R. RESEARCH · LABORATORIES
LOADING ZONE
S.T.A.R.
WHERE ARE WE?
BACK AT THE LABS.
I GUESS DR. MYERS WILL WANT TO TAKE A LOOK AT YOU, TOO.
BUT THAT MAN NEEDS A HOSPITAL...
TRAASH!
RRAARR!
JEEZ!
WHUMMP!
OUFF!
STOP HIM!
OUHH
FOR GOD'S SAKE, STOP HIM!
16

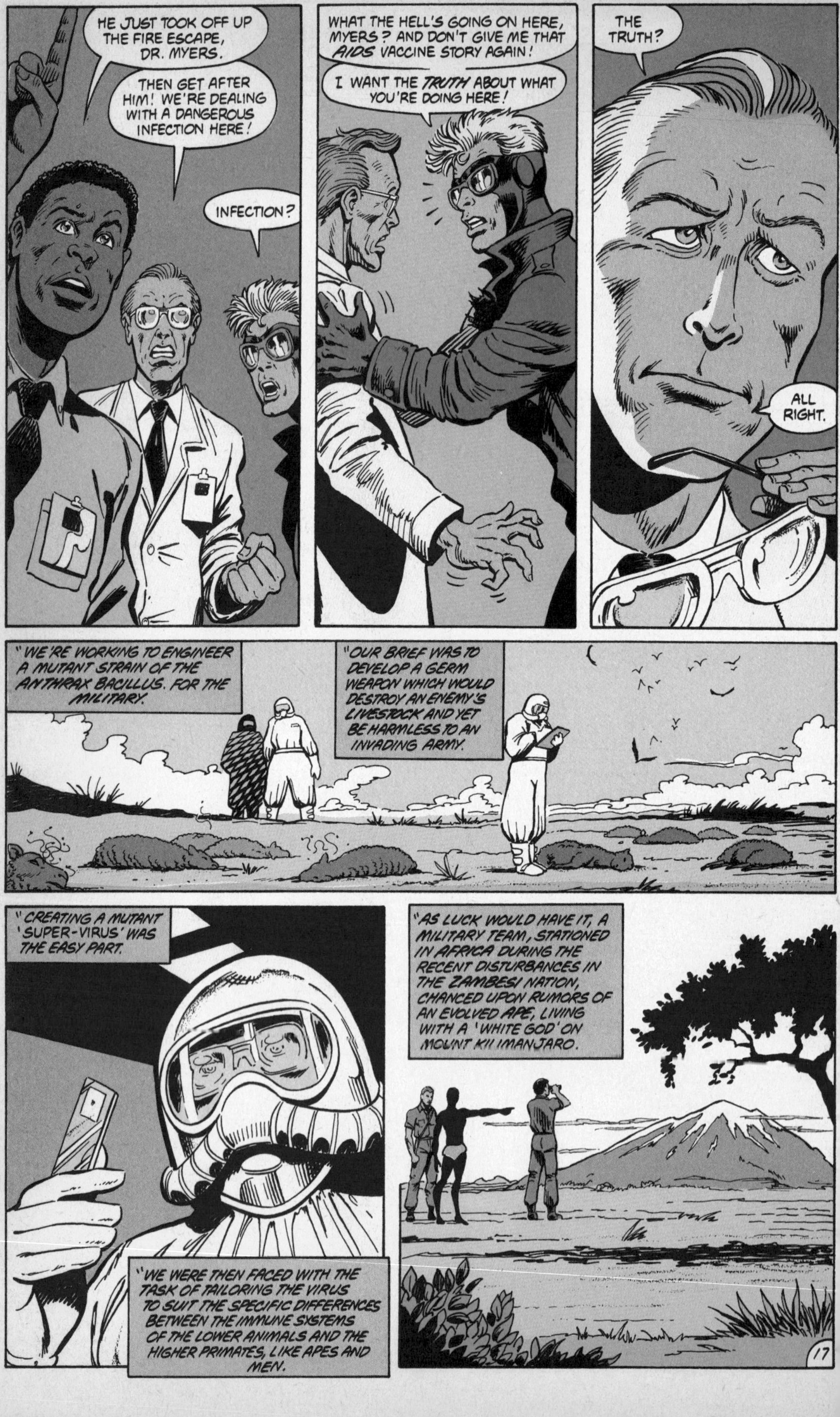
HE JUST TOOK OFF UP THE FIRE ESCAPE, DR. MYERS.
THEN GET AFTER HIM! WE'RE DEALING WITH A DANGEROUS INFECTION HERE!
INFECTION?
WHAT THE HELL'S GOING ON HERE, MYERS? AND DON'T GIVE ME THAT AIDS VACCINE STORY AGAIN!
I WANT THE TRUTH ABOUT WHAT YOU'RE DOING HERE!
THE TRUTH?
ALL RIGHT.
"WE'RE WORKING TO ENGINEER A MUTANT STRAIN OF THE ANTHRAX BACILLUS. FOR THE MILITARY.
"OUR BRIEF WAS TO DEVELOP A GERM WEAPON WHICH WOULD DESTROY AN ENEMY'S LIVESTOCK AND YET BE HARMLESS TO AN INVADING ARMY.
"CREATING A MUTANT 'SUPER-VIRUS' WAS THE EASY PART.
"WE WERE THEN FACED WITH THE TASK OF TAILORING THE VIRUS TO SUIT THE SPECIFIC DIFFERENCES BETWEEN THE IMMUNE SYSTEMS OF THE LOWER ANIMALS AND THE HIGHER PRIMATES, LIKE APES AND MEN.
"AS LUCK WOULD HAVE IT, A MILITARY TEAM, STATIONED IN AFRICA DURING THE RECENT DISTURBANCES IN THE ZAMBESI NATION, CHANCED UPON RUMORS OF AN EVOLVED APE, LIVING WITH A 'WHITE GOD' ON MOUNT KILIMANJARO.

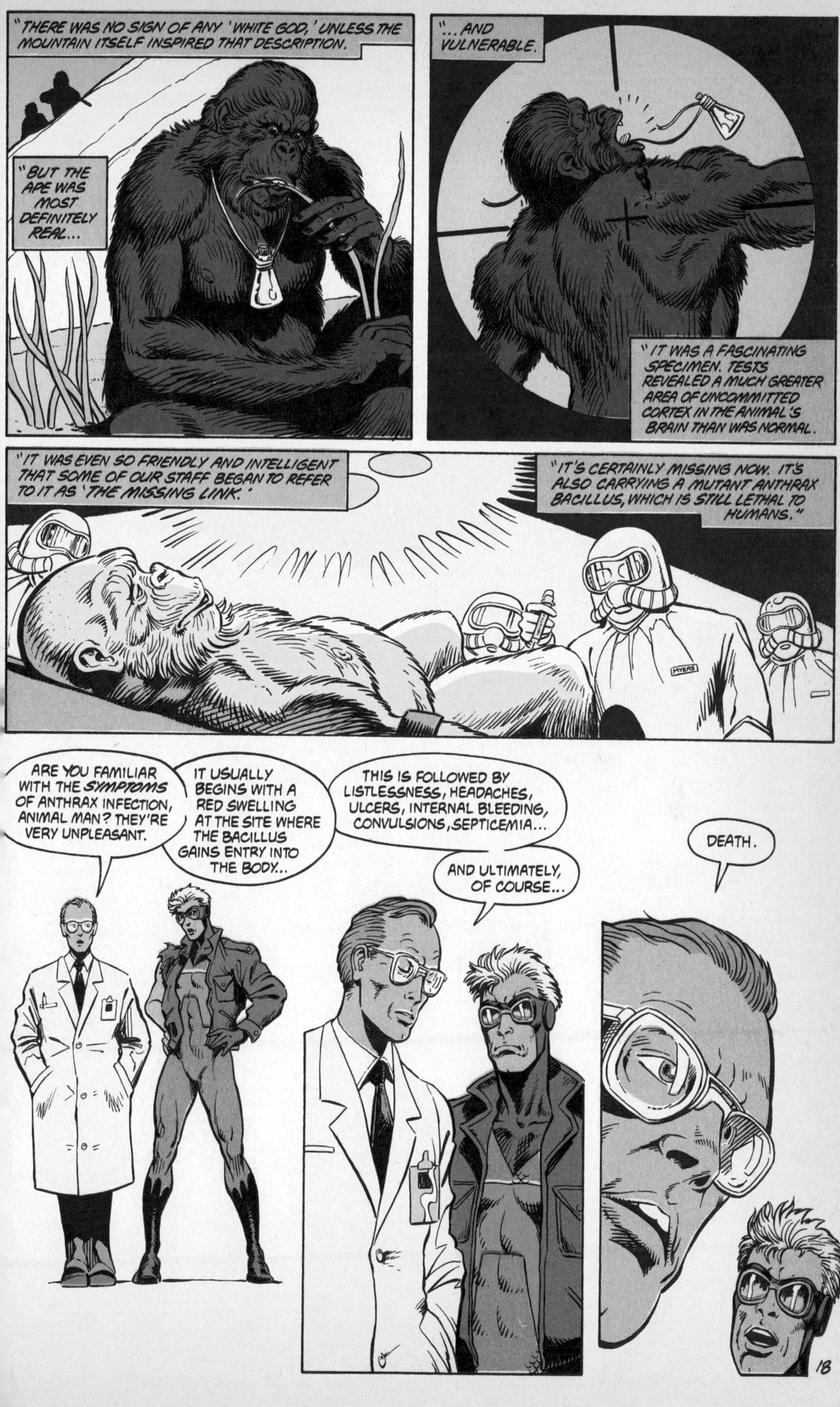

"THERE WAS NO SIGN OF ANY 'WHITE GOD,' UNLESS THE MOUNTAIN ITSELF INSPIRED THAT DESCRIPTION.
"BUT THE APE WAS MOST DEFINITELY REAL...
"...AND VULNERABLE.
"IT WAS A FASCINATING SPECIMEN. TESTS REVEALED A MUCH GREATER AREA OF UNCOMMITTED CORTEX IN THE ANIMAL'S BRAIN THAN WAS NORMAL.
"IT WAS EVEN SO FRIENDLY AND INTELLIGENT THAT SOME OF OUR STAFF BEGAN TO REFER TO IT AS 'THE MISSING LINK.'
"IT'S CERTAINLY MISSING NOW. IT'S ALSO CARRYING A MUTANT ANTHRAX BACILLUS, WHICH IS STILL LETHAL TO HUMANS."
MYERS
ARE YOU FAMILIAR WITH THE SYMPTOMS OF ANTHRAX INFECTION, ANIMAL MAN? THEY'RE VERY UNPLEASANT.
IT USUALLY BEGINS WITH A RED SWELLING AT THE SITE WHERE THE BACILLUS GAINS ENTRY INTO THE BODY...
THIS IS FOLLOWED BY LISTLESSNESS, HEADACHES, ULCERS, INTERNAL BLEEDING, CONVULSIONS, SEPTICEMIA...
AND ULTIMATELY, OF COURSE...
DEATH.

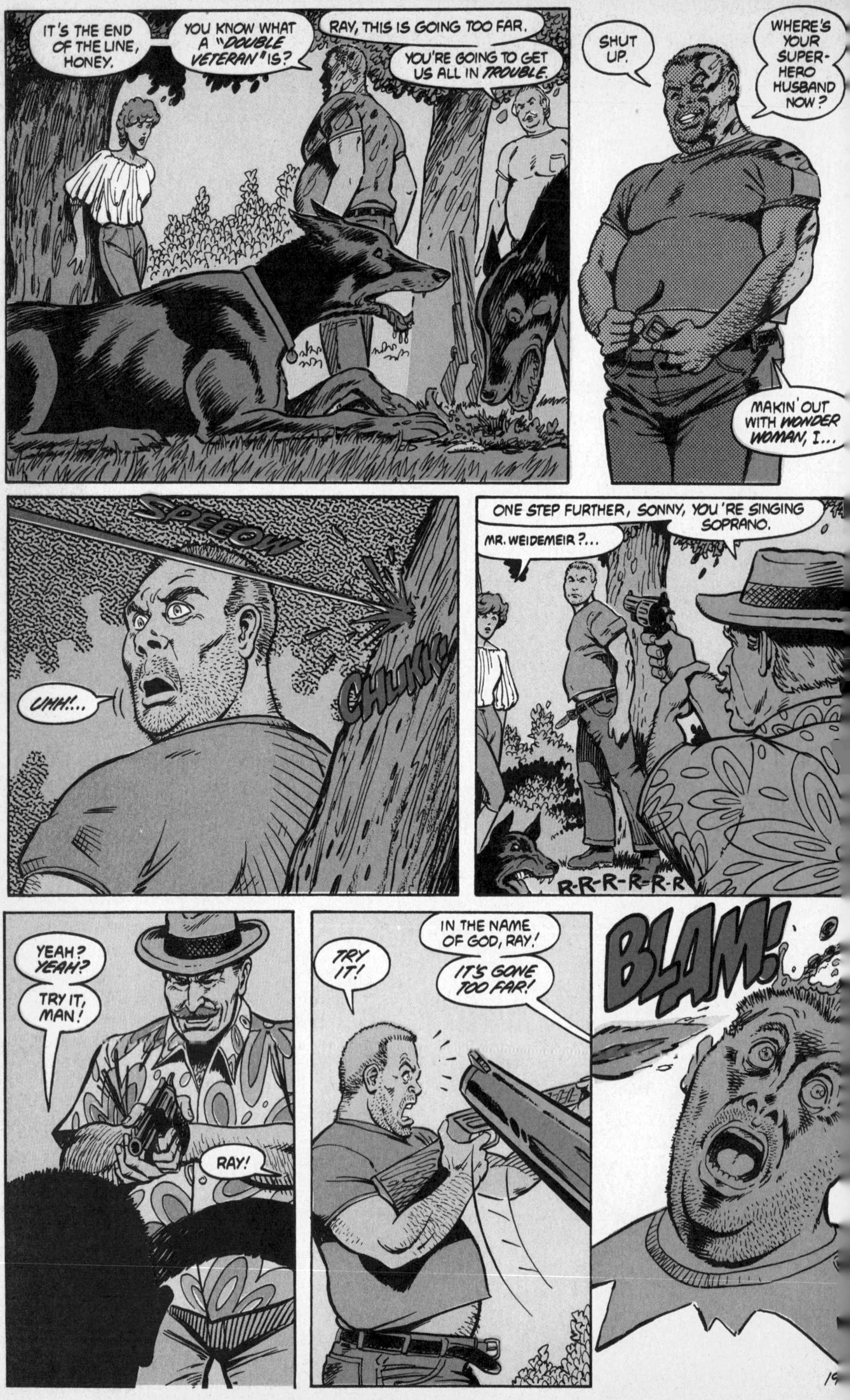
IT'S THE END OF THE LINE, HONEY.
YOU KNOW WHAT A "DOUBLE VETERAN" IS?
RAY, THIS IS GOING TOO FAR.
YOU'RE GOING TO GET US ALL IN TROUBLE.
SHUT UP.
WHERE'S YOUR SUPER-HERO HUSBAND NOW?
MAKIN' OUT WITH WONDER WOMAN, I...
SPEEOW
CHUKK
UHH!...
ONE STEP FURTHER, SONNY, YOU'RE SINGING SOPRANO.
MR. WEIDEMEIR?...
R-R-R-R-R-R
YEAH? YEAH?
TRY IT, MAN!
RAY!
TRY IT!
IN THE NAME OF GOD, RAY!
IT'S GONE TOO FAR!
BLAM!

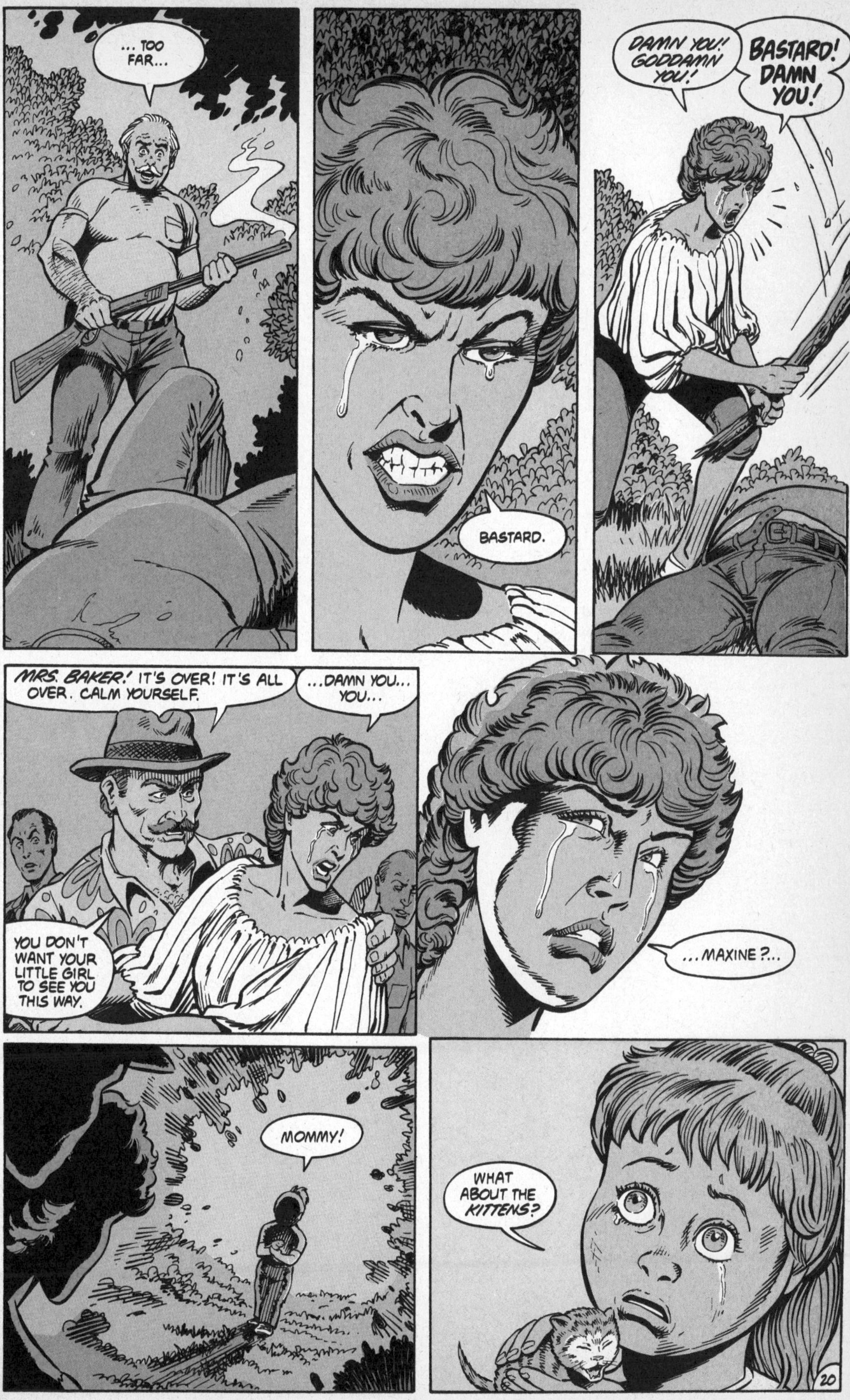

... TOO FAR...
BASTARD.
DAMN YOU!! GODDAMN YOU!!
BASTARD! DAMN YOU!
MRS. BAKER! IT'S OVER! IT'S ALL OVER. CALM YOURSELF.
...DAMN YOU... YOU...
YOU DON'T WANT YOUR LITTLE GIRL TO SEE YOU THIS WAY.
...MAXINE?...
MOMMY!
WHAT ABOUT THE KITTENS?
20

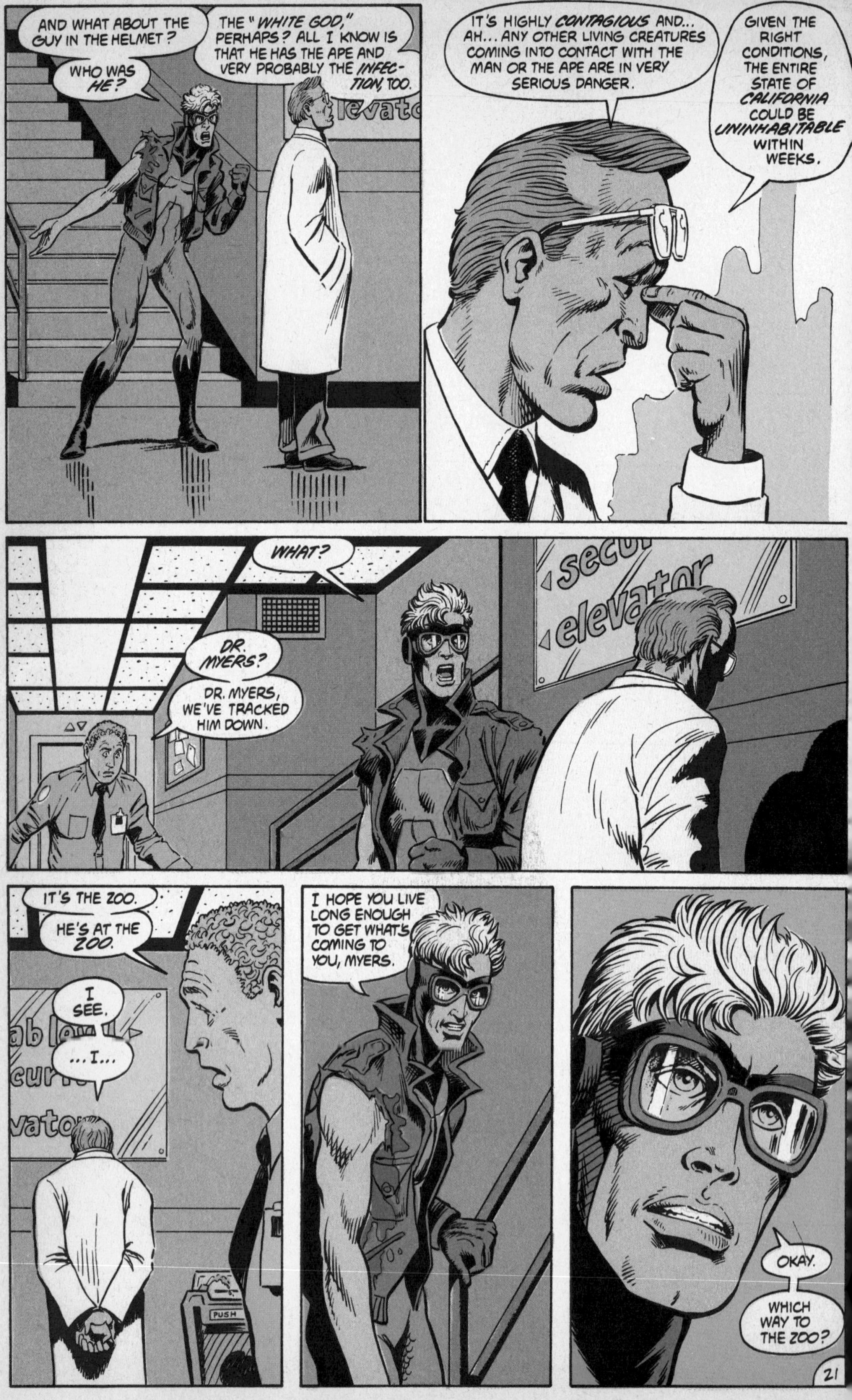
AND WHAT ABOUT THE GUY IN THE HELMET?
WHO WAS HE?
THE "WHITE GOD," PERHAPS? ALL I KNOW IS THAT HE HAS THE APE AND VERY PROBABLY THE INFECTION, TOO.
IT'S HIGHLY CONTAGIOUS AND... AH... ANY OTHER LIVING CREATURES COMING INTO CONTACT WITH THE MAN OR THE APE ARE IN VERY SERIOUS DANGER.
GIVEN THE RIGHT CONDITIONS, THE ENTIRE STATE OF CALIFORNIA COULD BE UNINHABITABLE WITHIN WEEKS.
WHAT?
DR. MYERS?
DR. MYERS, WE'VE TRACKED HIM DOWN.
IT'S THE ZOO.
HE'S AT THE ZOO.
I SEE.
...I...
I HOPE YOU LIVE LONG ENOUGH TO GET WHAT'S COMING TO YOU, MYERS.
OKAY.
WHICH WAY TO THE ZOO?
PUSH

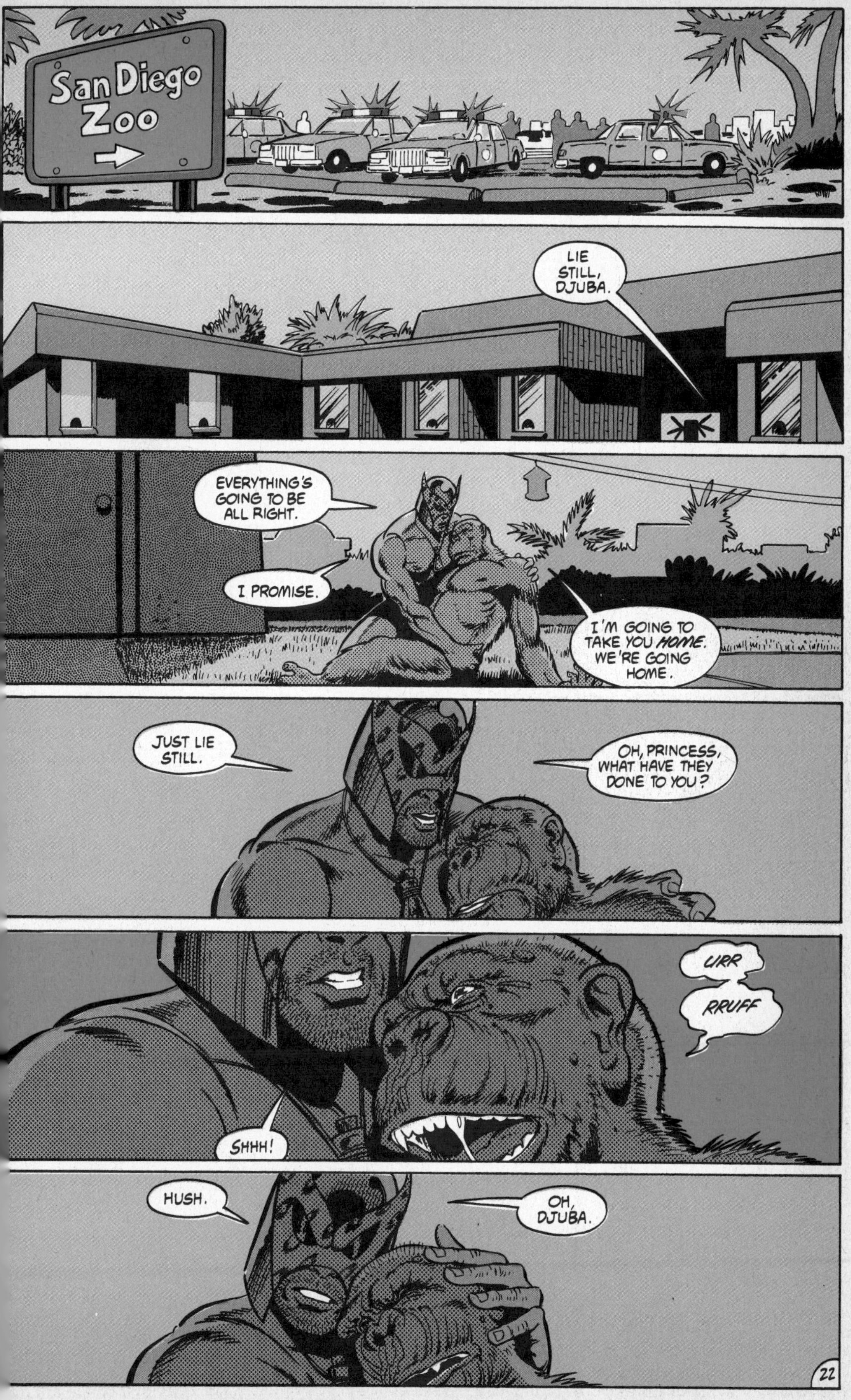
San Diego Zoo
LIE STILL, DJUBA.
EVERYTHING'S GOING TO BE ALL RIGHT.
I PROMISE.
I'M GOING TO TAKE YOU HOME. WE'RE GOING HOME.
JUST LIE STILL.
OH, PRINCESS, WHAT HAVE THEY DONE TO YOU?
URR
RRUFF
SHHH!
HUSH.
OH, DJUBA.

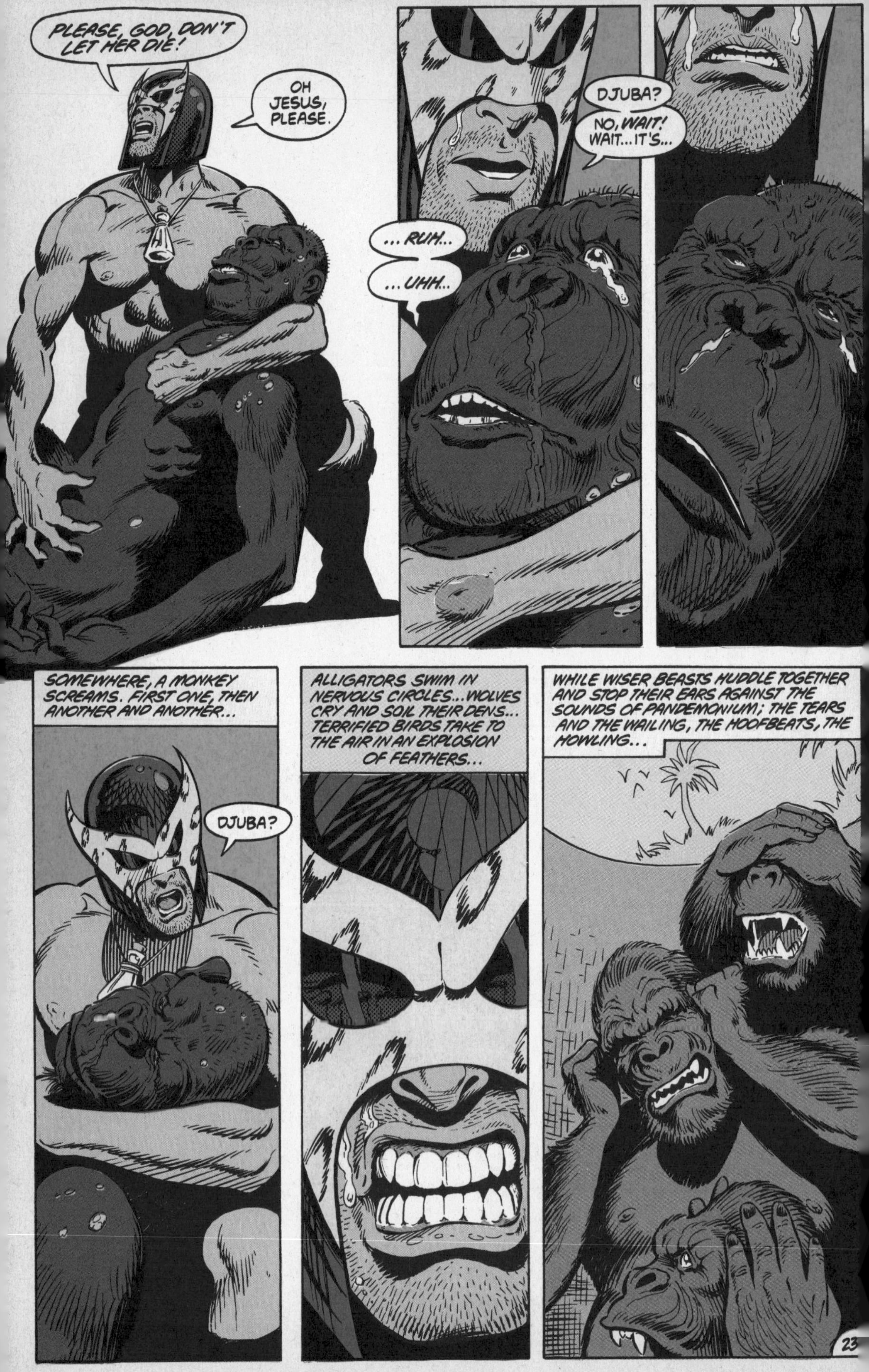

PLEASE, GOD, DON'T LET HER DIE!
OH JESUS, PLEASE.
DJUBA?
NO, WAIT! WAIT...IT'S...
...RUH...
...UHH...
SOMEWHERE, A MONKEY SCREAMS. FIRST ONE, THEN ANOTHER AND ANOTHER...
DJUBA?
ALLIGATORS SWIM IN NERVOUS CIRCLES...WOLVES CRY AND SOIL THEIR DENS... TERRIFIED BIRDS TAKE TO THE AIR IN AN EXPLOSION OF FEATHERS...
WHILE WISER BEASTS HUDDLE TOGETHER AND STOP THEIR EARS AGAINST THE SOUNDS OF PANDEMONIUM; THE TEARS AND THE WAILING, THE HOOFBEATS, THE HOWLING...

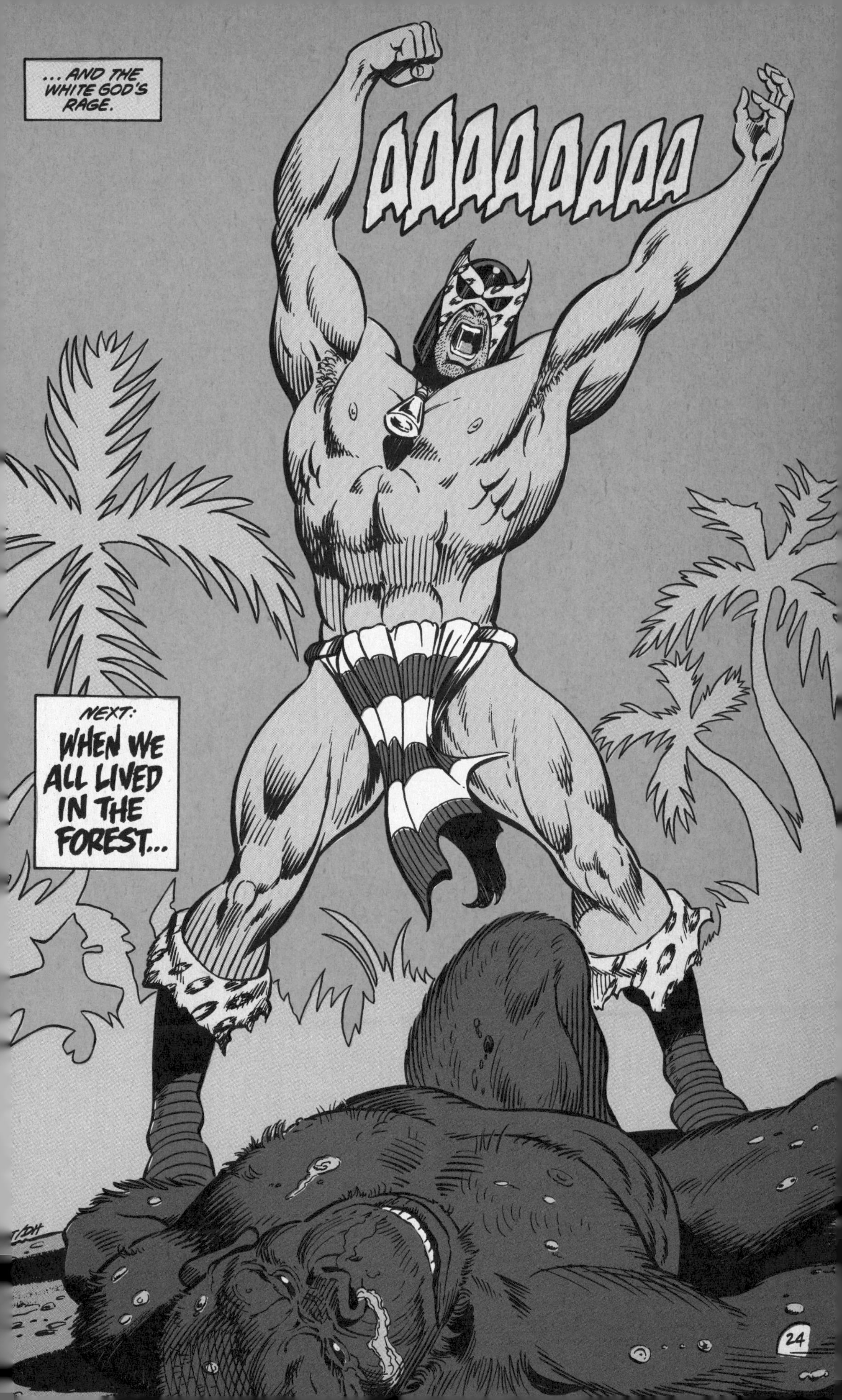
... AND THE WHITE GOD'S RAGE.
AAAAAAAA
NEXT:
WHEN WE ALL LIVED IN THE FOREST...
24

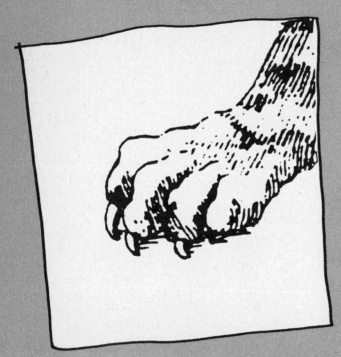

CHAPTER
FOUR

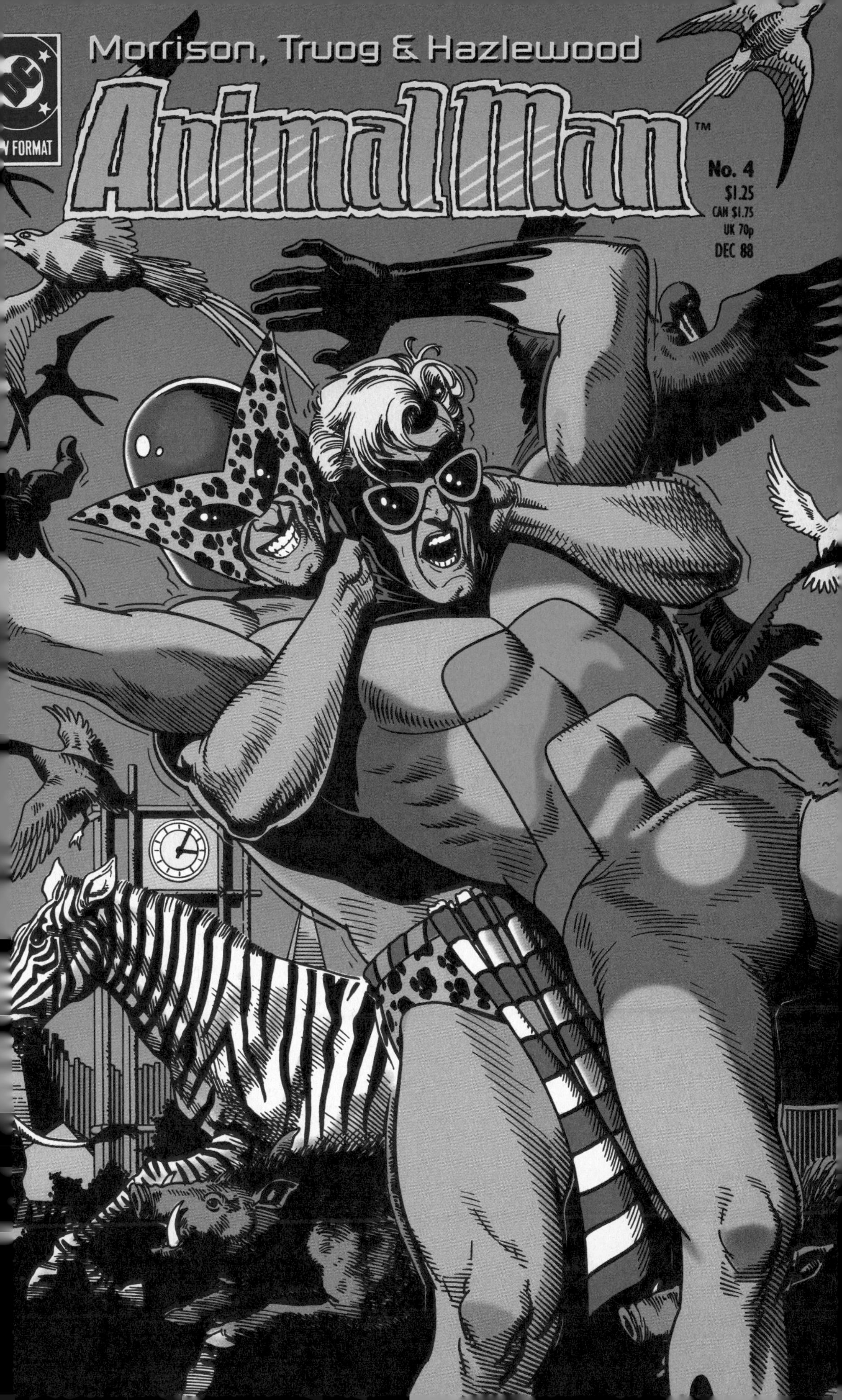

Morrison, Truog & Hazlewood
Animal Man
No. 4
$1.25
CAN $1.75
UK 70p
DEC 88

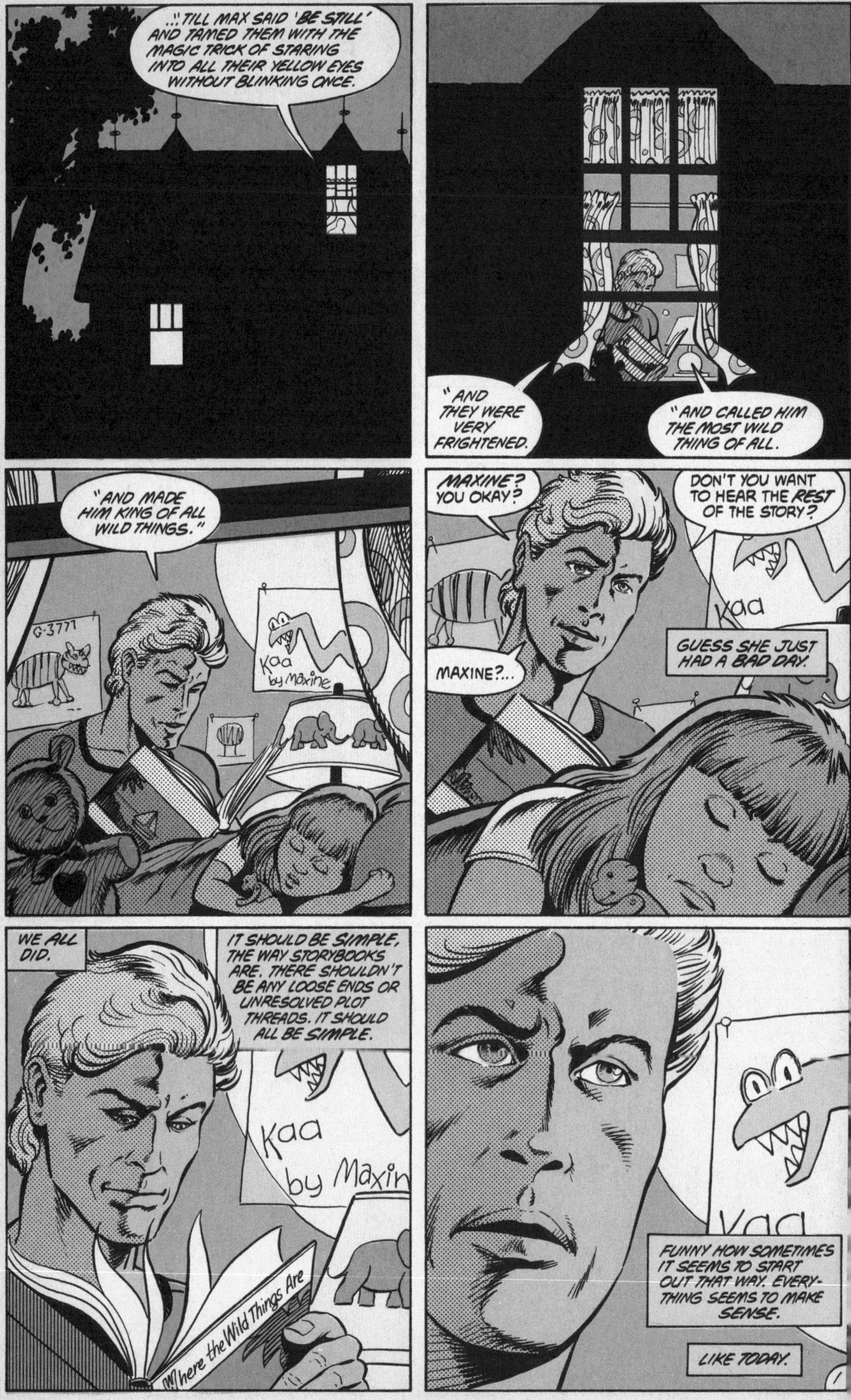
...'TILL MAX SAID 'BE STILL' AND TAMED THEM WITH THE MAGIC TRICK OF STARING INTO ALL THEIR YELLOW EYES WITHOUT BLINKING ONCE.
"AND THEY WERE VERY FRIGHTENED.
"AND CALLED HIM THE MOST WILD THING OF ALL.
"AND MADE HIM KING OF ALL WILD THINGS."
G-3777
Kaa by Maxine
MAXINE? YOU OKAY?
DON'T YOU WANT TO HEAR THE REST OF THE STORY?
Kaa
GUESS SHE JUST HAD A BAD DAY.
MAXINE?...
WE ALL DID.
IT SHOULD BE SIMPLE, THE WAY STORYBOOKS ARE. THERE SHOULDN'T BE ANY LOOSE ENDS OR UNRESOLVED PLOT THREADS. IT SHOULD ALL BE SIMPLE.
Kaa by Maxin
Where the Wild Things Are
Kaa
FUNNY HOW SOMETIMES IT SEEMS TO START OUT THAT WAY. EVERYTHING SEEMS TO MAKE SENSE.
LIKE TODAY.

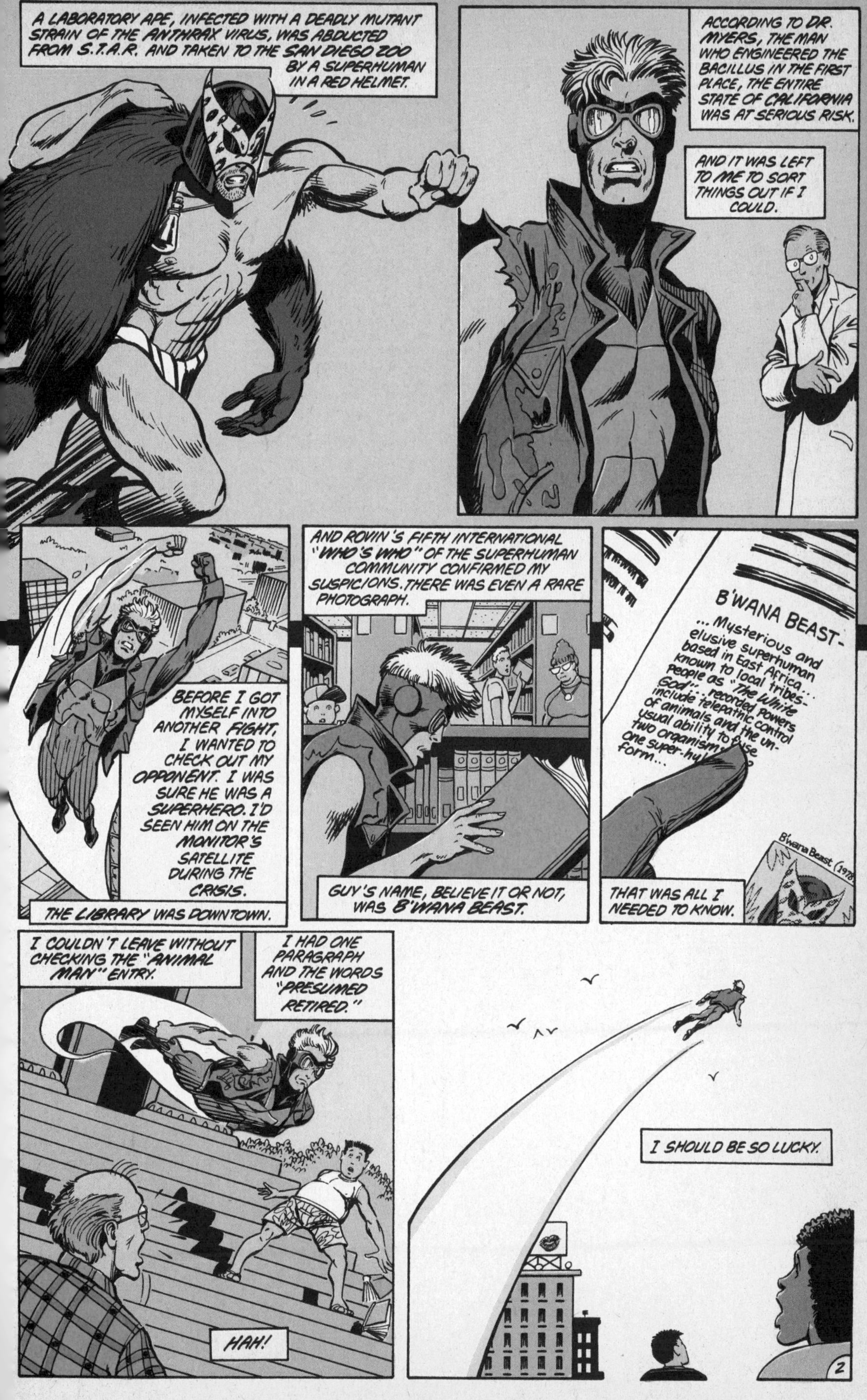
A LABORATORY APE, INFECTED WITH A DEADLY MUTANT STRAIN OF THE ANTHRAX VIRUS, WAS ABDUCTED FROM S.T.A.R. AND TAKEN TO THE SAN DIEGO ZOO BY A SUPERHUMAN IN A RED HELMET.
ACCORDING TO DR. MYERS, THE MAN WHO ENGINEERED THE BACILLUS IN THE FIRST PLACE, THE ENTIRE STATE OF CALIFORNIA WAS AT SERIOUS RISK.
AND IT WAS LEFT TO ME TO SORT THINGS OUT IF I COULD.
BEFORE I GOT MYSELF INTO ANOTHER FIGHT, I WANTED TO CHECK OUT MY OPPONENT. I WAS SURE HE WAS A SUPERHERO. I'D SEEN HIM ON THE MONITOR'S SATELLITE DURING THE CRISIS.
THE LIBRARY WAS DOWNTOWN.
AND ROVIN'S FIFTH INTERNATIONAL "WHO'S WHO" OF THE SUPERHUMAN COMMUNITY CONFIRMED MY SUSPICIONS. THERE WAS EVEN A RARE PHOTOGRAPH.
GUY'S NAME, BELIEVE IT OR NOT, WAS B'WANA BEAST.
B'WANA BEAST
... Mysterious and elusive superhuman based in East Africa... known to local tribes-people as "The White God"... recorded powers include telepathic control of animals and the unusual ability to fuse two organisms
one super-hu
form...
B'wana Beast (1978
THAT WAS ALL I NEEDED TO KNOW.
I COULDN'T LEAVE WITHOUT CHECKING THE "ANIMAL MAN" ENTRY.
I HAD ONE PARAGRAPH AND THE WORDS "PRESUMED RETIRED."
HAH!
I SHOULD BE SO LUCKY.

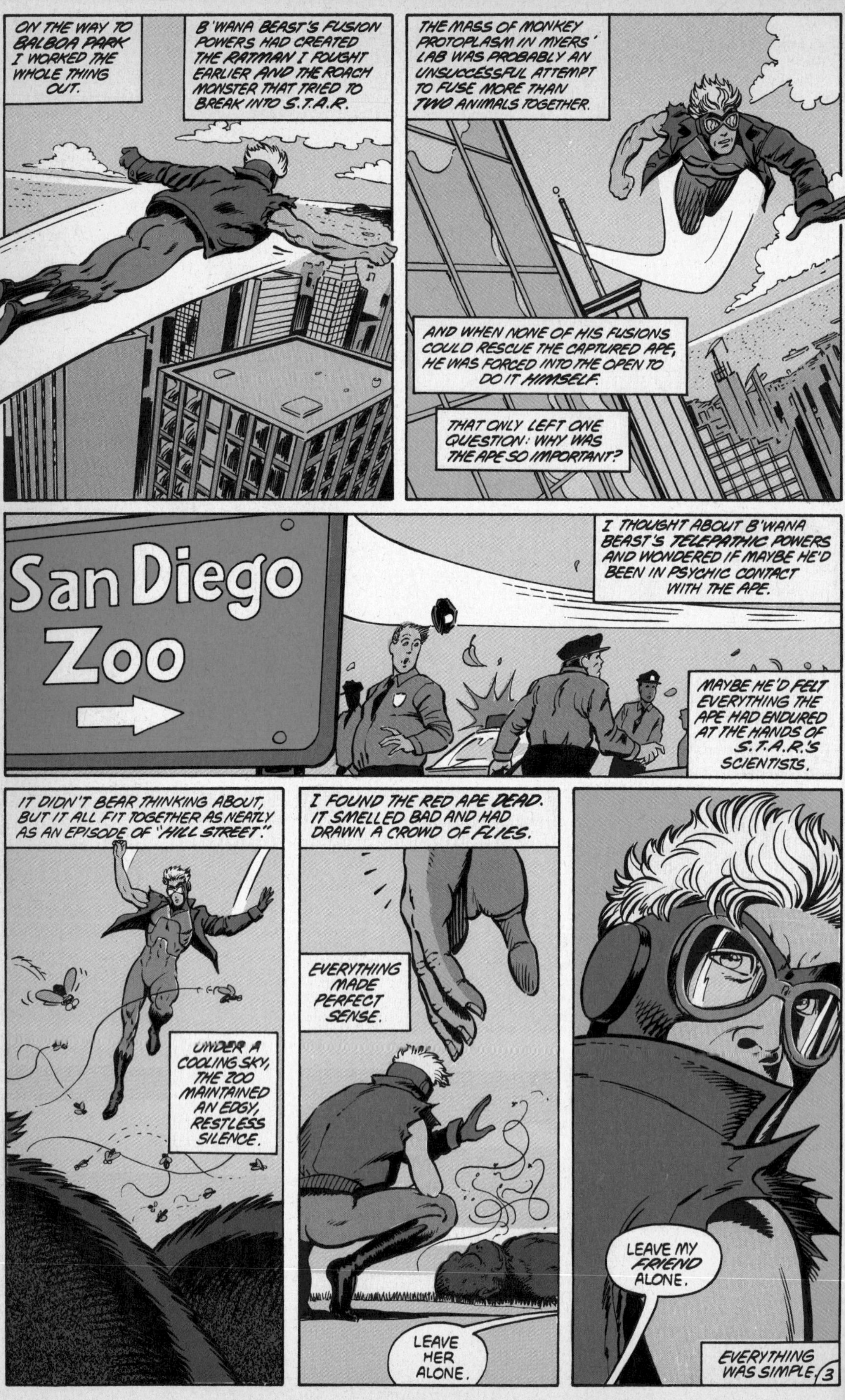
ON THE WAY TO BALBOA PARK I WORKED THE WHOLE THING OUT.
B'WANA BEAST'S FUSION POWERS HAD CREATED THE RATMAN I FOUGHT EARLIER AND THE ROACH MONSTER THAT TRIED TO BREAK INTO S.T.A.R.
THE MASS OF MONKEY PROTOPLASM IN MYERS' LAB WAS PROBABLY AN UNSUCCESSFUL ATTEMPT TO FUSE MORE THAN TWO ANIMALS TOGETHER.
AND WHEN NONE OF HIS FUSIONS COULD RESCUE THE CAPTURED APE, HE WAS FORCED INTO THE OPEN TO DO IT HIMSELF.
THAT ONLY LEFT ONE QUESTION: WHY WAS THE APE SO IMPORTANT?
San Diego Zoo
I THOUGHT ABOUT B'WANA BEAST'S TELEPATHIC POWERS AND WONDERED IF MAYBE HE'D BEEN IN PSYCHIC CONTACT WITH THE APE.
MAYBE HE'D FELT EVERYTHING THE APE HAD ENDURED AT THE HANDS OF S.T.A.R.'S SCIENTISTS.
IT DIDN'T BEAR THINKING ABOUT, BUT IT ALL FIT TOGETHER AS NEATLY AS AN EPISODE OF "HILL STREET."
UNDER A COOLING SKY, THE ZOO MAINTAINED AN EDGY, RESTLESS SILENCE.
I FOUND THE RED APE DEAD. IT SMELLED BAD AND HAD DRAWN A CROWD OF FLIES.
EVERYTHING MADE PERFECT SENSE.
LEAVE HER ALONE.
LEAVE MY FRIEND ALONE.
EVERYTHING WAS SIMPLE.
3

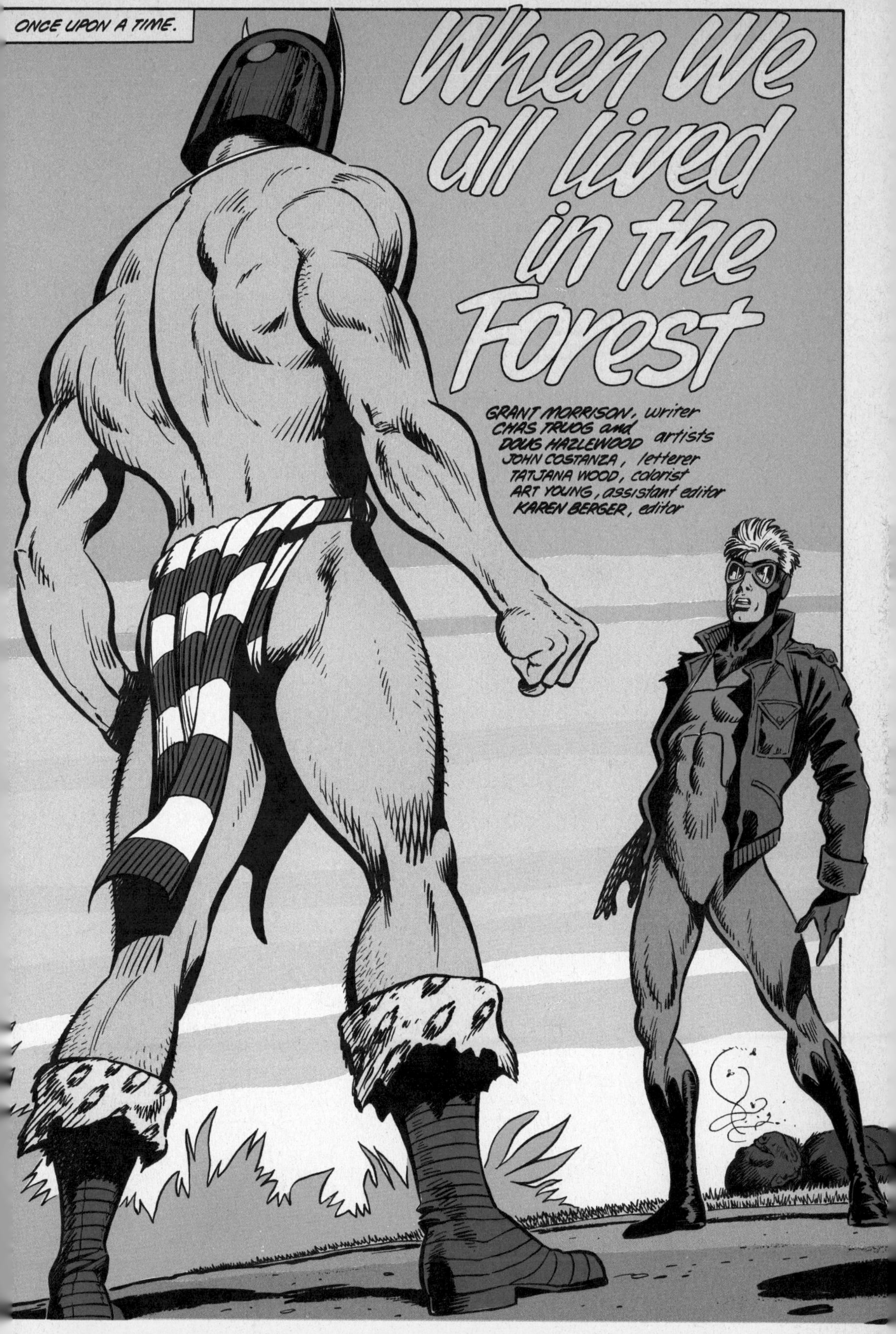
ONCE UPON A TIME.
When We all lived in the Forest
GRANT MORRISON, writer
CHAS TRUOG and DOUG HAZLEWOOD artists
JOHN COSTANZA, letterer
TATJANA WOOD, colorist
ART YOUNG, assistant editor
KAREN BERGER, editor

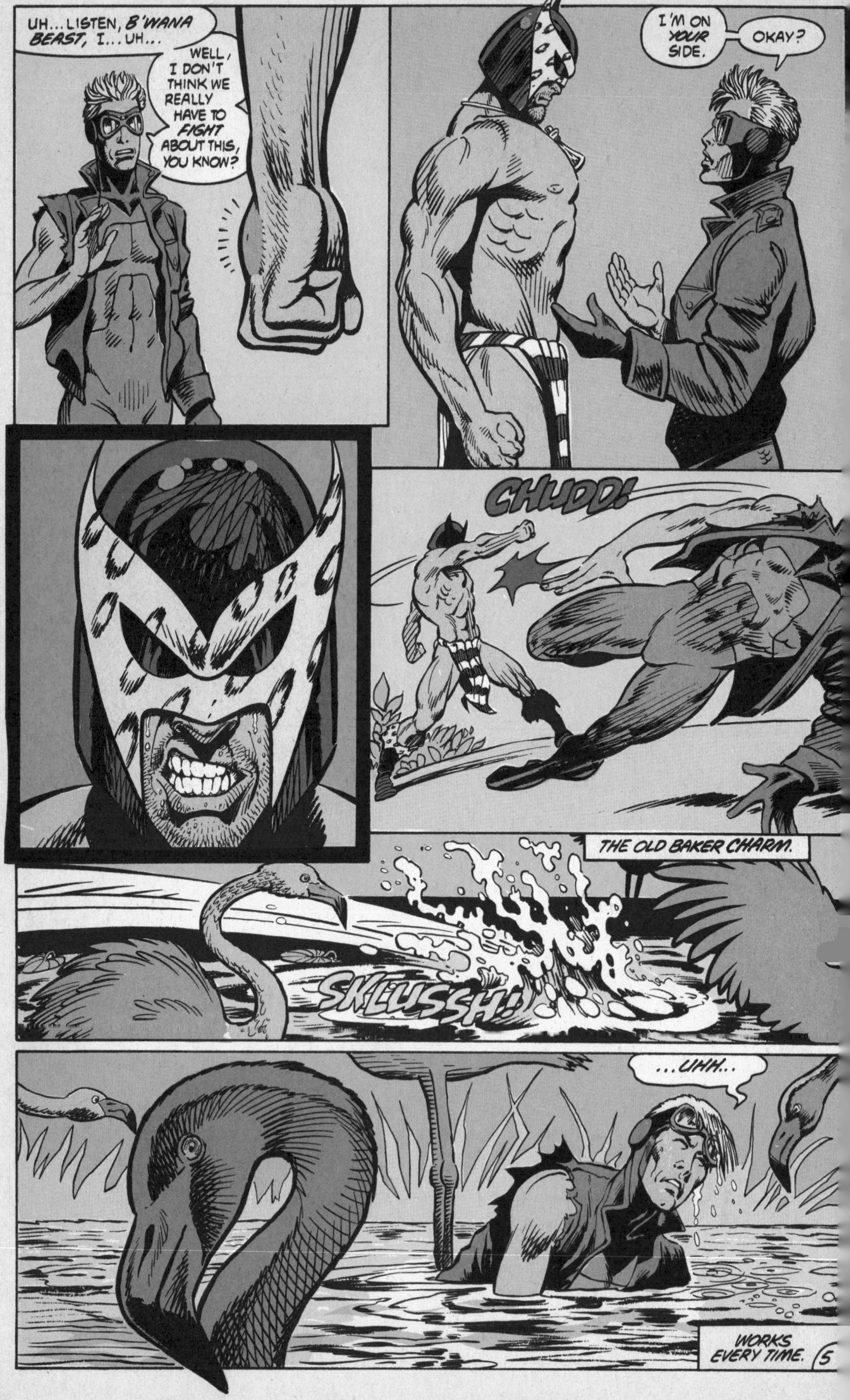
UH... LISTEN, B'WANA BEAST, I... UH...
WELL, I DON'T THINK WE REALLY HAVE TO FIGHT ABOUT THIS, YOU KNOW?
I'M ON YOUR SIDE.
OKAY?
CHUDD!
THE OLD BAKER CHARM.
SKLUSSH!
...UHH...
WORKS EVERY TIME.
5

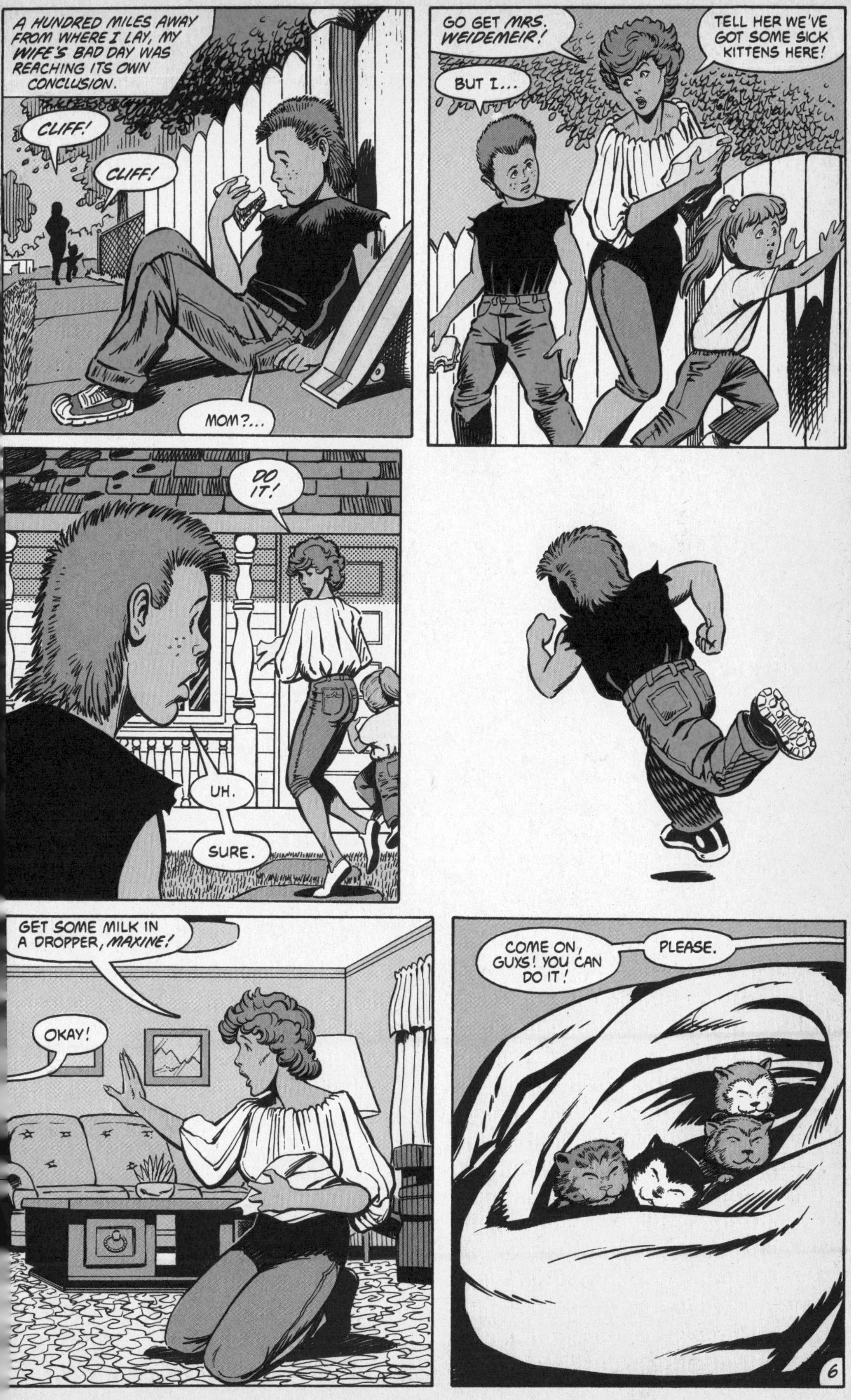
A HUNDRED MILES AWAY FROM WHERE I LAY, MY WIFE'S BAD DAY WAS REACHING ITS OWN CONCLUSION.
CLIFF!
CLIFF!
MOM?...
GO GET MRS. WEIDEMEIR!
BUT I...
TELL HER WE'VE GOT SOME SICK KITTENS HERE!
DO IT!
UH.
SURE.
GET SOME MILK IN A DROPPER, MAXINE!
OKAY!
COME ON, GUYS! YOU CAN DO IT!
PLEASE.
6

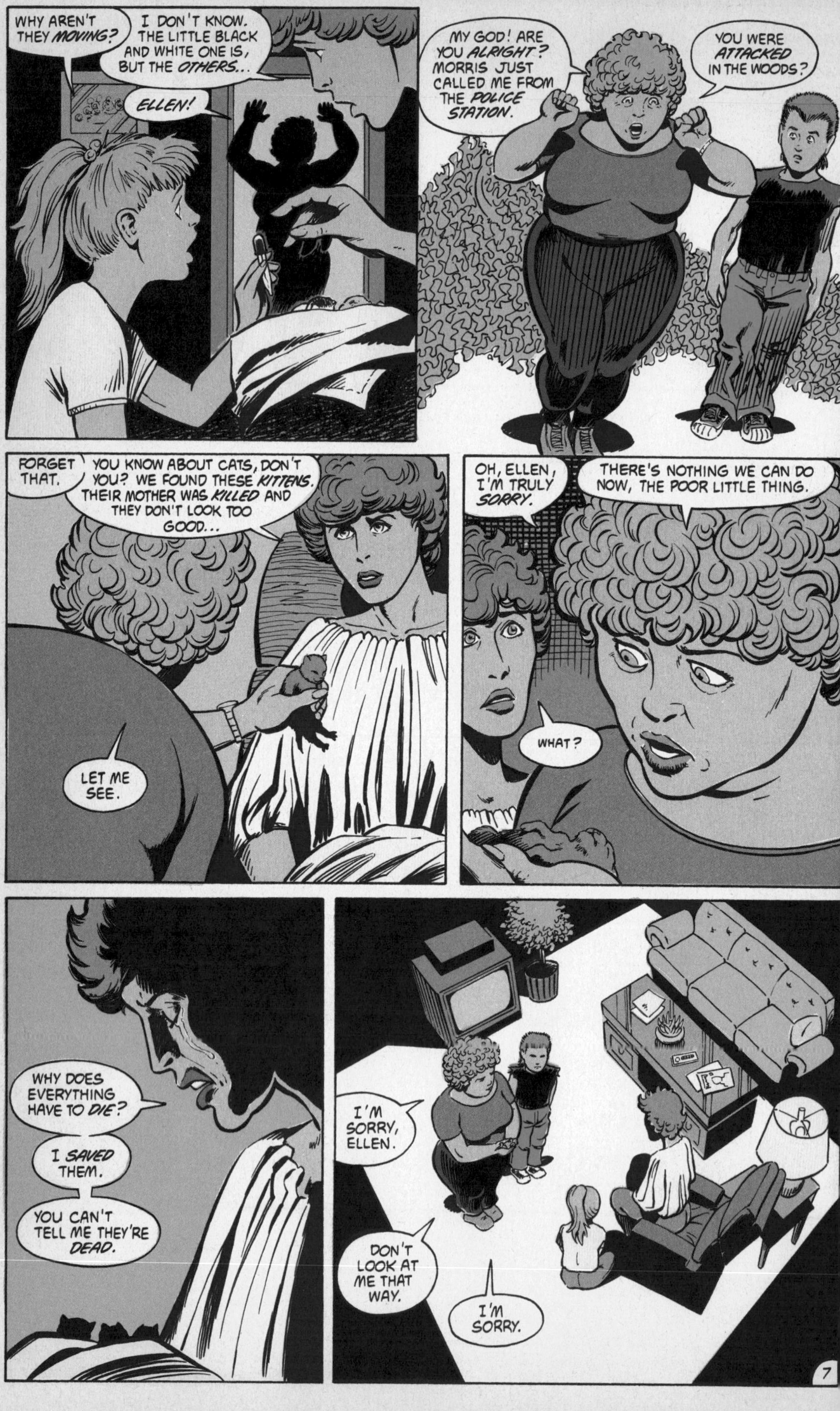
WHY AREN'T THEY MOVING?
I DON'T KNOW. THE LITTLE BLACK AND WHITE ONE IS, BUT THE OTHERS...
ELLEN!
MY GOD! ARE YOU ALRIGHT? MORRIS JUST CALLED ME FROM THE POLICE STATION.
YOU WERE ATTACKED IN THE WOODS?
FORGET THAT.
YOU KNOW ABOUT CATS, DON'T YOU? WE FOUND THESE KITTENS. THEIR MOTHER WAS KILLED AND THEY DON'T LOOK TOO GOOD...
LET ME SEE.
OH, ELLEN, I'M TRULY SORRY.
THERE'S NOTHING WE CAN DO NOW, THE POOR LITTLE THING.
WHAT?
WHY DOES EVERYTHING HAVE TO DIE?
I SAVED THEM.
YOU CAN'T TELL ME THEY'RE DEAD.
I'M SORRY, ELLEN.
DON'T LOOK AT ME THAT WAY.
I'M SORRY.
7

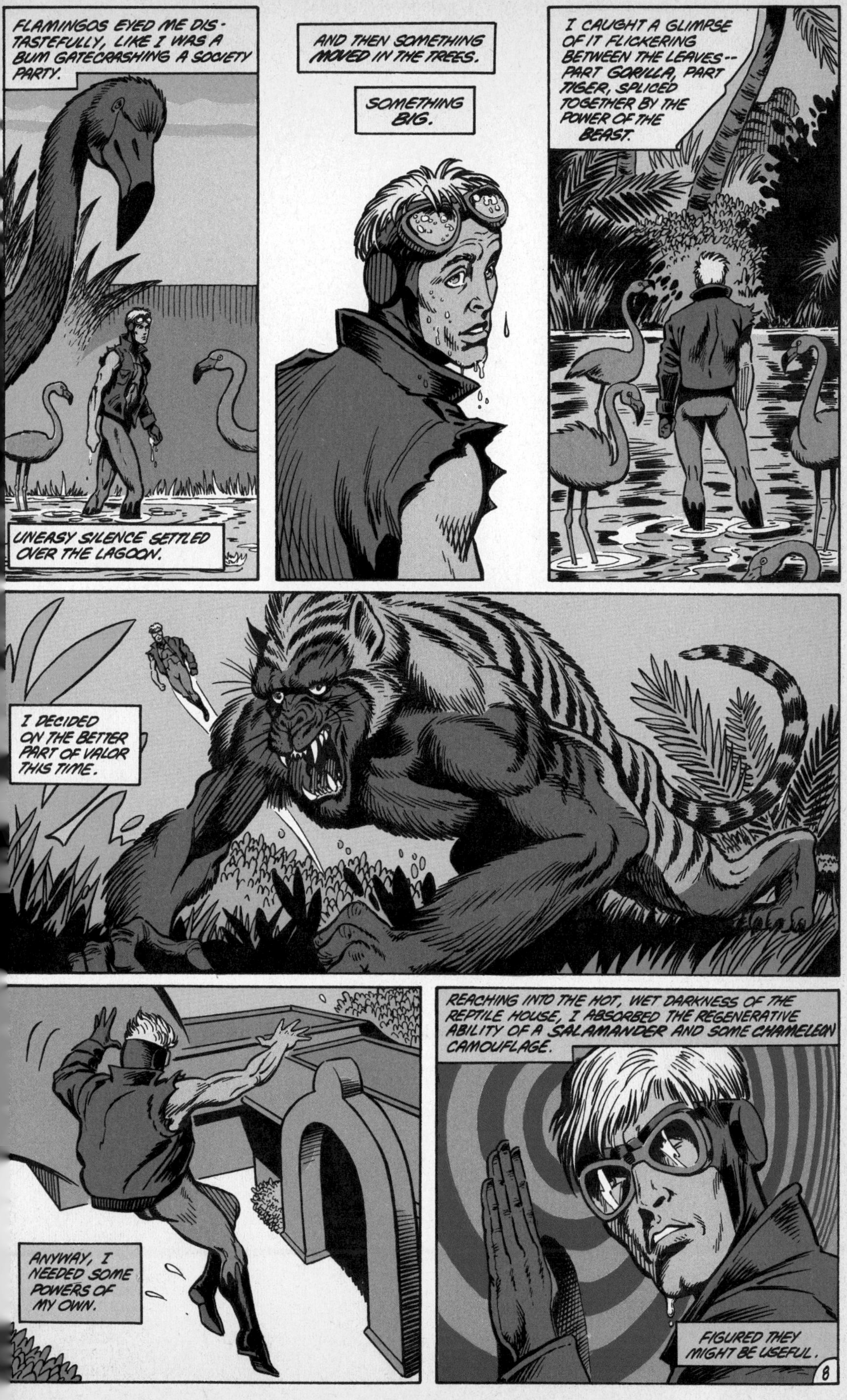
FLAMINGOS EYED ME DIS-TASTEFULLY, LIKE I WAS A BUM GATECRASHING A SOCIETY PARTY.
UNEASY SILENCE SETTLED OVER THE LAGOON.
AND THEN SOMETHING MOVED IN THE TREES.
SOMETHING BIG.
I CAUGHT A GLIMPSE OF IT FLICKERING BETWEEN THE LEAVES-- PART GORILLA, PART TIGER, SPLICED TOGETHER BY THE POWER OF THE BEAST.
I DECIDED ON THE BETTER PART OF VALOR THIS TIME.
ANYWAY, I NEEDED SOME POWERS OF MY OWN.
REACHING INTO THE HOT, WET DARKNESS OF THE REPTILE HOUSE, I ABSORBED THE REGENERATIVE ABILITY OF A SALAMANDER AND SOME CHAMELEON CAMOUFLAGE.
FIGURED THEY MIGHT BE USEFUL.
8

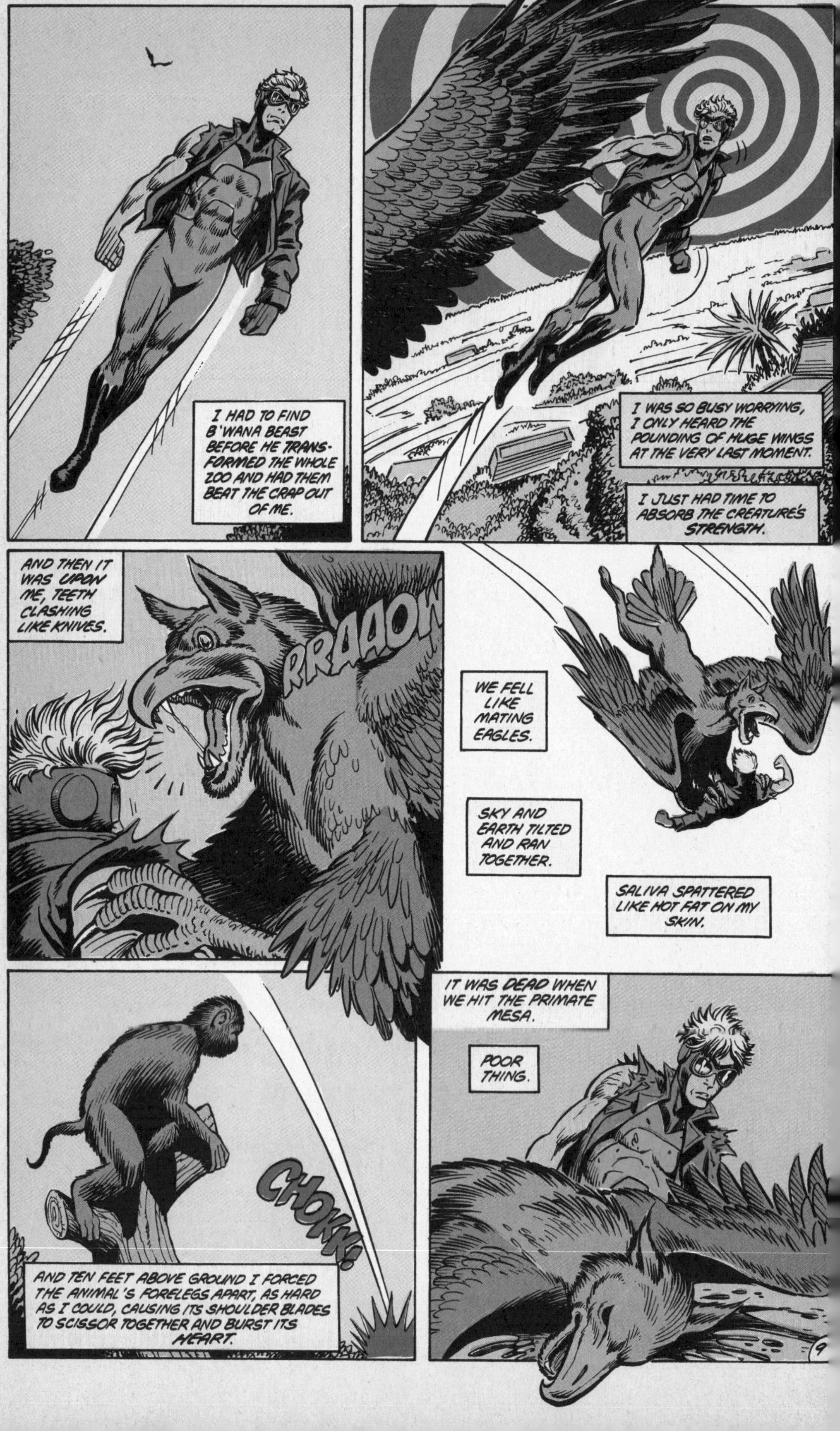

I HAD TO FIND B'WANA BEAST BEFORE HE TRANS-FORMED THE WHOLE ZOO AND HAD THEM BEAT THE CRAP OUT OF ME.
I WAS SO BUSY WORRYING, I ONLY HEARD THE POUNDING OF HUGE WINGS AT THE VERY LAST MOMENT.
I JUST HAD TIME TO ABSORB THE CREATURE'S STRENGTH.
AND THEN IT WAS UPON ME, TEETH CLASHING LIKE KNIVES.
RRAAOW
WE FELL LIKE MATING EAGLES.
SKY AND EARTH TILTED AND RAN TOGETHER.
SALIVA SPATTERED LIKE HOT FAT ON MY SKIN.
CHOKK!
AND TEN FEET ABOVE GROUND I FORCED THE ANIMAL'S FORELEGS APART, AS HARD AS I COULD, CAUSING ITS SHOULDER BLADES TO SCISSOR TOGETHER AND BURST ITS HEART.
IT WAS DEAD WHEN WE HIT THE PRIMATE MESA.
POOR THING.

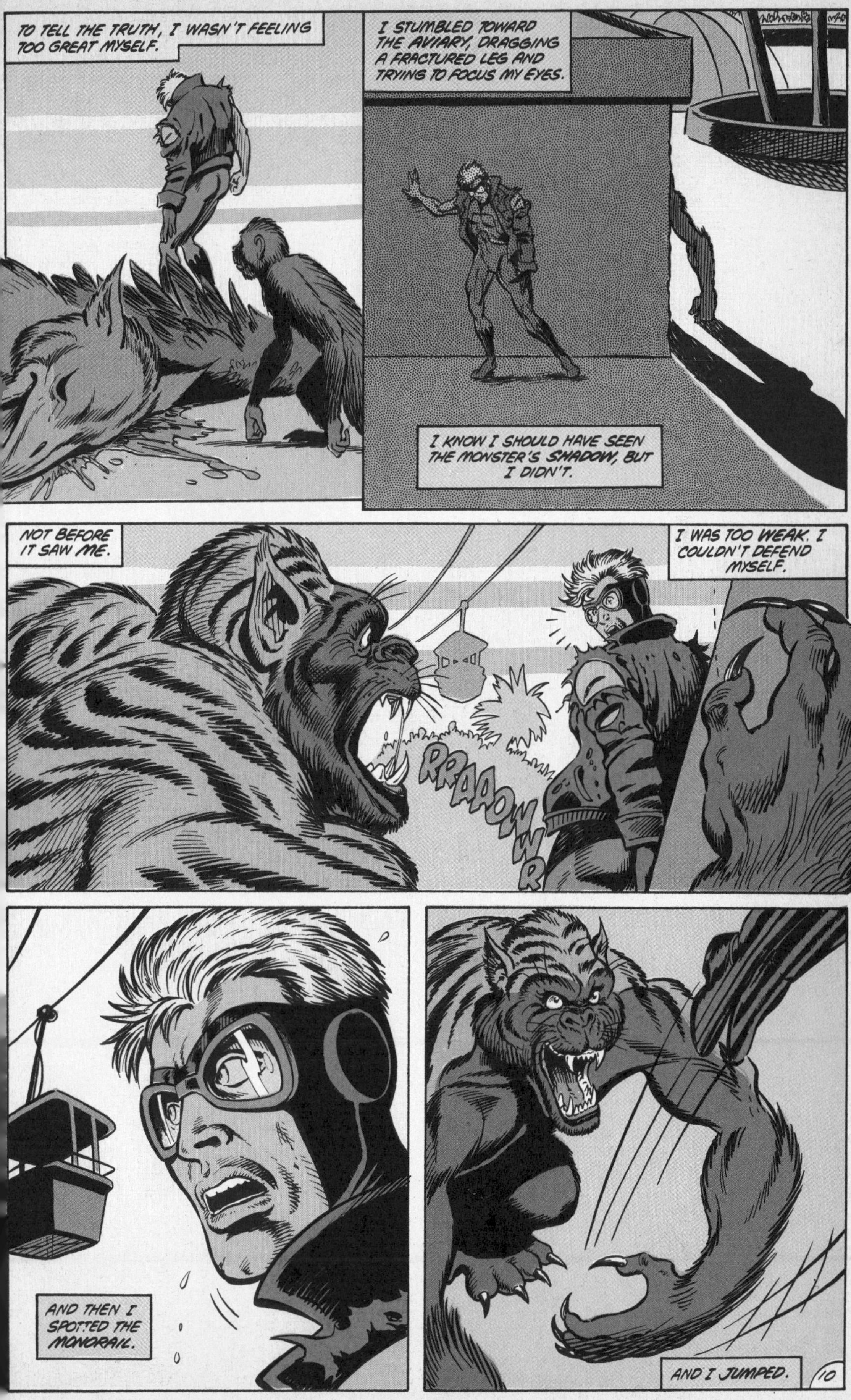
TO TELL THE TRUTH, I WASN'T FEELING TOO GREAT MYSELF.
I STUMBLED TOWARD THE AVIARY, DRAGGING A FRACTURED LEG AND TRYING TO FOCUS MY EYES.
I KNOW I SHOULD HAVE SEEN THE MONSTER'S SHADOW, BUT I DIDN'T.
NOT BEFORE IT SAW ME.
I WAS TOO WEAK. I COULDN'T DEFEND MYSELF.
RRAAOWWR
AND THEN I SPOTTED THE MONORAIL.
AND I JUMPED.
10

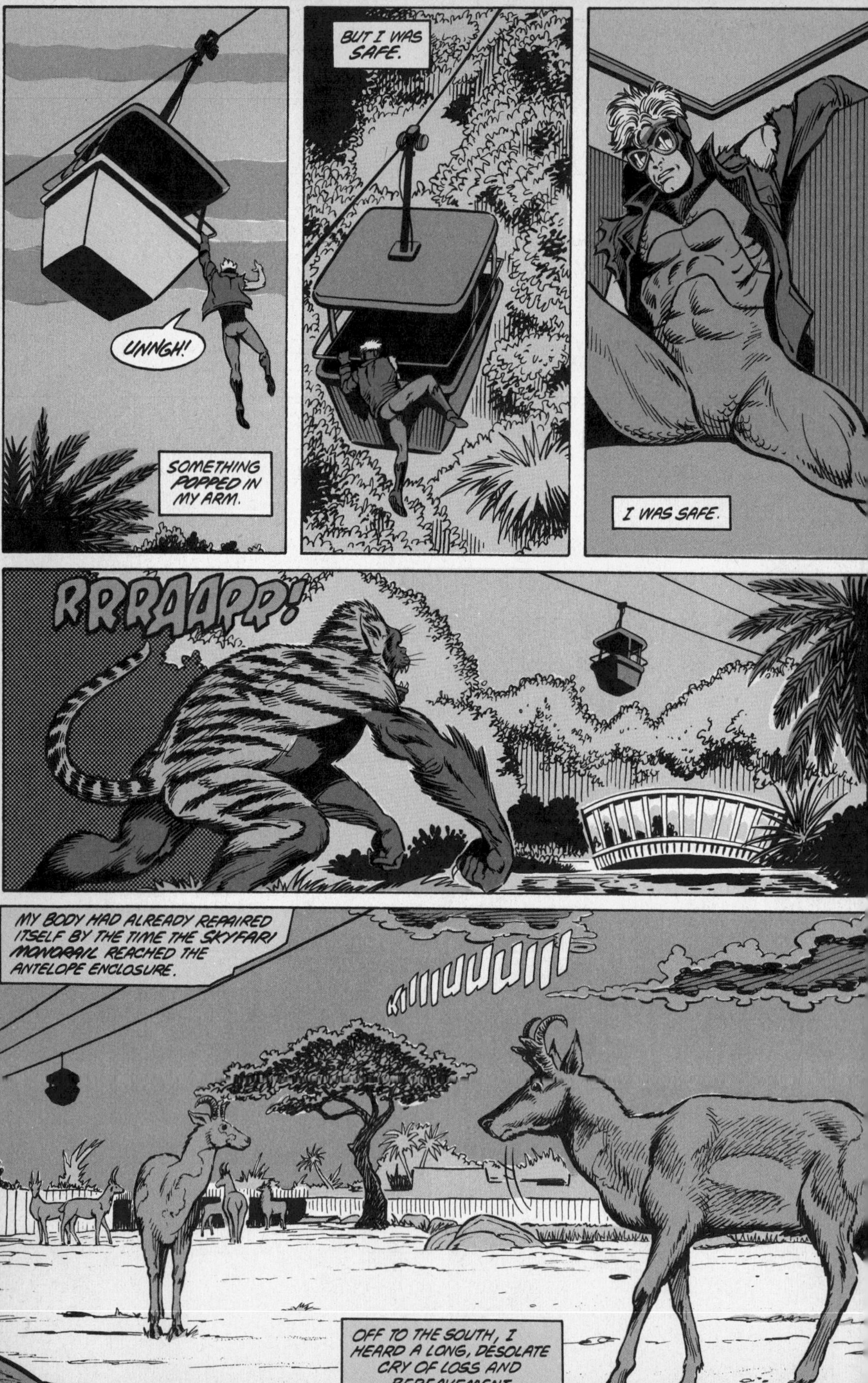
UNNGH!
SOMETHING POPPED IN MY ARM.
BUT I WAS SAFE.
I WAS SAFE.
RRRAARR!
MY BODY HAD ALREADY REPAIRED ITSELF BY THE TIME THE SKYFARI MONORAIL REACHED THE ANTELOPE ENCLOSURE.
KIIIUUUUIII
OFF TO THE SOUTH, I HEARD A LONG, DESOLATE CRY OF LOSS AND BEREAVEMENT.

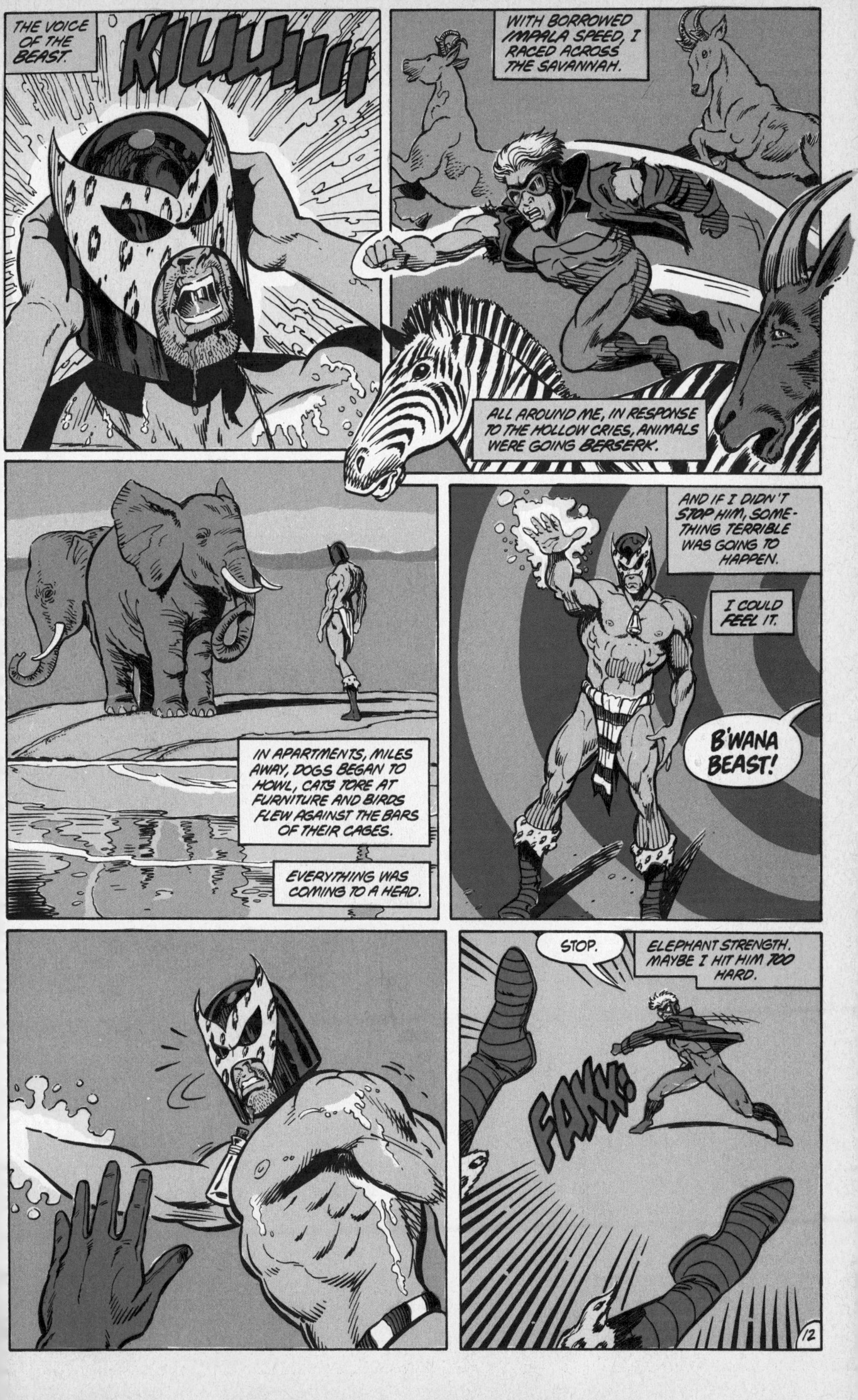
THE VOICE OF THE BEAST.
KIIUUIIII
WITH BORROWED IMPALA SPEED, I RACED ACROSS THE SAVANNAH.
ALL AROUND ME, IN RESPONSE TO THE HOLLOW CRIES, ANIMALS WERE GOING BERSERK.
IN APARTMENTS, MILES AWAY, DOGS BEGAN TO HOWL, CATS TORE AT FURNITURE AND BIRDS FLEW AGAINST THE BARS OF THEIR CAGES.
EVERYTHING WAS COMING TO A HEAD.
AND IF I DIDN'T STOP HIM, SOMETHING TERRIBLE WAS GOING TO HAPPEN.
I COULD FEEL IT.
B'WANA BEAST!
STOP.
ELEPHANT STRENGTH. MAYBE I HIT HIM TOO HARD.
FAKK!
12

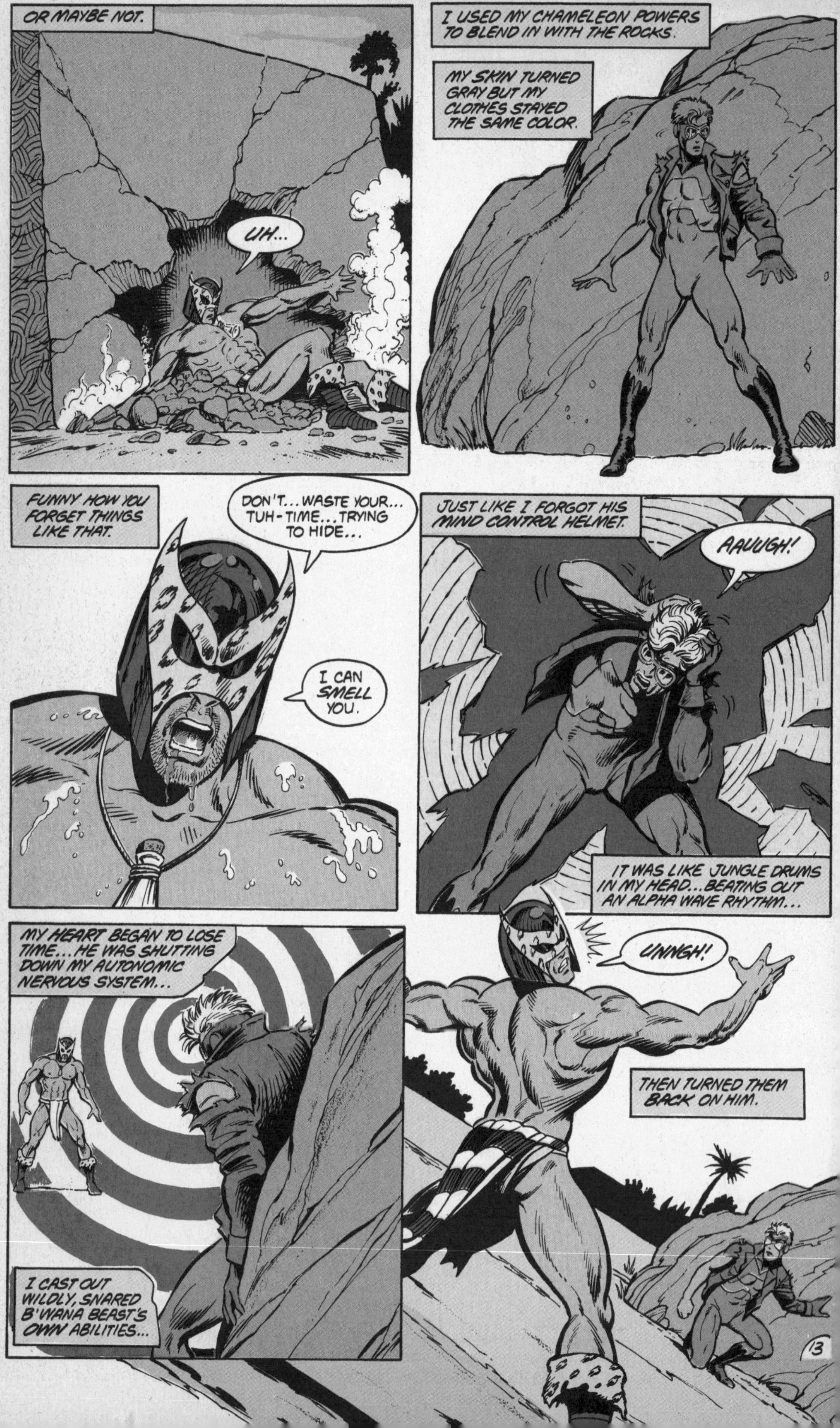
OR MAYBE NOT.
UH...
I USED MY CHAMELEON POWERS TO BLEND IN WITH THE ROCKS.
MY SKIN TURNED GRAY BUT MY CLOTHES STAYED THE SAME COLOR.
FUNNY HOW YOU FORGET THINGS LIKE THAT.
DON'T... WASTE YOUR... TUH-TIME... TRYING TO HIDE...
I CAN SMELL YOU.
JUST LIKE I FORGOT HIS MIND CONTROL HELMET.
AAUUGH!
IT WAS LIKE JUNGLE DRUMS IN MY HEAD... BEATING OUT AN ALPHA WAVE RHYTHM...
MY HEART BEGAN TO LOSE TIME... HE WAS SHUTTING DOWN MY AUTONOMIC NERVOUS SYSTEM...
I CAST OUT WILDLY, SNARED B'WANA BEAST'S OWN ABILITIES...
UNNGH!
THEN TURNED THEM BACK ON HIM.
13

AND WE WERE DEADLOCKED.

THOUGHTS WRESTLED IN THE EMPTY AIR BETWEEN US.

PERFECTLY MATCHED, WE EACH SEARCHED FOR SOME FLAW IN THE OTHER'S DEFENSE.

SOME CHINK IN THE ARMOR.

SOME GAP.

SOME WEAKNESS.

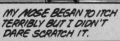

MY NOSE BEGAN TO ITCH TERRIBLY BUT I DIDN'T DARE SCRATCH IT.

AND THEN, IN THE MIDST OF OUR VIOLENT TELEPATHY, HE FALTERED, BLOOD SURGED UP IN HIS THROAT.

AND SUDDENLY IT WAS ALL OVER.

URRR

14

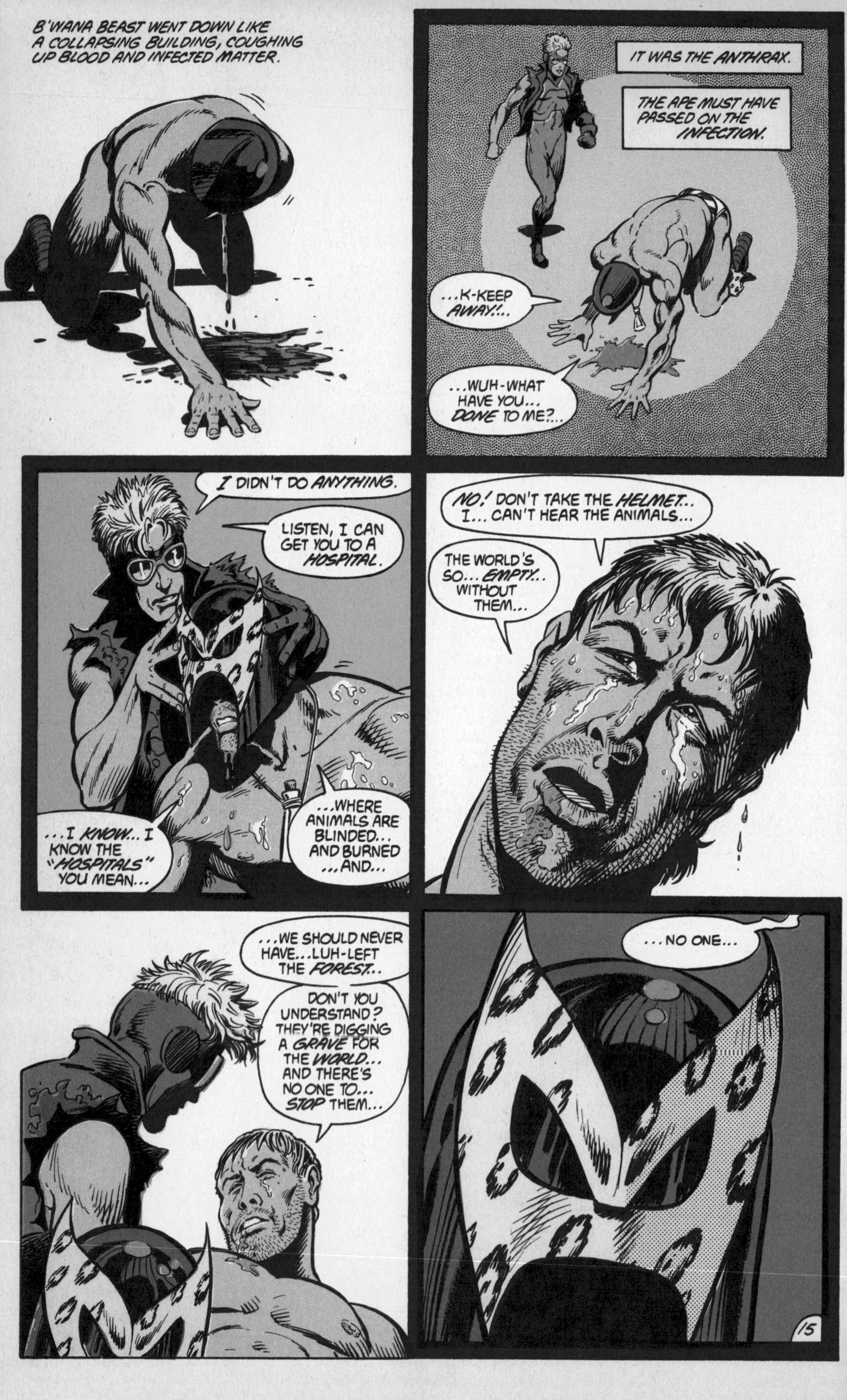

B'WANA BEAST WENT DOWN LIKE A COLLAPSING BUILDING, COUGHING UP BLOOD AND INFECTED MATTER.
IT WAS THE ANTHRAX.
THE APE MUST HAVE PASSED ON THE INFECTION.
...K-KEEP AWAY!...
...WUH-WHAT HAVE YOU... DONE TO ME?...
I DIDN'T DO ANYTHING.
LISTEN, I CAN GET YOU TO A HOSPITAL.
...I KNOW... I KNOW THE "HOSPITALS" YOU MEAN...
...WHERE ANIMALS ARE BLINDED... AND BURNED ...AND...
NO! DON'T TAKE THE HELMET... I... CAN'T HEAR THE ANIMALS...
THE WORLD'S SO... EMPTY... WITHOUT THEM...
...WE SHOULD NEVER HAVE...LUH-LEFT THE FOREST...
DON'T YOU UNDERSTAND? THEY'RE DIGGING A GRAVE FOR THE WORLD... AND THERE'S NO ONE TO... STOP THEM...
...NO ONE...
15

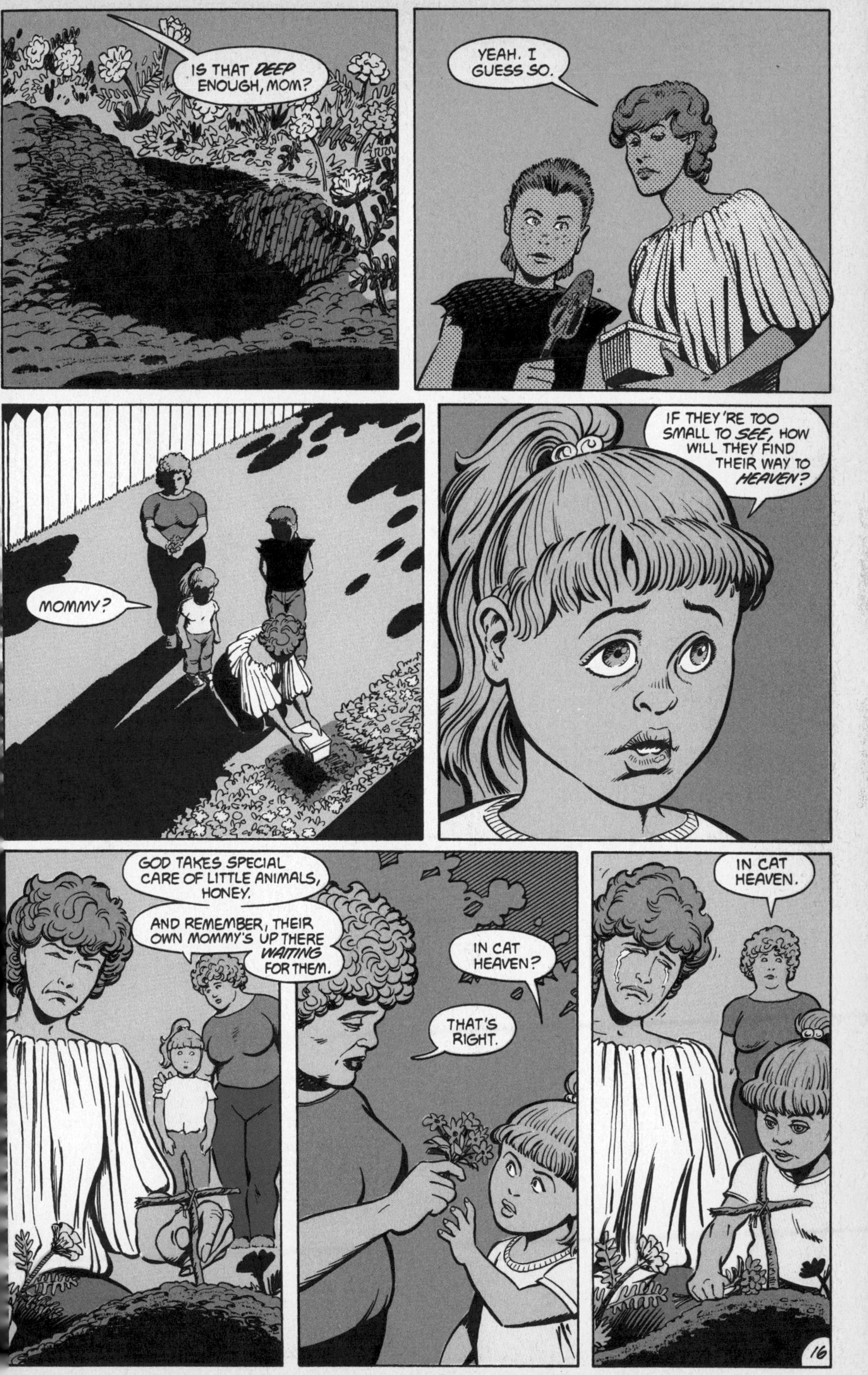
IS THAT *DEEP* ENOUGH, MOM?
YEAH. I GUESS SO.
MOMMY?
IF THEY'RE TOO SMALL TO *SEE*, HOW WILL THEY FIND THEIR WAY TO *HEAVEN*?
GOD TAKES SPECIAL CARE OF LITTLE ANIMALS, HONEY.
AND REMEMBER, THEIR OWN MOMMY'S UP THERE *WAITING* FOR THEM.
IN CAT HEAVEN?
THAT'S RIGHT.
IN CAT HEAVEN.

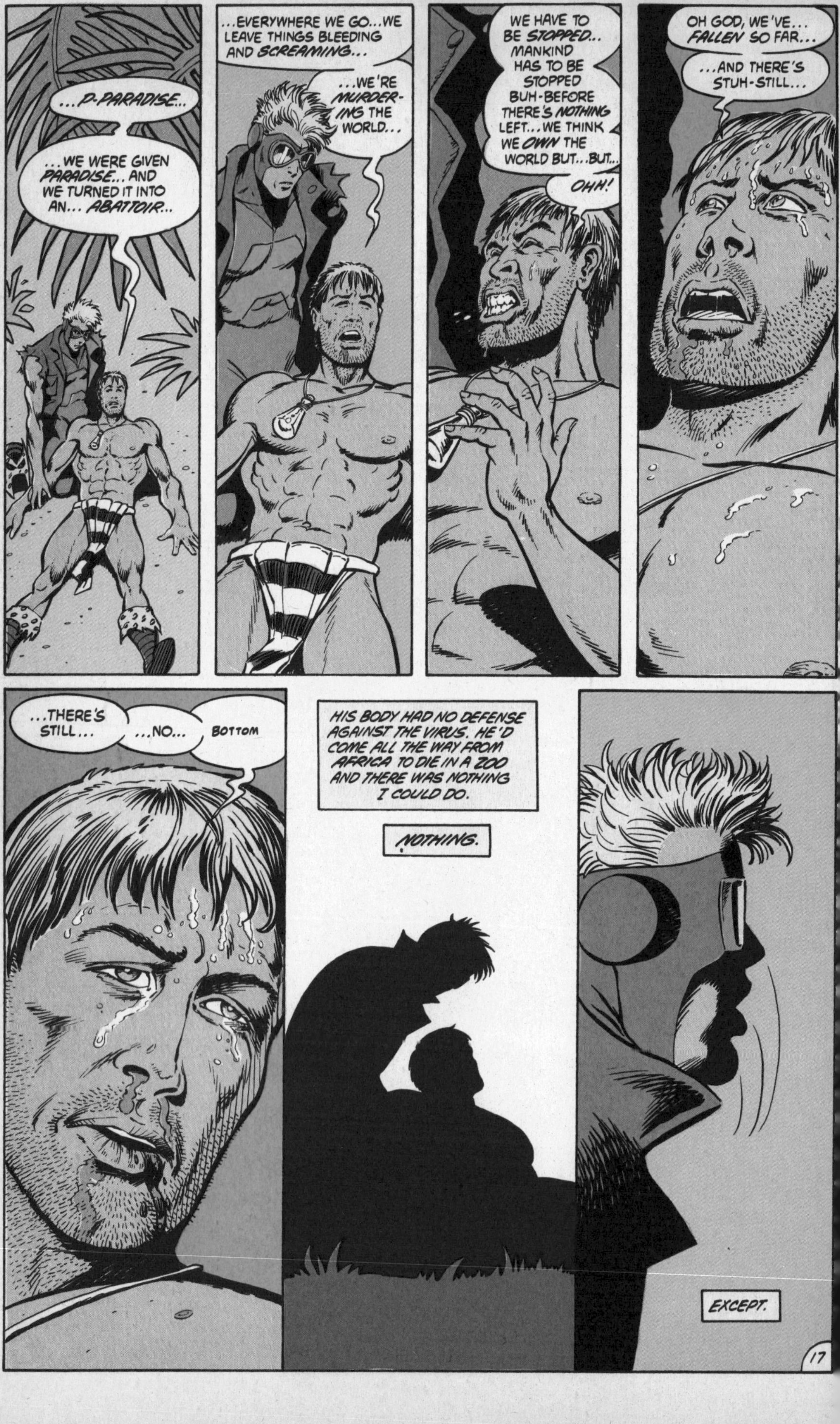
...P-PARADISE...
...WE WERE GIVEN PARADISE... AND WE TURNED IT INTO AN... ABATTOIR...
...EVERYWHERE WE GO...WE LEAVE THINGS BLEEDING AND SCREAMING...
...WE'RE MURDERING THE WORLD...
WE HAVE TO BE STOPPED... MANKIND HAS TO BE STOPPED BUH-BEFORE THERE'S NOTHING LEFT...WE THINK WE OWN THE WORLD BUT...BUT...
OHH!
OH GOD, WE'VE... FALLEN SO FAR...
...AND THERE'S STUH-STILL...
...THERE'S STILL...
...NO...
BOTTOM
HIS BODY HAD NO DEFENSE AGAINST THE VIRUS. HE'D COME ALL THE WAY FROM AFRICA TO DIE IN A ZOO AND THERE WAS NOTHING I COULD DO.
NOTHING.
EXCEPT.

EXCEPT I STILL HAD B'WANA BEAST'S POWERS.

INCLUDING THE POWER TO FUSE ORGANISMS INTO SUPER-HYBRID FORMS.

IT WORKED WITH RATS, TIGERS, WOLVES...

WHY NOT WHITE BLOOD CELLS?

SO I CLOSED MY EYES.

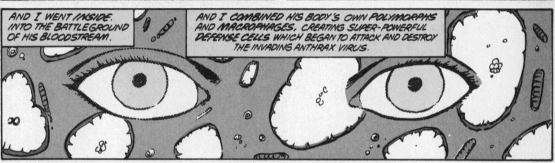

AND I WENT INSIDE. INTO THE BATTLEGROUND OF HIS BLOODSTREAM.

AND I COMBINED HIS BODY'S OWN POLYMORPHS AND MACROPHAGES, CREATING SUPER-POWERFUL DEFENSE CELLS WHICH BEGAN TO ATTACK AND DESTROY THE INVADING ANTHRAX VIRUS.

ALL AT ONCE, HIS WHOLE BODY RELAXED AND THE TIGHTNESS LEFT HIS FACE. HE WAS GOING TO LIVE.

IN THE END, IT WAS THAT SIMPLE... LIKE STORYBOOK MAGIC.

I GUESS I SHOULD HAVE BEEN PLEASED BUT I FELT NOTHING. TOO MUCH HAD HAPPENED.

I'D HAD MY FILL OF HORRORS AND MIRACLES, SO I JUST LEFT B'WANA BEAST PROPPED AGAINST A WALL.

WELL, WHAT WAS I SUPPOSED TO DO?

TAKE HIM TO JAIL LIKE A GOOD SUPER-HERO?

18

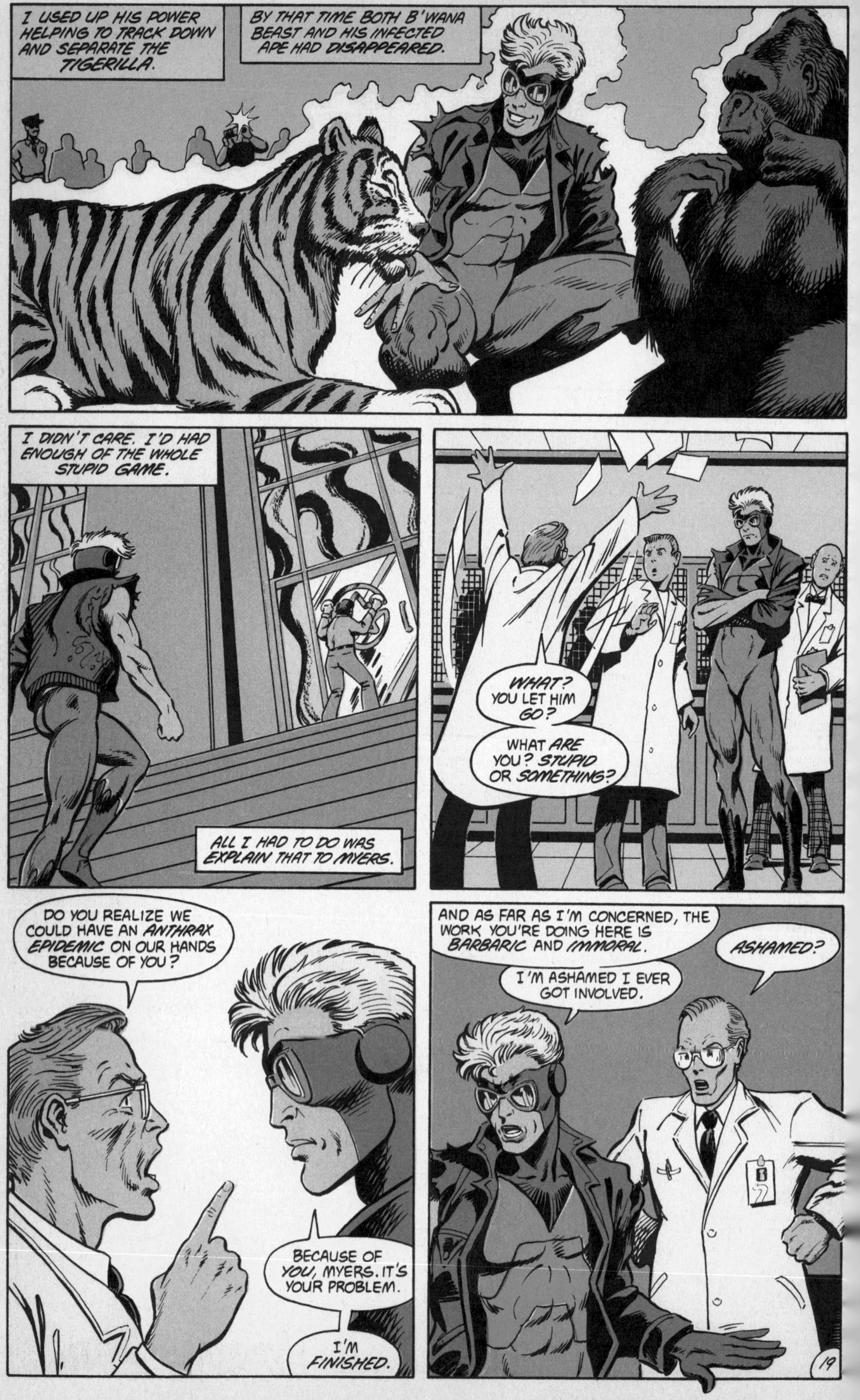
I USED UP HIS POWER HELPING TO TRACK DOWN AND SEPARATE THE TIGERILLA.
BY THAT TIME BOTH B'WANA BEAST AND HIS INFECTED APE HAD DISAPPEARED.
I DIDN'T CARE. I'D HAD ENOUGH OF THE WHOLE STUPID GAME.
ALL I HAD TO DO WAS EXPLAIN THAT TO MYERS.
WHAT? YOU LET HIM GO?
WHAT ARE YOU? STUPID OR SOMETHING?
DO YOU REALIZE WE COULD HAVE AN ANTHRAX EPIDEMIC ON OUR HANDS BECAUSE OF YOU?
BECAUSE OF YOU, MYERS. IT'S YOUR PROBLEM.
I'M FINISHED.
AND AS FAR AS I'M CONCERNED, THE WORK YOU'RE DOING HERE IS BARBARIC AND IMMORAL.
I'M ASHAMED I EVER GOT INVOLVED.
ASHAMED?
19

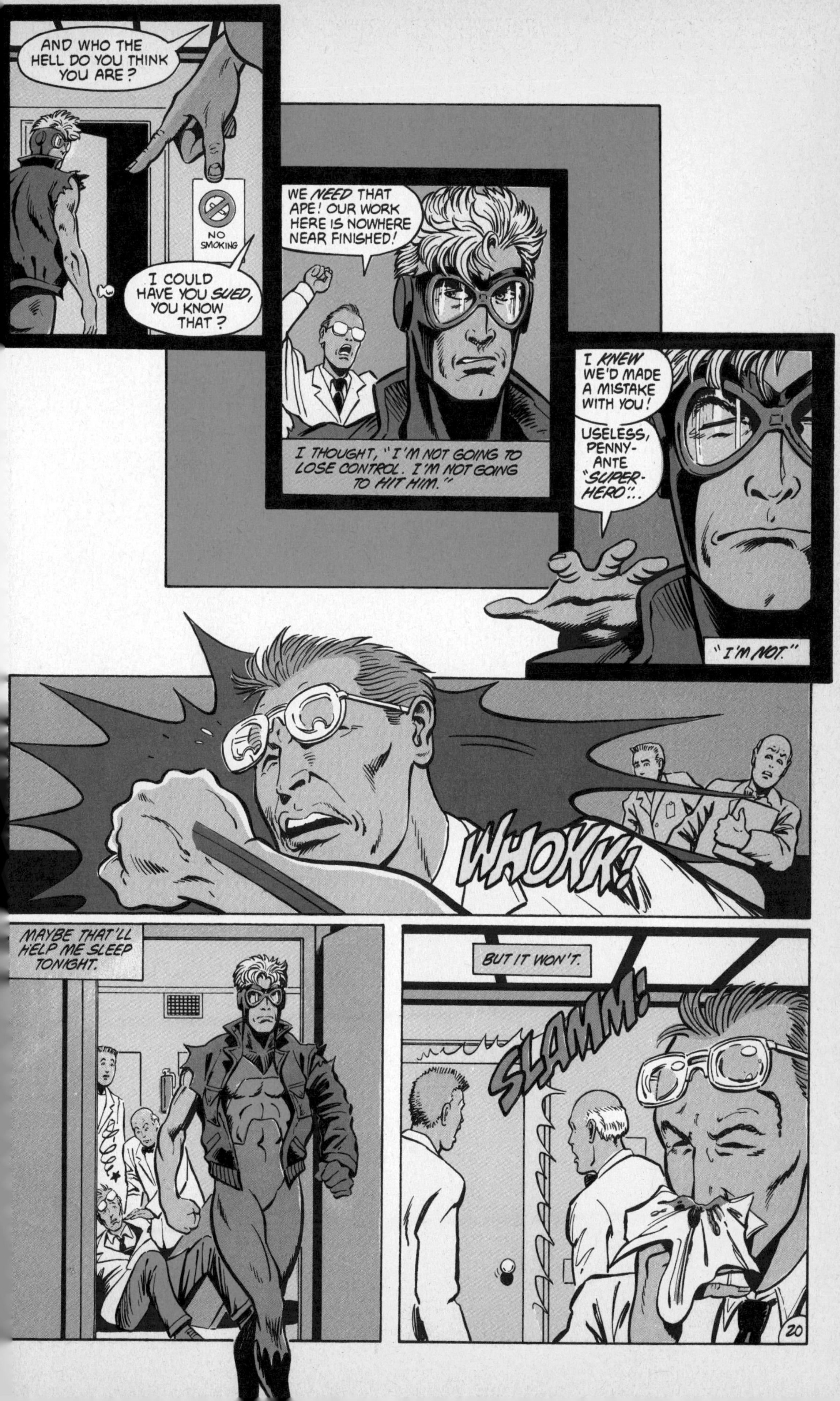
AND WHO THE HELL DO YOU THINK YOU ARE?
NO SMOKING
I COULD HAVE YOU SUED, YOU KNOW THAT?
WE NEED THAT APE! OUR WORK HERE IS NOWHERE NEAR FINISHED!
I THOUGHT, "I'M NOT GOING TO LOSE CONTROL. I'M NOT GOING TO HIT HIM."
I KNEW WE'D MADE A MISTAKE WITH YOU!
USELESS, PENNY-ANTE "SUPER-HERO"...
"I'M NOT."
WHOKK!
MAYBE THAT'LL HELP ME SLEEP TONIGHT.
BUT IT WON'T.
SLAMM!
20

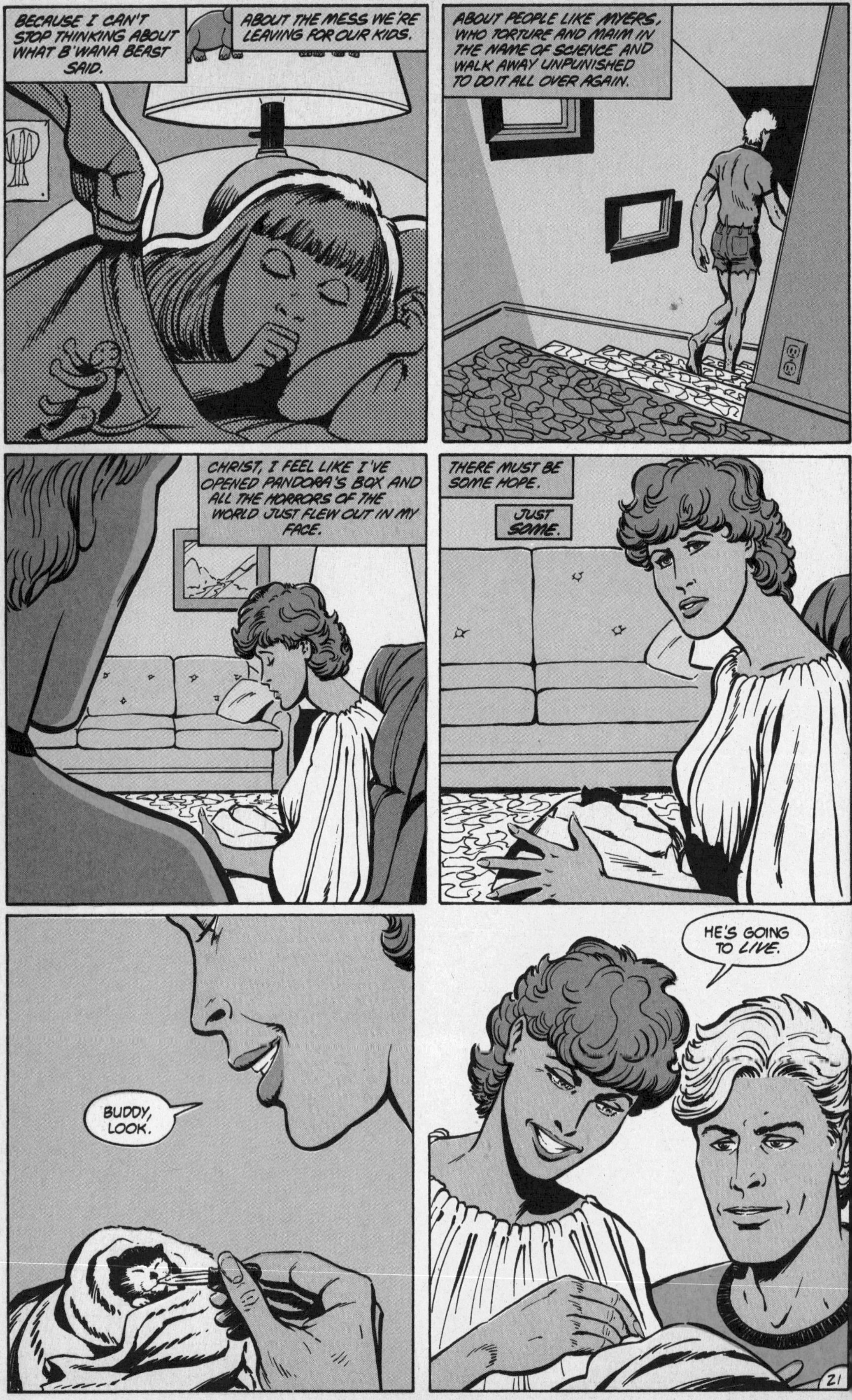
BECAUSE I CAN'T STOP THINKING ABOUT WHAT B'WANA BEAST SAID.
ABOUT THE MESS WE'RE LEAVING FOR OUR KIDS.
ABOUT PEOPLE LIKE MYERS, WHO TORTURE AND MAIM IN THE NAME OF SCIENCE AND WALK AWAY UNPUNISHED TO DO IT ALL OVER AGAIN.
CHRIST, I FEEL LIKE I'VE OPENED PANDORA'S BOX AND ALL THE HORRORS OF THE WORLD JUST FLEW OUT IN MY FACE.
THERE MUST BE SOME HOPE.
JUST SOME.
BUDDY, LOOK.
HE'S GOING TO LIVE.
21

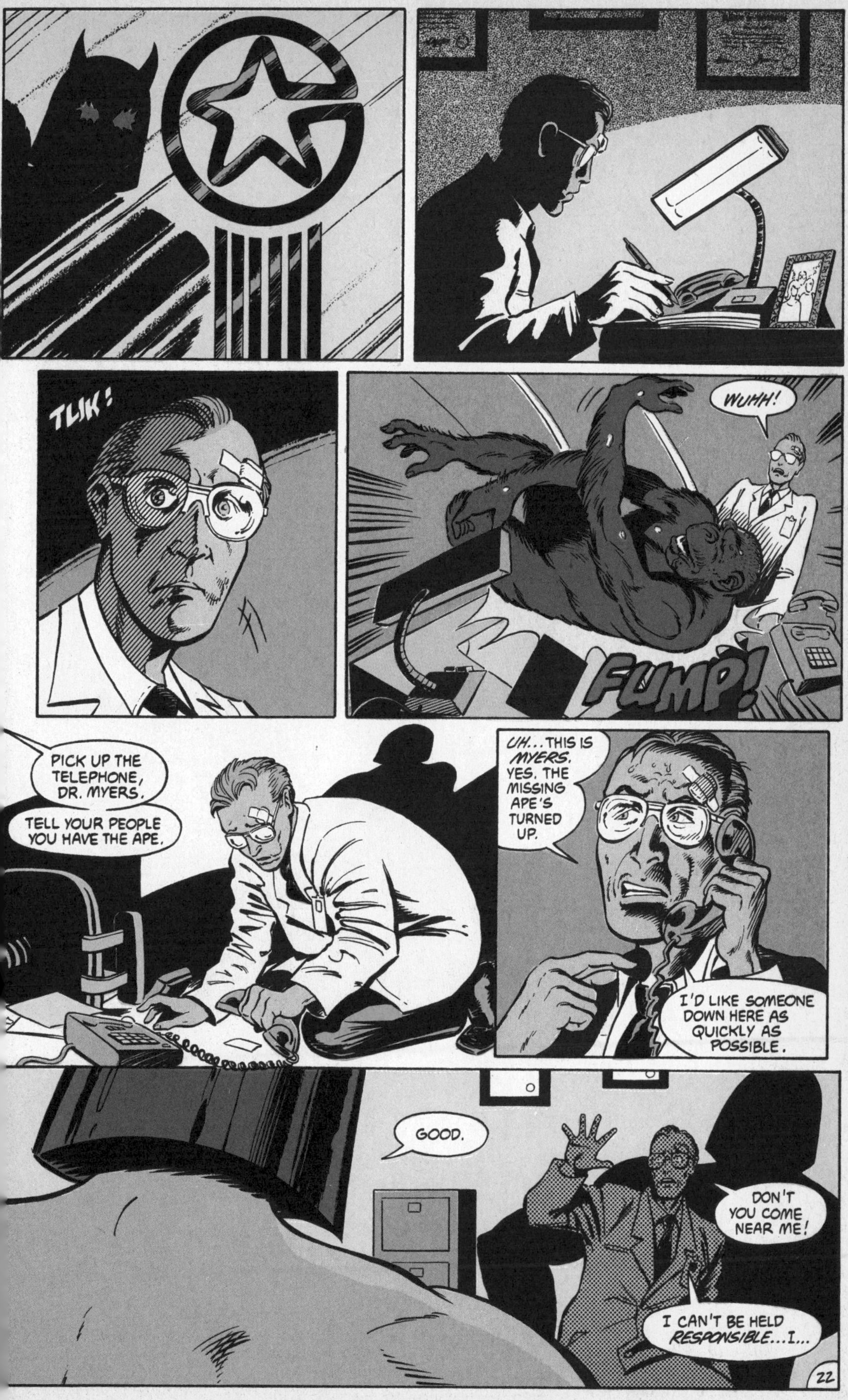
TLIK!
WUHH!
FUMP!
PICK UP THE TELEPHONE, DR. MYERS.
TELL YOUR PEOPLE YOU HAVE THE APE.
UH...THIS IS MYERS. YES. THE MISSING APE'S TURNED UP.
I'D LIKE SOMEONE DOWN HERE AS QUICKLY AS POSSIBLE.
GOOD.
DON'T YOU COME NEAR ME!
I CAN'T BE HELD RESPONSIBLE...I...
22

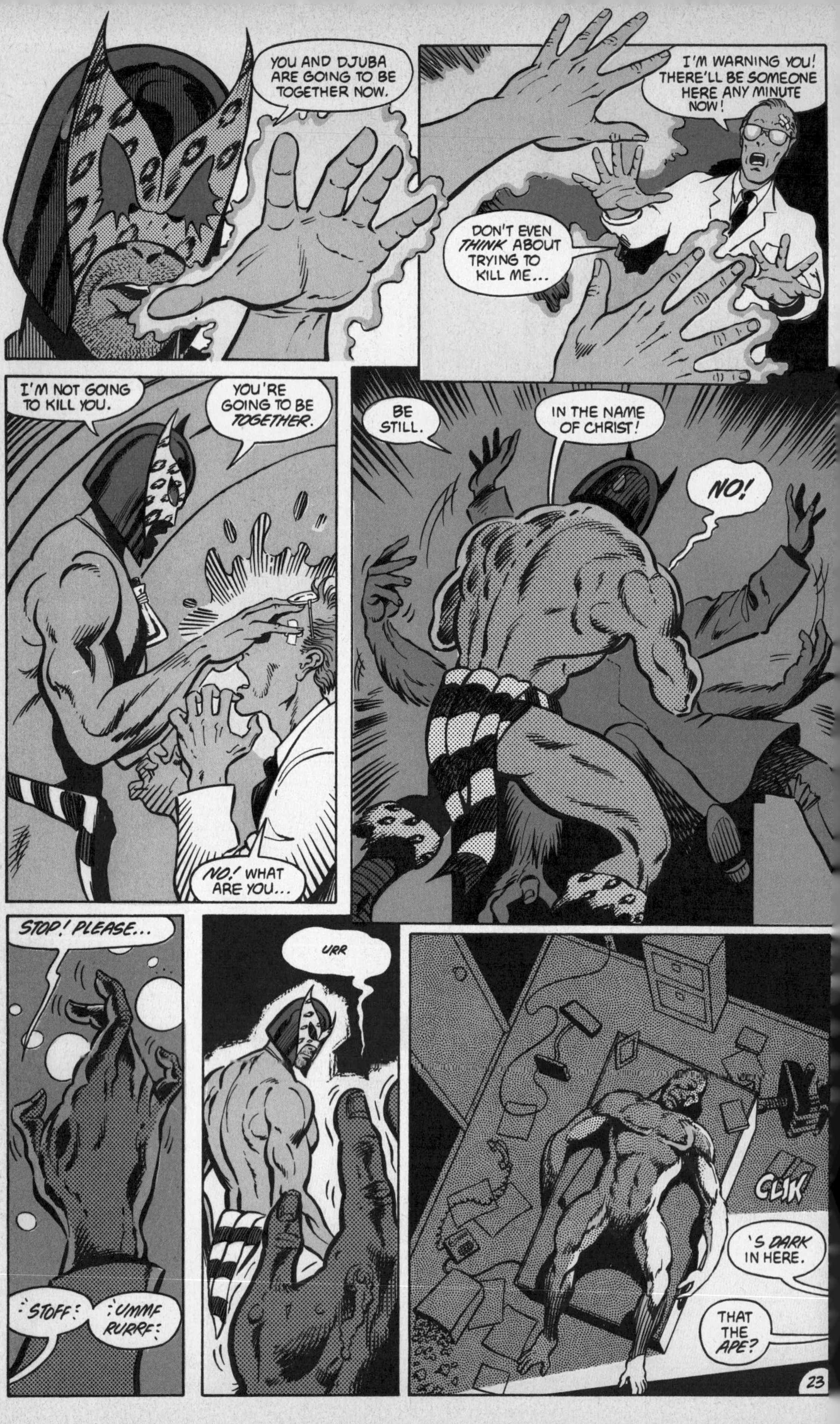
YOU AND DJUBA ARE GOING TO BE TOGETHER NOW.
I'M WARNING YOU! THERE'LL BE SOMEONE HERE ANY MINUTE NOW!
DON'T EVEN THINK ABOUT TRYING TO KILL ME...
I'M NOT GOING TO KILL YOU.
YOU'RE GOING TO BE TOGETHER.
NO! WHAT ARE YOU...
BE STILL.
IN THE NAME OF CHRIST!
NO!
STOP! PLEASE...
STOFF
UMMF RURRF
URR
CLIK
'S DARK IN HERE.
THAT THE APE?

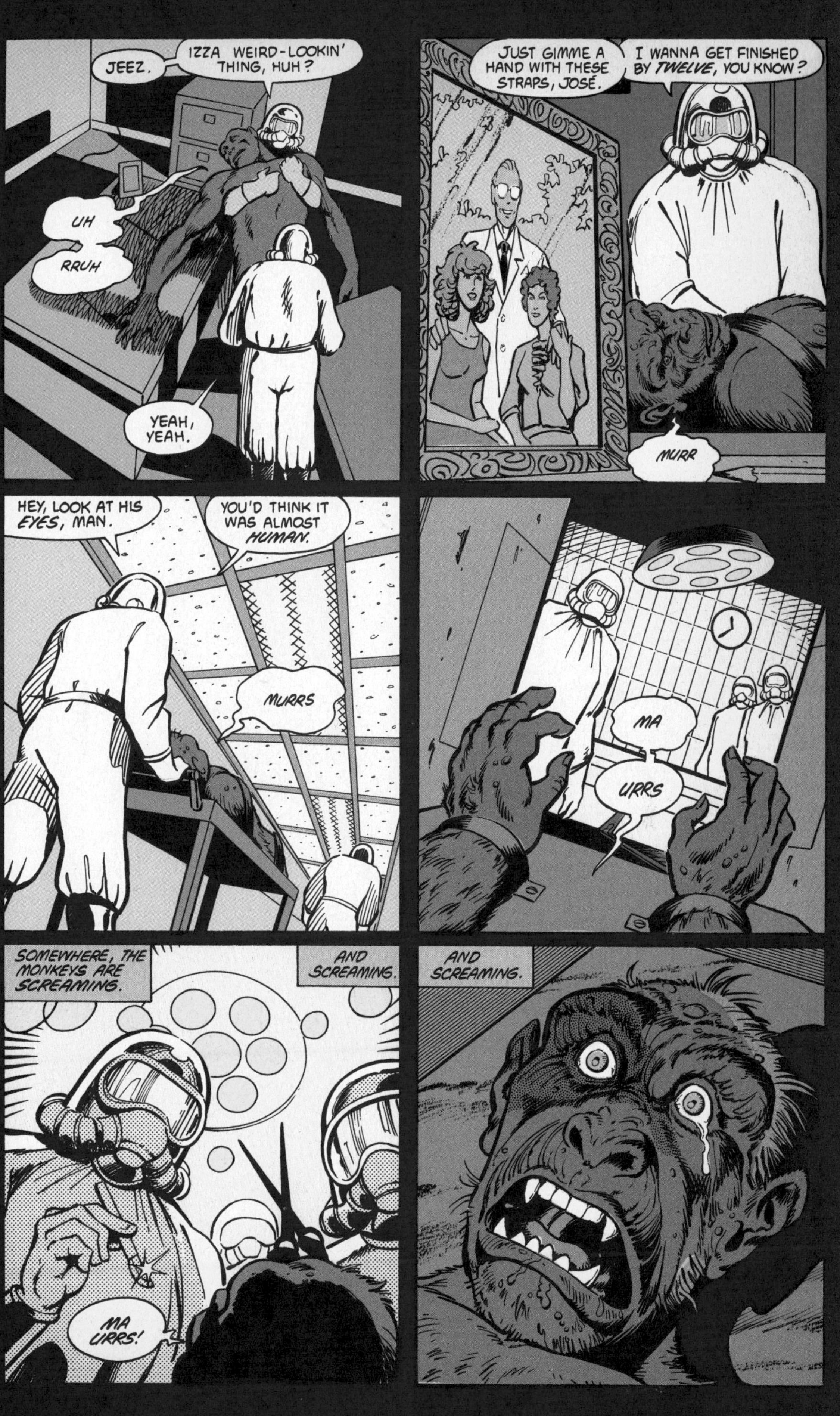
JEEZ.
IZZA WEIRD-LOOKIN' THING, HUH?
UH
RRUH
YEAH, YEAH.
JUST GIMME A HAND WITH THESE STRAPS, JOSÉ.
I WANNA GET FINISHED BY TWELVE, YOU KNOW?
MURR
HEY, LOOK AT HIS EYES, MAN.
YOU'D THINK IT WAS ALMOST HUMAN.
MURRS
MA
URRS
SOMEWHERE, THE MONKEYS ARE SCREAMING.
AND SCREAMING.
MA URRS!
AND SCREAMING.

CHAPTER
FIVE

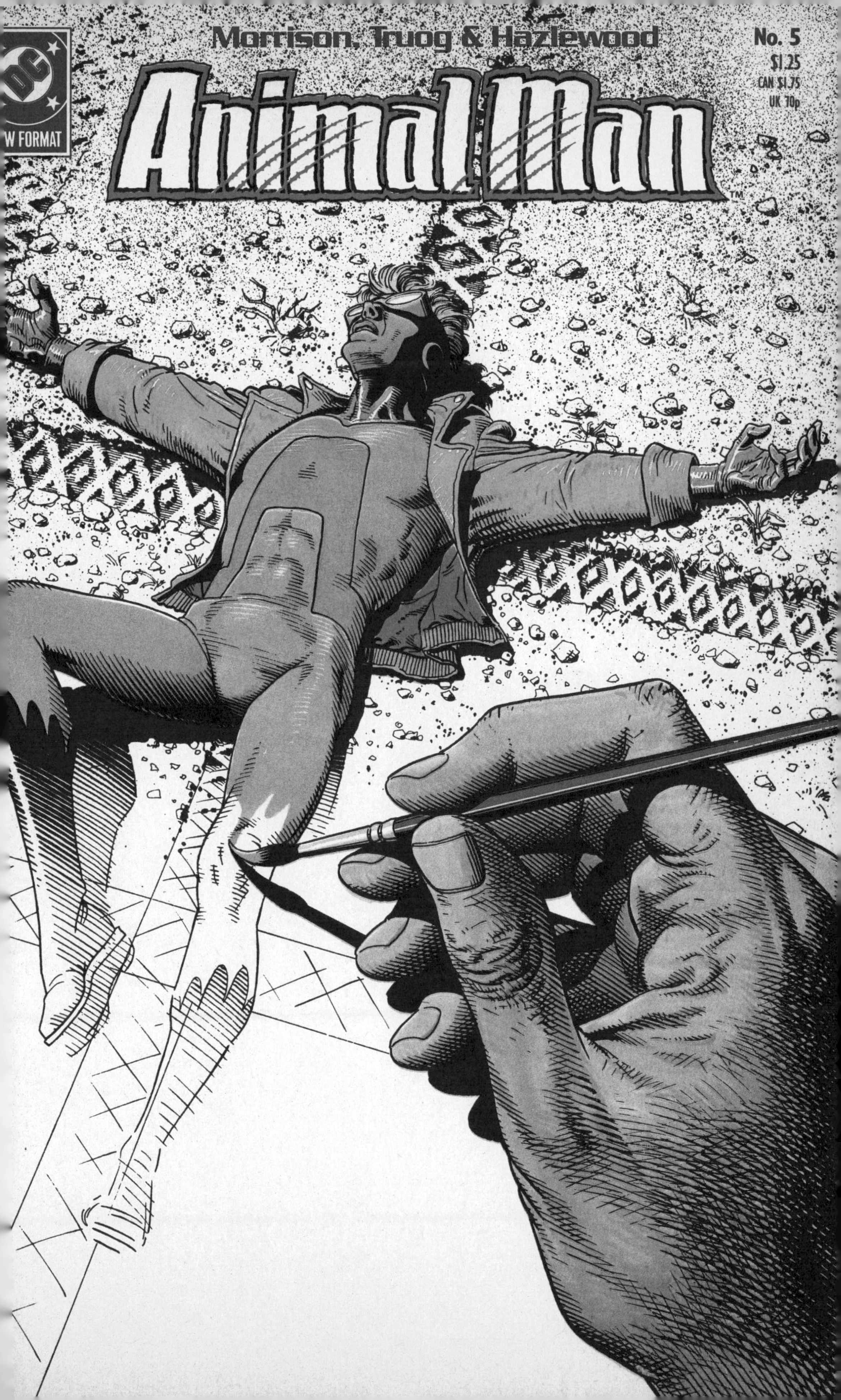
W FORMAT
Morrison, Truog & Hazlewood
No. 5
$1.25
CAN $1.75
UK 70p
Animal Man
TM

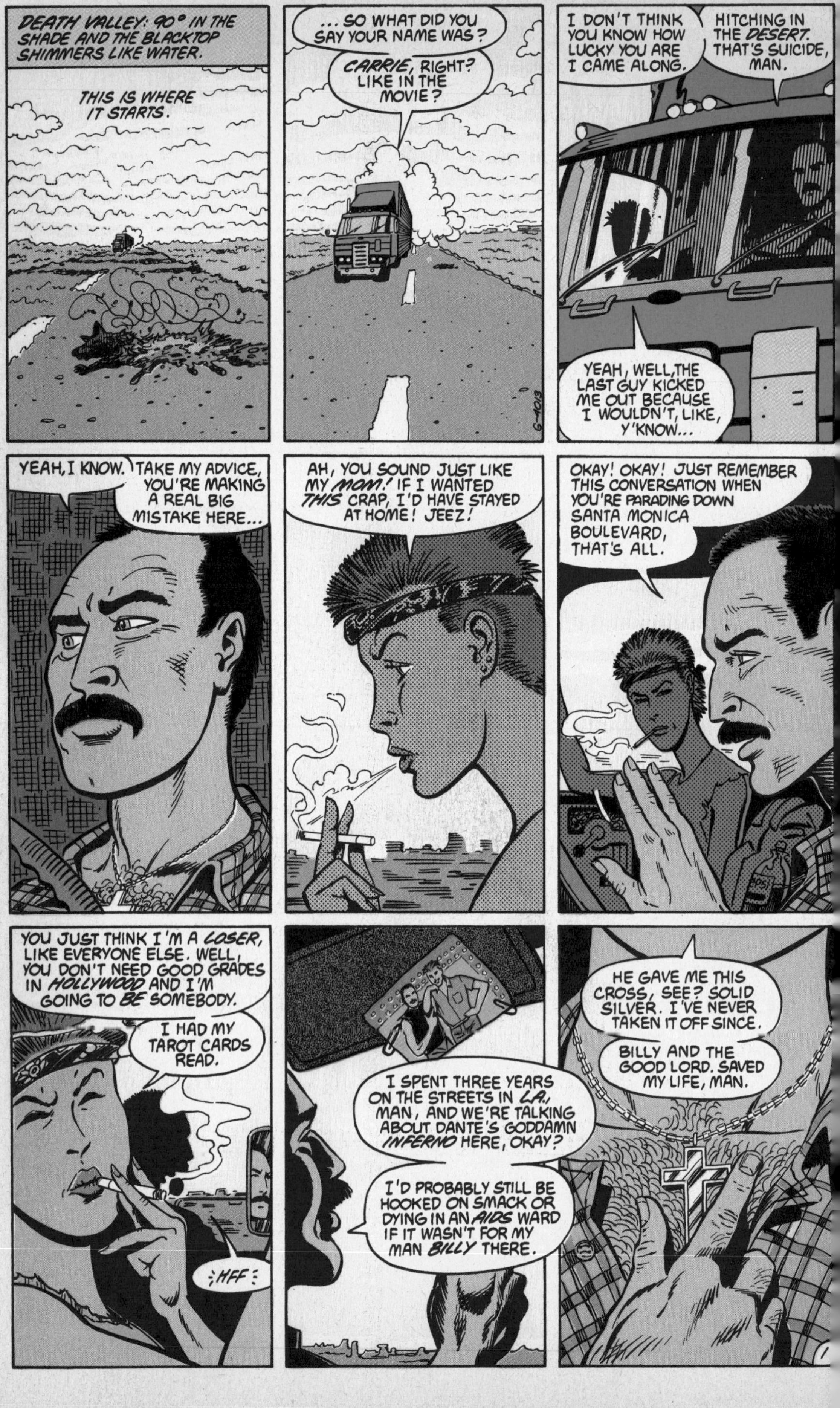
DEATH VALLEY: 90° IN THE SHADE AND THE BLACKTOP SHIMMERS LIKE WATER.
THIS IS WHERE IT STARTS.
... SO WHAT DID YOU SAY YOUR NAME WAS?
CARRIE, RIGHT? LIKE IN THE MOVIE?
I DON'T THINK YOU KNOW HOW LUCKY YOU ARE I CAME ALONG.
HITCHING IN THE DESERT. THAT'S SUICIDE, MAN.
YEAH, WELL, THE LAST GUY KICKED ME OUT BECAUSE I WOULDN'T, LIKE, Y'KNOW...
YEAH, I KNOW.
TAKE MY ADVICE, YOU'RE MAKING A REAL BIG MISTAKE HERE...
AH, YOU SOUND JUST LIKE MY MOM! IF I WANTED THIS CRAP, I'D HAVE STAYED AT HOME! JEEZ!
OKAY! OKAY! JUST REMEMBER THIS CONVERSATION WHEN YOU'RE PARADING DOWN SANTA MONICA BOULEVARD, THAT'S ALL.
YOU JUST THINK I'M A LOSER, LIKE EVERYONE ELSE. WELL, YOU DON'T NEED GOOD GRADES IN HOLLYWOOD AND I'M GOING TO BE SOMEBODY.
I HAD MY TAROT CARDS READ.
HFF
I SPENT THREE YEARS ON THE STREETS IN L.A., MAN, AND WE'RE TALKING ABOUT DANTE'S GODDAMN INFERNO HERE, OKAY?
I'D PROBABLY STILL BE HOOKED ON SMACK OR DYING IN AN AIDS WARD IF IT WASN'T FOR MY MAN BILLY THERE.
HE GAVE ME THIS CROSS, SEE? SOLID SILVER. I'VE NEVER TAKEN IT OFF SINCE.
BILLY AND THE GOOD LORD. SAVED MY LIFE, MAN.

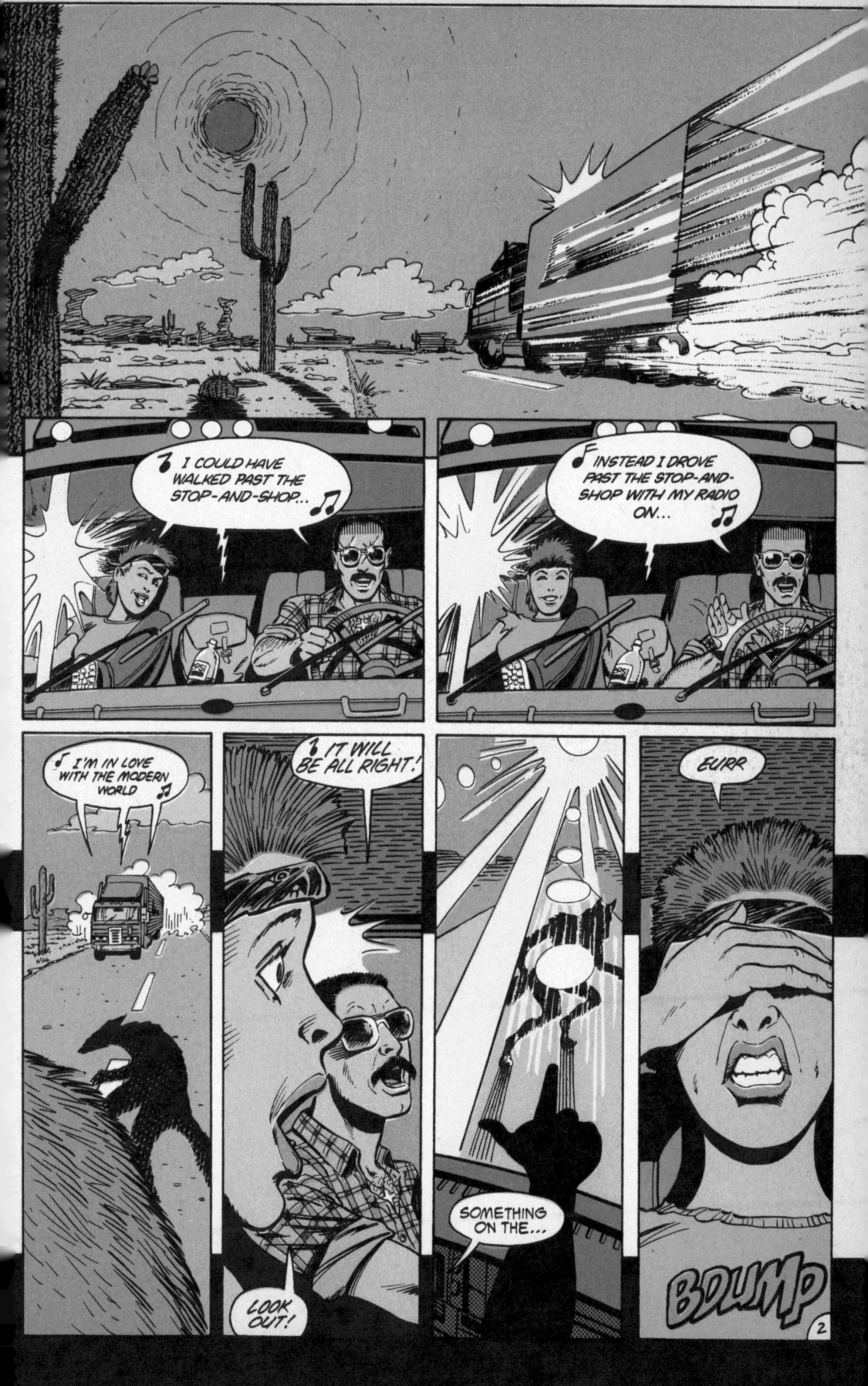
I COULD HAVE WALKED PAST THE STOP-AND-SHOP...
INSTEAD I DROVE PAST THE STOP-AND-SHOP WITH MY RADIO ON...
I'M IN LOVE WITH THE MODERN WORLD
IT WILL BE ALL RIGHT!
LOOK OUT!
SOMETHING ON THE...
EURR
BDUMP

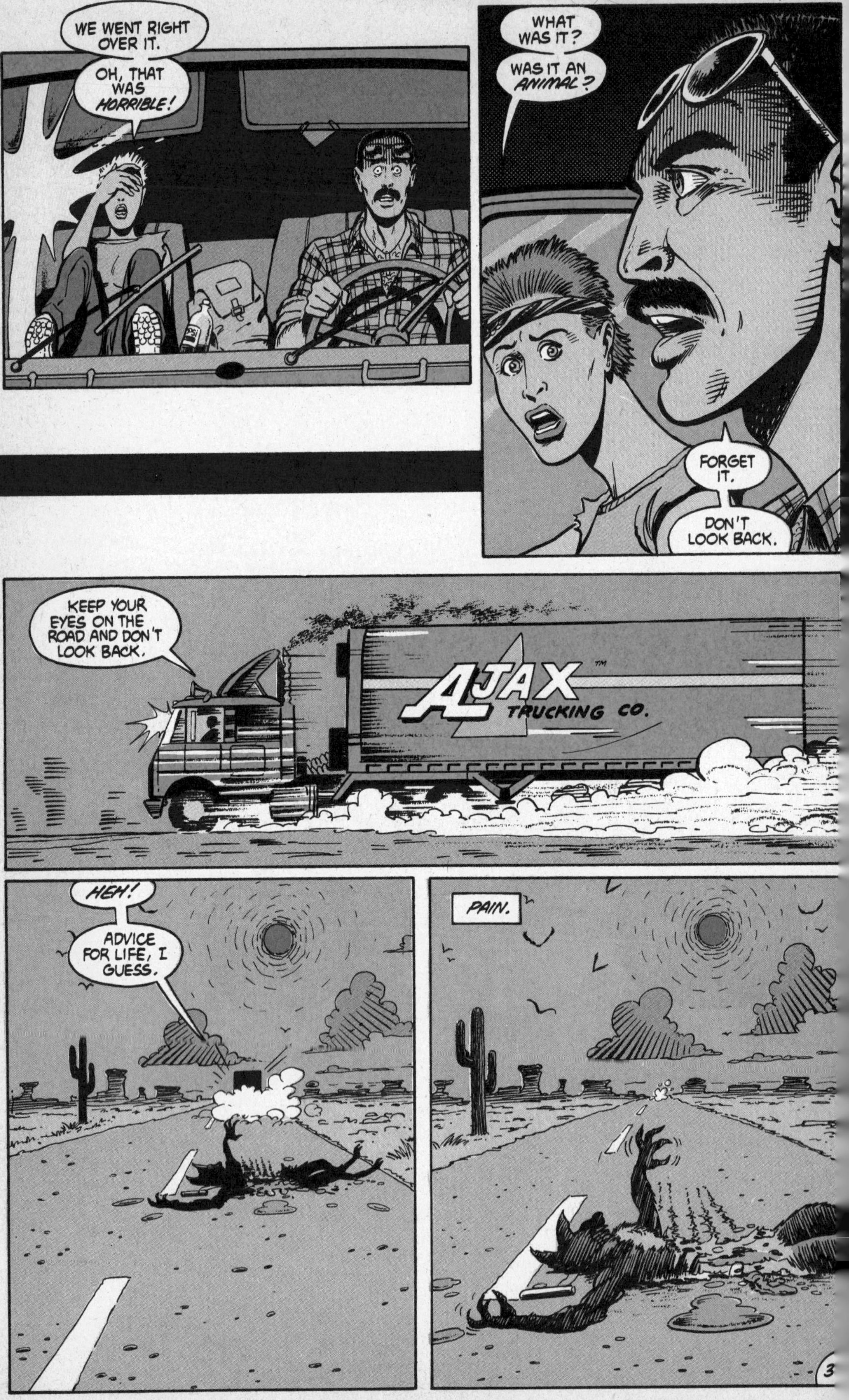
WE WENT RIGHT OVER IT.
OH, THAT WAS HORRIBLE!
WHAT WAS IT?
WAS IT AN ANIMAL?
FORGET IT.
DON'T LOOK BACK.
KEEP YOUR EYES ON THE ROAD AND DON'T LOOK BACK.
AJAX™ TRUCKING CO.
HEH!
ADVICE FOR LIFE, I GUESS.
PAIN.

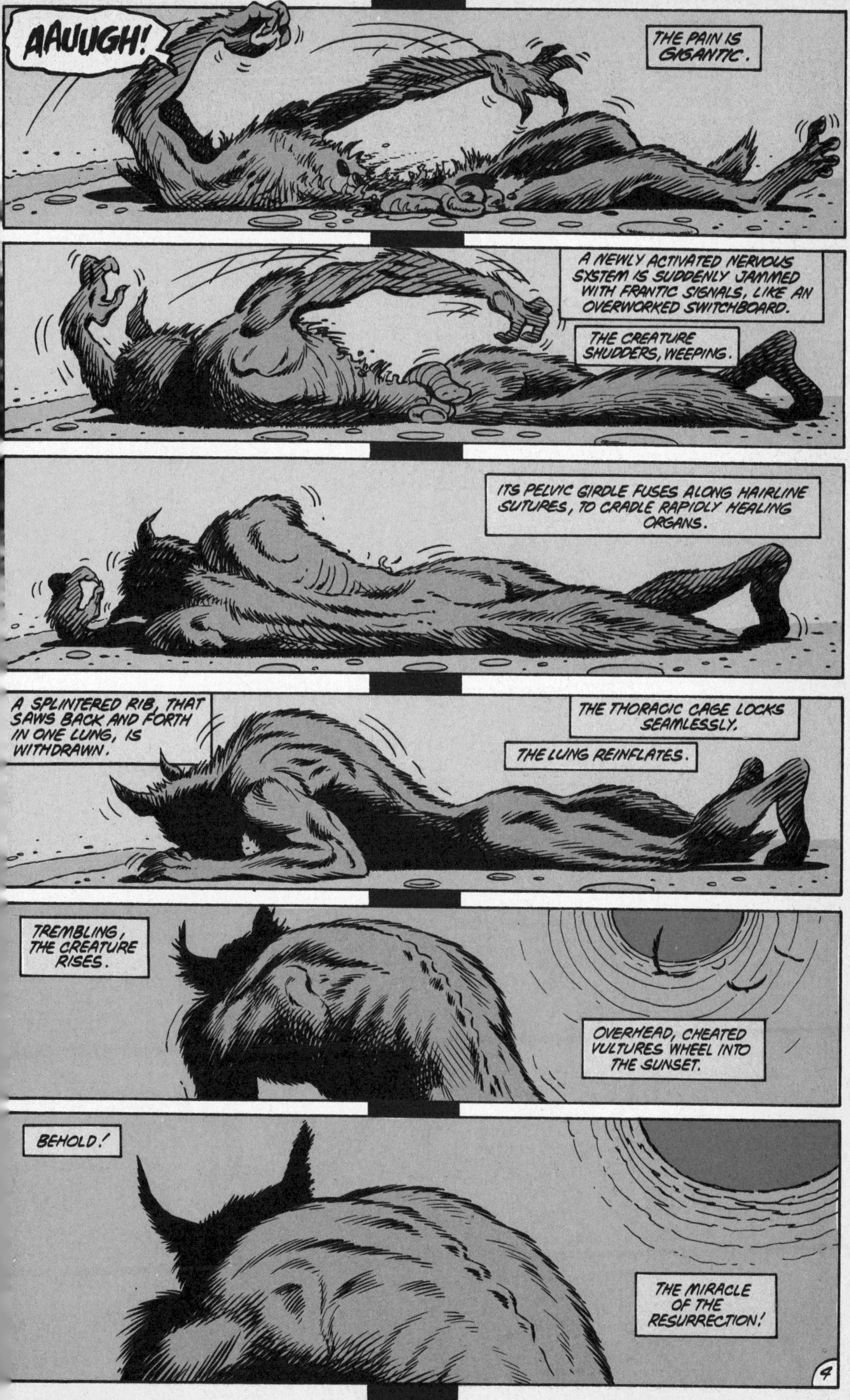
AAUUGH!
THE PAIN IS GIGANTIC.
A NEWLY ACTIVATED NERVOUS SYSTEM IS SUDDENLY JAMMED WITH FRANTIC SIGNALS, LIKE AN OVERWORKED SWITCHBOARD.
THE CREATURE SHUDDERS, WEEPING.
ITS PELVIC GIRDLE FUSES ALONG HAIRLINE SUTURES, TO CRADLE RAPIDLY HEALING ORGANS.
A SPLINTERED RIB, THAT SAWS BACK AND FORTH IN ONE LUNG, IS WITHDRAWN.
THE THORACIC CAGE LOCKS SEAMLESSLY.
THE LUNG REINFLATES.
TREMBLING, THE CREATURE RISES.
OVERHEAD, CHEATED VULTURES WHEEL INTO THE SUNSET.
BEHOLD!
THE MIRACLE OF THE RESURRECTION!
4

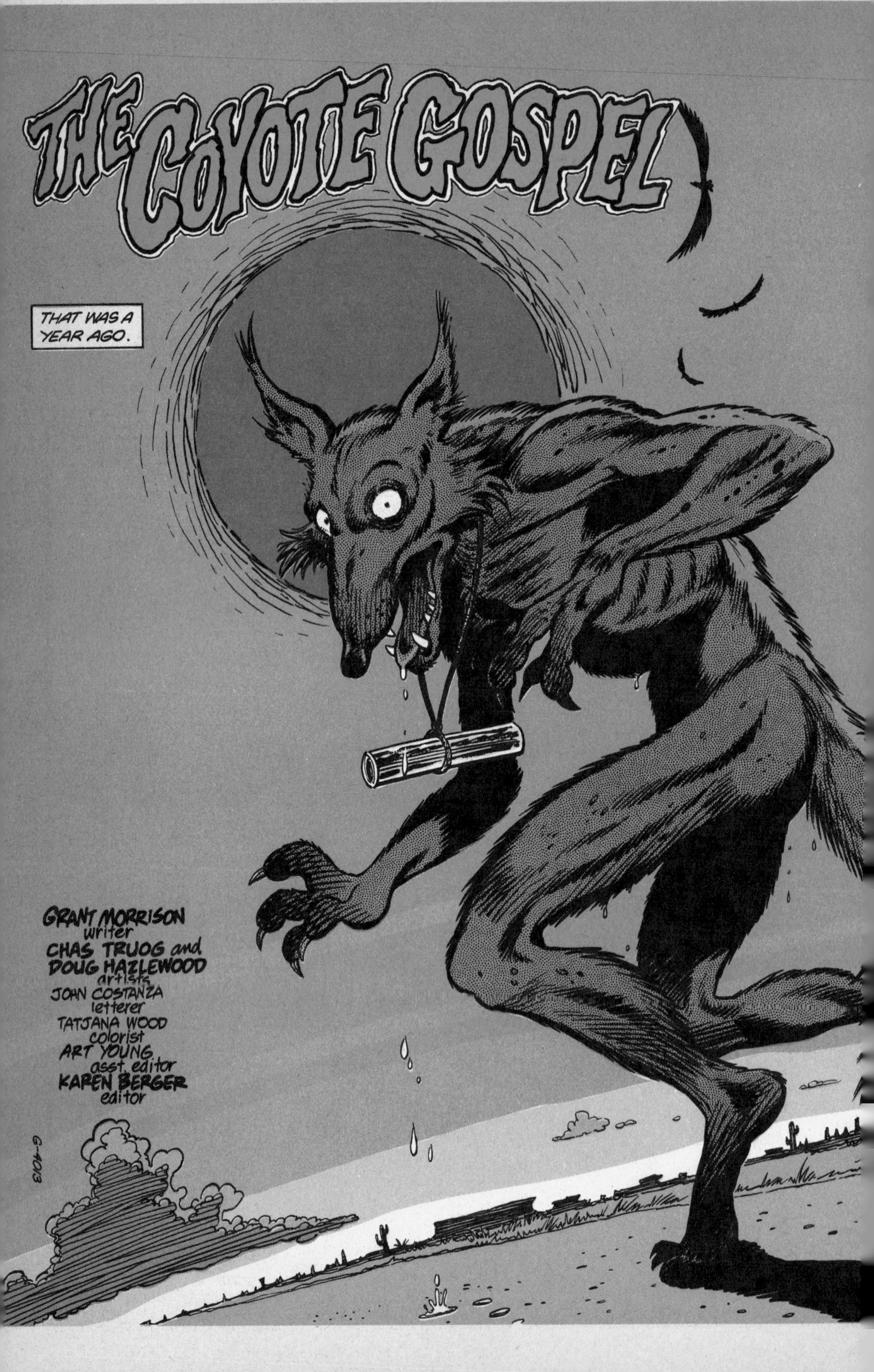
THE COYOTE GOSPEL
THAT WAS A YEAR AGO.
GRANT MORRISON writer
CHAS TRUOG and DOUG HAZLEWOOD artists
JOHN COSTANZA letterer
TATJANA WOOD colorist
ART YOUNG asst. editor
KAREN BERGER editor
G-4013

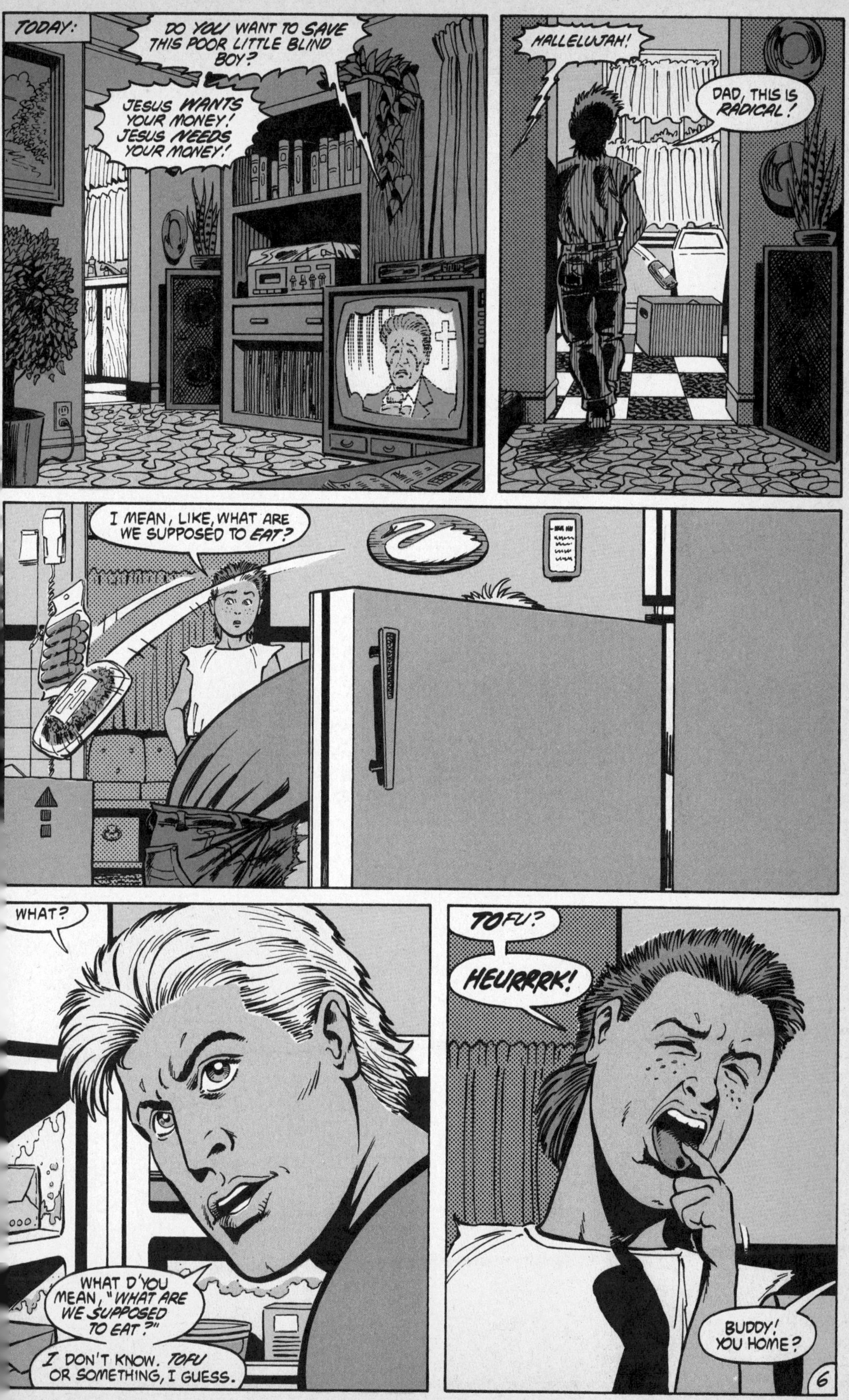
TODAY:
DO YOU WANT TO SAVE THIS POOR LITTLE BLIND BOY?
JESUS WANTS YOUR MONEY! JESUS NEEDS YOUR MONEY!
HALLELUJAH!
DAD, THIS IS RADICAL!
I MEAN, LIKE, WHAT ARE WE SUPPOSED TO EAT?
WHAT?
WHAT D'YOU MEAN, "WHAT ARE WE SUPPOSED TO EAT?"
I DON'T KNOW. TOFU OR SOMETHING, I GUESS.
TOFU?
HEURRRK!
BUDDY! YOU HOME?
6

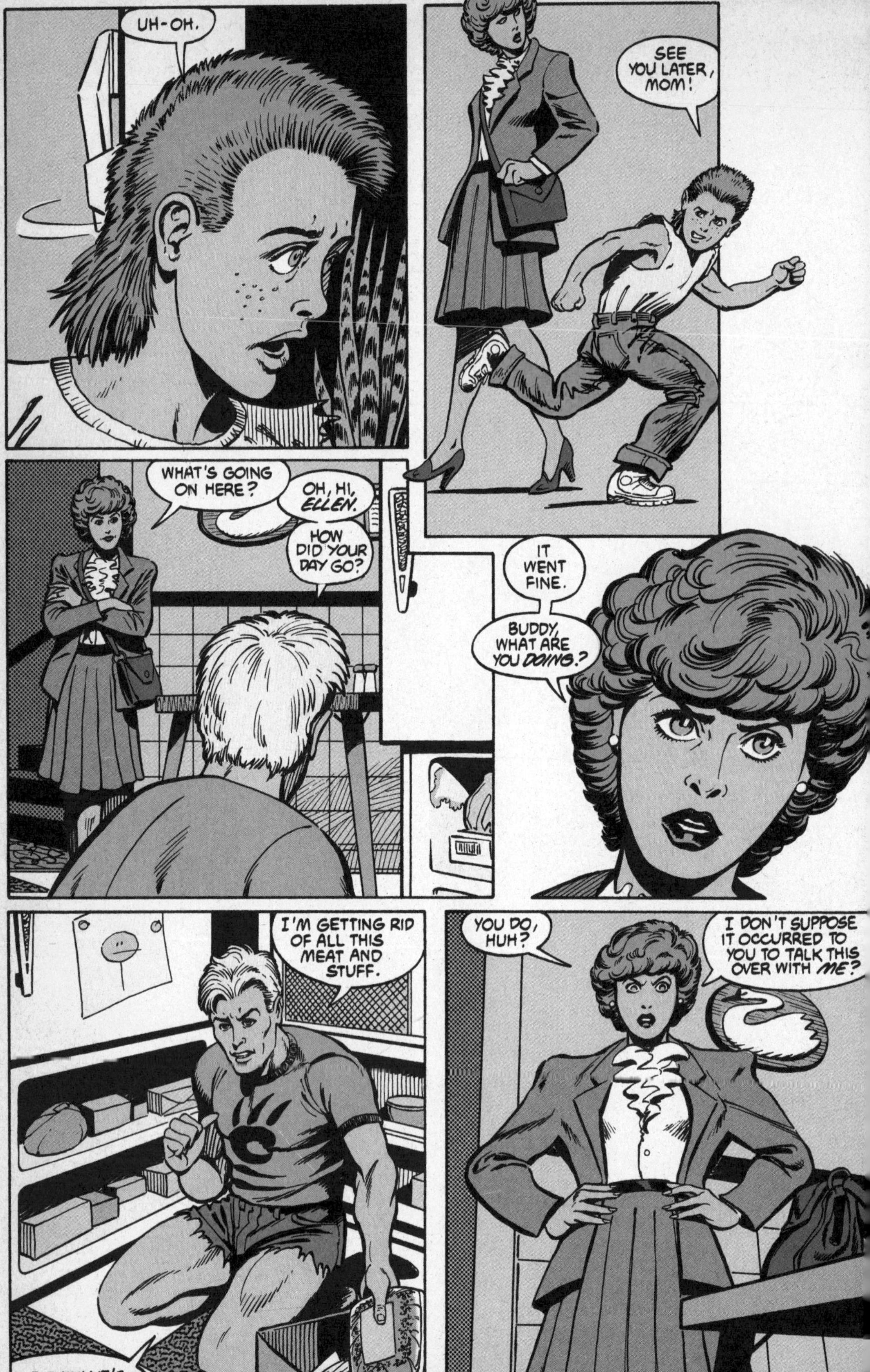

UH-OH.
SEE YOU LATER, MOM!
WHAT'S GOING ON HERE?
OH, HI, ELLEN.
HOW DID YOUR DAY GO?
IT WENT FINE.
BUDDY, WHAT ARE YOU DOING?
I'M GETTING RID OF ALL THIS MEAT AND STUFF.
I THINK IT'S TIME WE WENT VEGETARIAN.
YOU DO, HUH?
I DON'T SUPPOSE IT OCCURRED TO YOU TO TALK THIS OVER WITH ME?

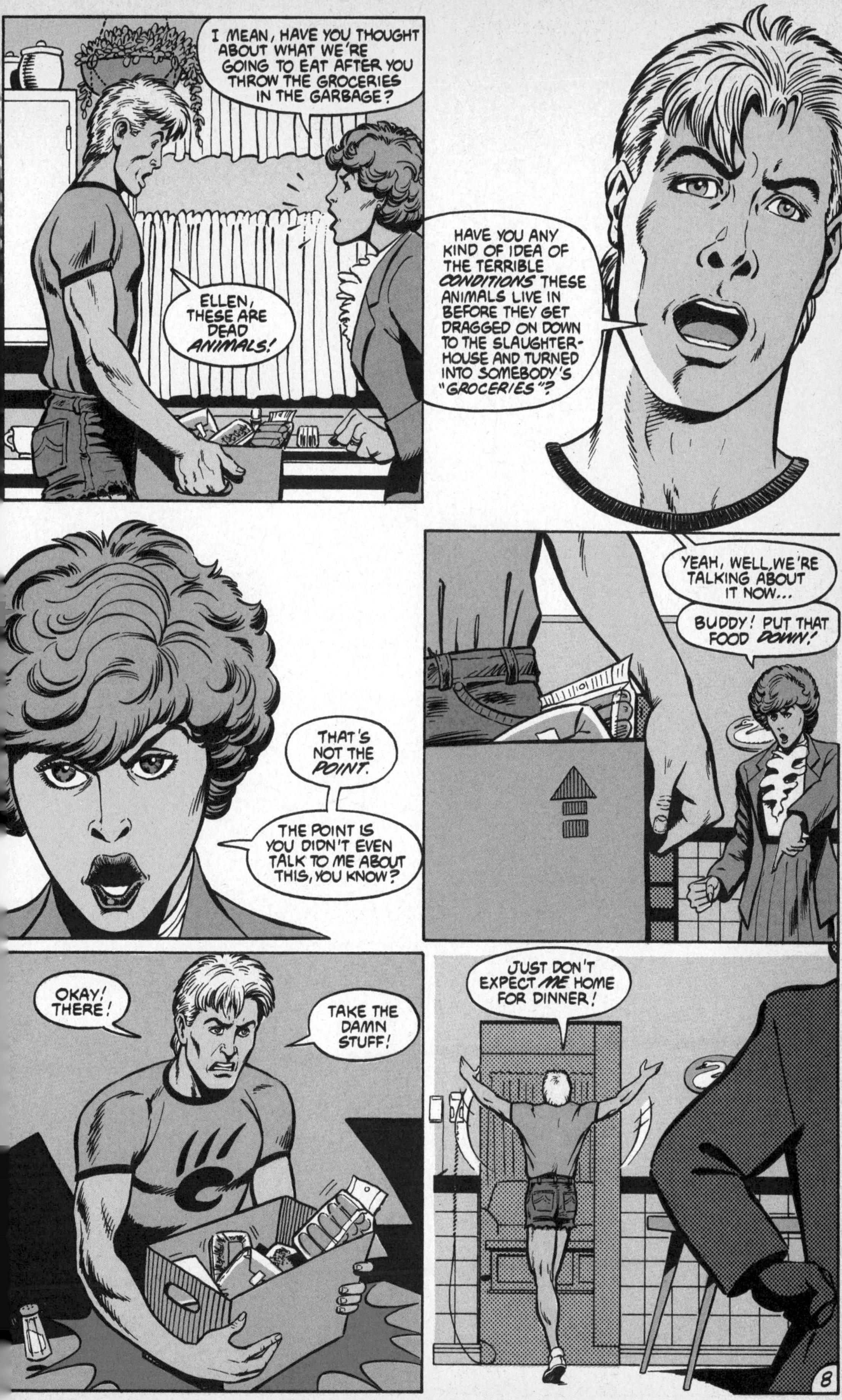
I MEAN, HAVE YOU THOUGHT ABOUT WHAT WE'RE GOING TO EAT AFTER YOU THROW THE GROCERIES IN THE GARBAGE?
ELLEN, THESE ARE DEAD ANIMALS!
HAVE YOU ANY KIND OF IDEA OF THE TERRIBLE CONDITIONS THESE ANIMALS LIVE IN BEFORE THEY GET DRAGGED ON DOWN TO THE SLAUGHTER-HOUSE AND TURNED INTO SOMEBODY'S "GROCERIES"?
THAT'S NOT THE POINT.
THE POINT IS YOU DIDN'T EVEN TALK TO ME ABOUT THIS, YOU KNOW?
YEAH, WELL, WE'RE TALKING ABOUT IT NOW...
BUDDY! PUT THAT FOOD DOWN!
OKAY! THERE!
TAKE THE DAMN STUFF!
JUST DON'T EXPECT ME HOME FOR DINNER!
8

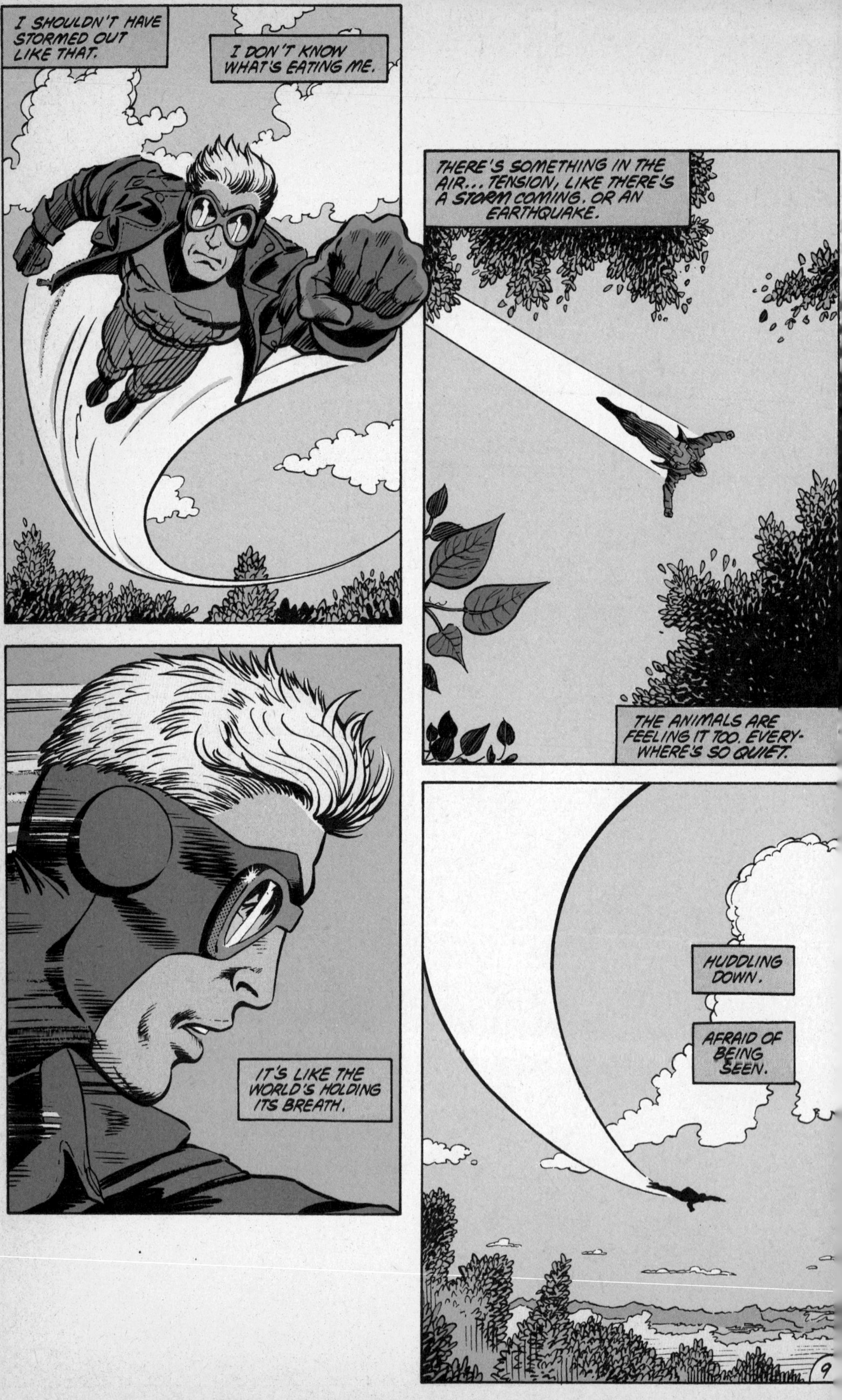
I SHOULDN'T HAVE STORMED OUT LIKE THAT.
I DON'T KNOW WHAT'S EATING ME.
THERE'S SOMETHING IN THE AIR... TENSION, LIKE THERE'S A STORM COMING. OR AN EARTHQUAKE.
THE ANIMALS ARE FEELING IT TOO. EVERY-WHERE'S SO QUIET.
IT'S LIKE THE WORLD'S HOLDING ITS BREATH.
HUDDLING DOWN.
AFRAID OF BEING SEEN.

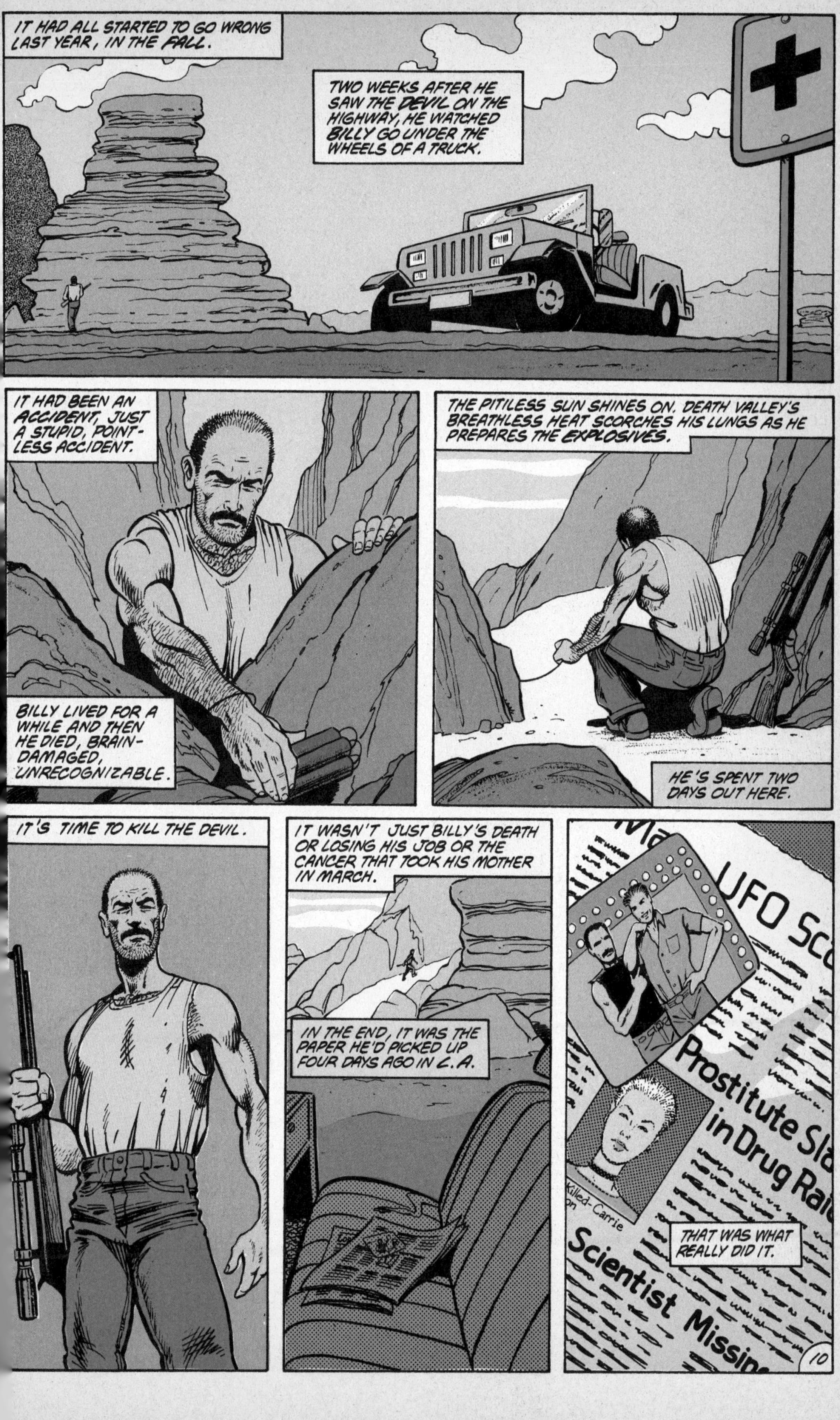
IT HAD ALL STARTED TO GO WRONG LAST YEAR, IN THE FALL.
TWO WEEKS AFTER HE SAW THE DEVIL ON THE HIGHWAY, HE WATCHED BILLY GO UNDER THE WHEELS OF A TRUCK.
IT HAD BEEN AN ACCIDENT, JUST A STUPID, POINTLESS ACCIDENT.
BILLY LIVED FOR A WHILE AND THEN HE DIED, BRAIN-DAMAGED, UNRECOGNIZABLE.
THE PITILESS SUN SHINES ON. DEATH VALLEY'S BREATHLESS HEAT SCORCHES HIS LUNGS AS HE PREPARES THE EXPLOSIVES.
HE'S SPENT TWO DAYS OUT HERE.
IT'S TIME TO KILL THE DEVIL.
IT WASN'T JUST BILLY'S DEATH OR LOSING HIS JOB OR THE CANCER THAT TOOK HIS MOTHER IN MARCH.
IN THE END, IT WAS THE PAPER HE'D PICKED UP FOUR DAYS AGO IN L.A.
UFO Sc
Prostitute Sla
in Drug Rai
Killed-Carrie
Scientist Missin
THAT WAS WHAT REALLY DID IT.

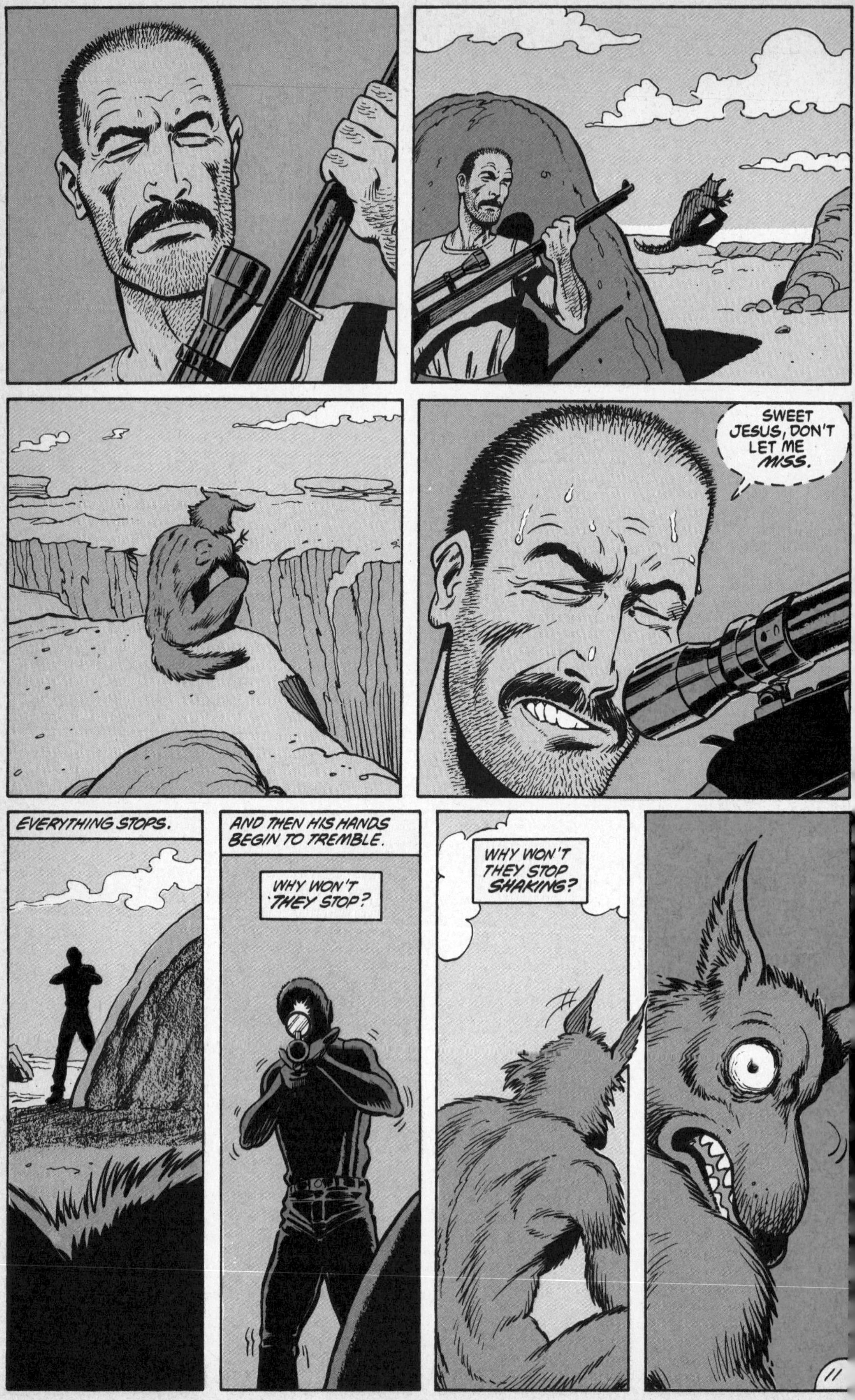
SWEET JESUS, DON'T LET ME MISS.
EVERYTHING STOPS.
AND THEN HIS HANDS BEGIN TO TREMBLE.
WHY WON'T THEY STOP?
WHY WON'T THEY STOP SHAKING?
11

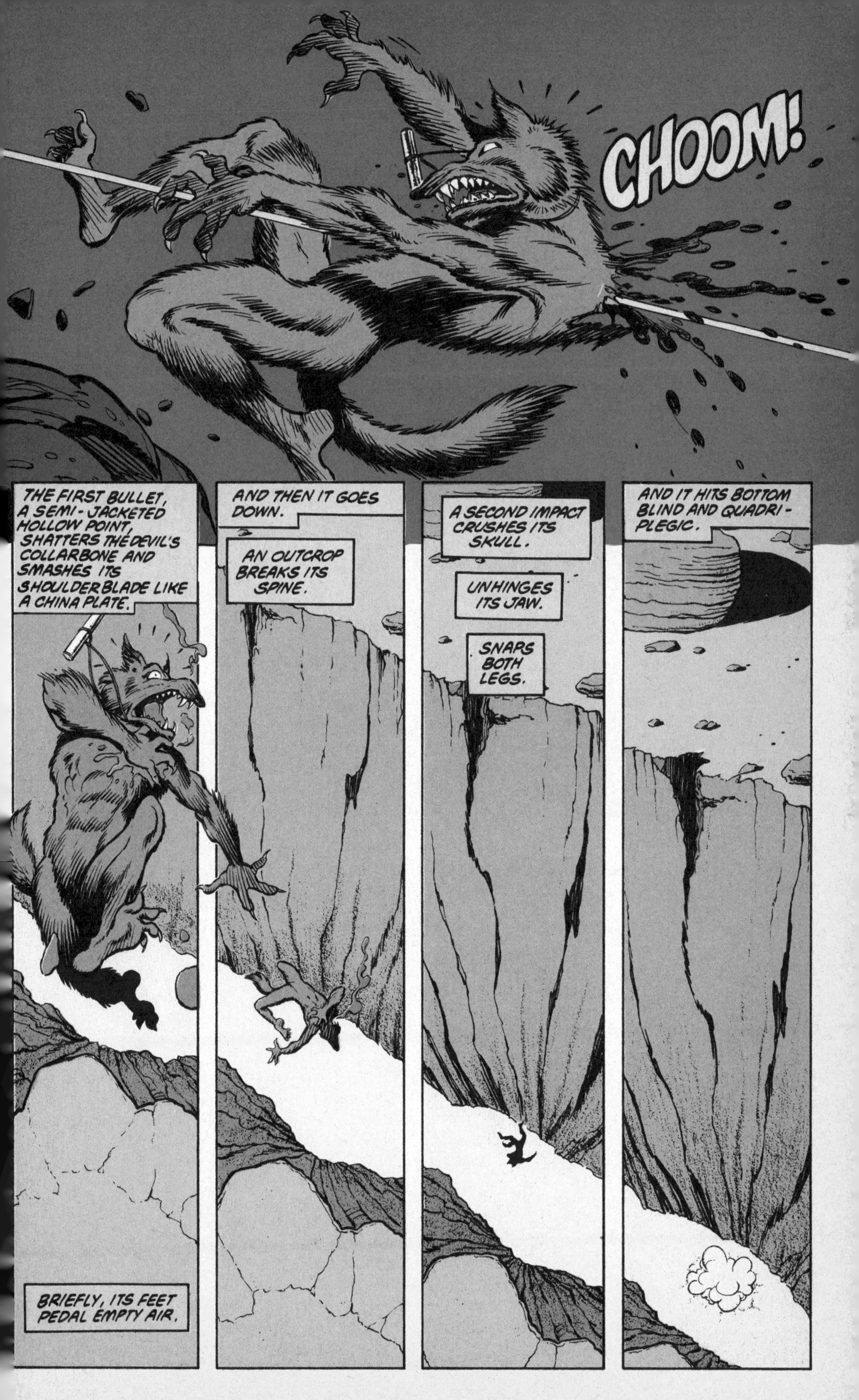
CHOOM!
THE FIRST BULLET, A SEMI-JACKETED HOLLOW POINT, SHATTERS THE DEVIL'S COLLARBONE AND SMASHES ITS SHOULDERBLADE LIKE A CHINA PLATE.
BRIEFLY, ITS FEET PEDAL EMPTY AIR.
AND THEN IT GOES DOWN.
AN OUTCROP BREAKS ITS SPINE.
A SECOND IMPACT CRUSHES ITS SKULL.
UNHINGES ITS JAW.
SNAPS BOTH LEGS.
AND IT HITS BOTTOM BLIND AND QUADRI-PLEGIC.

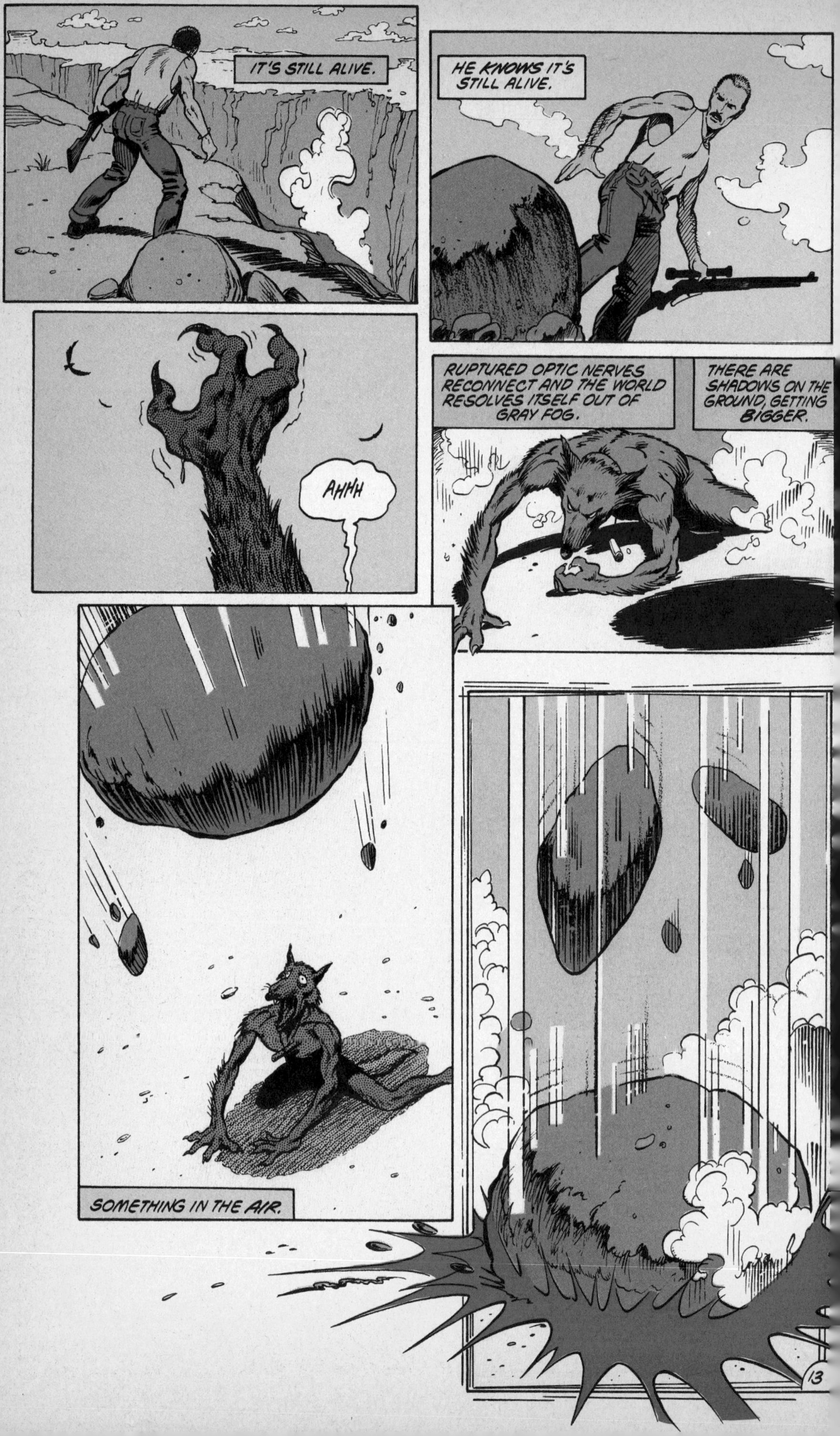
IT'S STILL ALIVE.
HE KNOWS IT'S STILL ALIVE.
AHHH
RUPTURED OPTIC NERVES RECONNECT AND THE WORLD RESOLVES ITSELF OUT OF GRAY FOG.
THERE ARE SHADOWS ON THE GROUND, GETTING BIGGER.
SOMETHING IN THE AIR.

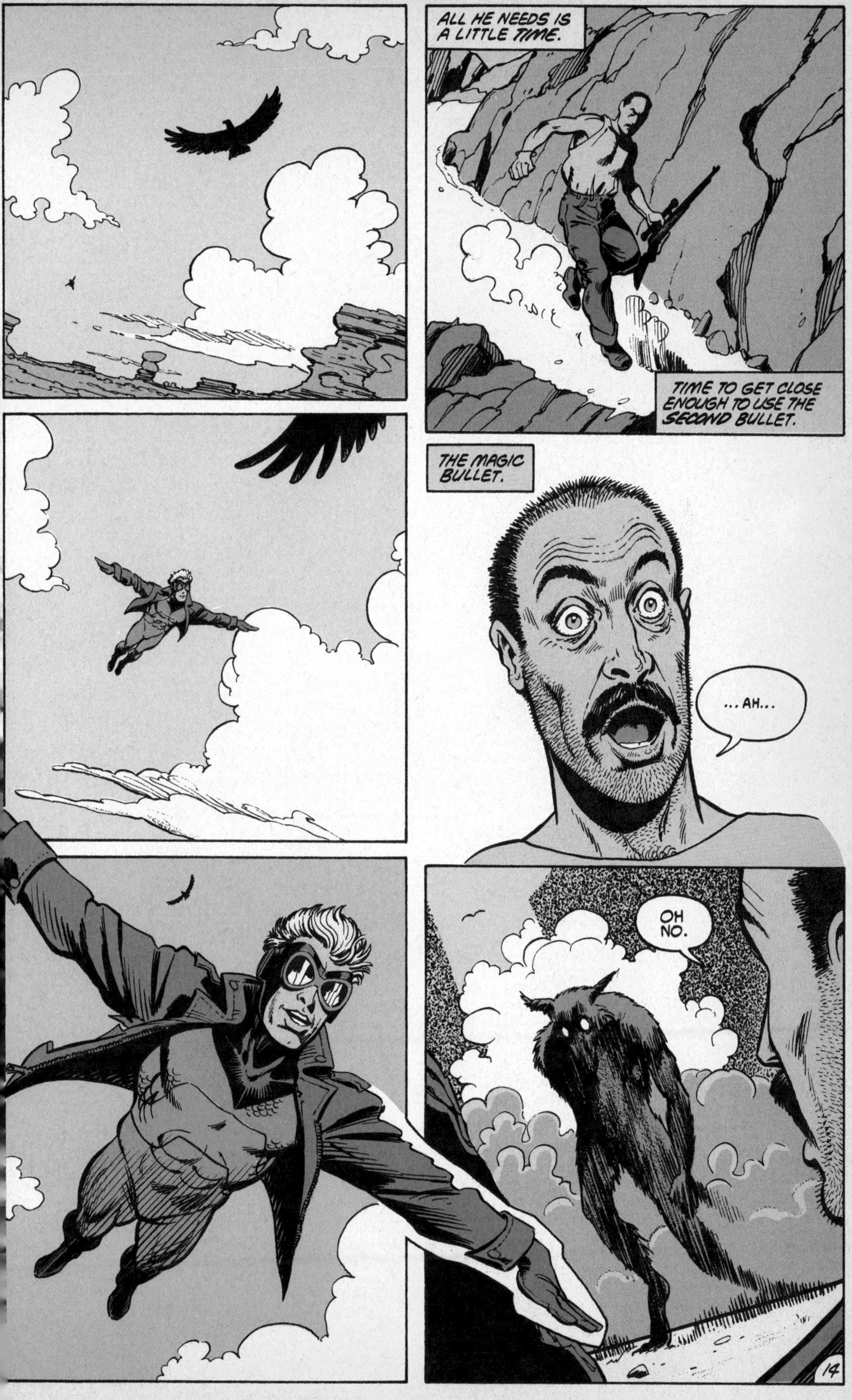
ALL HE NEEDS IS A LITTLE TIME.
TIME TO GET CLOSE ENOUGH TO USE THE SECOND BULLET.
THE MAGIC BULLET.
...AH...
OH NO.
14

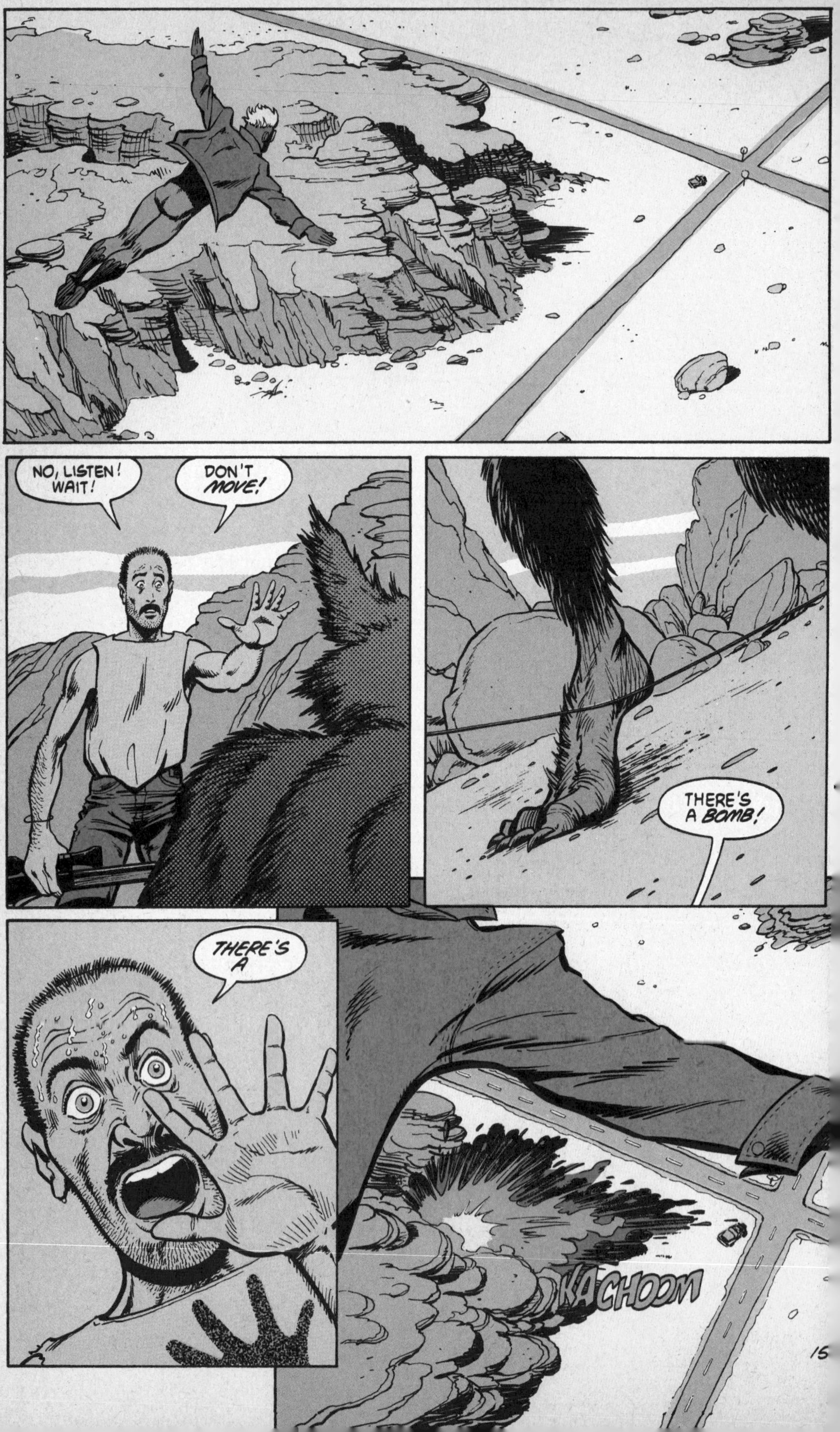
NO, LISTEN! WAIT!
DON'T MOVE!
THERE'S A BOMB!
THERE'S A
KACHOOM

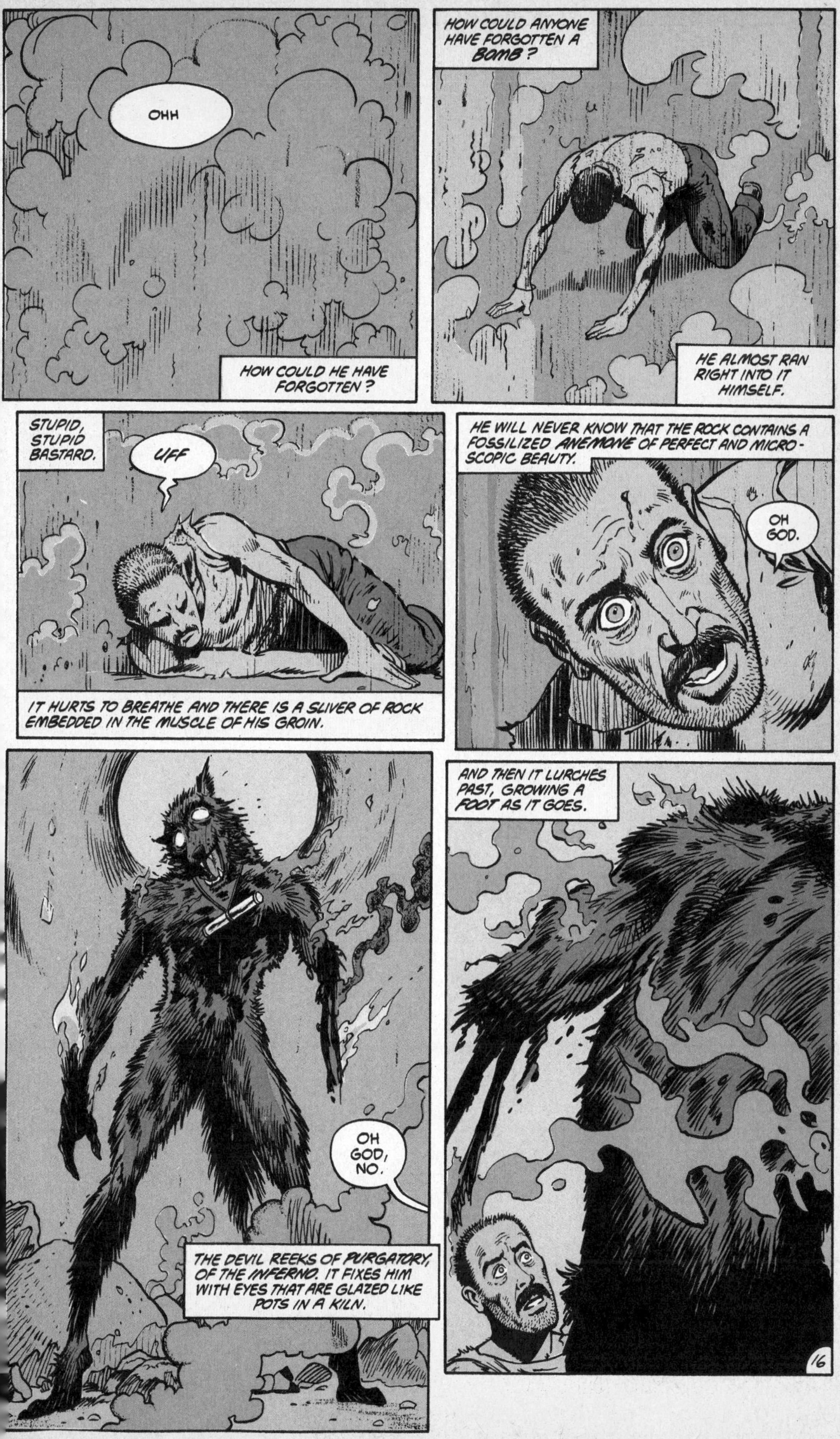
OHH
HOW COULD HE HAVE FORGOTTEN?
HOW COULD ANYONE HAVE FORGOTTEN A BOMB?
HE ALMOST RAN RIGHT INTO IT HIMSELF.
STUPID, STUPID BASTARD.
UFF
IT HURTS TO BREATHE AND THERE IS A SLIVER OF ROCK EMBEDDED IN THE MUSCLE OF HIS GROIN.
HE WILL NEVER KNOW THAT THE ROCK CONTAINS A FOSSILIZED ANEMONE OF PERFECT AND MICRO-SCOPIC BEAUTY.
OH GOD.
OH GOD, NO.
THE DEVIL REEKS OF PURGATORY, OF THE INFERNO. IT FIXES HIM WITH EYES THAT ARE GLAZED LIKE POTS IN A KILN.
AND THEN IT LURCHES PAST, GROWING A FOOT AS IT GOES.
16

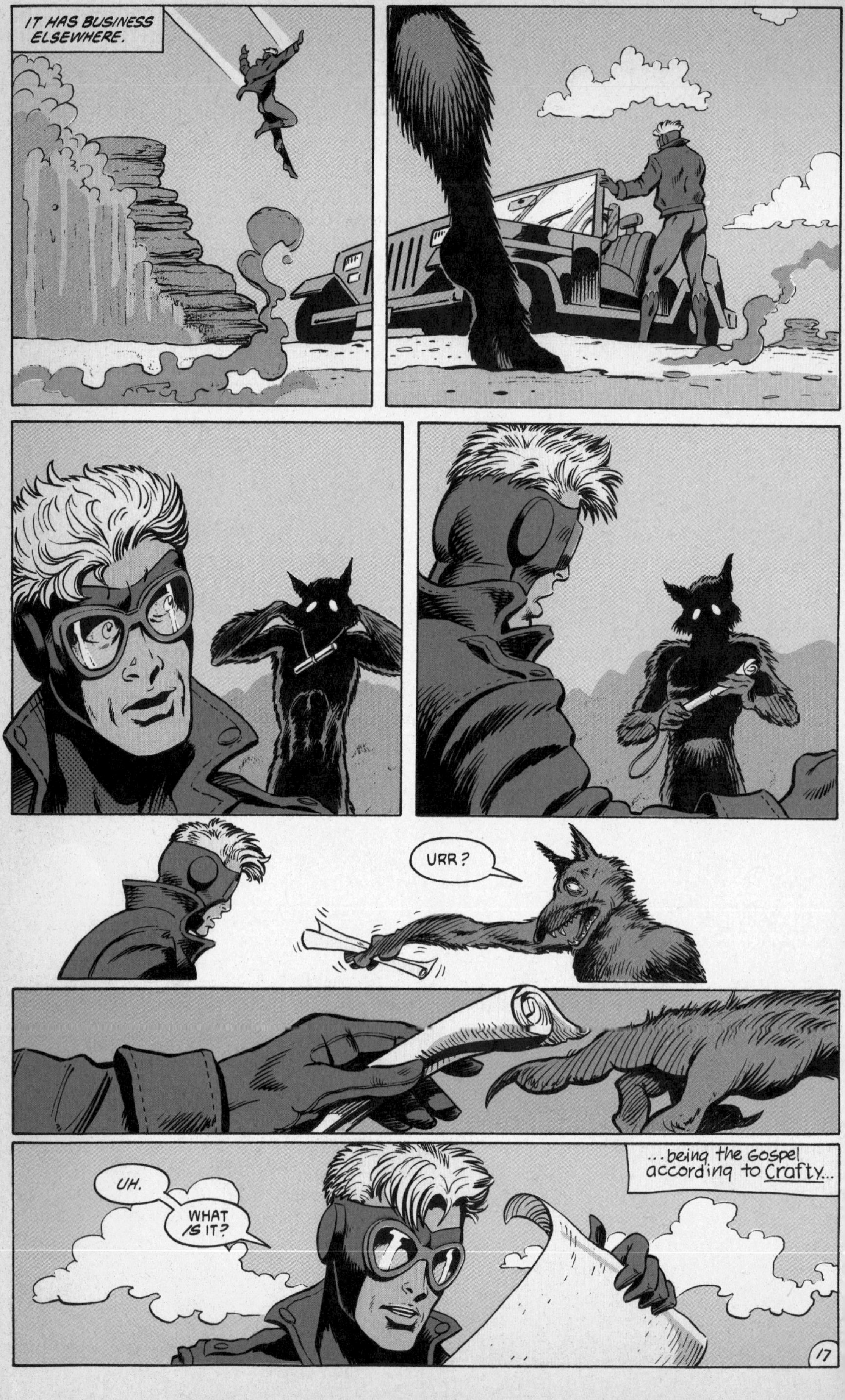
IT HAS BUSINESS ELSEWHERE.
URR?
...being the Gospel according to Crafty...
UH.
WHAT IS IT?

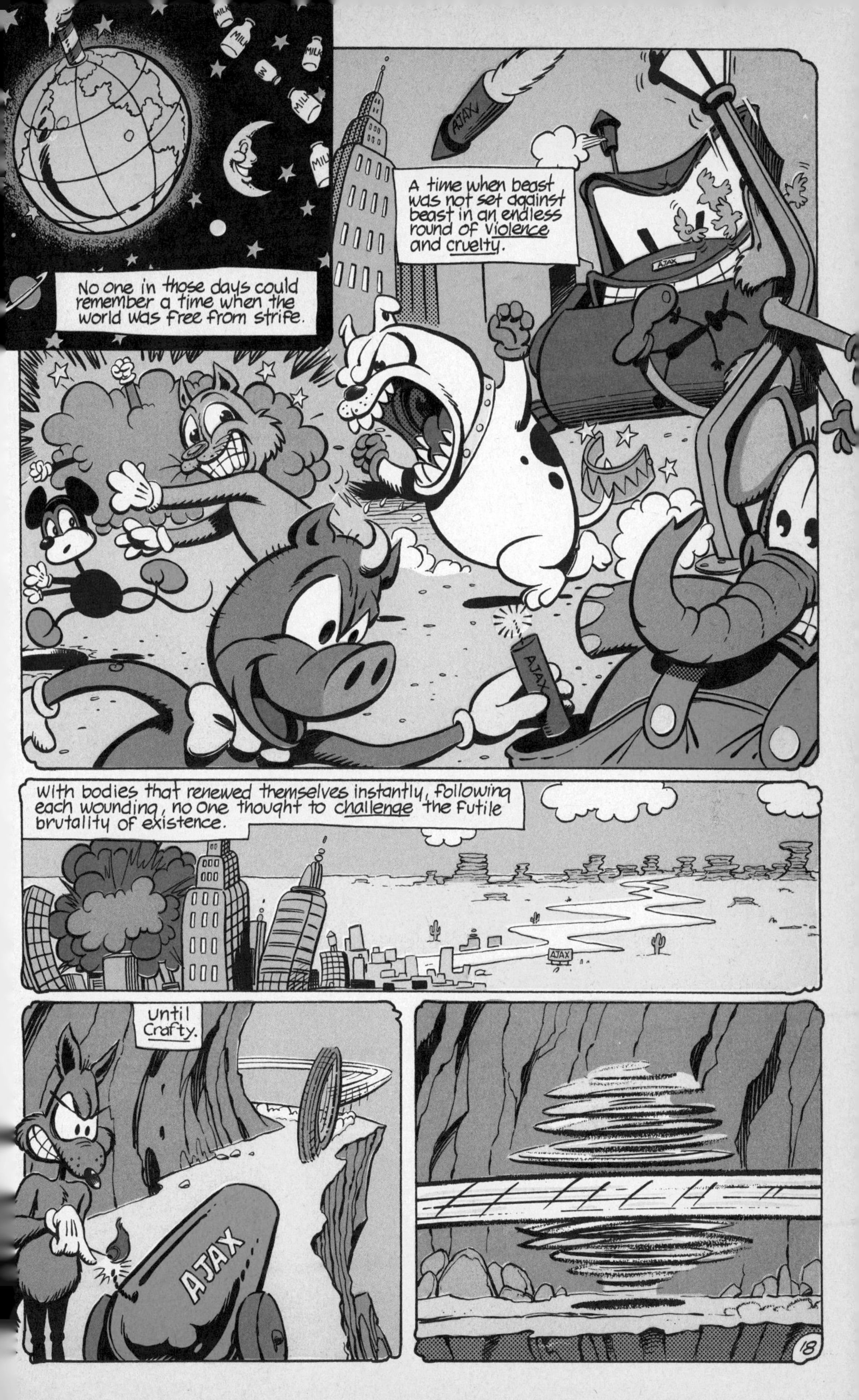

MILK
No one in those days could remember a time when the world was free from strife.
AJAX
A time when beast was not set against beast in an endless round of violence and cruelty.
AJAX
AJAX
With bodies that renewed themselves instantly, following each wounding, no one thought to challenge the futile brutality of existence.
AJAX
Until Crafty.
AJAX

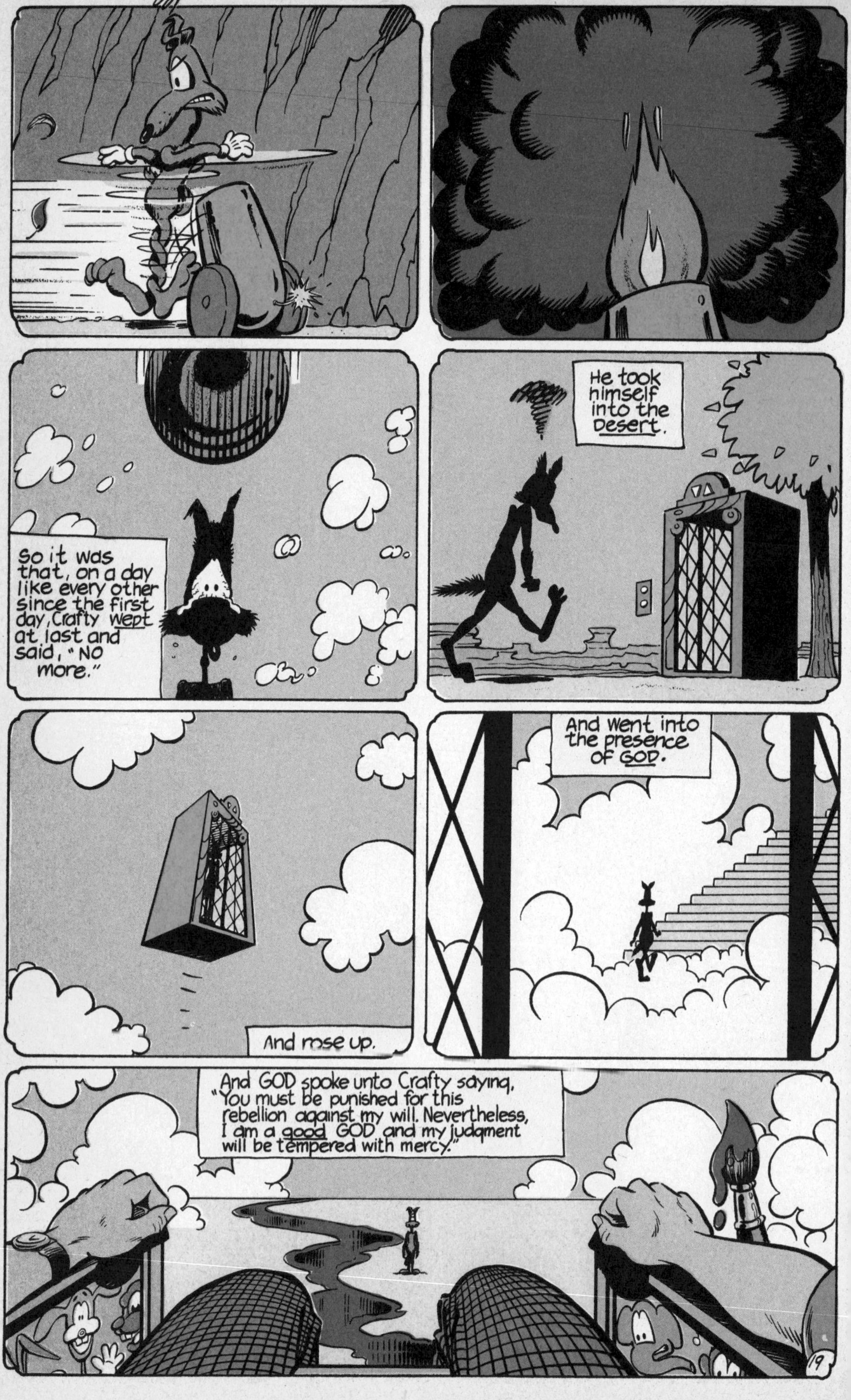

So it was that, on a day like every other since the first day, Crafty wept at last and said, "No more."
He took himself into the Desert.
And rose up.
And went into the presence of GOD.
And GOD spoke unto Crafty saying, "You must be punished for this rebellion against my will. Nevertheless, I am a good GOD and my judgment will be tempered with mercy."

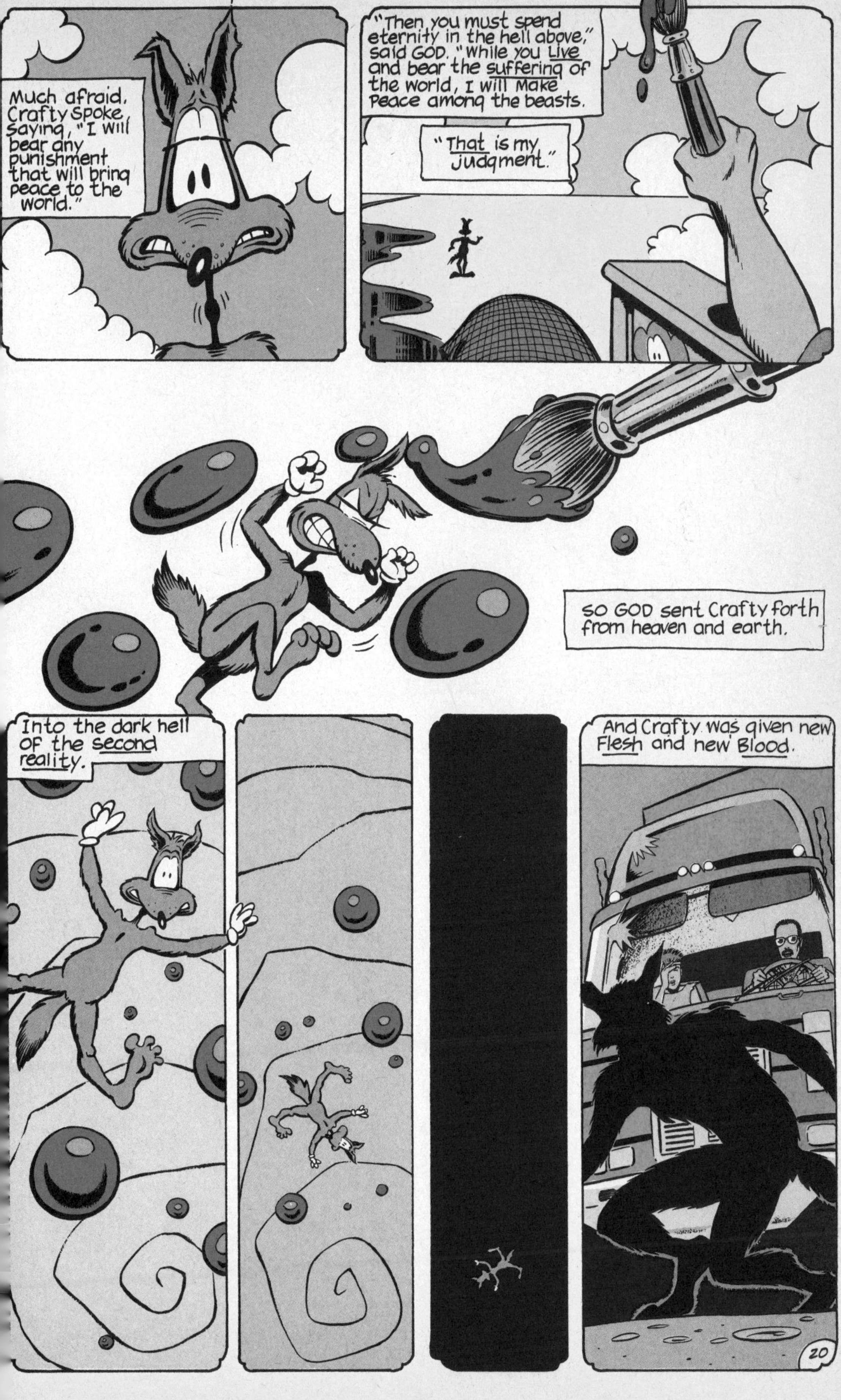

Much afraid, Crafty spoke, saying, "I will bear any punishment that will bring peace to the world."
"Then you must spend eternity in the hell above," said GOD. "While you Live and bear the suffering of the world, I will make Peace among the beasts.
"That is my judgment."
So GOD sent Crafty forth from heaven and earth.
Into the dark hell of the second reality.
And Crafty was given new Flesh and new Blood.

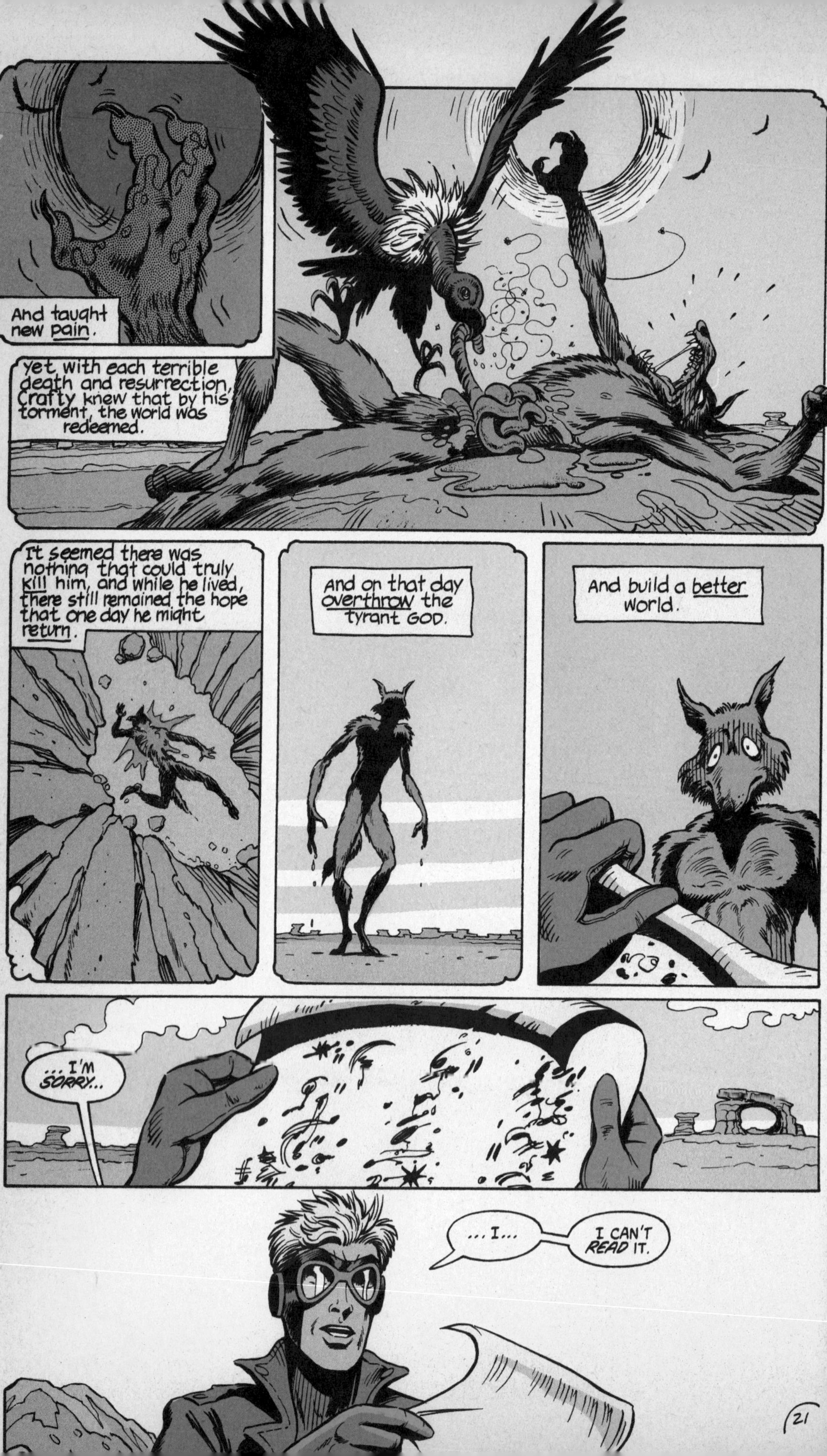
And taught new pain.
yet with each terrible death and resurrection, Crafty knew that by his torment, the world was redeemed.
It seemed there was nothing that could truly kill him, and while he lived, there still remained the hope that one day he might return.
And on that day overthrow the tyrant GOD.
And build a better world.
... I'M SORRY...
... I...
I CAN'T READ IT.

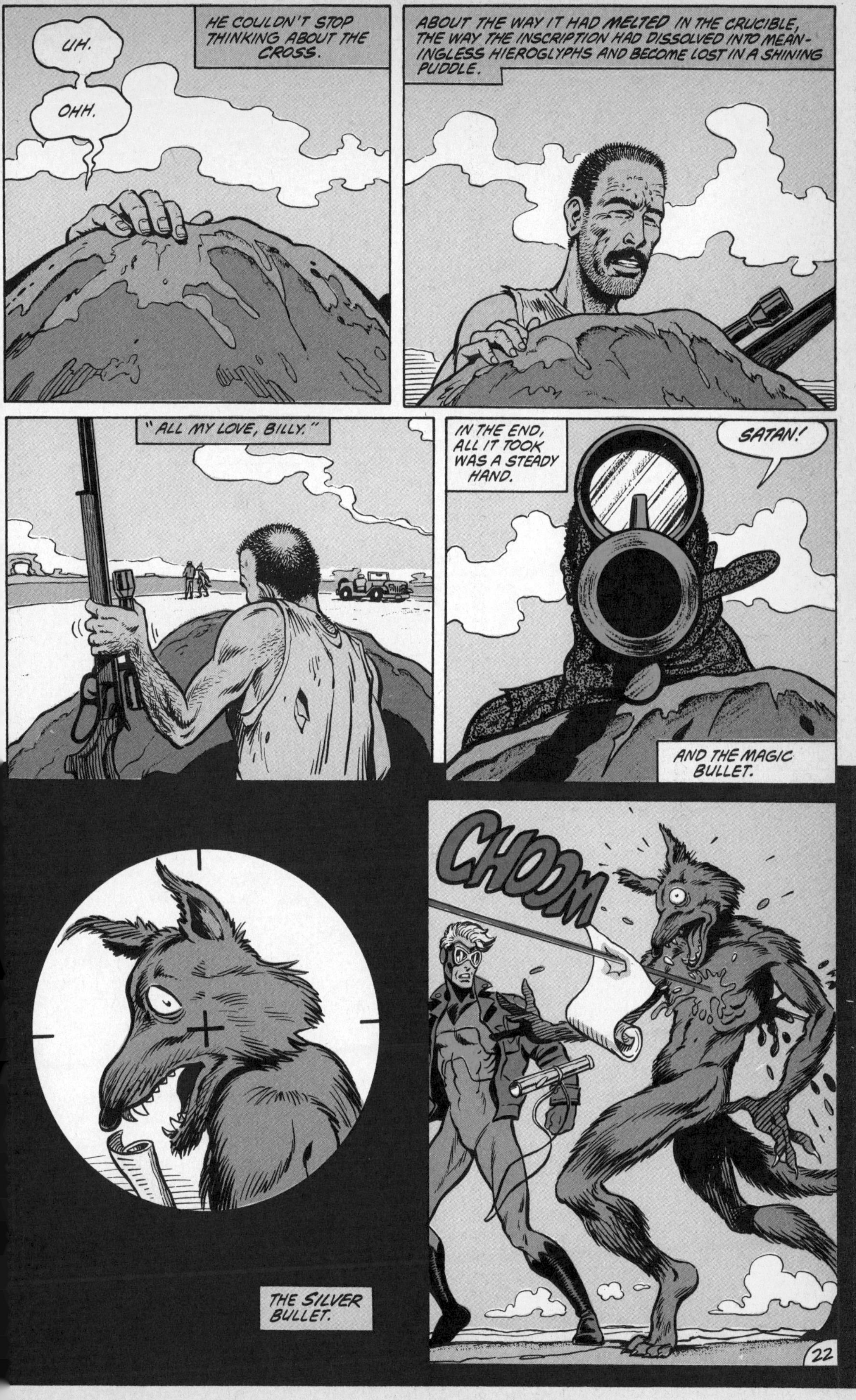
HE COULDN'T STOP THINKING ABOUT THE CROSS.
UH.
OHH.
ABOUT THE WAY IT HAD MELTED IN THE CRUCIBLE, THE WAY THE INSCRIPTION HAD DISSOLVED INTO MEAN-INGLESS HIEROGLYPHS AND BECOME LOST IN A SHINING PUDDLE.
"ALL MY LOVE, BILLY."
IN THE END, ALL IT TOOK WAS A STEADY HAND.
SATAN!
AND THE MAGIC BULLET.
THE SILVER BULLET.
CHOOM
22

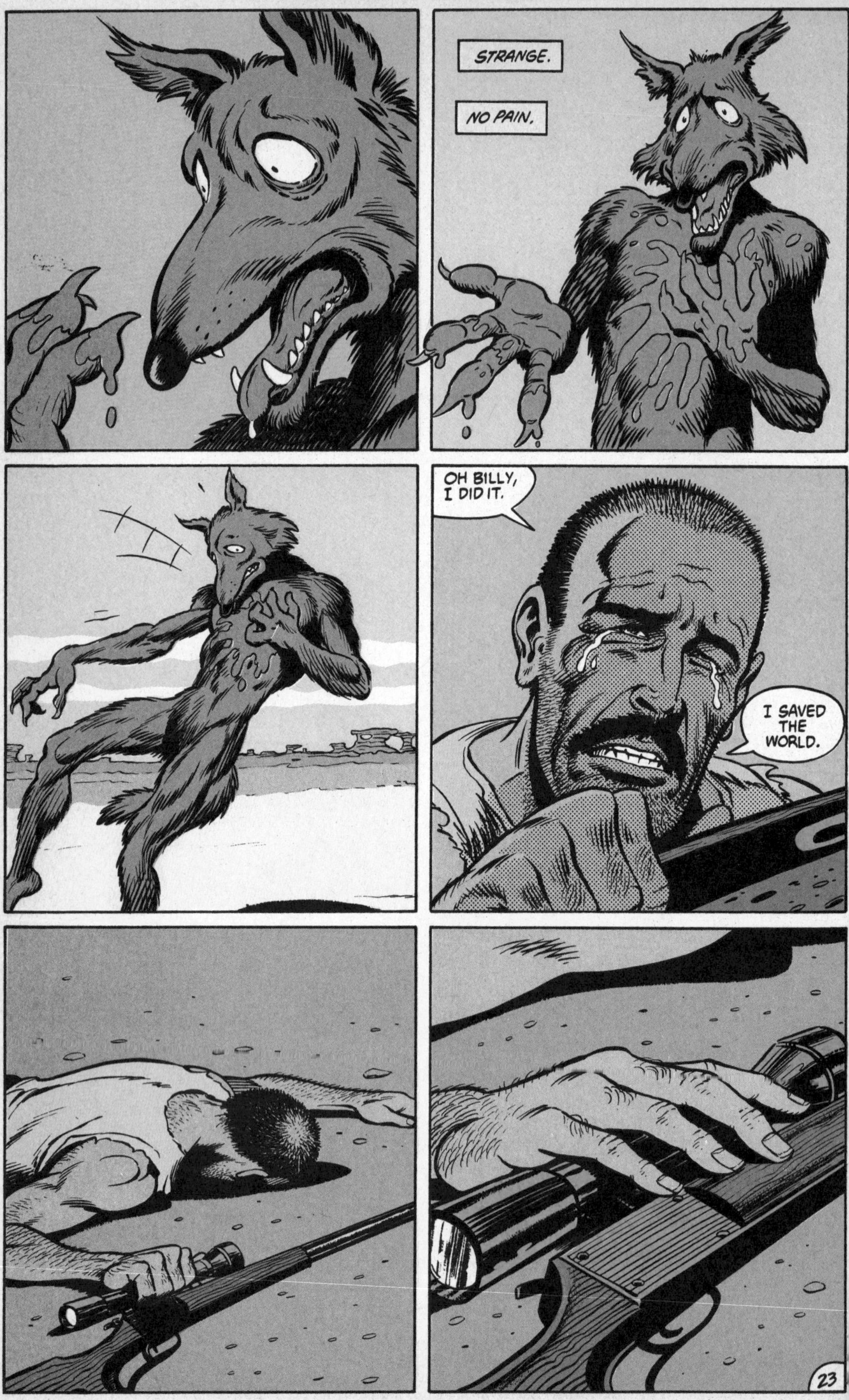
STRANGE.
NO PAIN.
OH BILLY, I DID IT.
I SAVED THE WORLD.

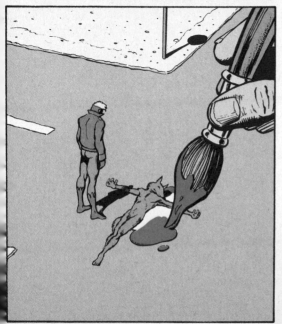

THE END, FOLKS!

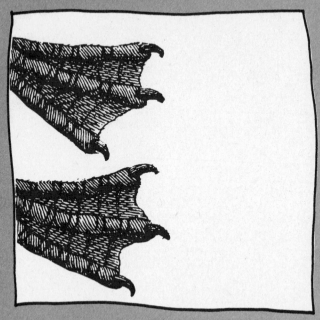

C H A P T E R

SIX

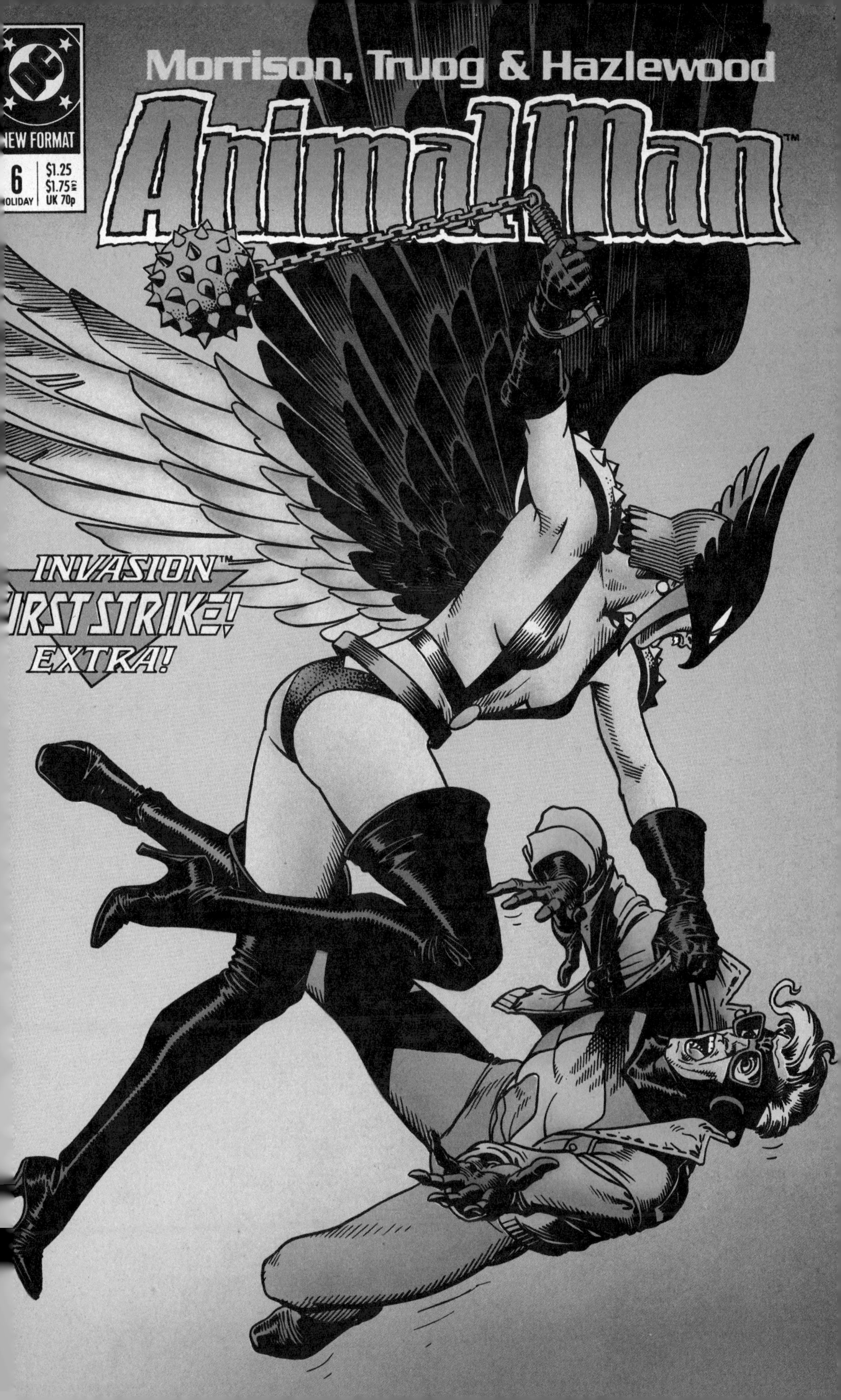
NEW FORMAT
6
HOLIDAY
$1.25
$1.75
UK 70p
Morrison, Truog & Hazlewood
Animal Man™
INVASION™
IRST STRIKE!
EXTRA!

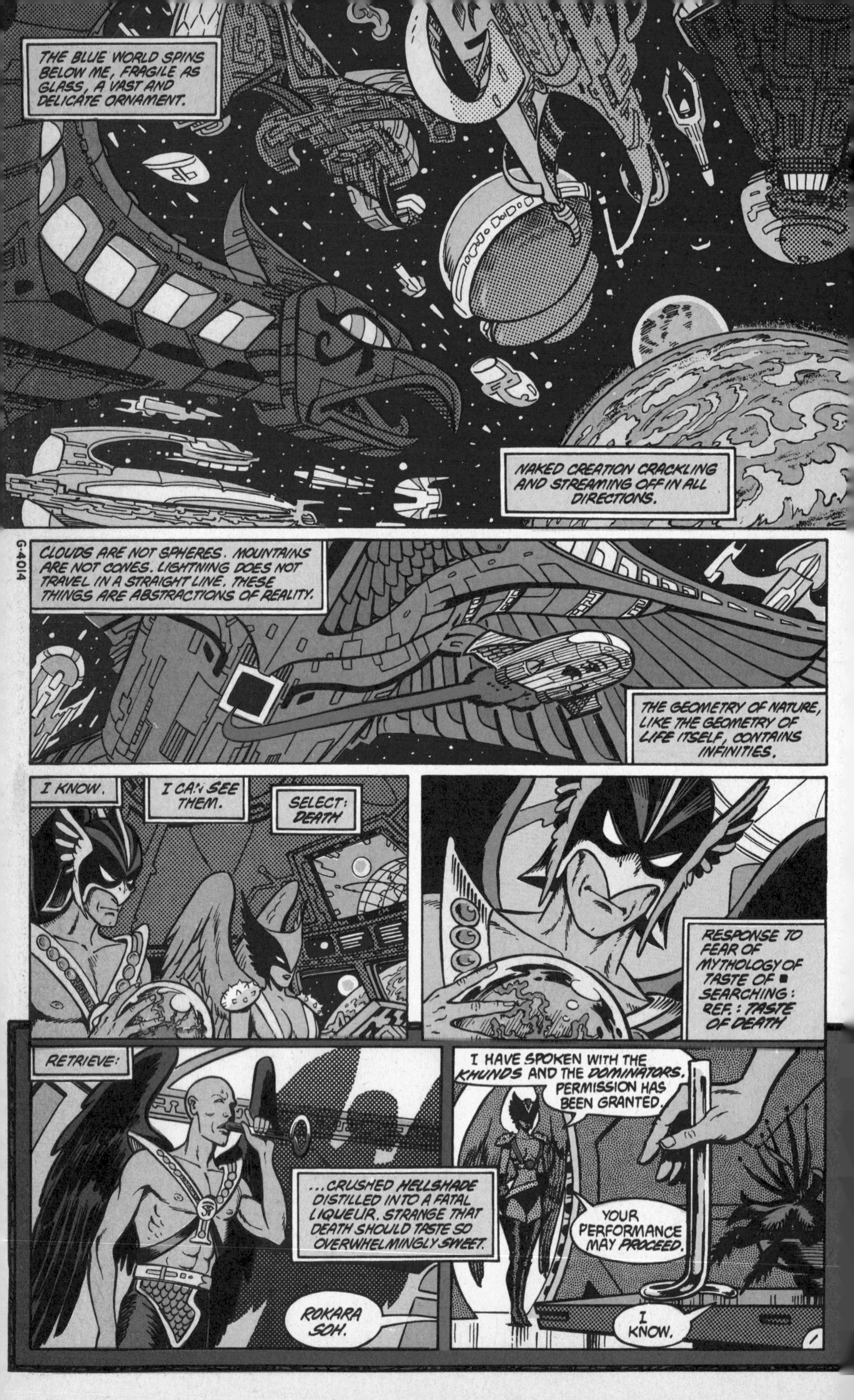
THE BLUE WORLD SPINS BELOW ME, FRAGILE AS GLASS, A VAST AND DELICATE ORNAMENT.
NAKED CREATION CRACKLING AND STREAMING OFF IN ALL DIRECTIONS.
CLOUDS ARE NOT SPHERES. MOUNTAINS ARE NOT CONES. LIGHTNING DOES NOT TRAVEL IN A STRAIGHT LINE. THESE THINGS ARE ABSTRACTIONS OF REALITY.
THE GEOMETRY OF NATURE, LIKE THE GEOMETRY OF LIFE ITSELF, CONTAINS INFINITIES.
I KNOW.
I CAN SEE THEM.
SELECT: DEATH
RESPONSE TO FEAR OF MYTHOLOGY OF TASTE OF SEARCHING: REF.: TASTE OF DEATH
RETRIEVE:
...CRUSHED HELLSHADE DISTILLED INTO A FATAL LIQUEUR. STRANGE THAT DEATH SHOULD TASTE SO OVERWHELMINGLY SWEET.
ROKARA SOH.
I HAVE SPOKEN WITH THE KHUNDS AND THE DOMINATORS. PERMISSION HAS BEEN GRANTED.
YOUR PERFORMANCE MAY PROCEED.
I KNOW.

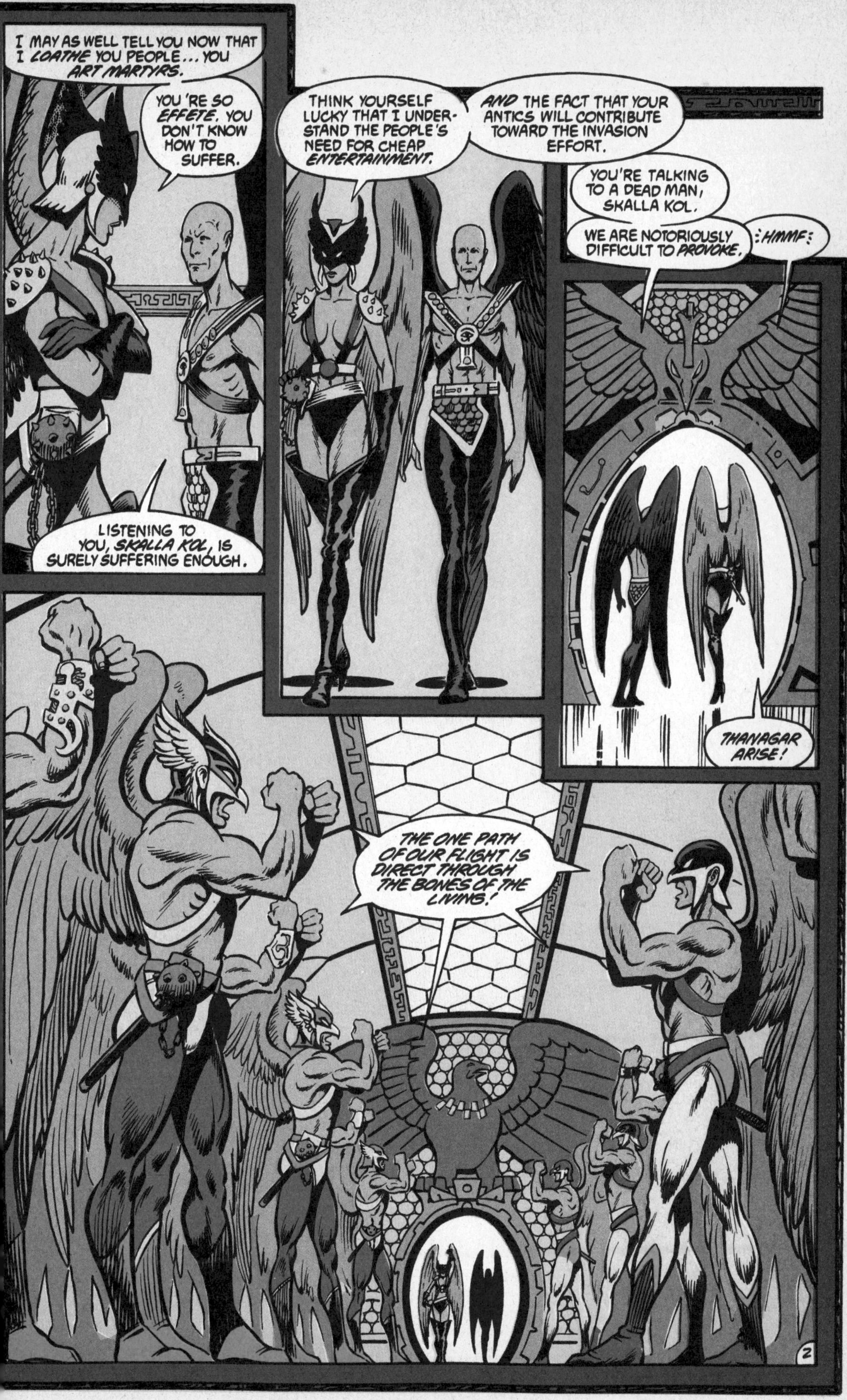
I MAY AS WELL TELL YOU NOW THAT I LOATHE YOU PEOPLE... YOU ART MARTYRS.
YOU'RE SO EFFETE. YOU DON'T KNOW HOW TO SUFFER.
LISTENING TO YOU, SKALLA KOL, IS SURELY SUFFERING ENOUGH.
THINK YOURSELF LUCKY THAT I UNDERSTAND THE PEOPLE'S NEED FOR CHEAP ENTERTAINMENT.
AND THE FACT THAT YOUR ANTICS WILL CONTRIBUTE TOWARD THE INVASION EFFORT.
YOU'RE TALKING TO A DEAD MAN, SKALLA KOL.
WE ARE NOTORIOUSLY DIFFICULT TO PROVOKE.
HMMF
THANAGAR ARISE!
THE ONE PATH OF OUR FLIGHT IS DIRECT THROUGH THE BONES OF THE LIVING!
2

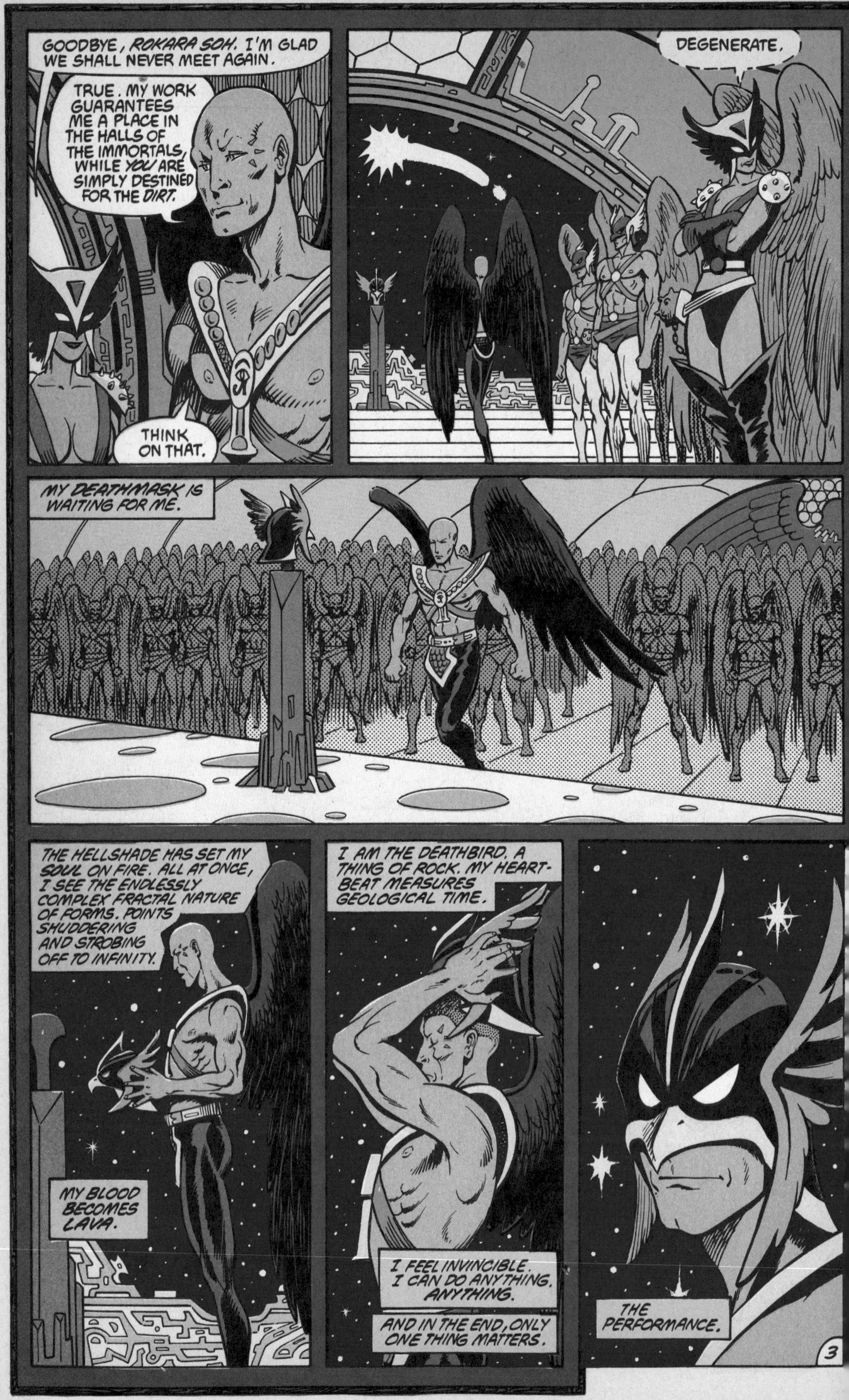

GOODBYE, ROKARA SOH. I'M GLAD WE SHALL NEVER MEET AGAIN.
TRUE. MY WORK GUARANTEES ME A PLACE IN THE HALLS OF THE IMMORTALS, WHILE YOU ARE SIMPLY DESTINED FOR THE DIRT.
THINK ON THAT.
DEGENERATE.
MY DEATHMASK IS WAITING FOR ME.
THE HELLSHADE HAS SET MY SOUL ON FIRE. ALL AT ONCE, I SEE THE ENDLESSLY COMPLEX FRACTAL NATURE OF FORMS. POINTS SHUDDERING AND STROBING OFF TO INFINITY.
MY BLOOD BECOMES LAVA.
I AM THE DEATHBIRD. A THING OF ROCK. MY HEART-BEAT MEASURES GEOLOGICAL TIME.
I FEEL INVINCIBLE. I CAN DO ANYTHING. ANYTHING.
AND IN THE END, ONLY ONE THING MATTERS.
THE PERFORMANCE.

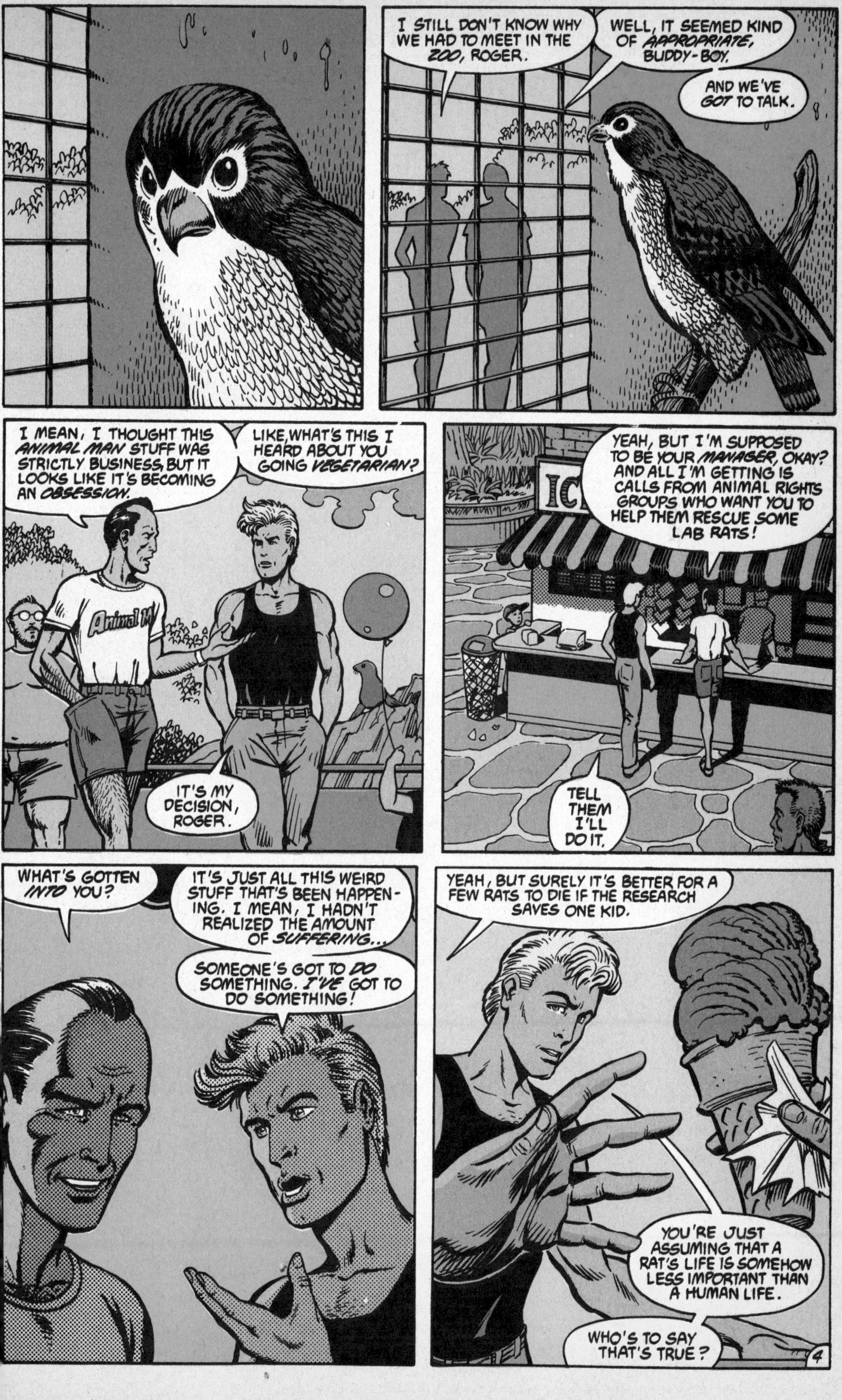
I STILL DON'T KNOW WHY WE HAD TO MEET IN THE ZOO, ROGER.
WELL, IT SEEMED KIND OF APPROPRIATE, BUDDY-BOY.
AND WE'VE GOT TO TALK.
I MEAN, I THOUGHT THIS ANIMAL MAN STUFF WAS STRICTLY BUSINESS, BUT IT LOOKS LIKE IT'S BECOMING AN OBSESSION.
LIKE, WHAT'S THIS I HEARD ABOUT YOU GOING VEGETARIAN?
IT'S MY DECISION, ROGER.
YEAH, BUT I'M SUPPOSED TO BE YOUR MANAGER, OKAY? AND ALL I'M GETTING IS CALLS FROM ANIMAL RIGHTS GROUPS WHO WANT YOU TO HELP THEM RESCUE SOME LAB RATS!
TELL THEM I'LL DO IT.
WHAT'S GOTTEN INTO YOU?
IT'S JUST ALL THIS WEIRD STUFF THAT'S BEEN HAPPENING. I MEAN, I HADN'T REALIZED THE AMOUNT OF SUFFERING...
SOMEONE'S GOT TO DO SOMETHING. I'VE GOT TO DO SOMETHING!
YEAH, BUT SURELY IT'S BETTER FOR A FEW RATS TO DIE IF THE RESEARCH SAVES ONE KID.
YOU'RE JUST ASSUMING THAT A RAT'S LIFE IS SOMEHOW LESS IMPORTANT THAN A HUMAN LIFE.
WHO'S TO SAY THAT'S TRUE?

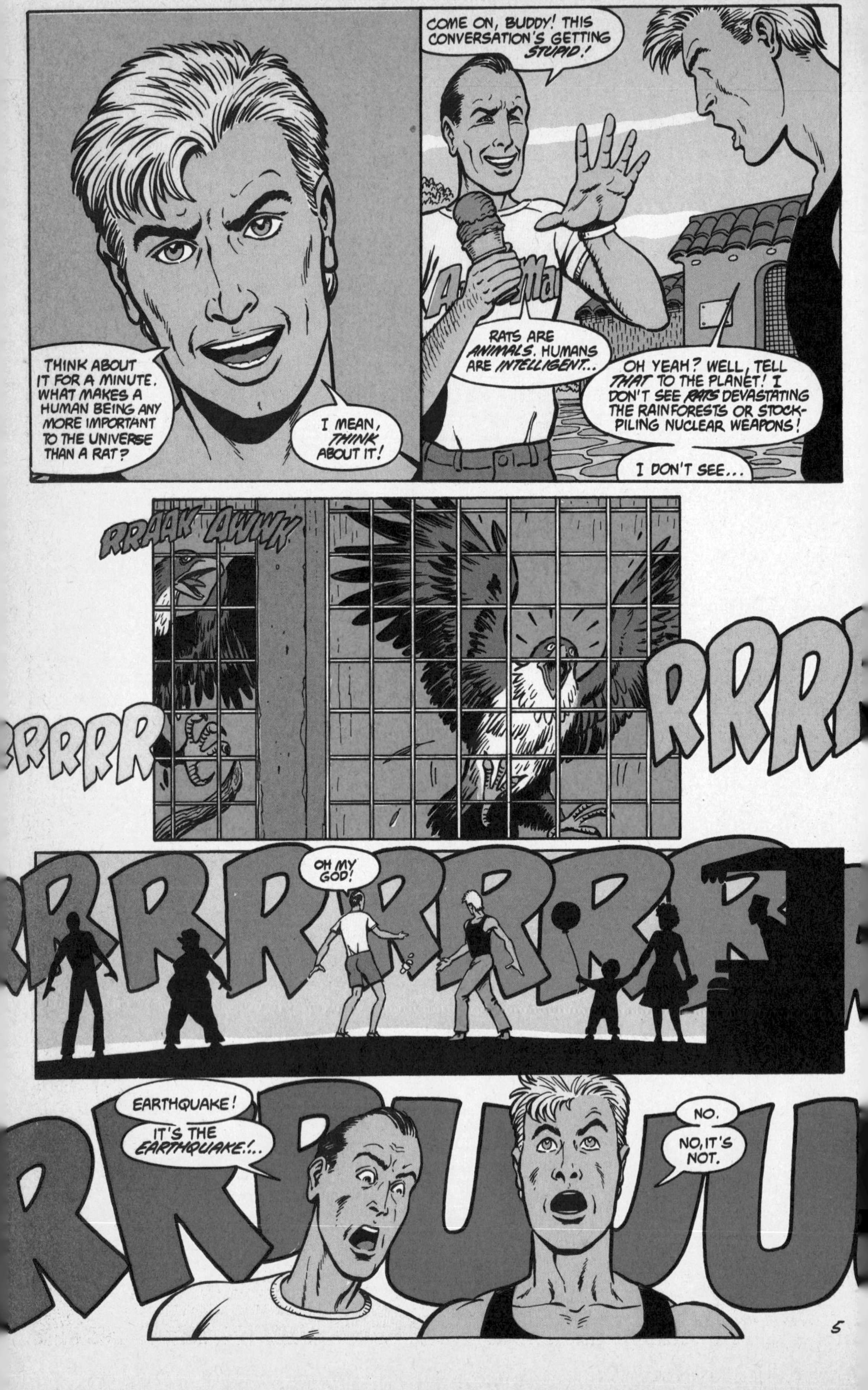
THINK ABOUT IT FOR A MINUTE. WHAT MAKES A HUMAN BEING ANY MORE IMPORTANT TO THE UNIVERSE THAN A RAT?
I MEAN, THINK ABOUT IT!
COME ON, BUDDY! THIS CONVERSATION'S GETTING STUPID!
RATS ARE ANIMALS. HUMANS ARE INTELLIGENT...
OH YEAH? WELL, TELL THAT TO THE PLANET! I DON'T SEE RATS DEVASTATING THE RAINFORESTS OR STOCK-PILING NUCLEAR WEAPONS!
I DON'T SEE...
RRAAK AWWK
RRRR
RRRR
RRRRRRRR
OH MY GOD!
RRRUUU
EARTHQUAKE!
IT'S THE EARTHQUAKE!...
NO.
NO, IT'S NOT.

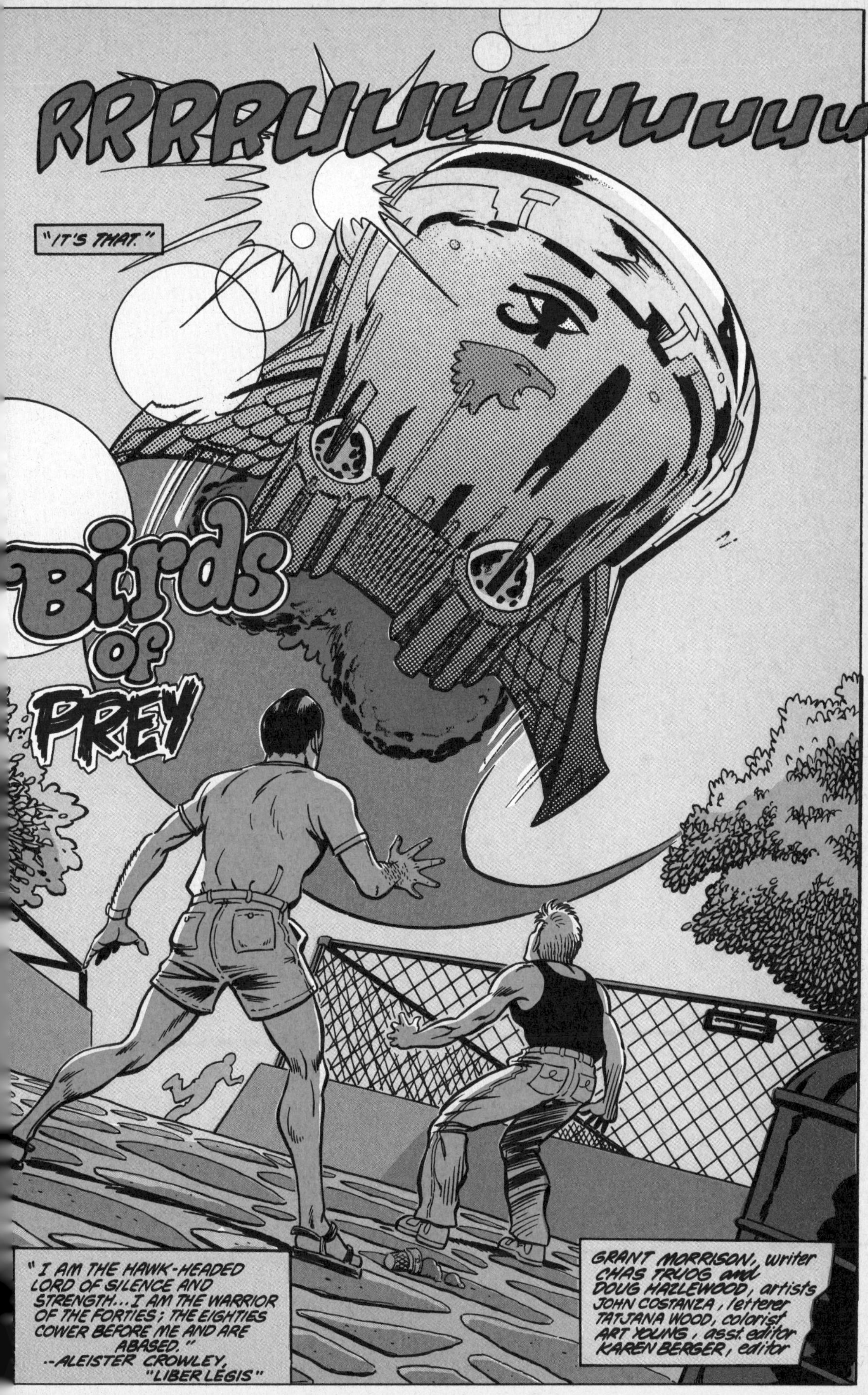
RRRRUUUUUUUUUU
"IT'S THAT."
Birds of PREY
"I AM THE HAWK-HEADED LORD OF SILENCE AND STRENGTH... I AM THE WARRIOR OF THE FORTIES; THE EIGHTIES COWER BEFORE ME AND ARE ABASED." --ALEISTER CROWLEY, "LIBER LÉGIS"
GRANT MORRISON, writer CHAS TRUOG and DOUG HAZLEWOOD, artists JOHN COSTANZA, letterer TATJANA WOOD, colorist ART YOUNG, asst. editor KAREN BERGER, editor

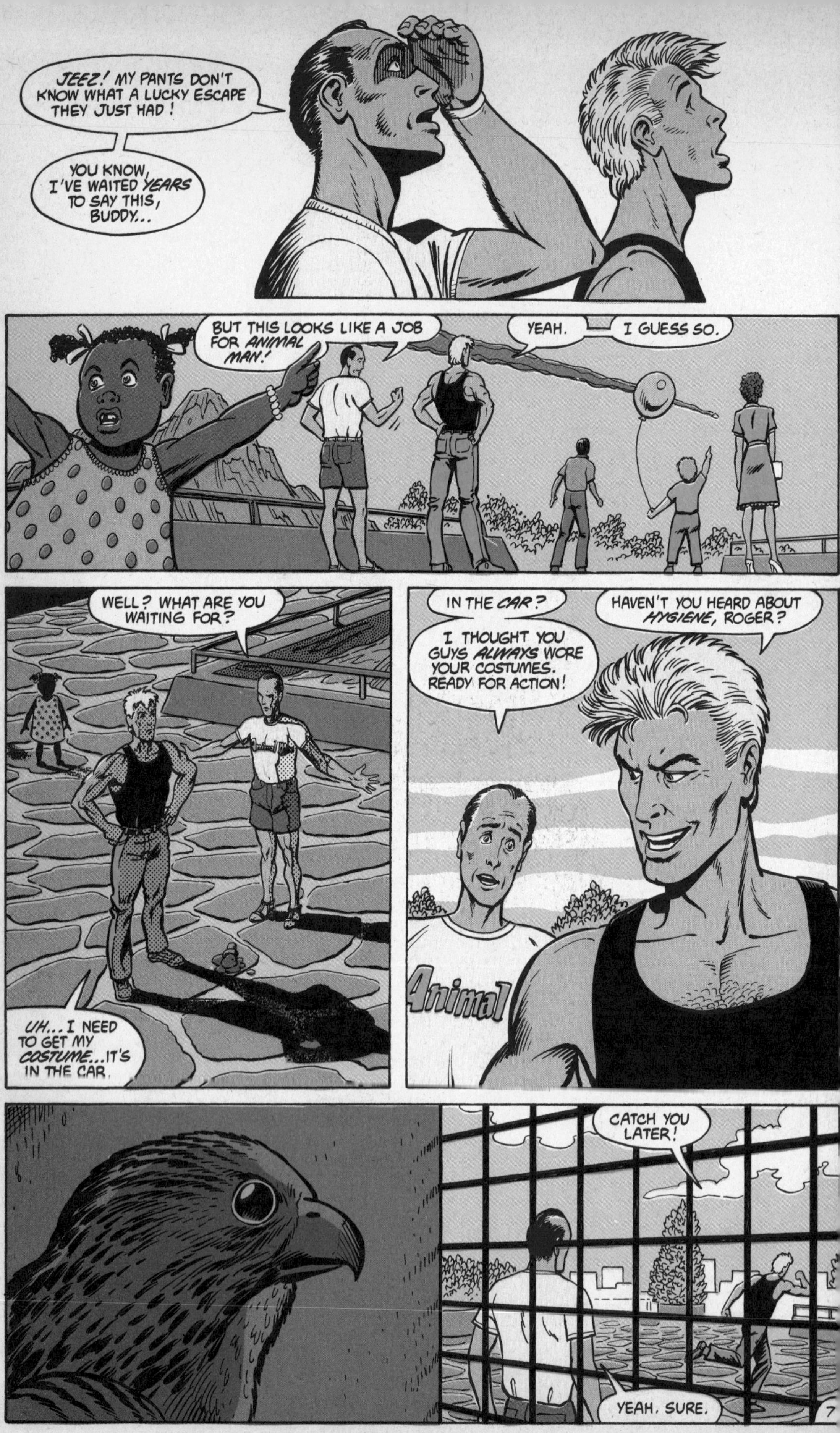
JEEZ! MY PANTS DON'T KNOW WHAT A LUCKY ESCAPE THEY JUST HAD!
YOU KNOW, I'VE WAITED YEARS TO SAY THIS, BUDDY...
BUT THIS LOOKS LIKE A JOB FOR ANIMAL MAN!
YEAH.
I GUESS SO.
WELL? WHAT ARE YOU WAITING FOR?
UH... I NEED TO GET MY COSTUME... IT'S IN THE CAR.
IN THE CAR?
I THOUGHT YOU GUYS ALWAYS WORE YOUR COSTUMES. READY FOR ACTION!
HAVEN'T YOU HEARD ABOUT HYGIENE, ROGER?
Animal
CATCH YOU LATER!
YEAH. SURE.

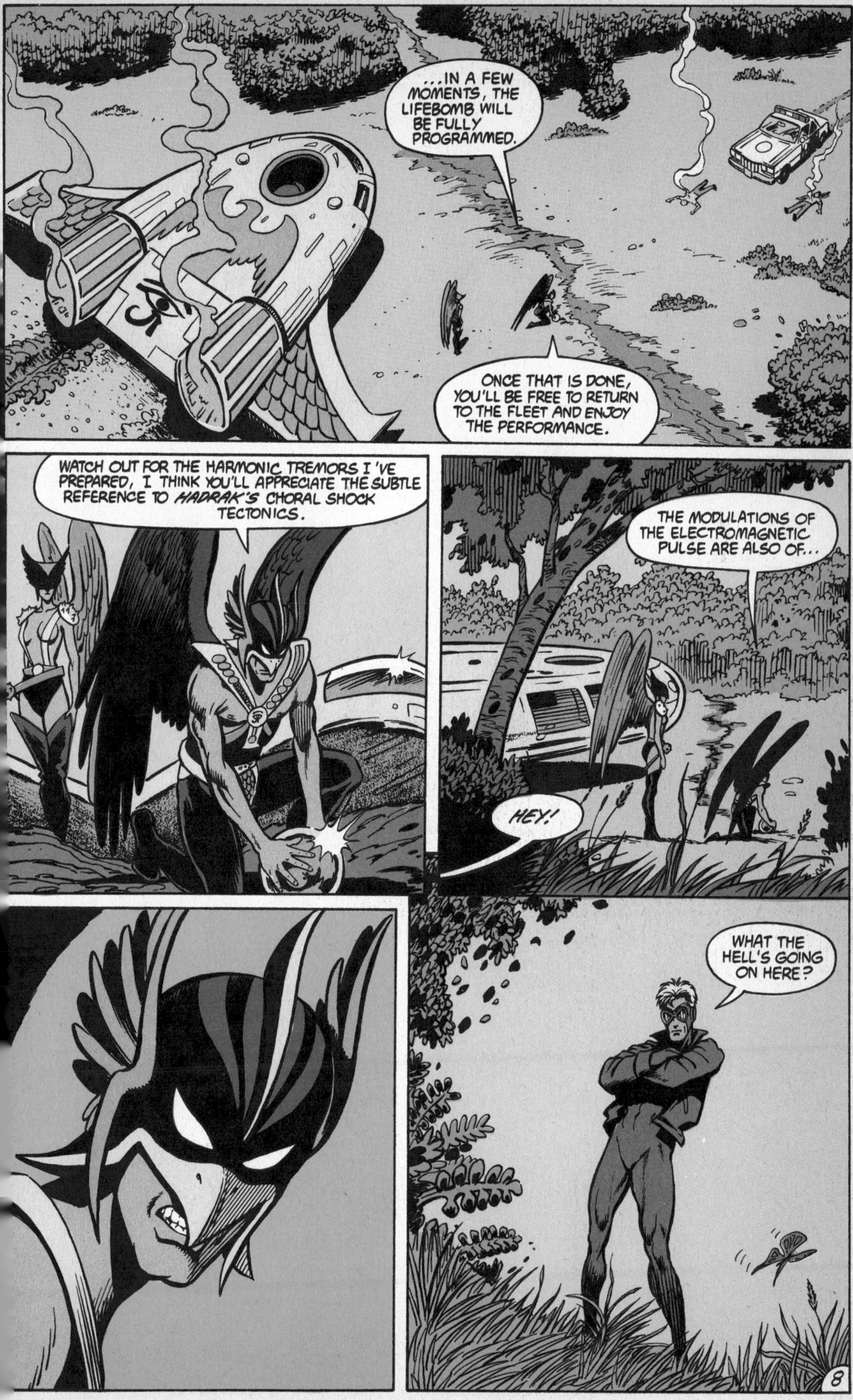
...IN A FEW MOMENTS, THE LIFEBOMB WILL BE FULLY PROGRAMMED.
ONCE THAT IS DONE, YOU'LL BE FREE TO RETURN TO THE FLEET AND ENJOY THE PERFORMANCE.
WATCH OUT FOR THE HARMONIC TREMORS I'VE PREPARED, I THINK YOU'LL APPRECIATE THE SUBTLE REFERENCE TO HADRAK'S CHORAL SHOCK TECTONICS.
THE MODULATIONS OF THE ELECTROMAGNETIC PULSE ARE ALSO OF...
HEY!
WHAT THE HELL'S GOING ON HERE?
8

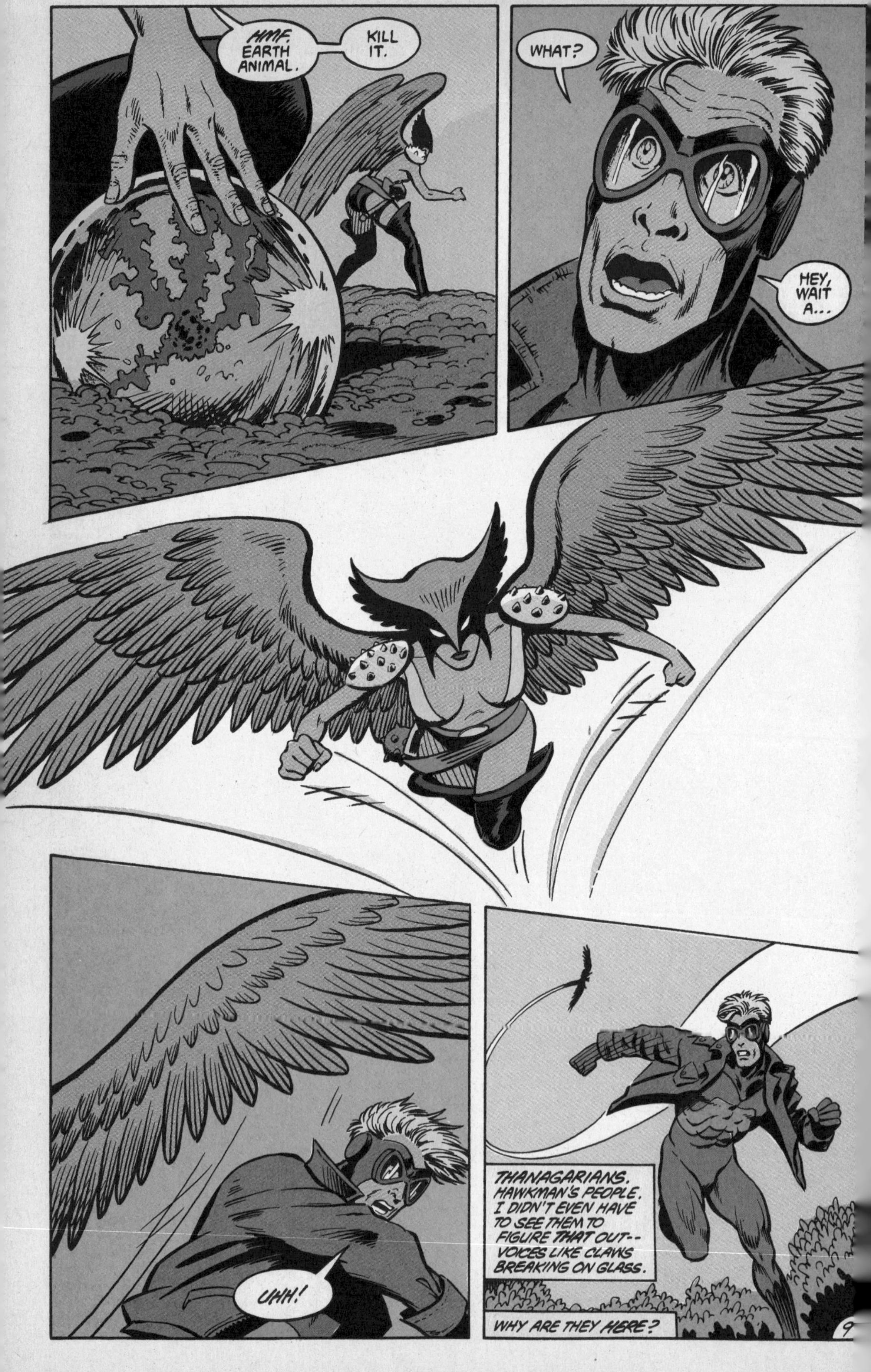
HMF. EARTH ANIMAL.
KILL IT.
WHAT?
HEY, WAIT A...
UHH!
THANAGARIANS. HAWKMAN'S PEOPLE. I DIDN'T EVEN HAVE TO SEE THEM TO FIGURE THAT OUT-- VOICES LIKE CLAWS BREAKING ON GLASS.
WHY ARE THEY HERE?
9

AND WHAT HAVE I GOTTEN MYSELF...

CHUNT!

AOWWW!

THRAKHT

UHH!

UNNNH

KILL ME.

SHE'S JUST GOING TO *KILL* ME.

KILL ME.

THE LAKE. UP AHEAD.

I CAN HEAR HER WINGS...HUGE...

HER SHADOW ON THE GRASS.

10

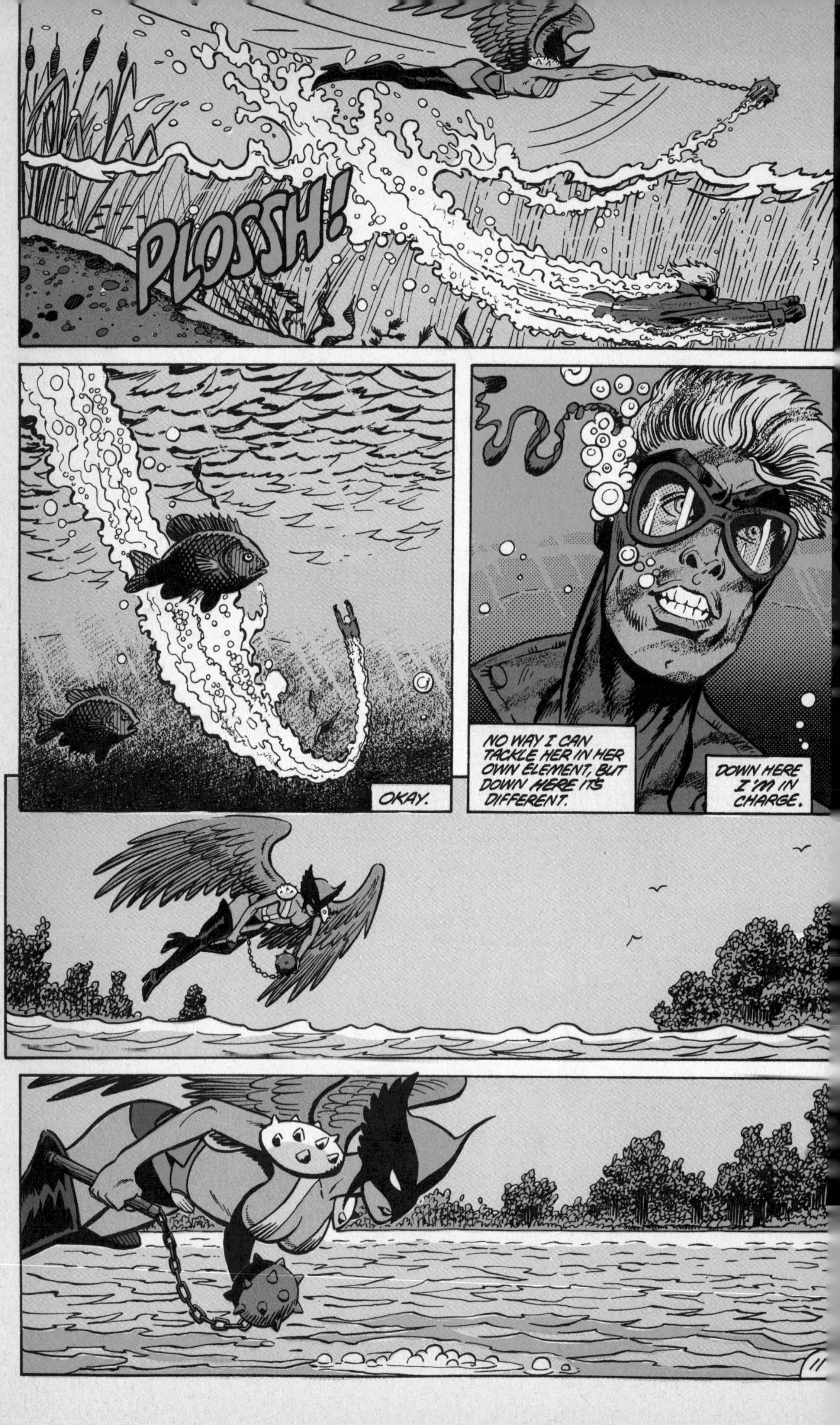
PLOSSH!
OKAY.
NO WAY I CAN TACKLE HER IN HER OWN ELEMENT, BUT DOWN HERE IT'S DIFFERENT.
DOWN HERE I'M IN CHARGE.

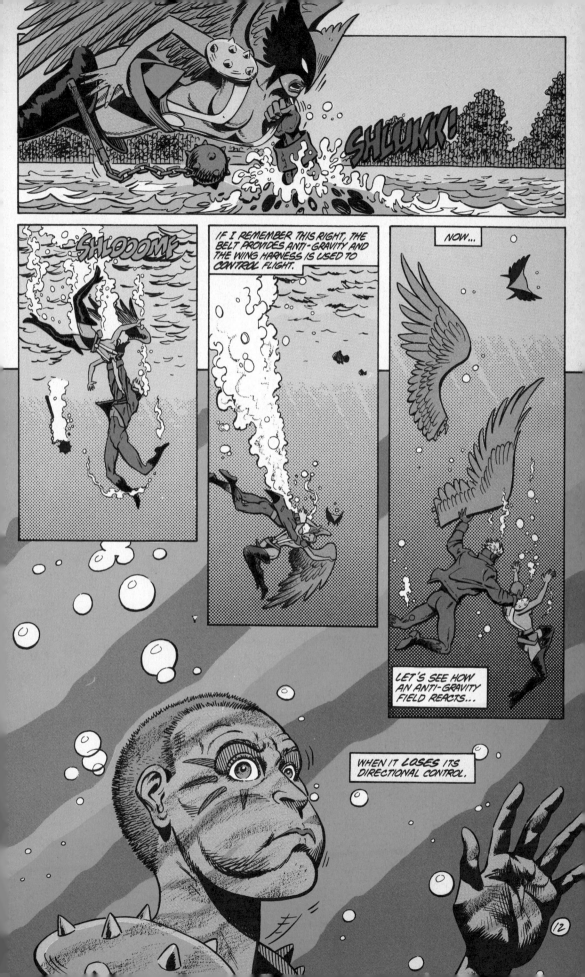

SHLUKK!

SHLODOM!

IF I REMEMBER THIS RIGHT, THE BELT PROVIDES ANTI-GRAVITY AND THE WING HARNESS IS USED TO *CONTROL* FLIGHT.

NOW...

LET'S SEE HOW AN ANTI-GRAVITY FIELD REACTS...

WHEN IT *LOSES* ITS DIRECTIONAL CONTROL.

12

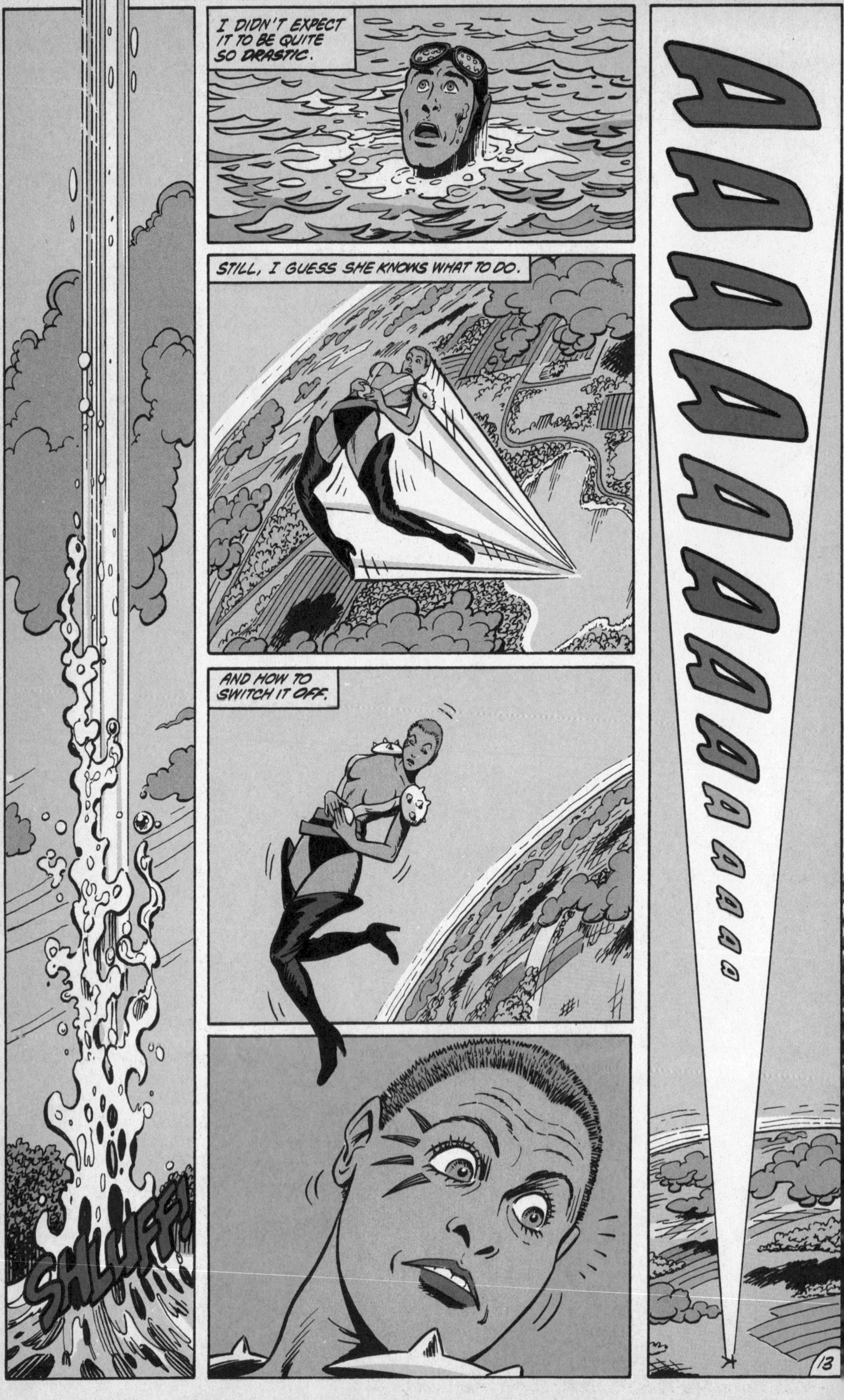
I DIDN'T EXPECT IT TO BE QUITE SO DRASTIC.
STILL, I GUESS SHE KNOWS WHAT TO DO.
AND HOW TO SWITCH IT OFF.
SHLUFF!
AAAAAAAAAAAAAA
13

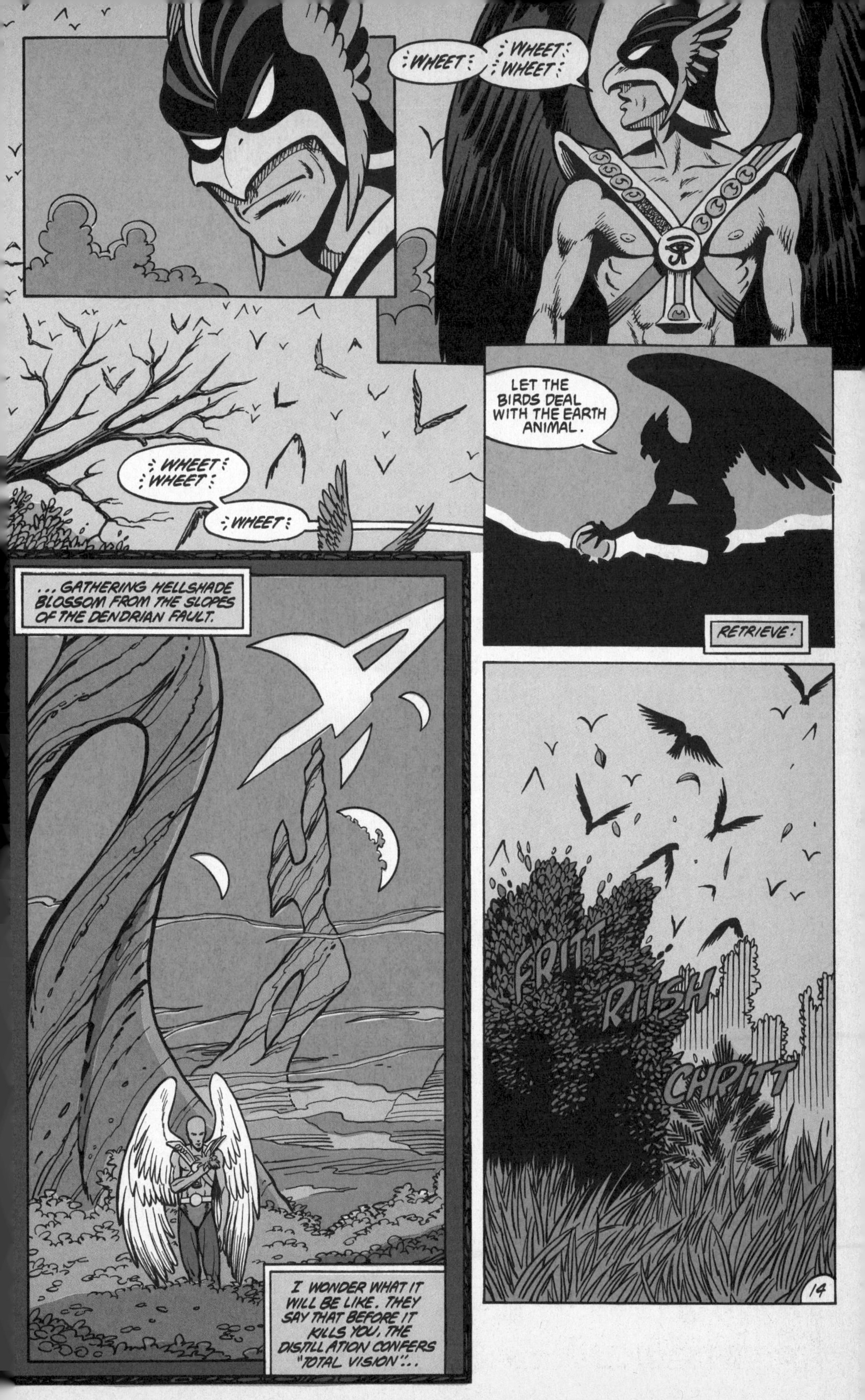
WHEET
WHEET WHEET
LET THE BIRDS DEAL WITH THE EARTH ANIMAL.
WHEET WHEET
WHEET
RETRIEVE:
... GATHERING HELLSHADE BLOSSOM FROM THE SLOPES OF THE DENDRIAN FAULT.
I WONDER WHAT IT WILL BE LIKE. THEY SAY THAT BEFORE IT KILLS YOU, THE DISTILLATION CONFERS "TOTAL VISION"...
FRITT
RIISH
CHRITT
14

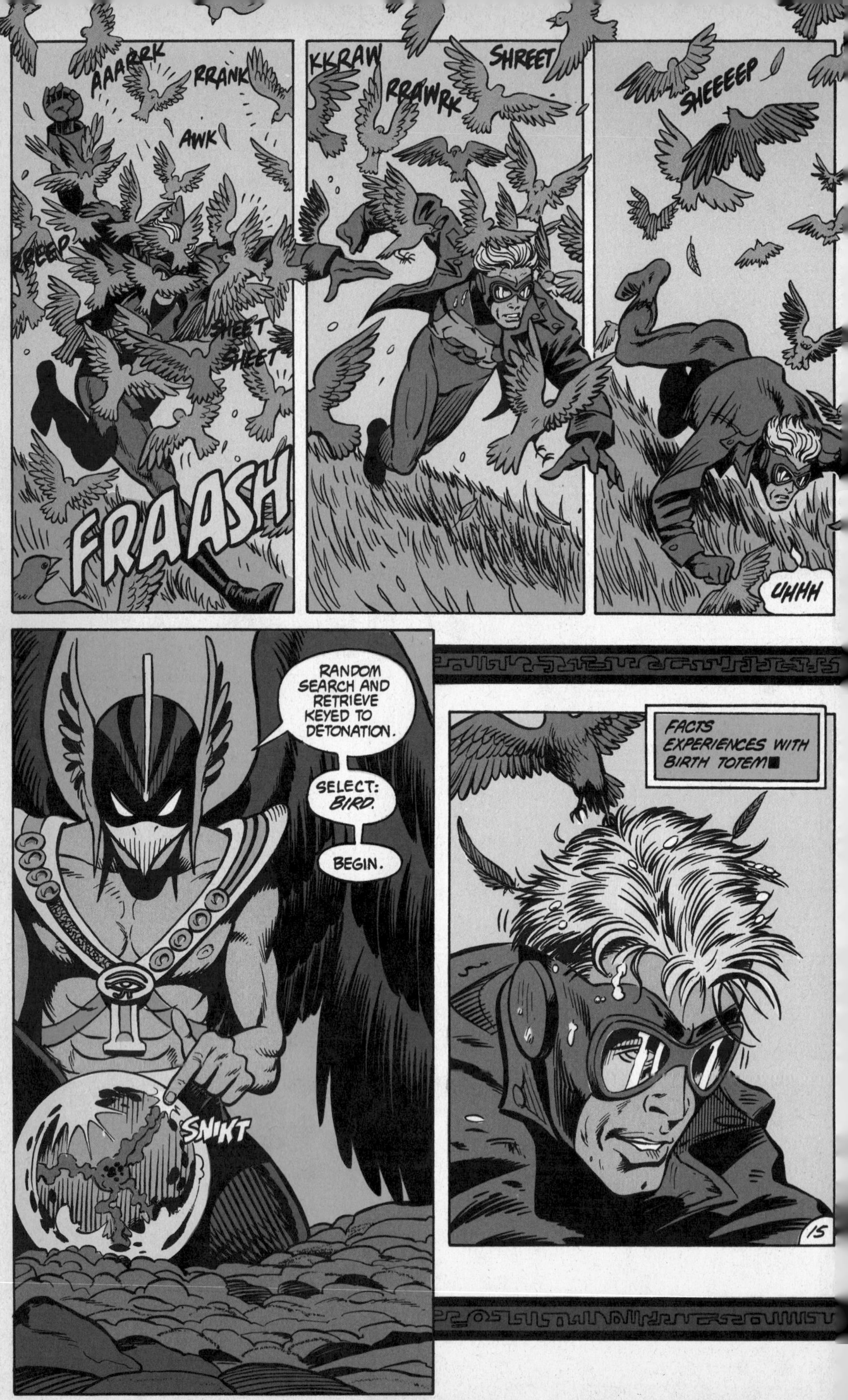
AAARRK
RRANK
AWK
KREEP
SHEET
SHEET
FRAASH
KKRAW
RRAWRK
SHREET
SHEEEEP
UHHH
RANDOM SEARCH AND RETRIEVE KEYED TO DETONATION.
SELECT: *BIRD.*
BEGIN.
SNIKT
FACTS EXPERIENCES WITH BIRTH TOTEM
15

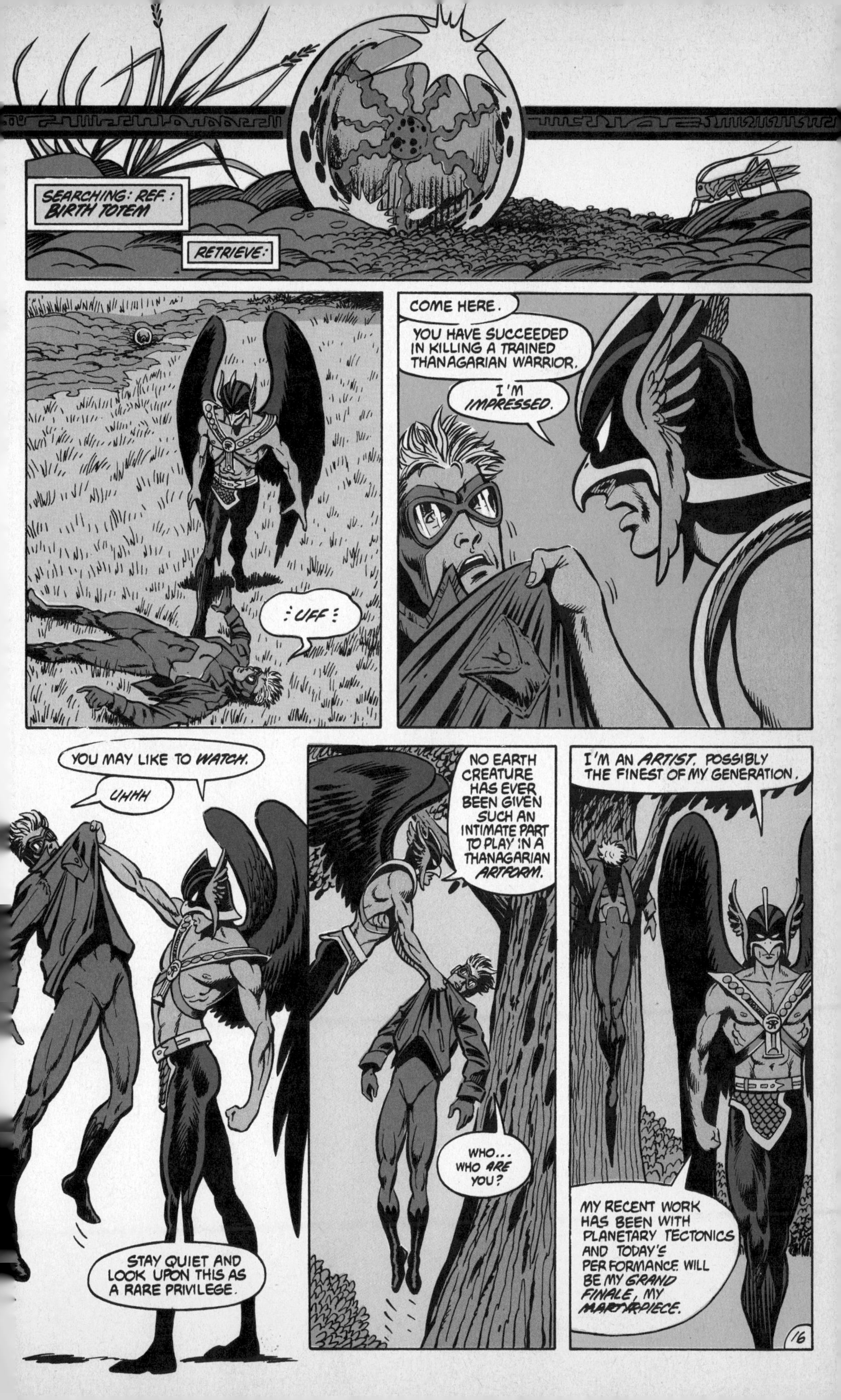

SEARCHING: REF.: BIRTH TOTEM
RETRIEVE:
:UFF:
COME HERE.
YOU HAVE SUCCEEDED IN KILLING A TRAINED THANAGARIAN WARRIOR.
I'M IMPRESSED.
YOU MAY LIKE TO WATCH.
UHHH
STAY QUIET AND LOOK UPON THIS AS A RARE PRIVILEGE.
NO EARTH CREATURE HAS EVER BEEN GIVEN SUCH AN INTIMATE PART TO PLAY IN A THANAGARIAN ARTFORM.
WHO... WHO ARE YOU?
I'M AN ARTIST, POSSIBLY THE FINEST OF MY GENERATION.
MY RECENT WORK HAS BEEN WITH PLANETARY TECTONICS AND TODAY'S PERFORMANCE WILL BE MY GRAND FINALE, MY MASTERPIECE.
16

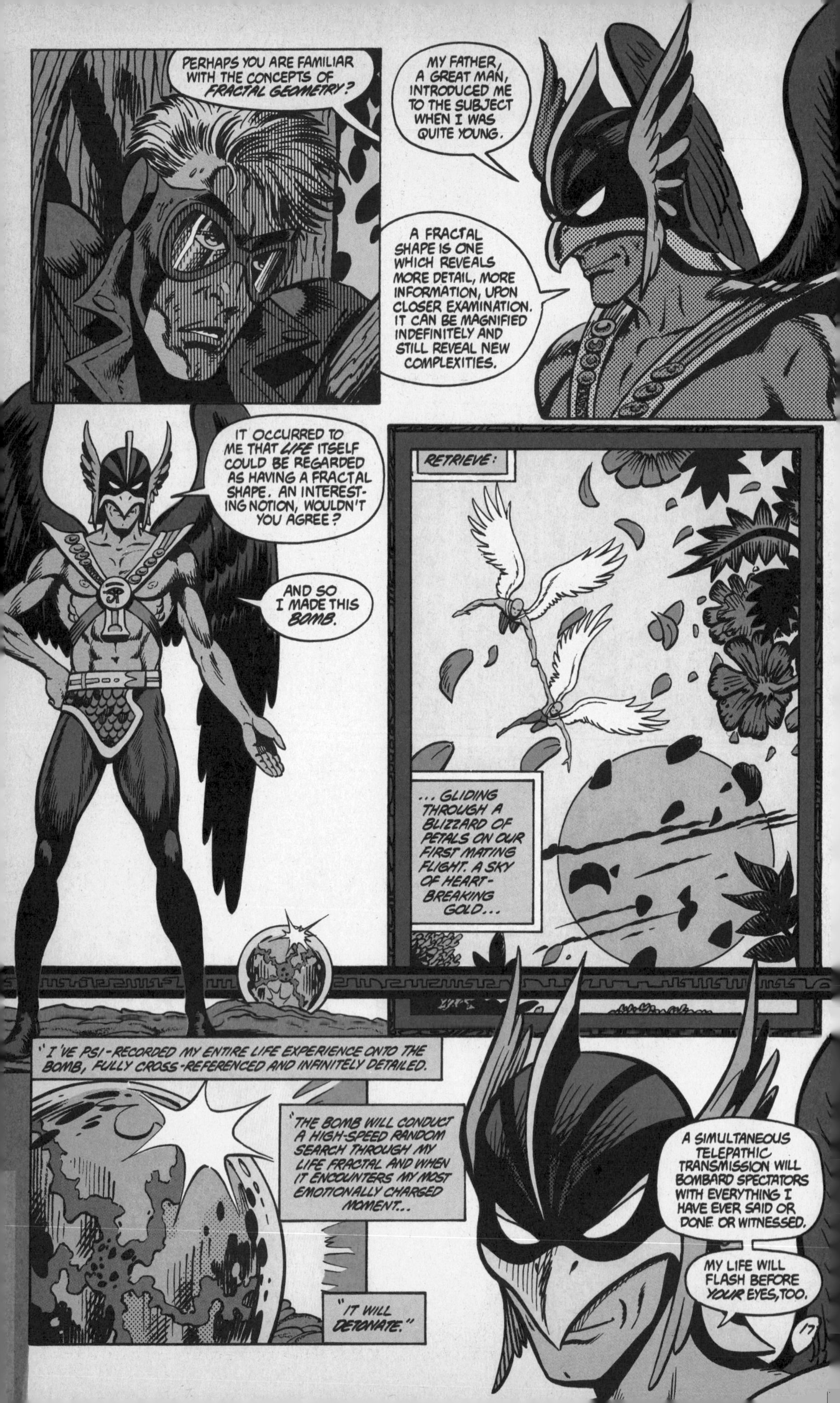
PERHAPS YOU ARE FAMILIAR WITH THE CONCEPTS OF FRACTAL GEOMETRY?
MY FATHER, A GREAT MAN, INTRODUCED ME TO THE SUBJECT WHEN I WAS QUITE YOUNG.
A FRACTAL SHAPE IS ONE WHICH REVEALS MORE DETAIL, MORE INFORMATION, UPON CLOSER EXAMINATION. IT CAN BE MAGNIFIED INDEFINITELY AND STILL REVEAL NEW COMPLEXITIES.
IT OCCURRED TO ME THAT LIFE ITSELF COULD BE REGARDED AS HAVING A FRACTAL SHAPE. AN INTERESTING NOTION, WOULDN'T YOU AGREE?
AND SO I MADE THIS BOMB.
RETRIEVE:
...GLIDING THROUGH A BLIZZARD OF PETALS ON OUR FIRST MATING FLIGHT. A SKY OF HEART-BREAKING GOLD...
"I'VE PSI-RECORDED MY ENTIRE LIFE EXPERIENCE ONTO THE BOMB, FULLY CROSS-REFERENCED AND INFINITELY DETAILED.
"THE BOMB WILL CONDUCT A HIGH-SPEED RANDOM SEARCH THROUGH MY LIFE FRACTAL AND WHEN IT ENCOUNTERS MY MOST EMOTIONALLY CHARGED MOMENT...
"IT WILL DETONATE."
A SIMULTANEOUS TELEPATHIC TRANSMISSION WILL BOMBARD SPECTATORS WITH EVERYTHING I HAVE EVER SAID OR DONE OR WITNESSED.
MY LIFE WILL FLASH BEFORE YOUR EYES, TOO.
17

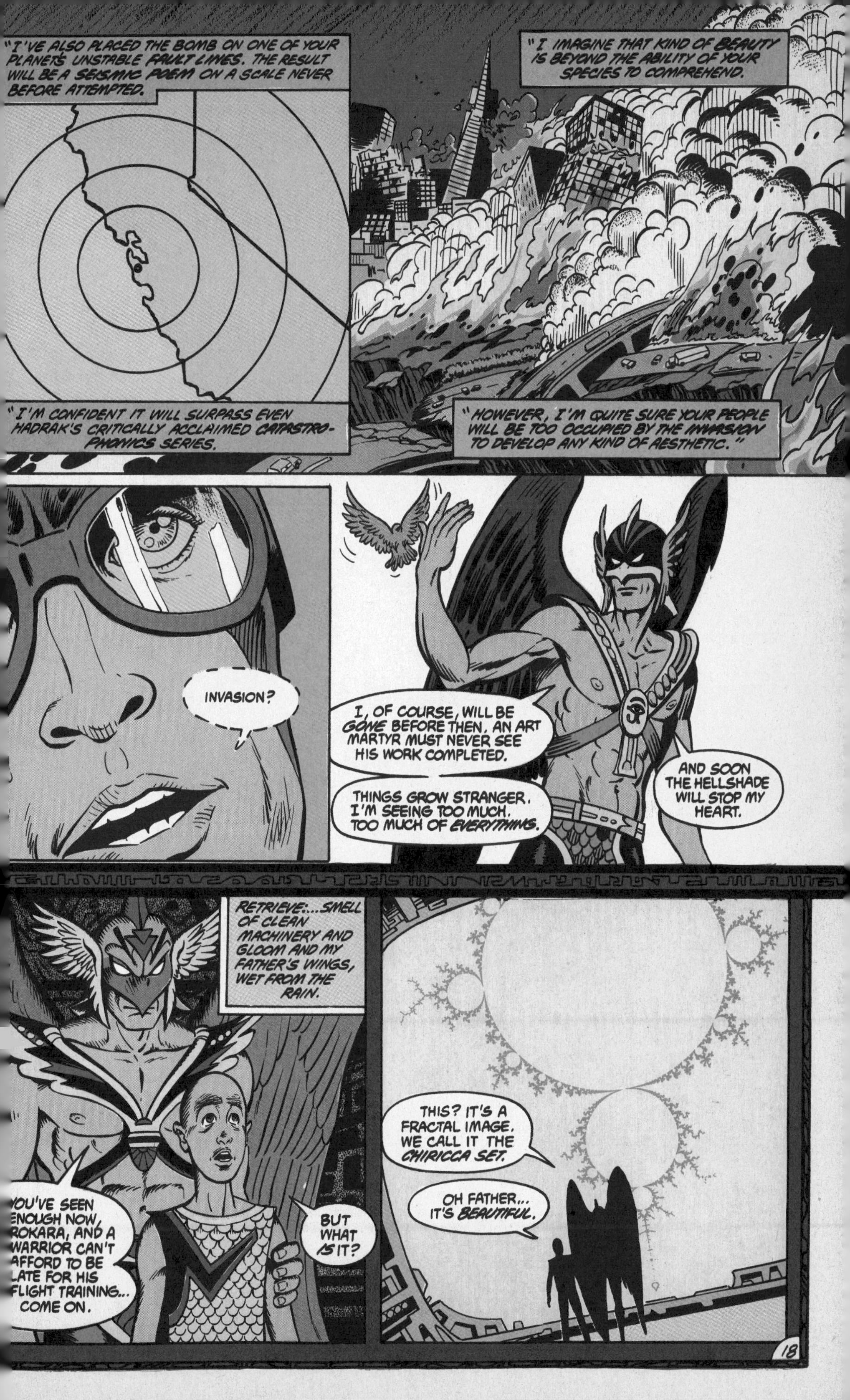
"I'VE ALSO PLACED THE BOMB ON ONE OF YOUR PLANET'S UNSTABLE FAULT LINES. THE RESULT WILL BE A SEISMIC POEM ON A SCALE NEVER BEFORE ATTEMPTED.
"I'M CONFIDENT IT WILL SURPASS EVEN HADRAK'S CRITICALLY ACCLAIMED CATASTRO-PHONICS SERIES.
"I IMAGINE THAT KIND OF BEAUTY IS BEYOND THE ABILITY OF YOUR SPECIES TO COMPREHEND.
"HOWEVER, I'M QUITE SURE YOUR PEOPLE WILL BE TOO OCCUPIED BY THE INVASION TO DEVELOP ANY KIND OF AESTHETIC."
INVASION?
I, OF COURSE, WILL BE GONE BEFORE THEN. AN ART MARTYR MUST NEVER SEE HIS WORK COMPLETED.
THINGS GROW STRANGER. I'M SEEING TOO MUCH. TOO MUCH OF EVERYTHING.
AND SOON THE HELLSHADE WILL STOP MY HEART.
RETRIEVE:...SMELL OF CLEAN MACHINERY AND GLOOM AND MY FATHER'S WINGS, WET FROM THE RAIN.
YOU'VE SEEN ENOUGH NOW, ROKARA, AND A WARRIOR CAN'T AFFORD TO BE LATE FOR HIS FLIGHT TRAINING... COME ON.
BUT WHAT IS IT?
THIS? IT'S A FRACTAL IMAGE. WE CALL IT THE CHIRICCA SET.
OH FATHER... IT'S BEAUTIFUL.
18

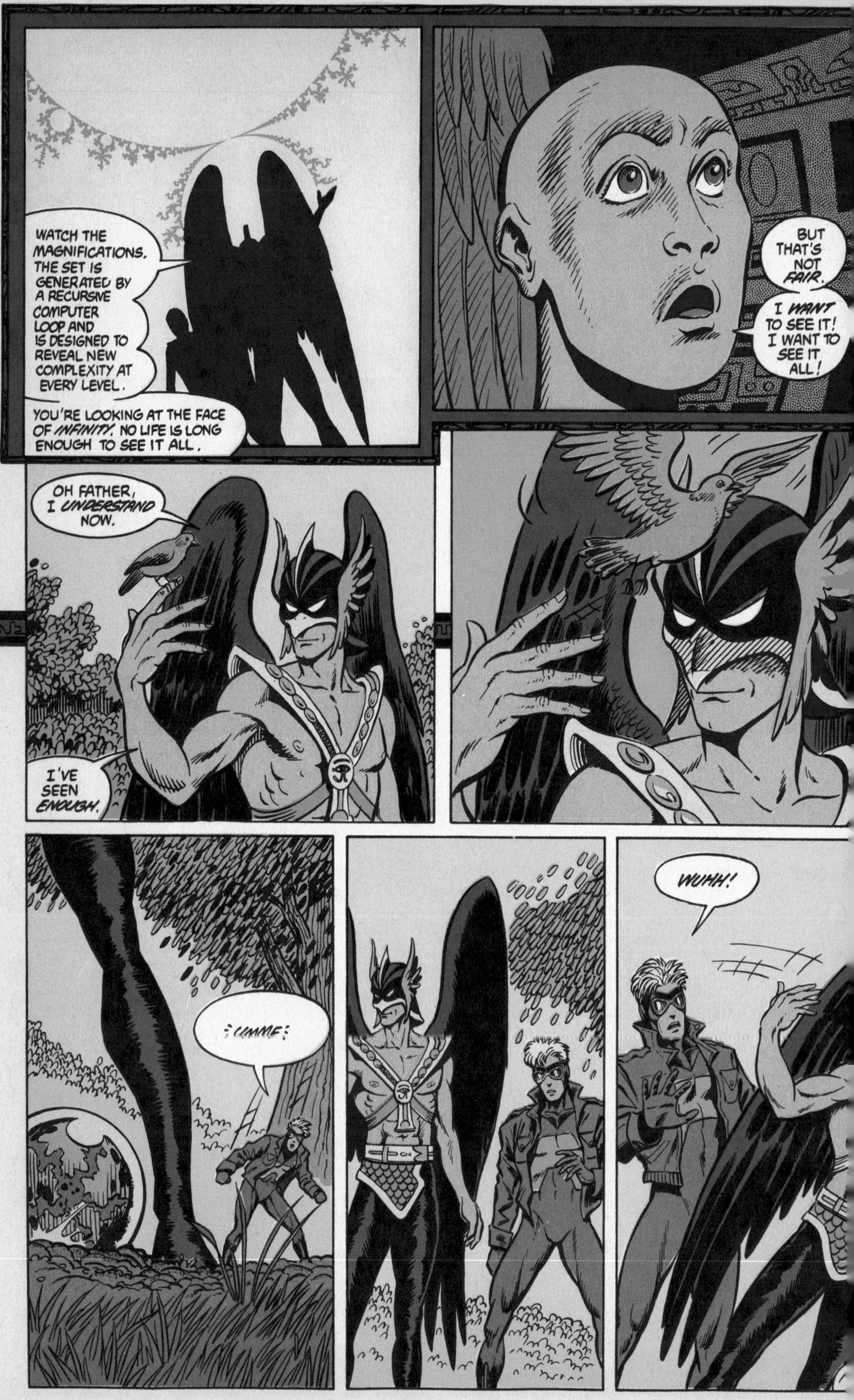
WATCH THE MAGNIFICATIONS. THE SET IS GENERATED BY A RECURSIVE COMPUTER LOOP AND IS DESIGNED TO REVEAL NEW COMPLEXITY AT EVERY LEVEL.
YOU'RE LOOKING AT THE FACE OF *INFINITY.* NO LIFE IS LONG ENOUGH TO SEE IT ALL.
BUT THAT'S NOT *FAIR.*
I *WANT* TO SEE IT! I WANT TO SEE IT ALL!
OH FATHER, I *UNDERSTAND* NOW.
I'VE SEEN *ENOUGH.*
:UMMF:
WUHH!

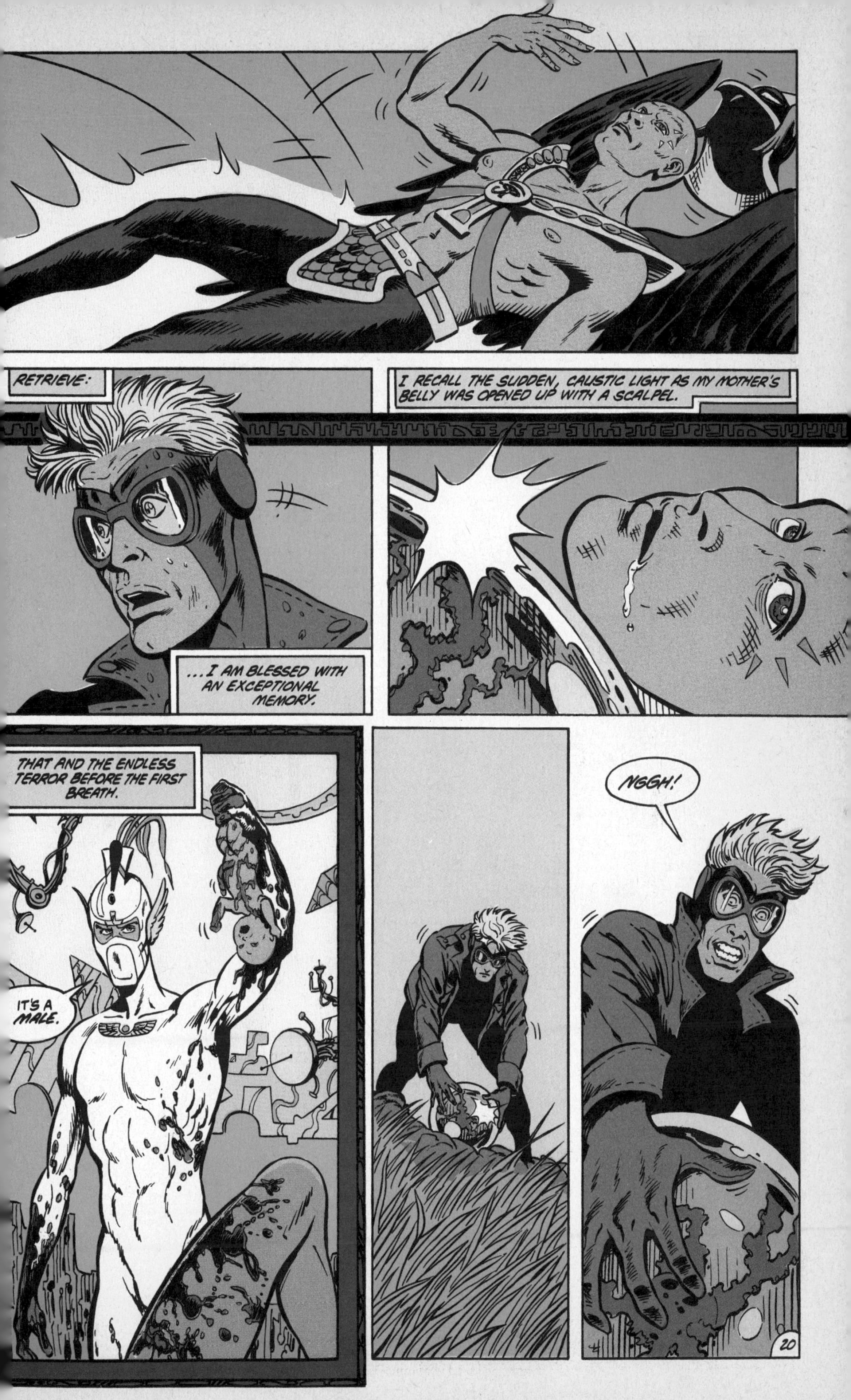
RETRIEVE:
I RECALL THE SUDDEN, CAUSTIC LIGHT AS MY MOTHER'S BELLY WAS OPENED UP WITH A SCALPEL.
...I AM BLESSED WITH AN EXCEPTIONAL MEMORY.
THAT AND THE ENDLESS TERROR BEFORE THE FIRST BREATH.
IT'S A MALE.
NGGH!
20

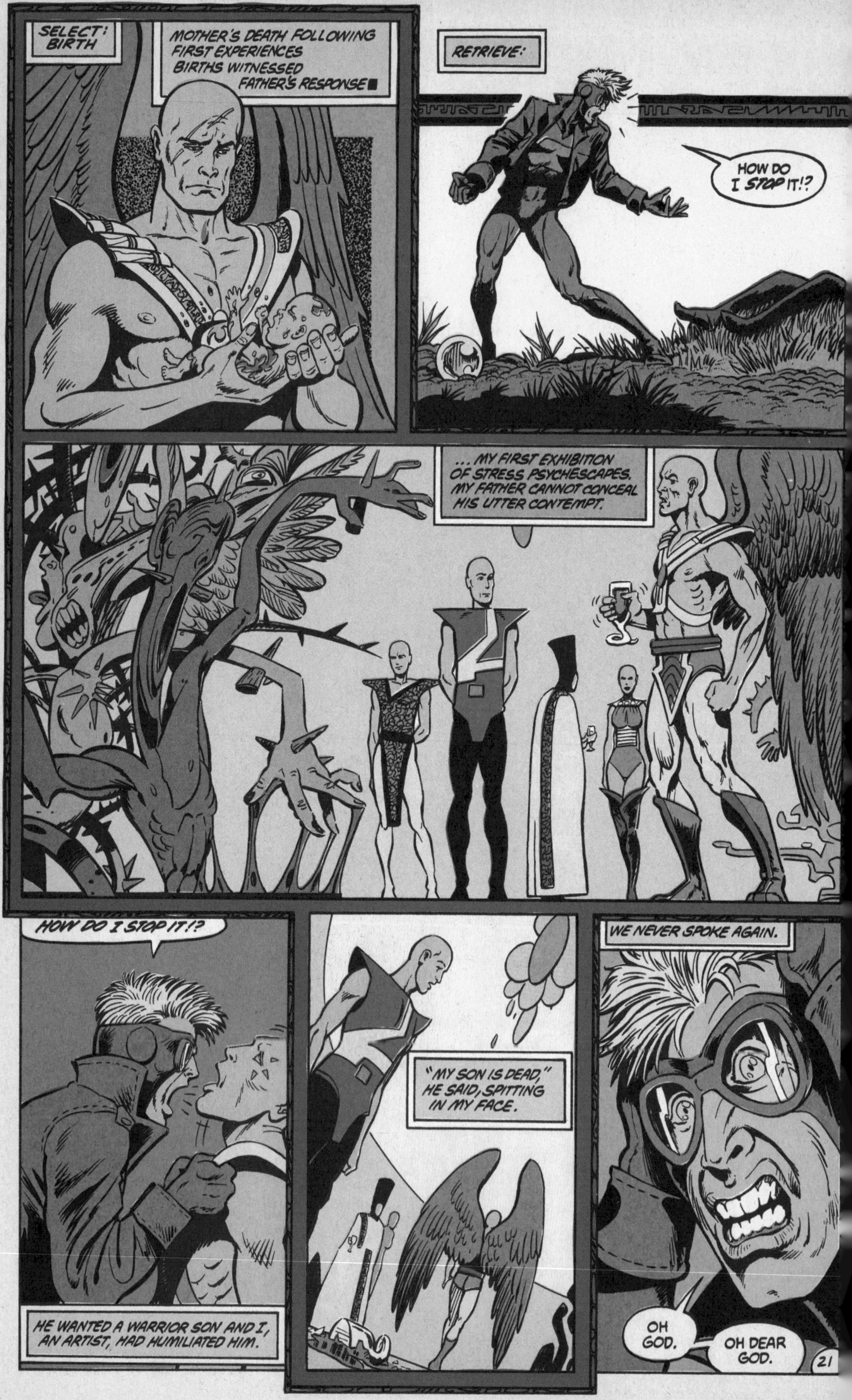
SELECT: BIRTH
MOTHER'S DEATH FOLLOWING
FIRST EXPERIENCES
BIRTHS WITNESSED
FATHER'S RESPONSE
RETRIEVE:
HOW DO I STOP IT!?
... MY FIRST EXHIBITION OF STRESS PSYCHESCAPES. MY FATHER CANNOT CONCEAL HIS UTTER CONTEMPT.
HOW DO I STOP IT!?
HE WANTED A WARRIOR SON AND I, AN ARTIST, HAD HUMILIATED HIM.
"MY SON IS DEAD," HE SAID, SPITTING IN MY FACE.
WE NEVER SPOKE AGAIN.
OH GOD.
OH DEAR GOD.

RETRIEVE... HEAT ON MY FACE AS I WATCH MY FATHER'S FUNERAL ASCENT.

STOP.

STOP.

RETRIEVE:... I WORK IN A FEVER, WITHOUT FOOD, WITHOUT SLEEP, SCORCHED BY THE HEAT OF THE PSYCHOPLASTIC KILNS.

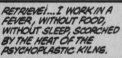

FOR GOD'S SAKE, JUST STOP!

DAYS PASS AND, IN A TRANCE STATE NOW, I WORK ON, DRIVEN, POSSESSED...

TURNING SLOWLY, GIVING OFF SPARKS, HE IS BORNE UP TO HEAVEN BY ANTI-GRAVITY.

MERCIFULLY, THE FIRE DRIES THE TEARS ON MY FACE. MY EMOTION GOES UNNOTICED.

AND ON THE FIFTH DAY I WAKE, EMPTIED AND DAZED.

SOME VAST SHAPE OBSCURES THE SUN.

STOP!

OH FATHER, I HAVE SO MANY THINGS I WANTED TO SAY TO YOU.

I AM COLD AND AFRAID. I NEED TO URINATE.

TERRIFIED, I RAISE MY HEAD.

I LOOK UP.

22

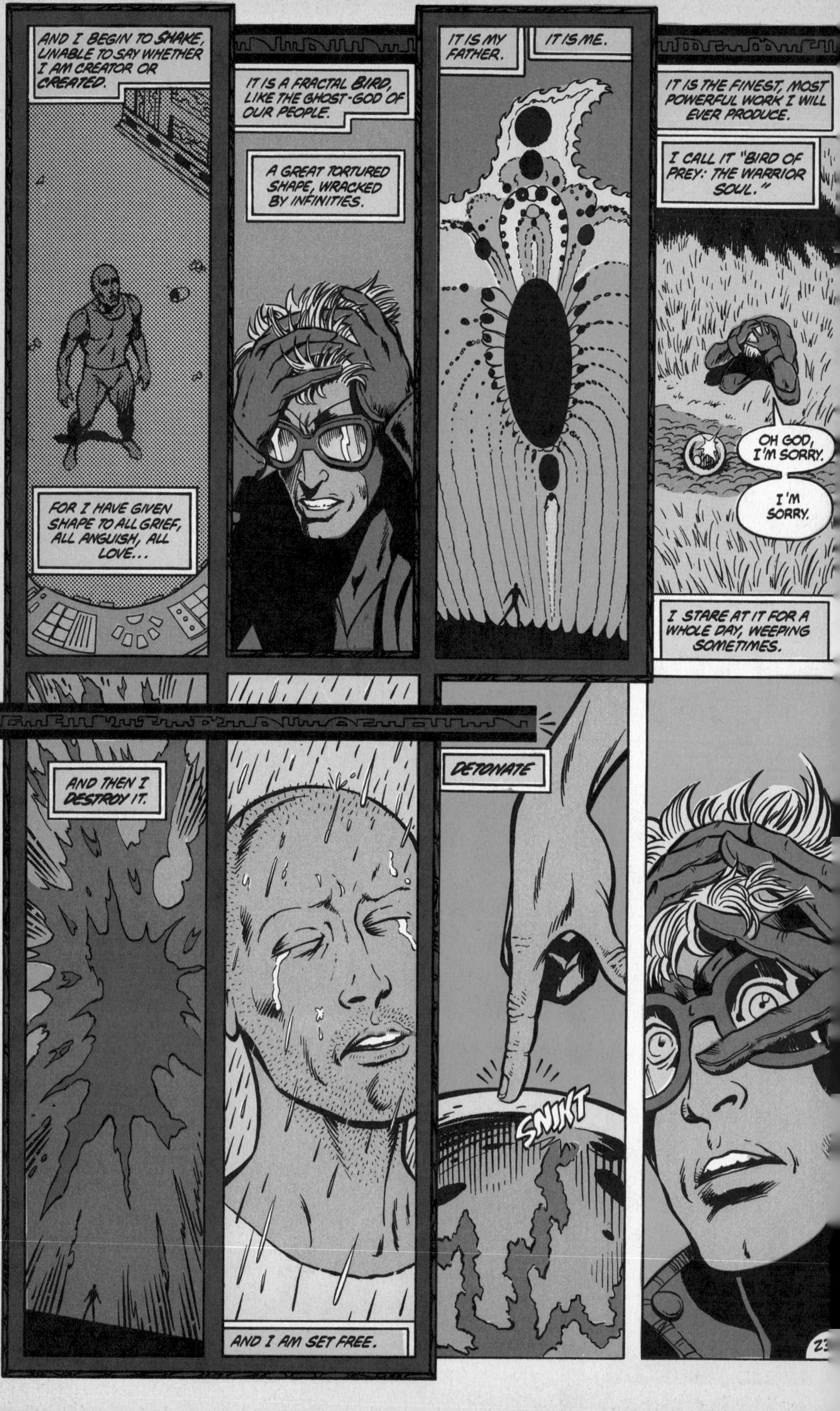
AND I BEGIN TO SHAKE, UNABLE TO SAY WHETHER I AM CREATOR OR CREATED.
FOR I HAVE GIVEN SHAPE TO ALL GRIEF, ALL ANGUISH, ALL LOVE...
IT IS A FRACTAL BIRD, LIKE THE GHOST-GOD OF OUR PEOPLE.
A GREAT TORTURED SHAPE, WRACKED BY INFINITIES.
IT IS MY FATHER.
IT IS ME.
IT IS THE FINEST, MOST POWERFUL WORK I WILL EVER PRODUCE.
I CALL IT "BIRD OF PREY: THE WARRIOR SOUL."
OH GOD, I'M SORRY.
I'M SORRY.
I STARE AT IT FOR A WHOLE DAY, WEEPING SOMETIMES.
AND THEN I DESTROY IT.
AND I AM SET FREE.
DETONATE
SNIKT

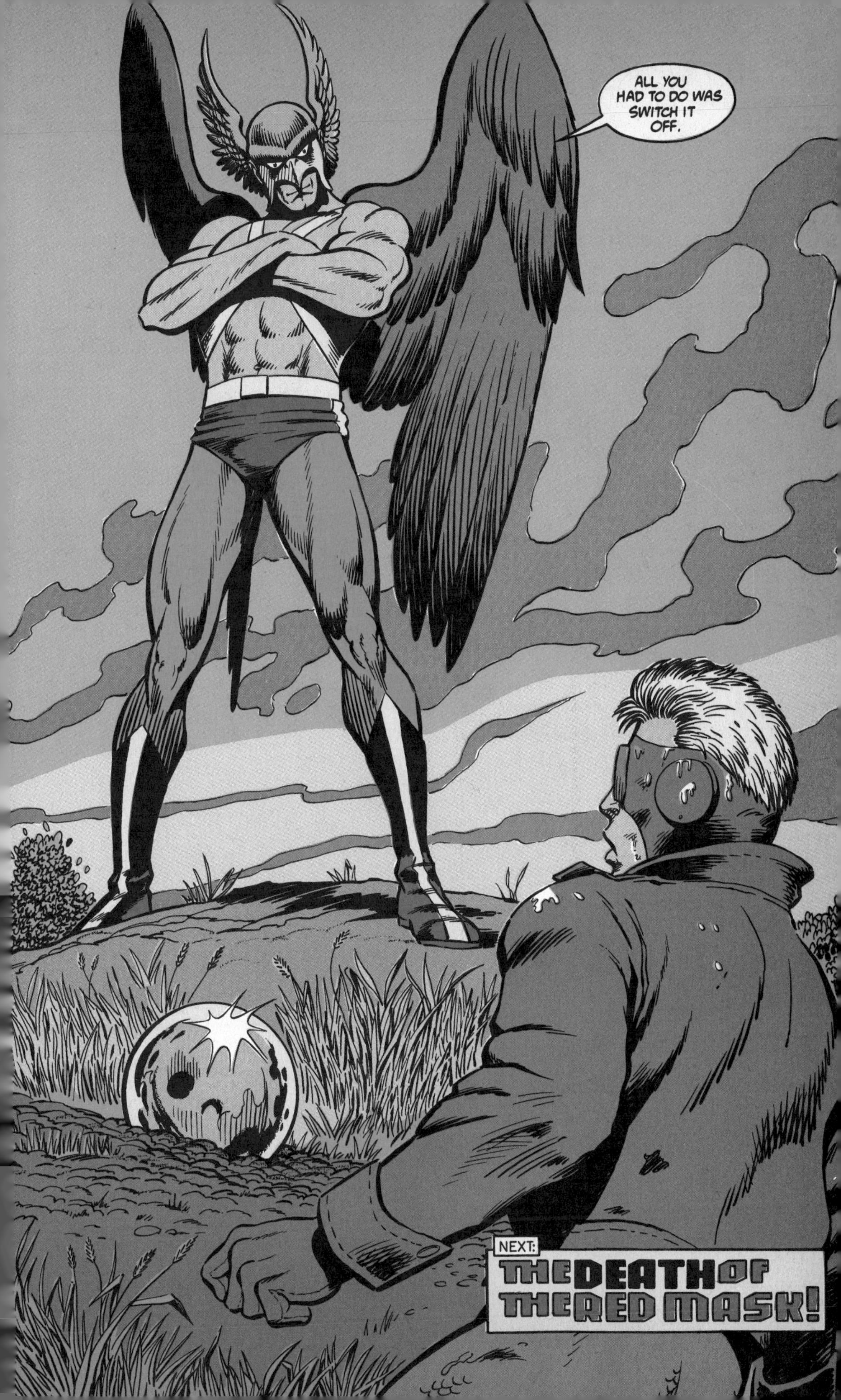
ALL YOU HAD TO DO WAS SWITCH IT OFF.
NEXT:
THE DEATH OF THE RED MASK!

CHAPTER
SEVEN

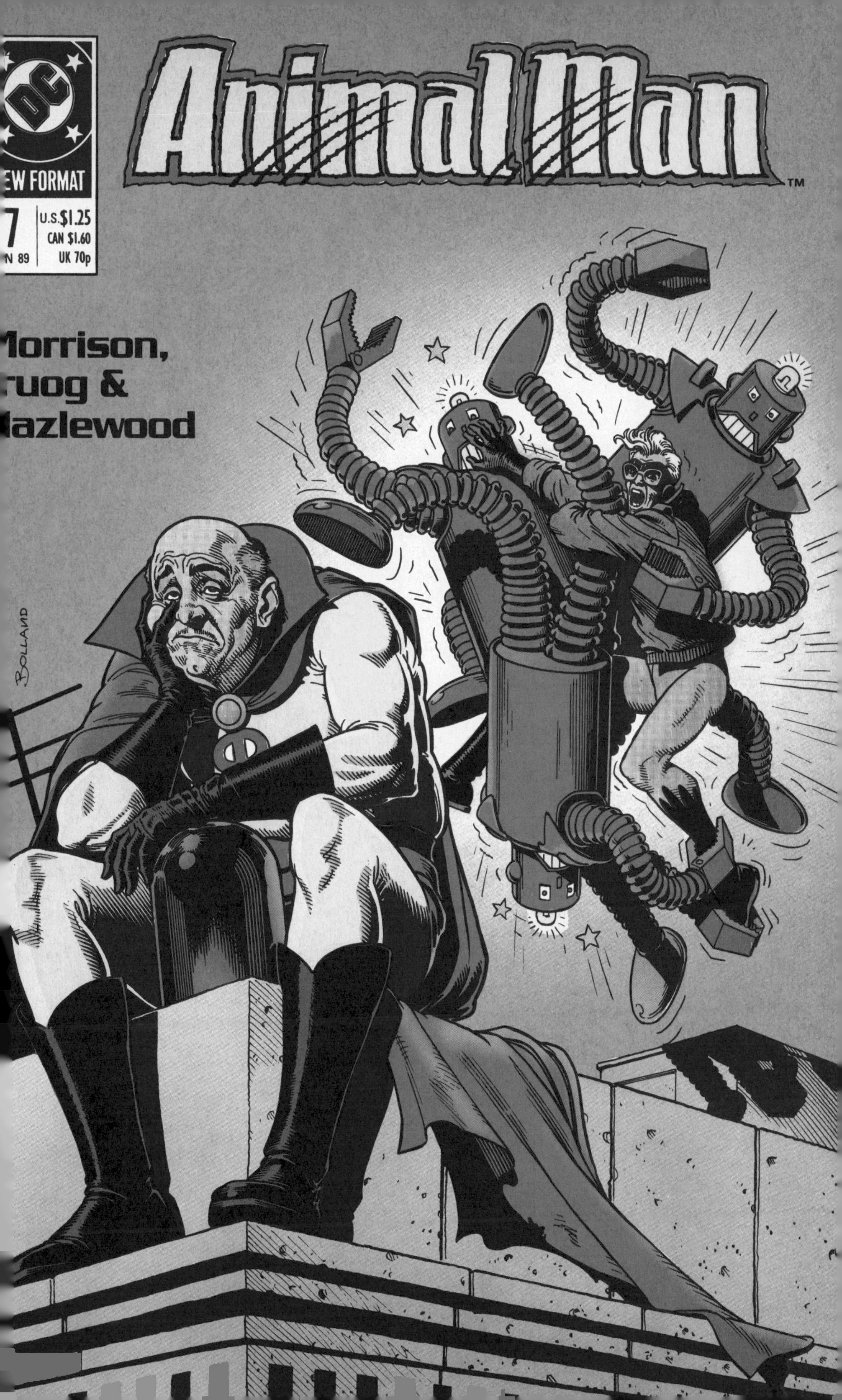

Animal Man™
EW FORMAT
7
N 89
U.S. $1.25
CAN $1.60
UK 70p
lorrison,
ruog &
lazlewood
BOLLAND

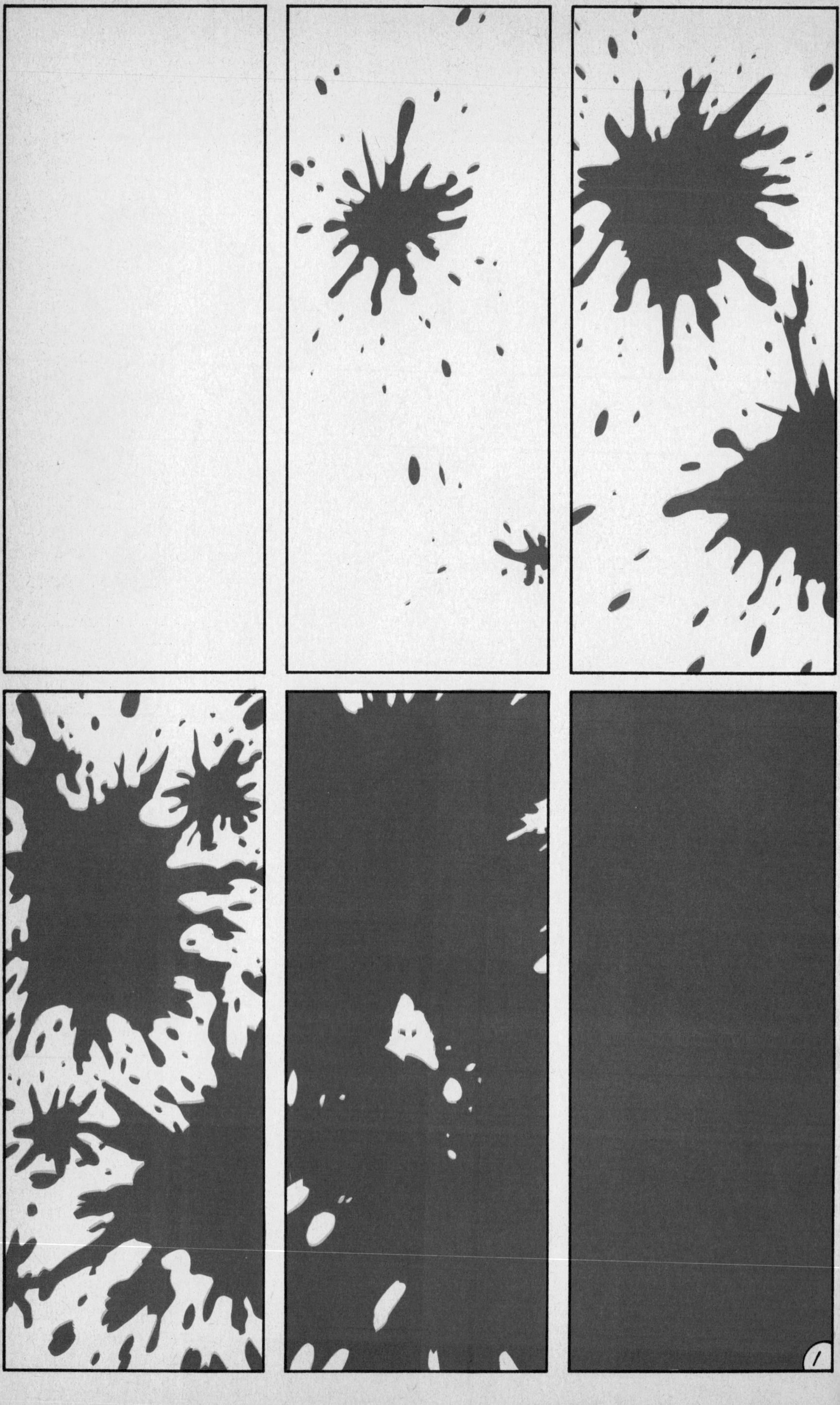
1

G-4141

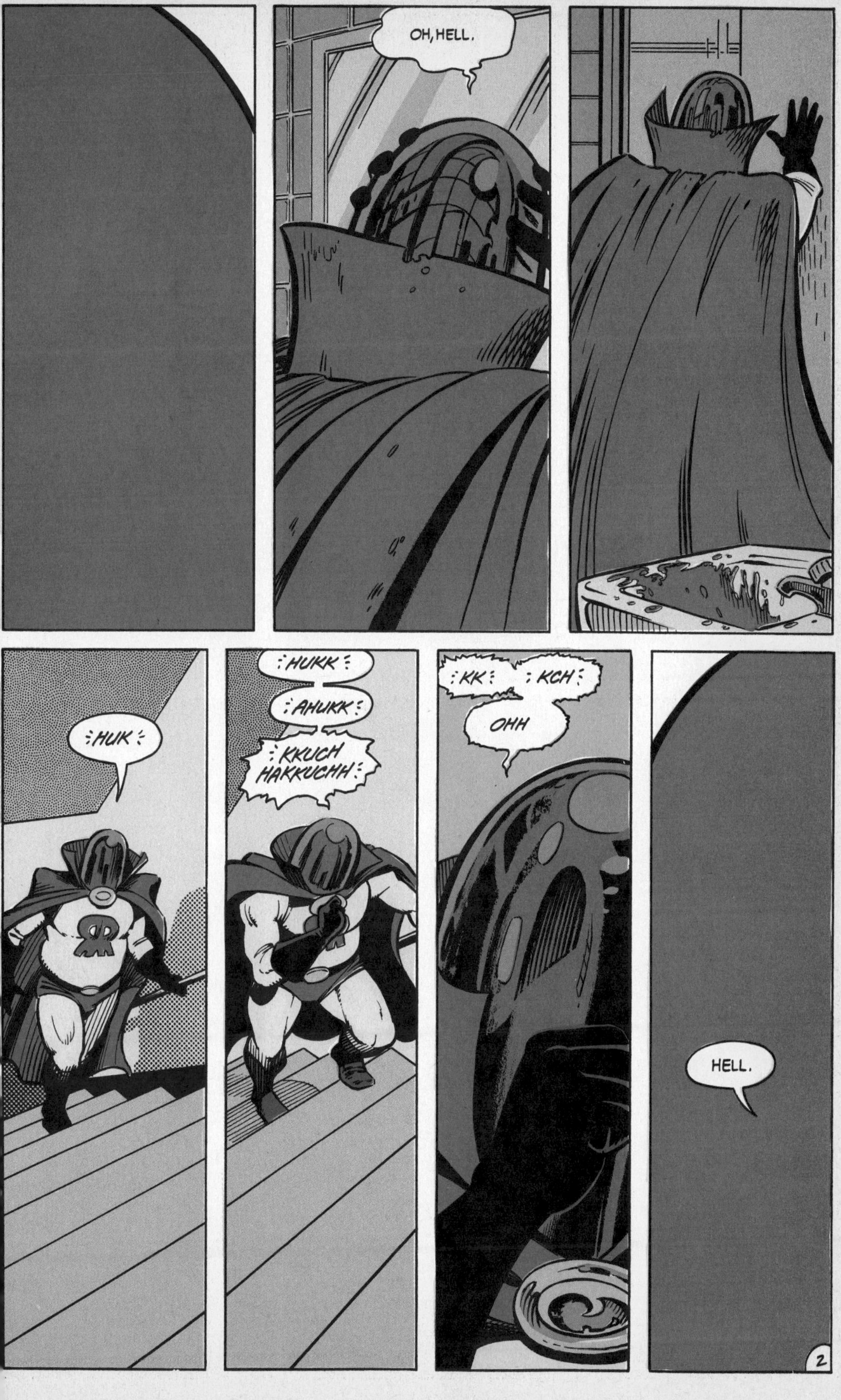
OH, HELL.
HUK
HUKK
AHUKK
KKUCH HAKKUCHH
KK
KCH
OHH
HELL.

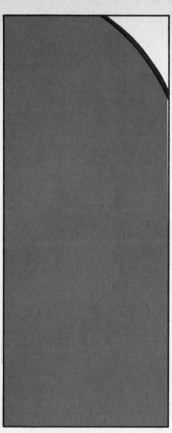

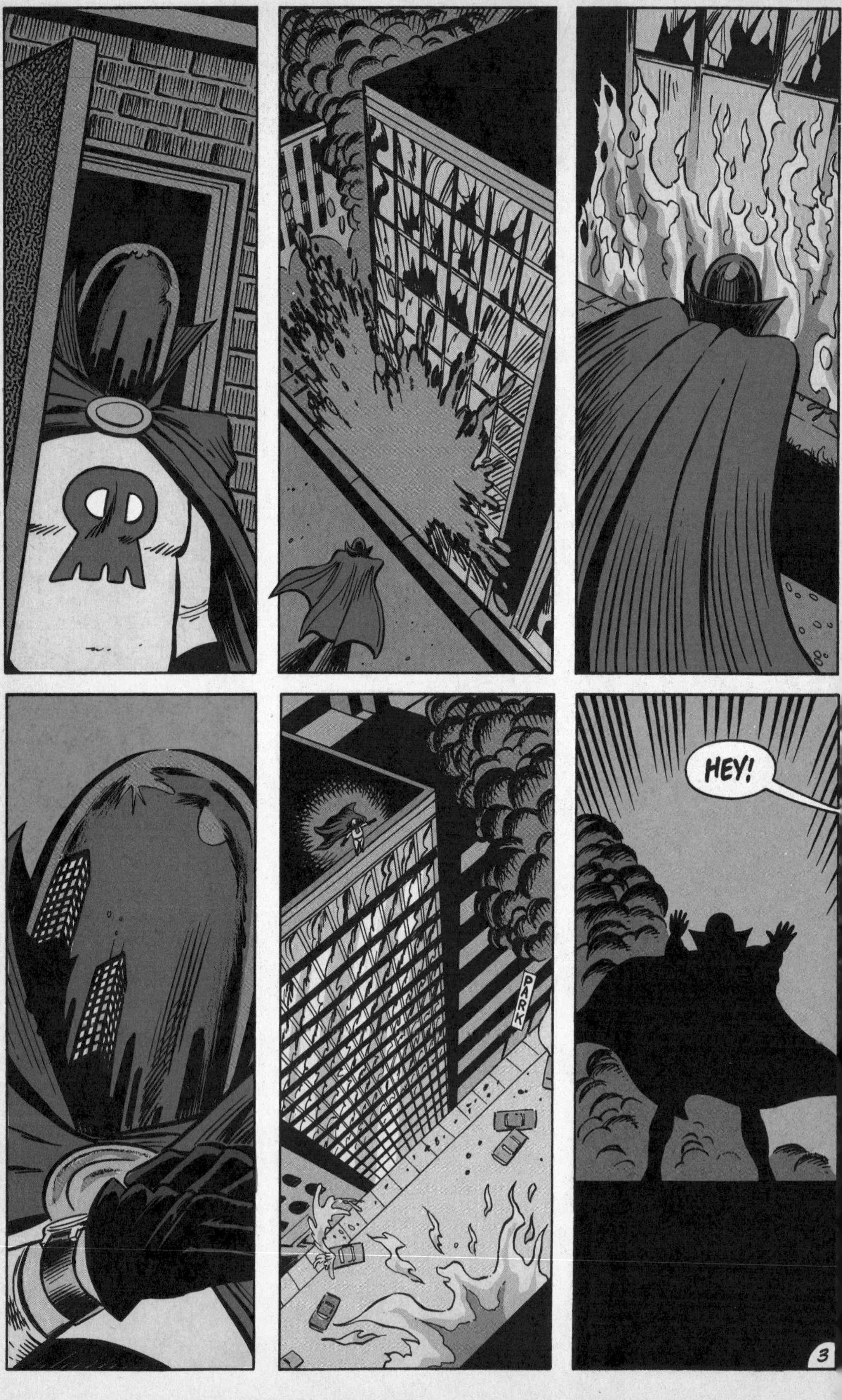
PARK
HEY!

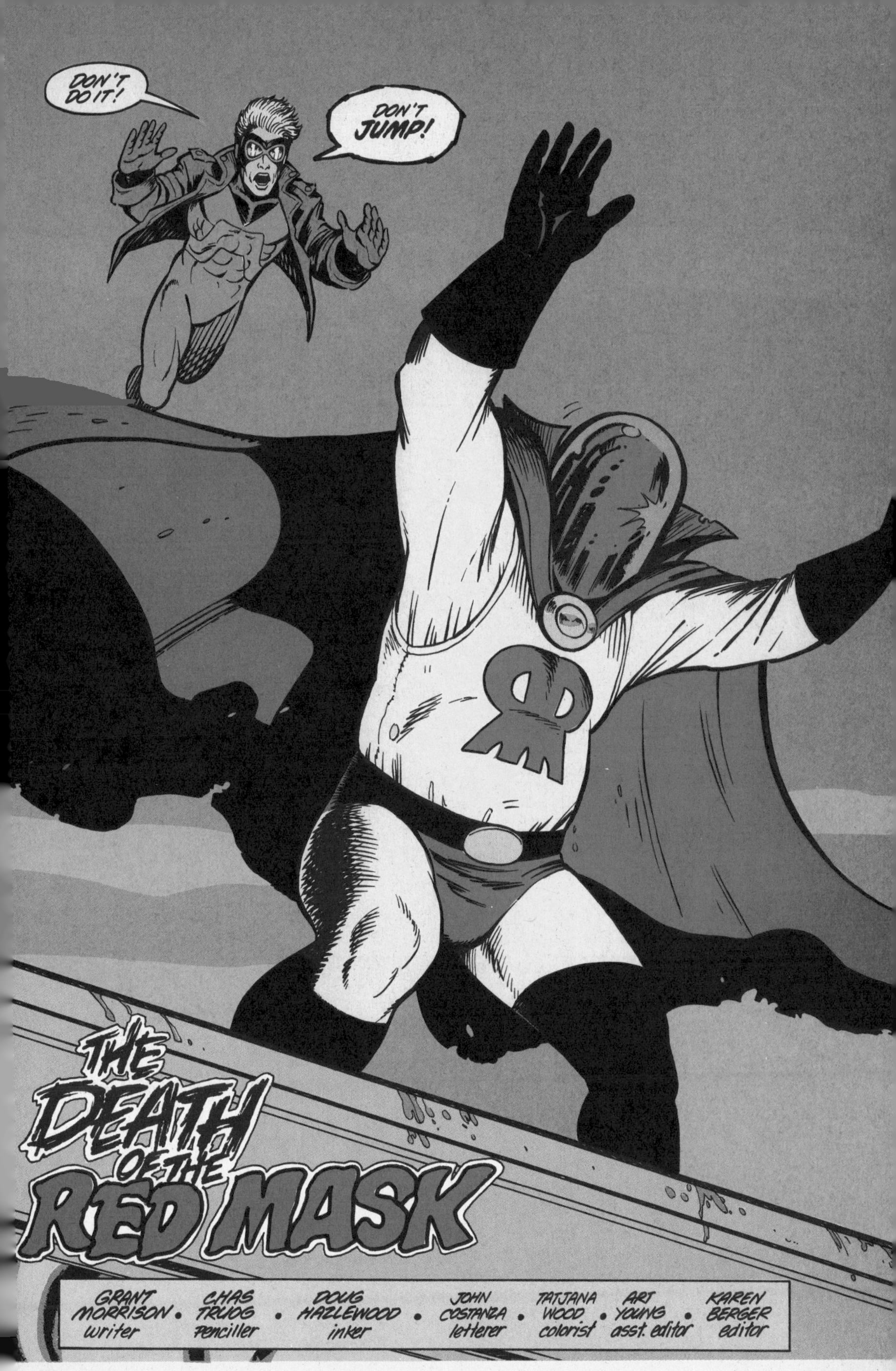
DON'T DO IT!
DON'T JUMP!
THE DEATH OF THE RED MASK
GRANT MORRISON writer • CHAS TRUOG penciller • DOUG HAZLEWOOD inker • JOHN COSTANZA letterer • TATJANA WOOD colorist • ART YOUNG asst. editor • KAREN BERGER editor

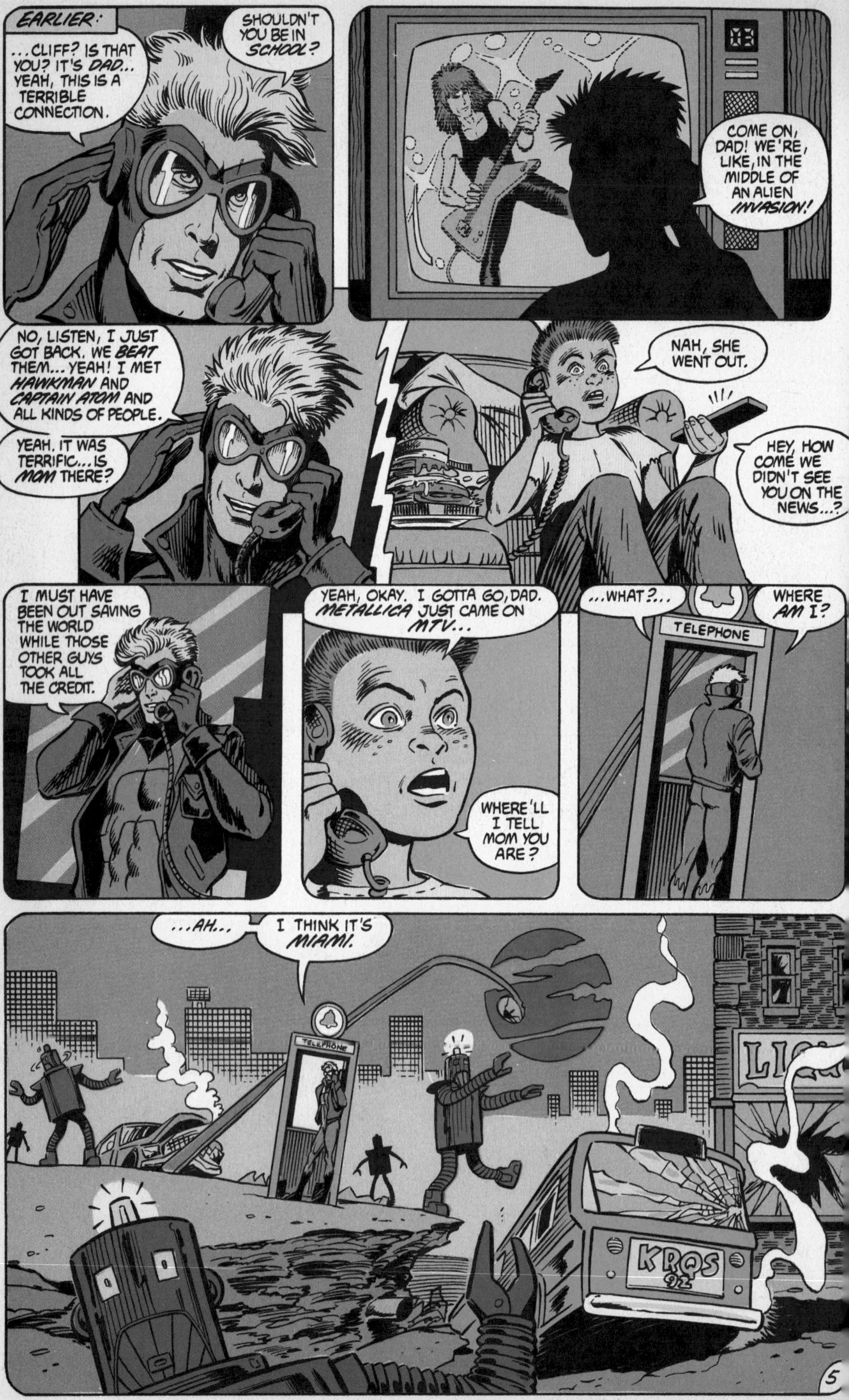
EARLIER:
...CLIFF? IS THAT YOU? IT'S DAD... YEAH, THIS IS A TERRIBLE CONNECTION.
SHOULDN'T YOU BE IN SCHOOL?
COME ON, DAD! WE'RE, LIKE, IN THE MIDDLE OF AN ALIEN INVASION!
NO, LISTEN, I JUST GOT BACK. WE BEAT THEM... YEAH! I MET HAWKMAN AND CAPTAIN ATOM AND ALL KINDS OF PEOPLE.
YEAH. IT WAS TERRIFIC... IS MOM THERE?
NAH, SHE WENT OUT.
HEY, HOW COME WE DIDN'T SEE YOU ON THE NEWS...?
I MUST HAVE BEEN OUT SAVING THE WORLD WHILE THOSE OTHER GUYS TOOK ALL THE CREDIT.
YEAH, OKAY. I GOTTA GO, DAD. METALLICA JUST CAME ON MTV...
WHERE'LL I TELL MOM YOU ARE?
...WHAT?...
TELEPHONE
WHERE AM I?
...AH...
I THINK IT'S MIAMI.
TELEPHONE
KRQS 92
5

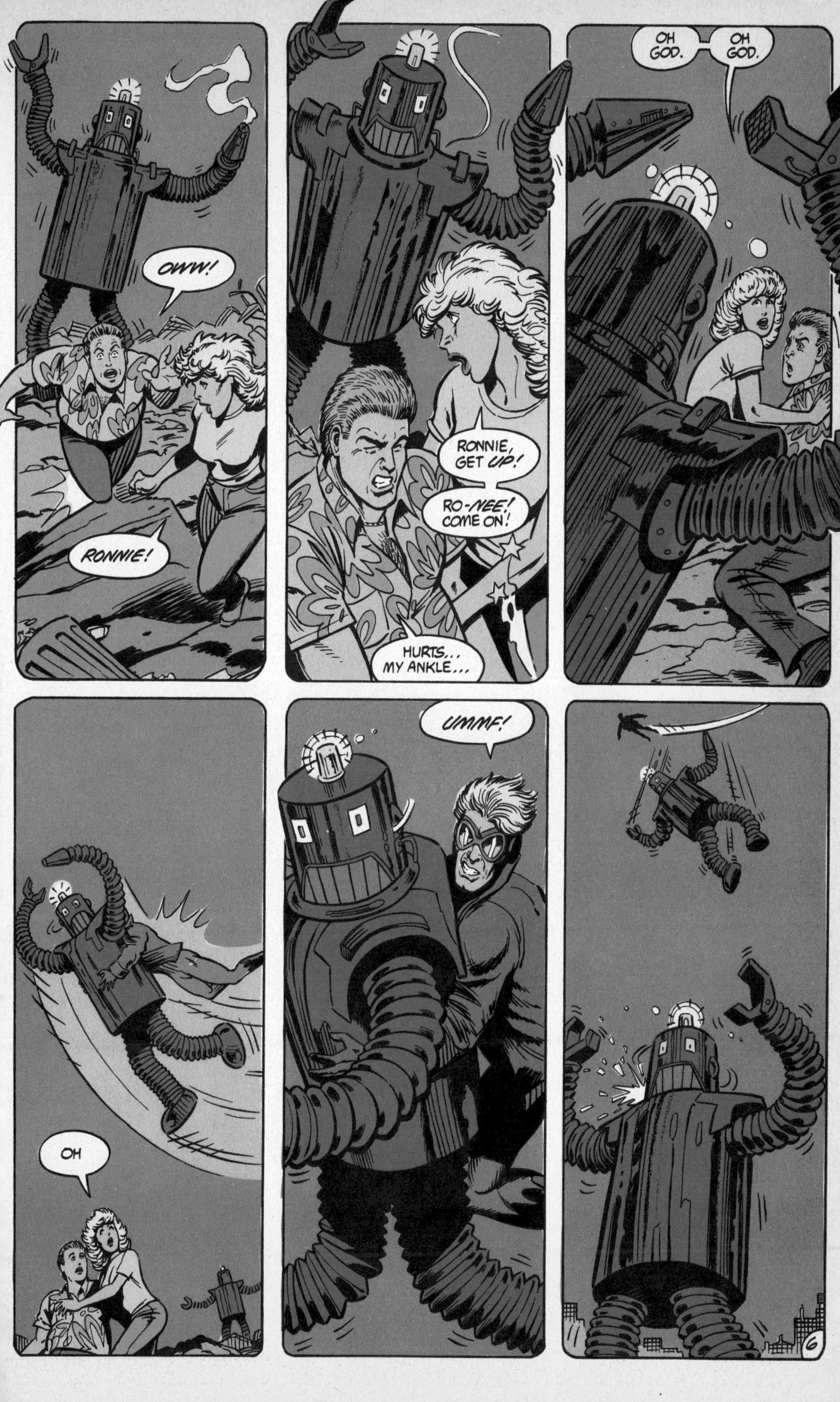
OWW!
RONNIE!
RONNIE, GET UP!
RO-NEE! COME ON!
HURTS... MY ANKLE...
OH GOD.
OH GOD.
OH
UMMF!
6

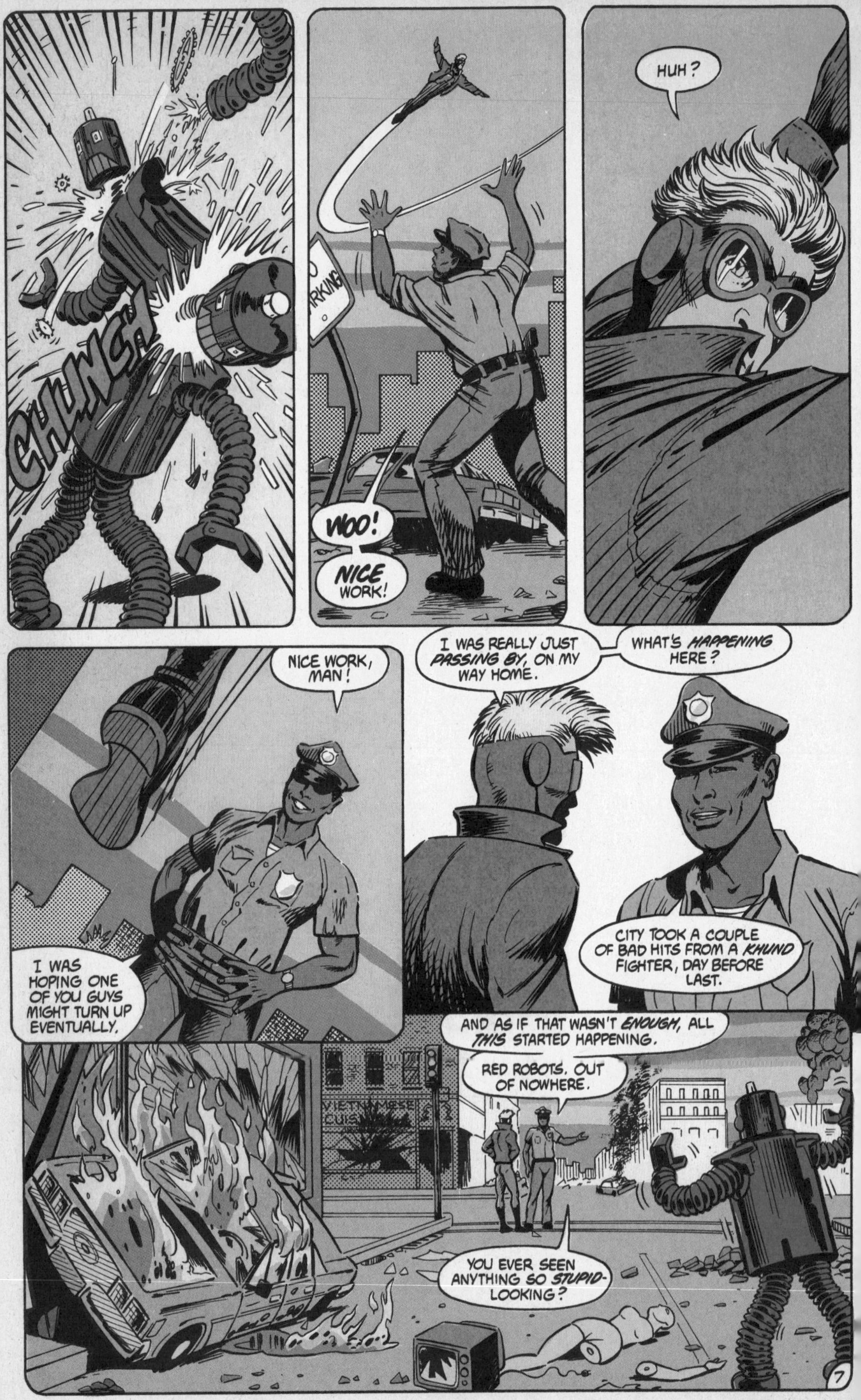

CHUNCH
NO PARKING
WOO!
NICE WORK!
HUH?
NICE WORK, MAN!
I WAS HOPING ONE OF YOU GUYS MIGHT TURN UP EVENTUALLY.
WHAT'S HAPPENING HERE?
I WAS REALLY JUST PASSING BY, ON MY WAY HOME.
CITY TOOK A COUPLE OF BAD HITS FROM A KHUND FIGHTER, DAY BEFORE LAST.
AND AS IF THAT WASN'T ENOUGH, ALL THIS STARTED HAPPENING.
RED ROBOTS. OUT OF NOWHERE.
YOU EVER SEEN ANYTHING SO STUPID-LOOKING?
VIETNAMESE CUISINE
7

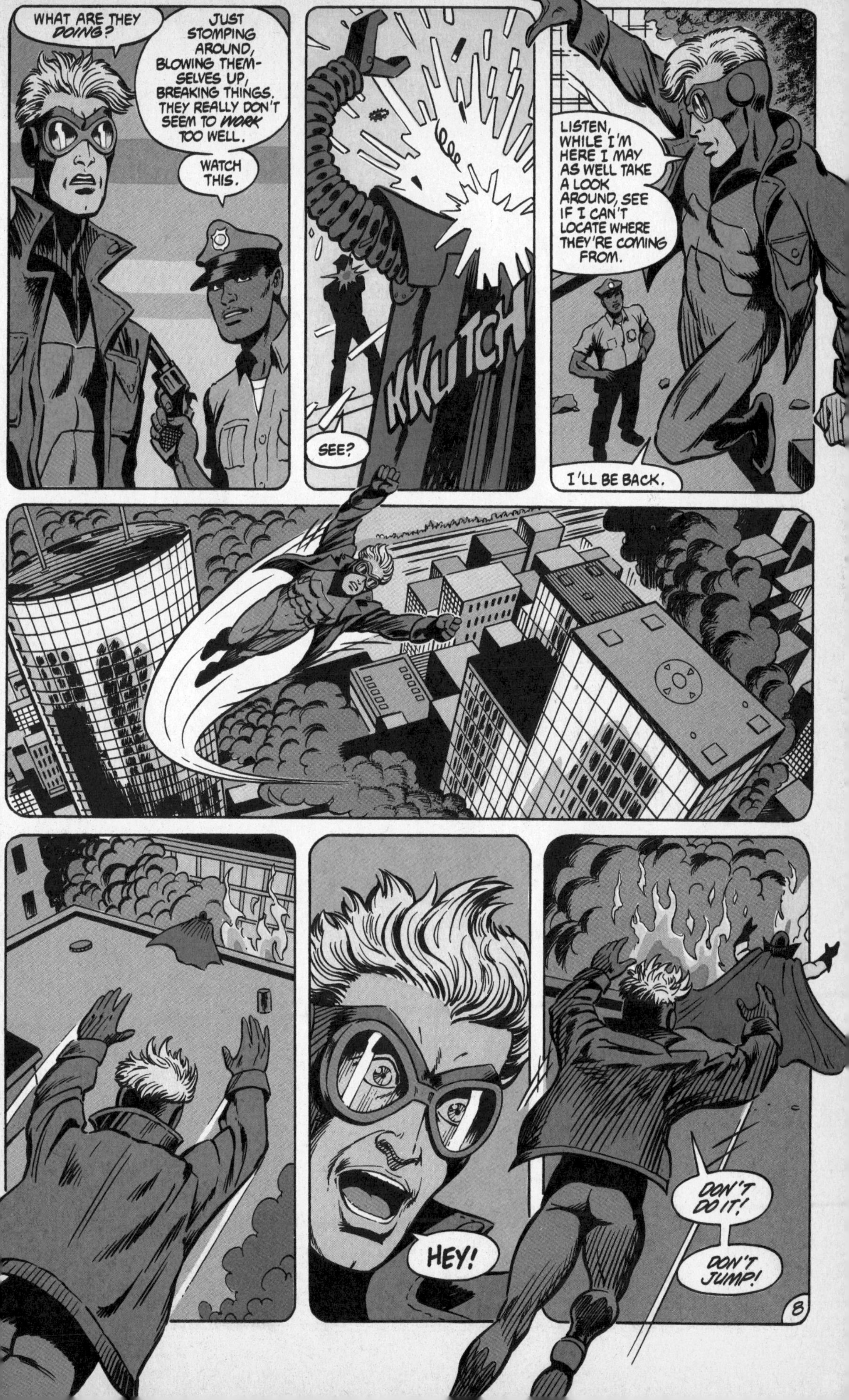
WHAT ARE THEY DOING?
JUST STOMPING AROUND, BLOWING THEMSELVES UP, BREAKING THINGS. THEY REALLY DON'T SEEM TO WORK TOO WELL.
WATCH THIS.
KKUTCH
SEE?
LISTEN, WHILE I'M HERE I MAY AS WELL TAKE A LOOK AROUND, SEE IF I CAN'T LOCATE WHERE THEY'RE COMING FROM.
I'LL BE BACK.
HEY!
DON'T DO IT!
DON'T JUMP!
8

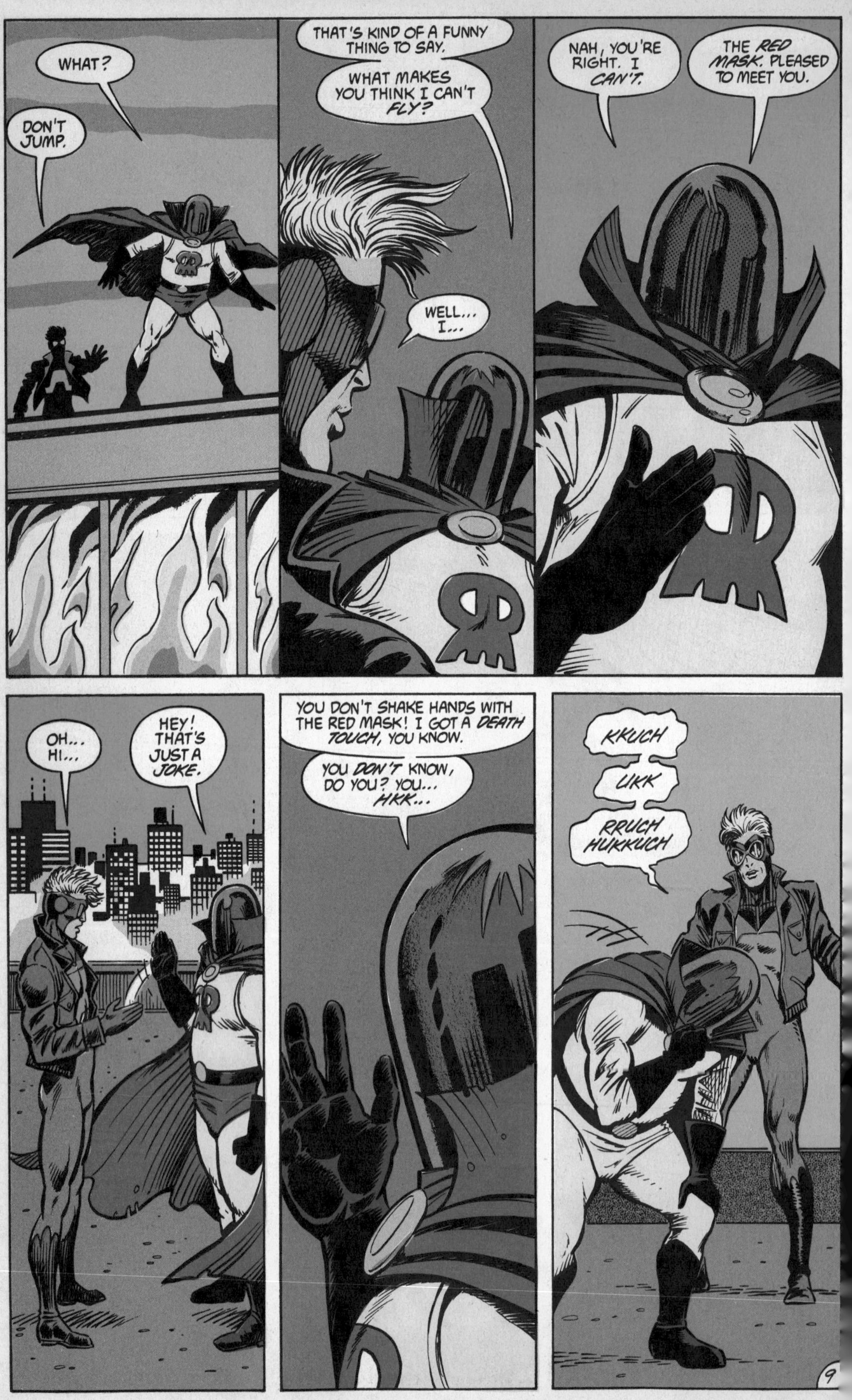
DON'T JUMP.
WHAT?
THAT'S KIND OF A FUNNY THING TO SAY.
WHAT MAKES YOU THINK I CAN'T FLY?
WELL... I...
NAH, YOU'RE RIGHT. I CAN'T.
THE RED MASK. PLEASED TO MEET YOU.
OH... HI...
HEY! THAT'S JUST A JOKE.
YOU DON'T SHAKE HANDS WITH THE RED MASK! I GOT A DEATH TOUCH, YOU KNOW.
YOU DON'T KNOW, DO YOU? YOU... HKK...
KKUCH
UKK
RRUCH HUKKUCH

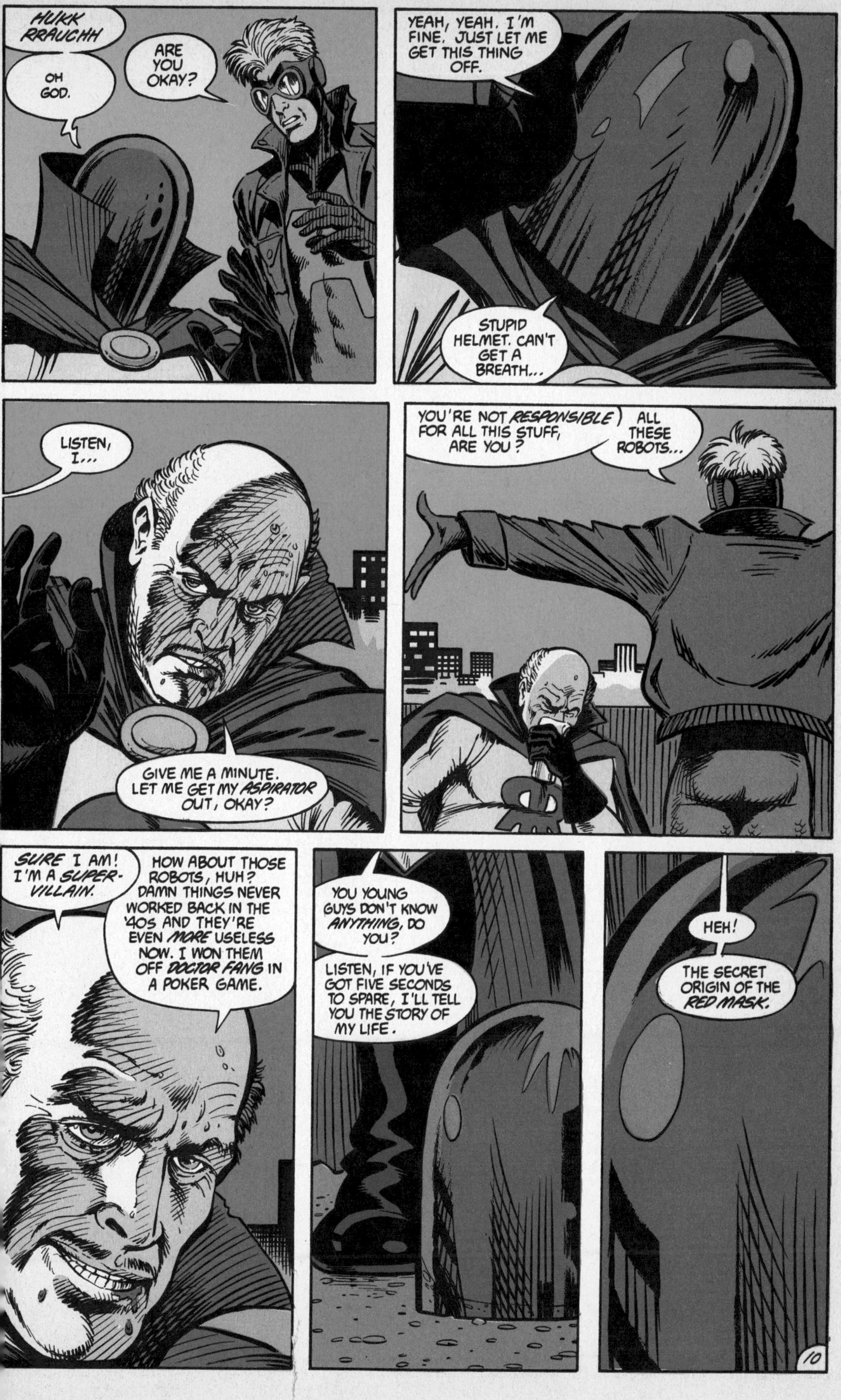
HUKK RRAUCHH
OH GOD.
ARE YOU OKAY?
YEAH, YEAH. I'M FINE. JUST LET ME GET THIS THING OFF.
STUPID HELMET. CAN'T GET A BREATH...
LISTEN, I...
GIVE ME A MINUTE. LET ME GET MY ASPIRATOR OUT, OKAY?
YOU'RE NOT RESPONSIBLE FOR ALL THIS STUFF, ARE YOU?
ALL THESE ROBOTS...
SURE I AM! I'M A SUPER-VILLAIN.
HOW ABOUT THOSE ROBOTS, HUH? DAMN THINGS NEVER WORKED BACK IN THE '40S AND THEY'RE EVEN MORE USELESS NOW. I WON THEM OFF DOCTOR FANG IN A POKER GAME.
YOU YOUNG GUYS DON'T KNOW ANYTHING, DO YOU?
LISTEN, IF YOU'VE GOT FIVE SECONDS TO SPARE, I'LL TELL YOU THE STORY OF MY LIFE.
HEH!
THE SECRET ORIGIN OF THE RED MASK.
10

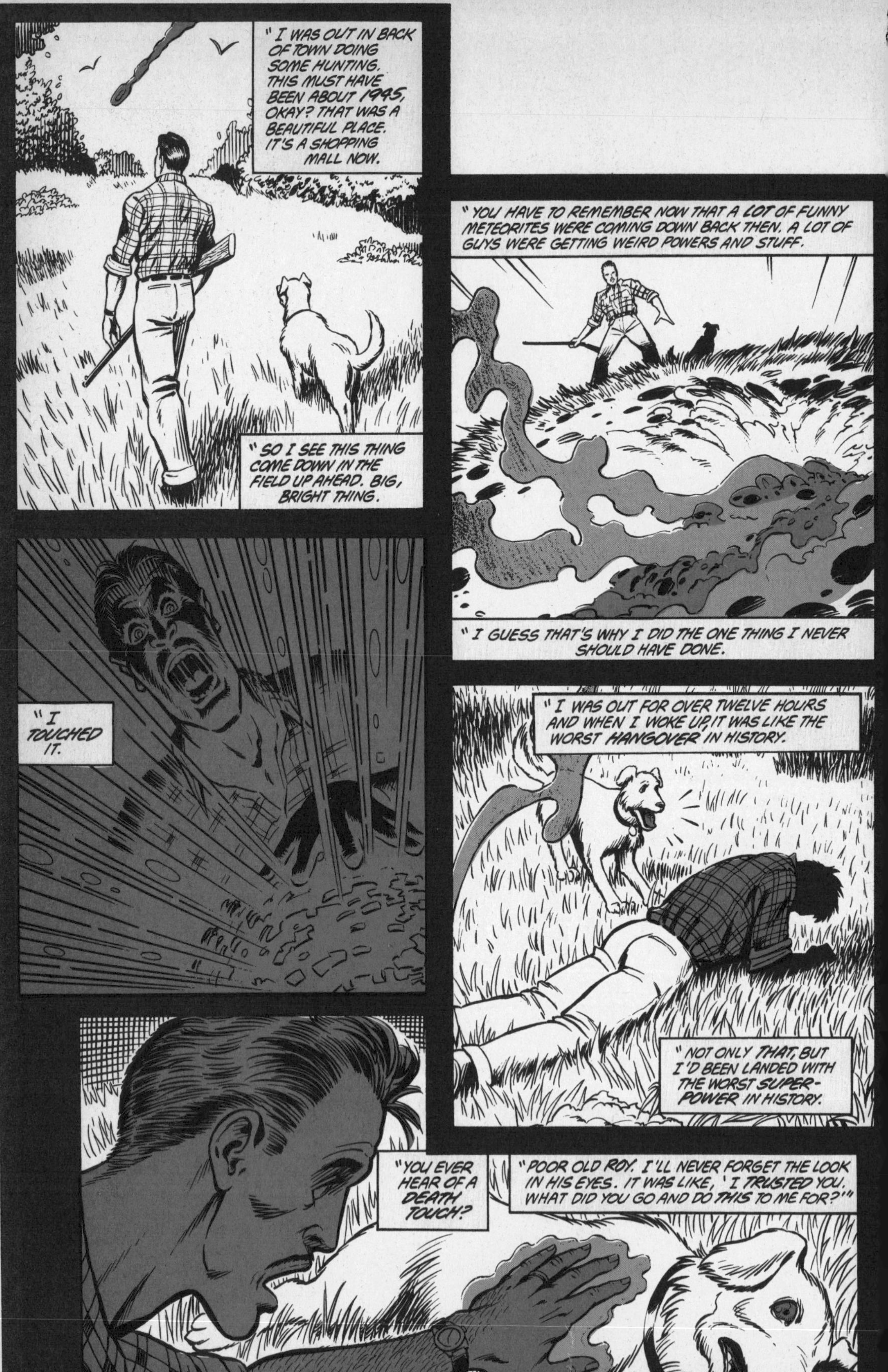
"I WAS OUT IN BACK OF TOWN DOING SOME HUNTING. THIS MUST HAVE BEEN ABOUT 1945, OKAY? THAT WAS A BEAUTIFUL PLACE. IT'S A SHOPPING MALL NOW.
"SO I SEE THIS THING COME DOWN IN THE FIELD UP AHEAD. BIG, BRIGHT THING.
"YOU HAVE TO REMEMBER NOW THAT A LOT OF FUNNY METEORITES WERE COMING DOWN BACK THEN. A LOT OF GUYS WERE GETTING WEIRD POWERS AND STUFF.
"I GUESS THAT'S WHY I DID THE ONE THING I NEVER SHOULD HAVE DONE.
"I TOUCHED IT.
"I WAS OUT FOR OVER TWELVE HOURS AND WHEN I WOKE UP, IT WAS LIKE THE WORST HANGOVER IN HISTORY.
"NOT ONLY THAT, BUT I'D BEEN LANDED WITH THE WORST SUPER-POWER IN HISTORY.
"YOU EVER HEAR OF A DEATH TOUCH?
"POOR OLD ROY. I'LL NEVER FORGET THE LOOK IN HIS EYES. IT WAS LIKE, 'I TRUSTED YOU. WHAT DID YOU GO AND DO THIS TO ME FOR?'"
11

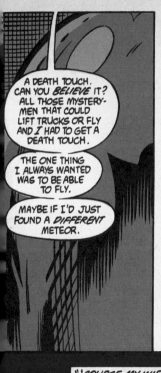

A DEATH TOUCH. CAN YOU *BELIEVE* IT? ALL THOSE MYSTERY-MEN THAT COULD LIFT TRUCKS OR FLY AND *I* HAD TO GET A DEATH TOUCH.

THE ONE THING I ALWAYS WANTED WAS TO BE ABLE TO FLY.

MAYBE IF I'D JUST FOUND A *DIFFERENT* METEOR.

I MEAN, LOOK AT YOU--*YOU* CAN FLY. I'LL BET THAT WAS AN ACCIDENT...

YEAH. SPACESHIP BLEW UP IN MY FACE. GAVE ME ANIMAL POWERS.

THERE YOU GO. THAT'S EXACTLY WHAT I'M SAYING. YOU GET YOUR ANIMAL POWERS, I GET A DEATH TOUCH.

FICKLE FINGER OF FATE.

"'COURSE MY WIFE LEFT ME. WELL, WHAT WOULD *YOU* HAVE DONE?

"SO, IN THE END, WHAT ELSE COULD I *DO* WITH A DEATH TOUCH?

"TO BE HONEST, I THINK SHE WAS SEEING THE *MAILMAN* ANYWAY.

"I BECAME A BAD GUY.

"CALLED MYSELF THE *RED MASK*. I WAS THINKING OF THAT EDGAR ALLAN POE STORY...THEY MADE A MOVIE OF IT WITH VINCENT PRICE.

"ANYWAY, THINGS WERE OKAY FOR A WHILE. I HUNG OUT WITH THIS GUY CALLED THE *VEIL* AND WE MADE OURSELVES SOME *DOUGH*.

"THE FUNNY THING ABOUT HIM WAS, HE ALWAYS WORE A TOUPEE. DON'T ASK ME WHY. NO ONE EVER *SAW* HIS HEAD UNDER THAT HOOD.

12

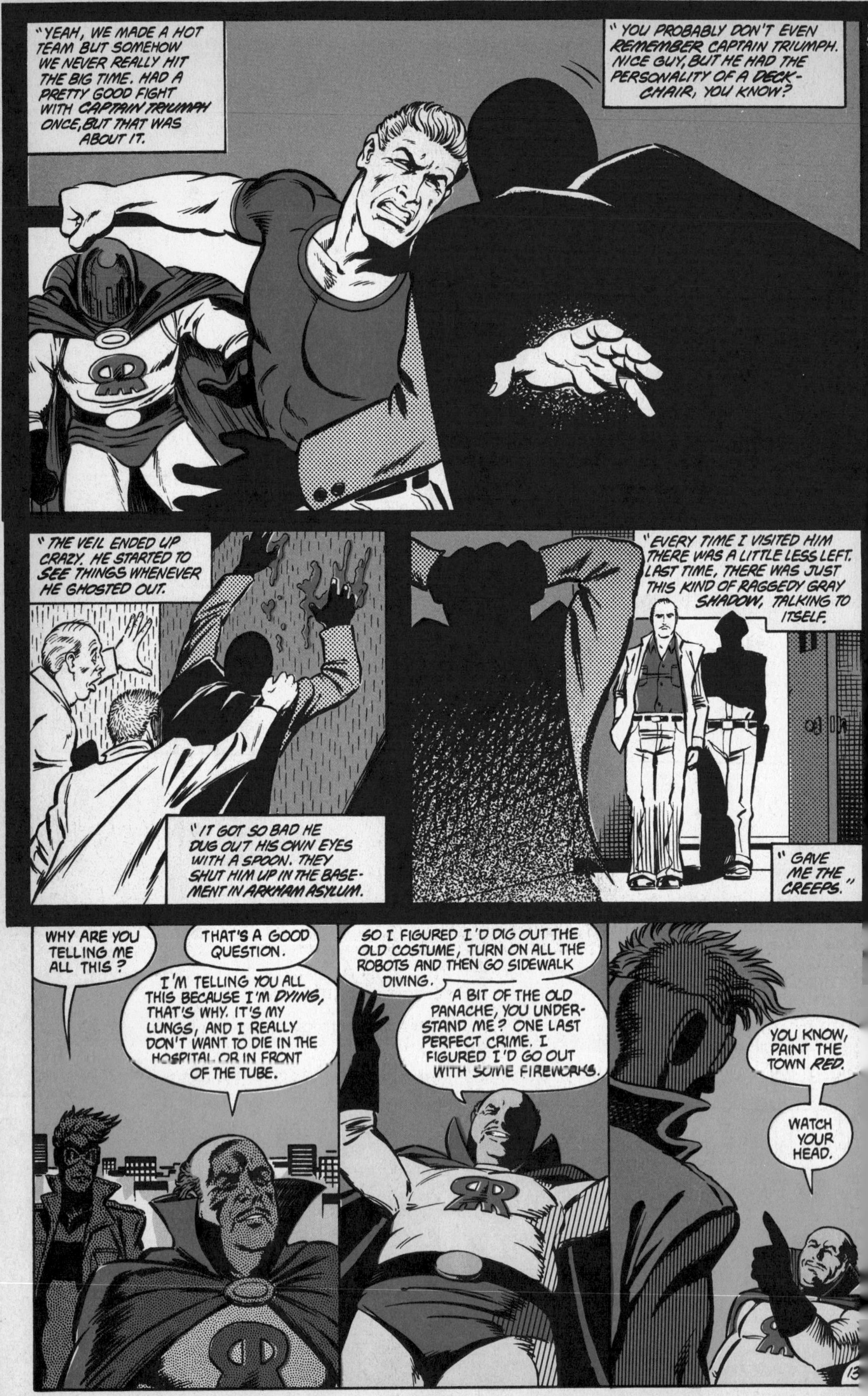
"YEAH, WE MADE A HOT TEAM BUT SOMEHOW WE NEVER REALLY HIT THE BIG TIME. HAD A PRETTY GOOD FIGHT WITH CAPTAIN TRIUMPH ONCE, BUT THAT WAS ABOUT IT.
"YOU PROBABLY DON'T EVEN REMEMBER CAPTAIN TRIUMPH. NICE GUY, BUT HE HAD THE PERSONALITY OF A DECK-CHAIR, YOU KNOW?
"THE VEIL ENDED UP CRAZY. HE STARTED TO SEE THINGS WHENEVER HE GHOSTED OUT.
"IT GOT SO BAD HE DUG OUT HIS OWN EYES WITH A SPOON. THEY SHUT HIM UP IN THE BASE-MENT IN ARKHAM ASYLUM.
"EVERY TIME I VISITED HIM THERE WAS A LITTLE LESS LEFT. LAST TIME, THERE WAS JUST THIS KIND OF RAGGEDY GRAY SHADOW, TALKING TO ITSELF.
"GAVE ME THE CREEPS."
WHY ARE YOU TELLING ME ALL THIS?
THAT'S A GOOD QUESTION.
I'M TELLING YOU ALL THIS BECAUSE I'M DYING, THAT'S WHY. IT'S MY LUNGS, AND I REALLY DON'T WANT TO DIE IN THE HOSPITAL OR IN FRONT OF THE TUBE.
SO I FIGURED I'D DIG OUT THE OLD COSTUME, TURN ON ALL THE ROBOTS AND THEN GO SIDEWALK DIVING.
A BIT OF THE OLD PANACHE, YOU UNDER-STAND ME? ONE LAST PERFECT CRIME. I FIGURED I'D GO OUT WITH SOME FIREWORKS.
YOU KNOW, PAINT THE TOWN RED.
WATCH YOUR HEAD.

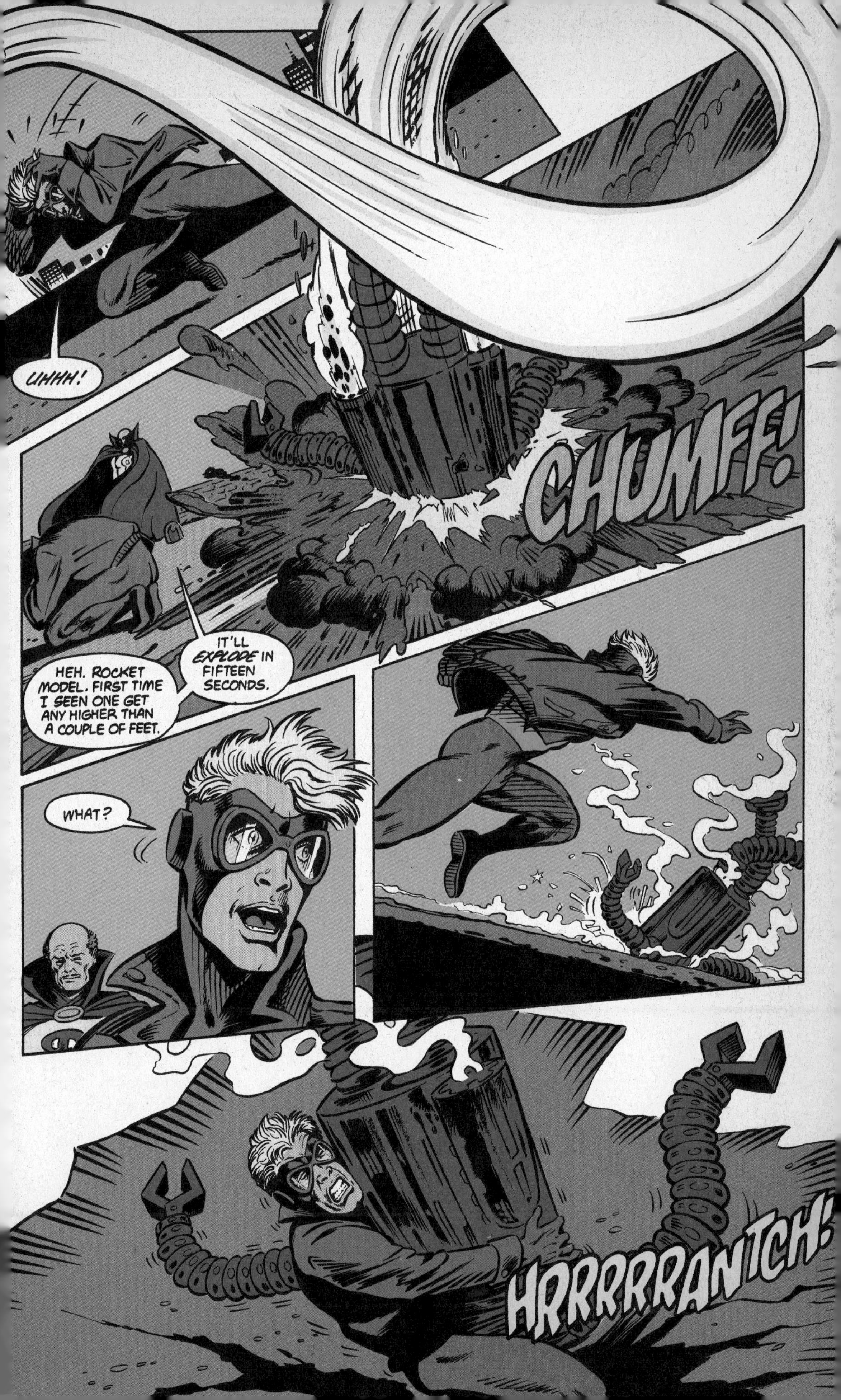
UHHH!
CHUMFF!
IT'LL EXPLODE IN FIFTEEN SECONDS.
HEH. ROCKET MODEL. FIRST TIME I SEEN ONE GET ANY HIGHER THAN A COUPLE OF FEET.
WHAT?
HRRRRRANTCH!

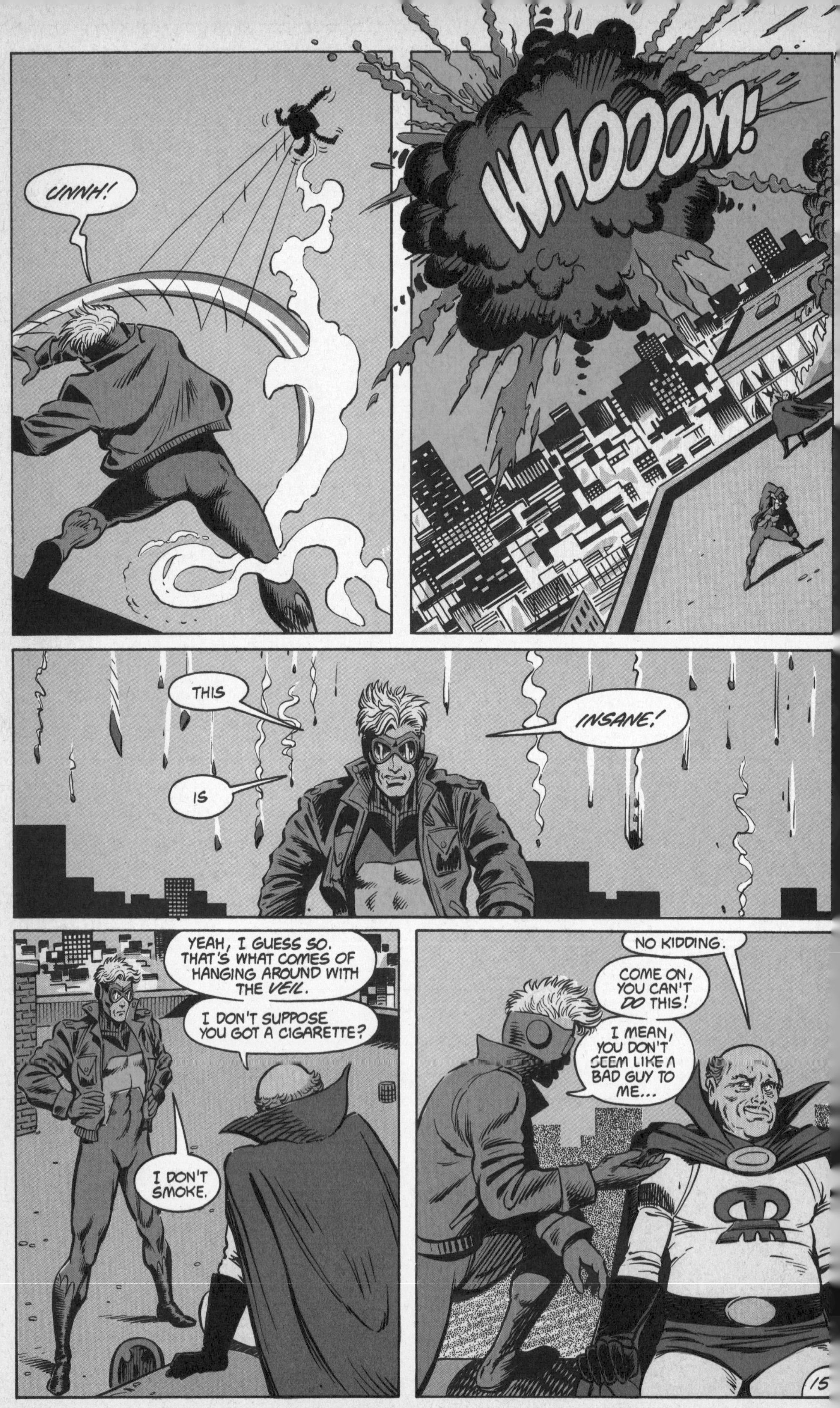
UNNH!
WHOOOM!
THIS
IS
INSANE!
YEAH, I GUESS SO. THAT'S WHAT COMES OF HANGING AROUND WITH THE VEIL.
I DON'T SUPPOSE YOU GOT A CIGARETTE?
I DON'T SMOKE.
NO KIDDING.
COME ON, YOU CAN'T DO THIS!
I MEAN, YOU DON'T SEEM LIKE A BAD GUY TO ME...
15

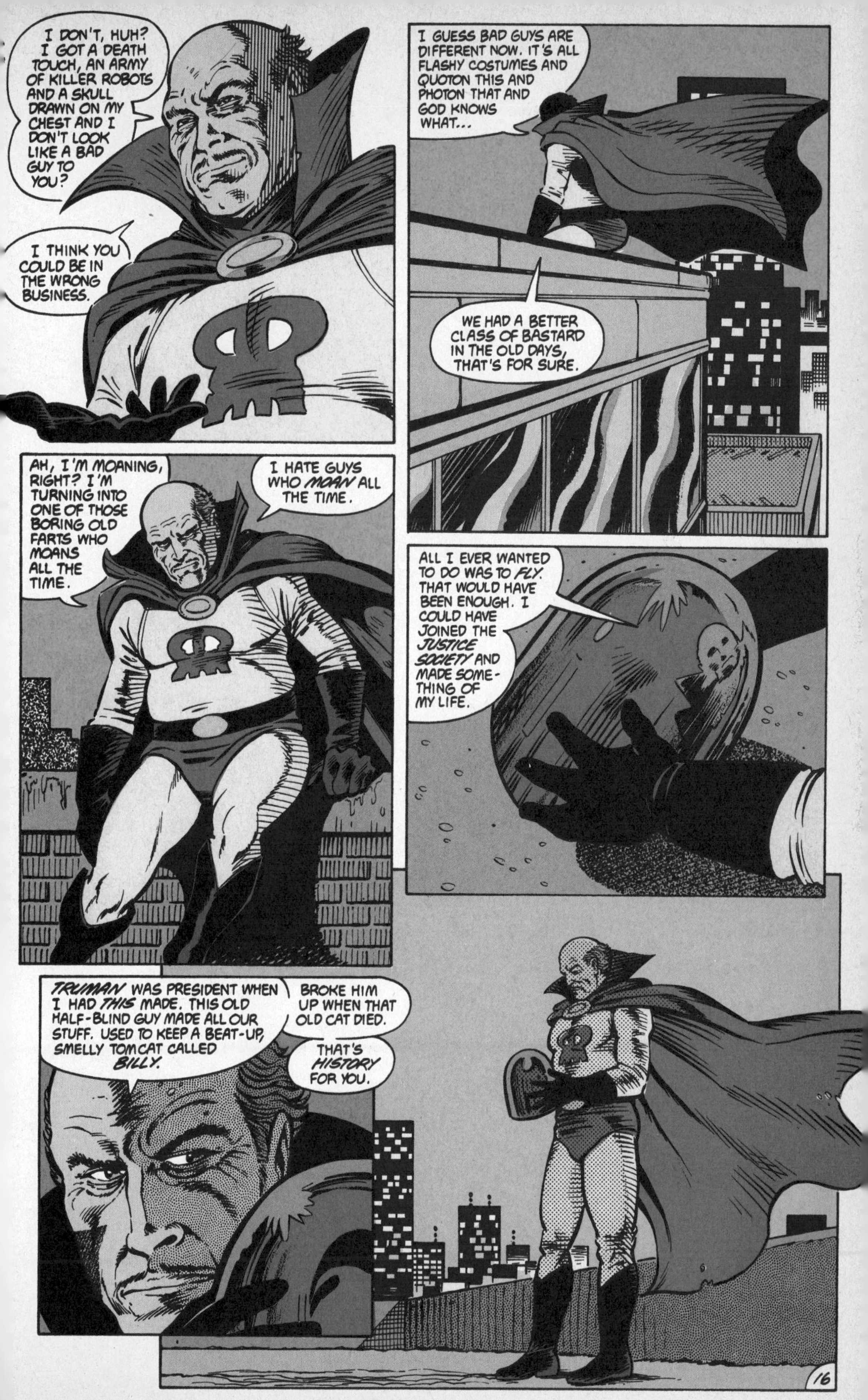

I DON'T, HUH? I GOT A DEATH TOUCH, AN ARMY OF KILLER ROBOTS AND A SKULL DRAWN ON MY CHEST AND I DON'T LOOK LIKE A BAD GUY TO YOU?
I THINK YOU COULD BE IN THE WRONG BUSINESS.
I GUESS BAD GUYS ARE DIFFERENT NOW. IT'S ALL FLASHY COSTUMES AND QUOTON THIS AND PHOTON THAT AND GOD KNOWS WHAT...
WE HAD A BETTER CLASS OF BASTARD IN THE OLD DAYS, THAT'S FOR SURE.
AH, I'M MOANING, RIGHT? I'M TURNING INTO ONE OF THOSE BORING OLD FARTS WHO MOANS ALL THE TIME.
I HATE GUYS WHO MOAN ALL THE TIME.
ALL I EVER WANTED TO DO WAS TO FLY. THAT WOULD HAVE BEEN ENOUGH. I COULD HAVE JOINED THE JUSTICE SOCIETY AND MADE SOMETHING OF MY LIFE.
TRUMAN WAS PRESIDENT WHEN I HAD THIS MADE. THIS OLD HALF-BLIND GUY MADE ALL OUR STUFF. USED TO KEEP A BEAT-UP, SMELLY TOMCAT CALLED BILLY.
BROKE HIM UP WHEN THAT OLD CAT DIED.
THAT'S HISTORY FOR YOU.

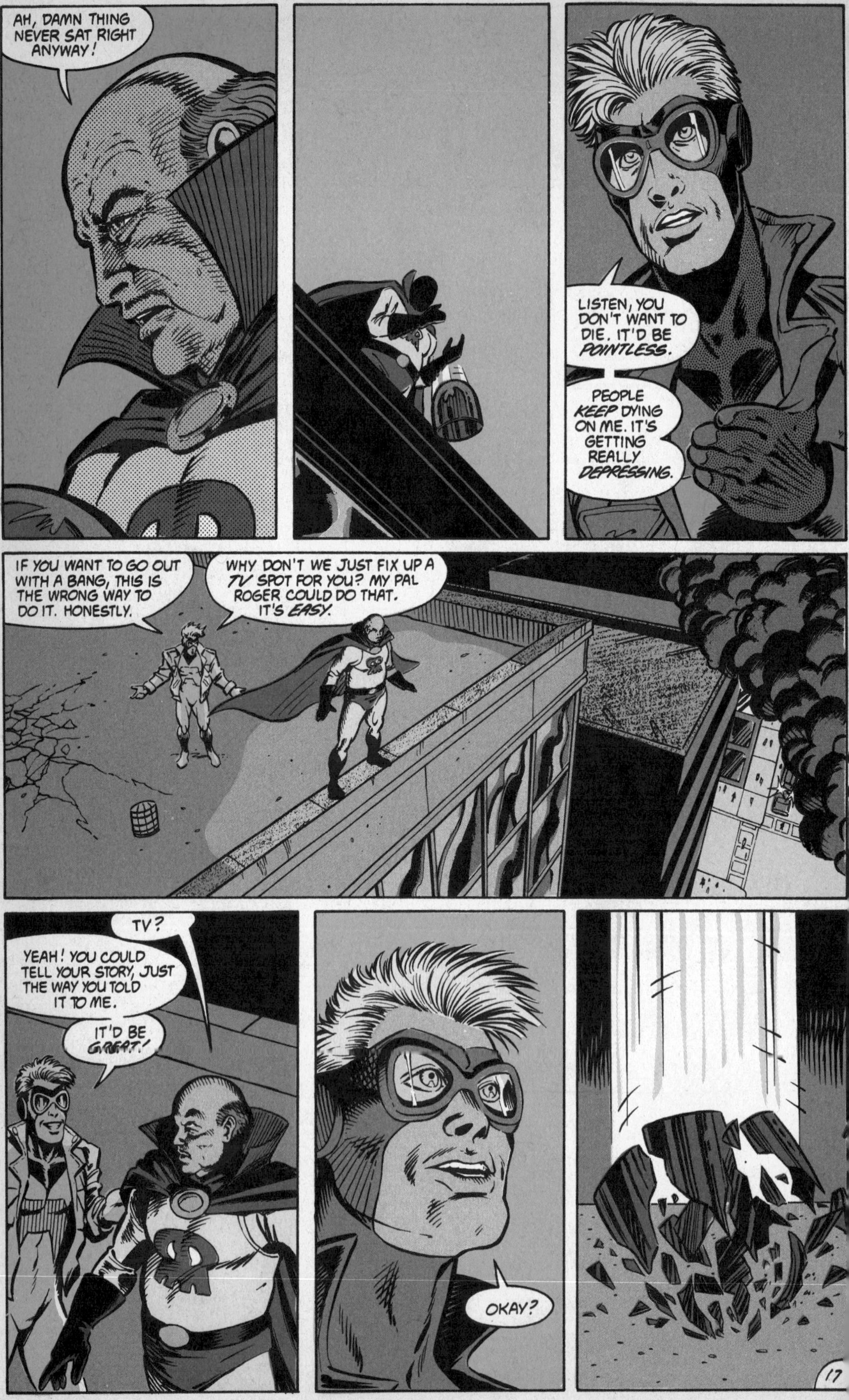
AH, DAMN THING NEVER SAT RIGHT ANYWAY!
LISTEN, YOU DON'T WANT TO DIE. IT'D BE POINTLESS.
PEOPLE KEEP DYING ON ME. IT'S GETTING REALLY DEPRESSING.
IF YOU WANT TO GO OUT WITH A BANG, THIS IS THE WRONG WAY TO DO IT. HONESTLY.
WHY DON'T WE JUST FIX UP A TV SPOT FOR YOU? MY PAL ROGER COULD DO THAT. IT'S EASY.
TV?
YEAH! YOU COULD TELL YOUR STORY, JUST THE WAY YOU TOLD IT TO ME.
IT'D BE GREAT!
OKAY?

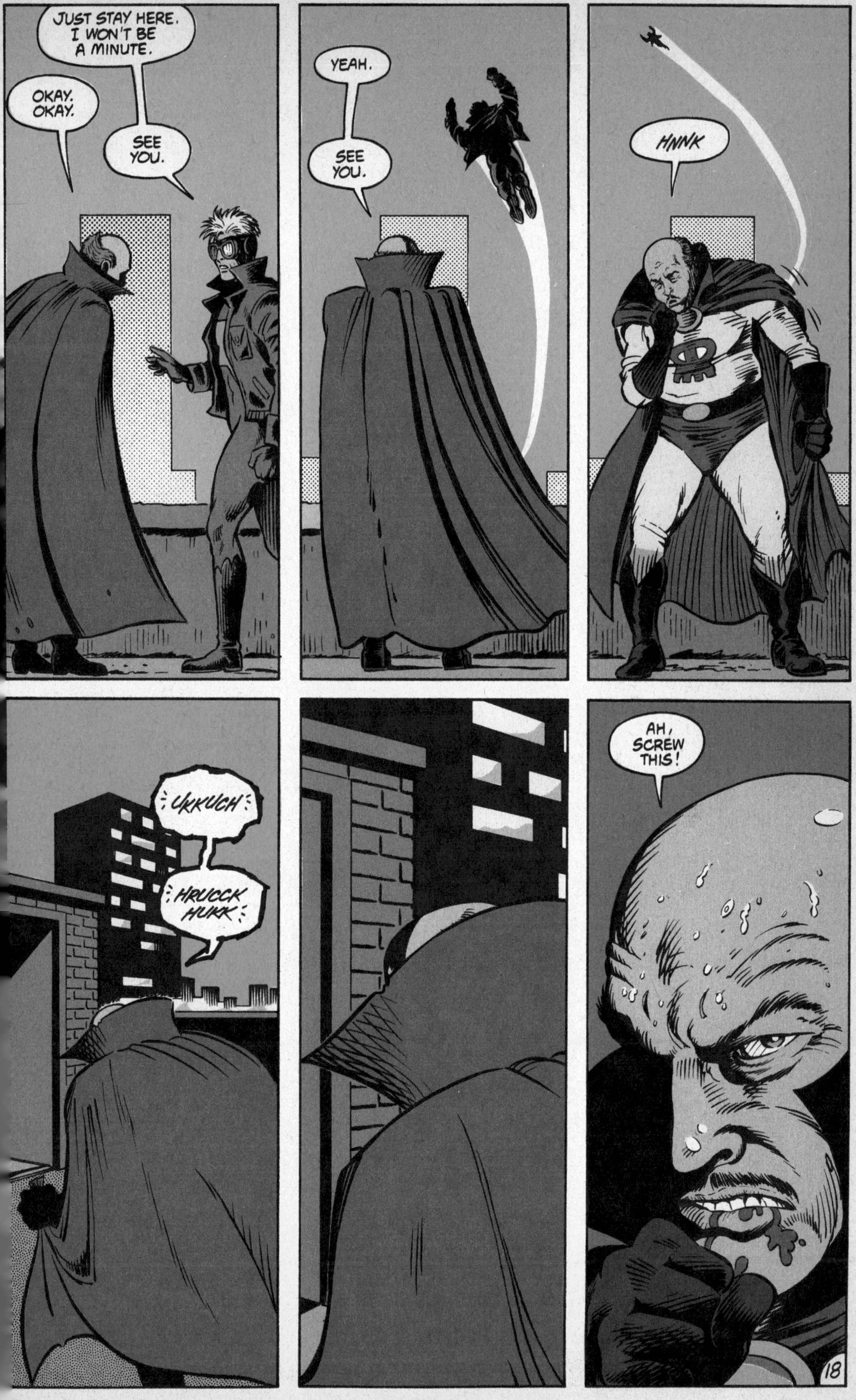
JUST STAY HERE. I WON'T BE A MINUTE.
OKAY. OKAY.
SEE YOU.
YEAH.
SEE YOU.
HNNK
UKKUCH
HRUCCK HUKK
AH, SCREW THIS!
18

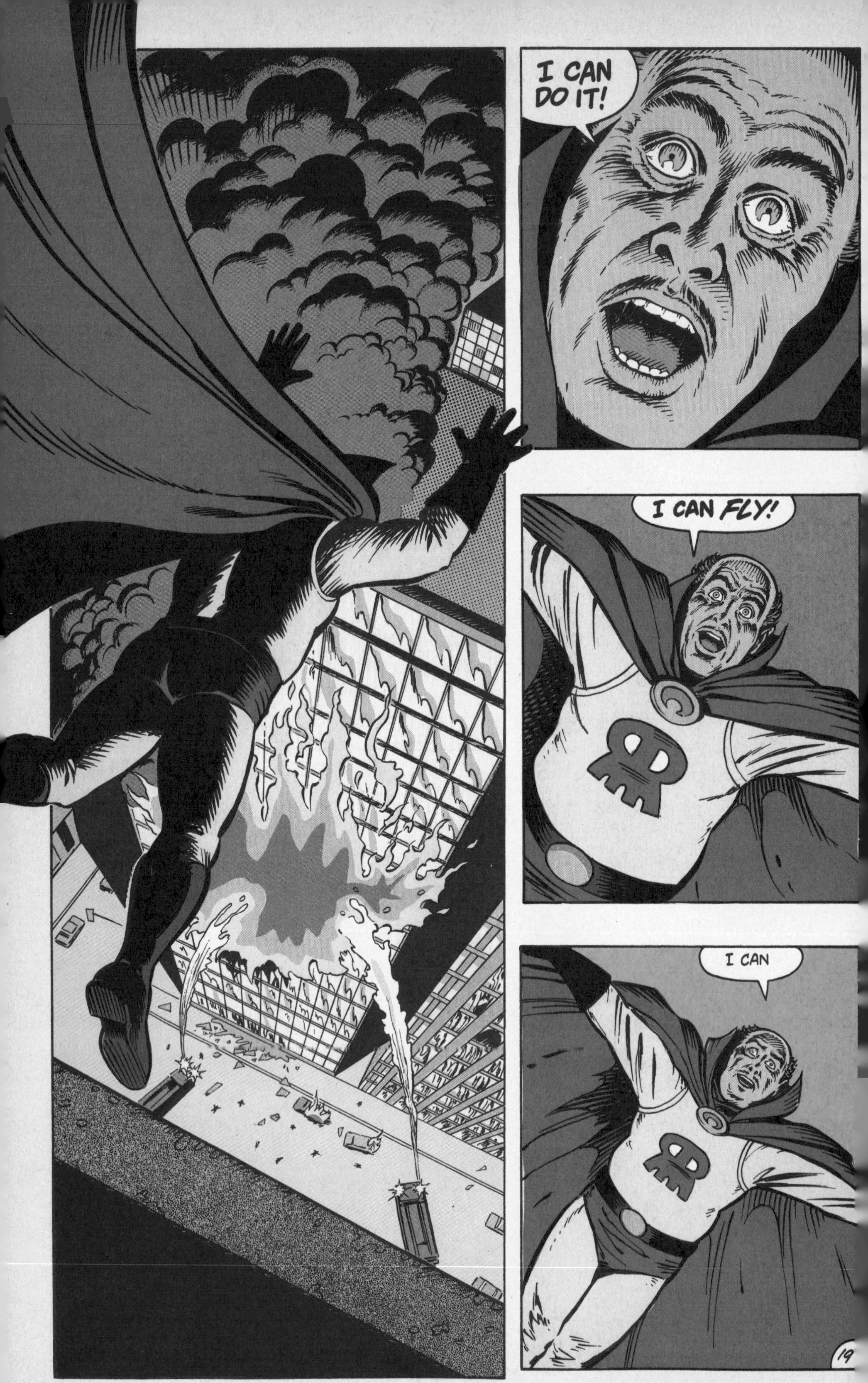
I CAN DO IT!
I CAN FLY!
I CAN

Epilogue:

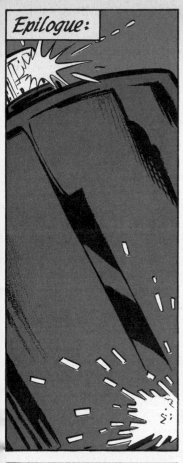

THAT THE LAST OF THEM?

22

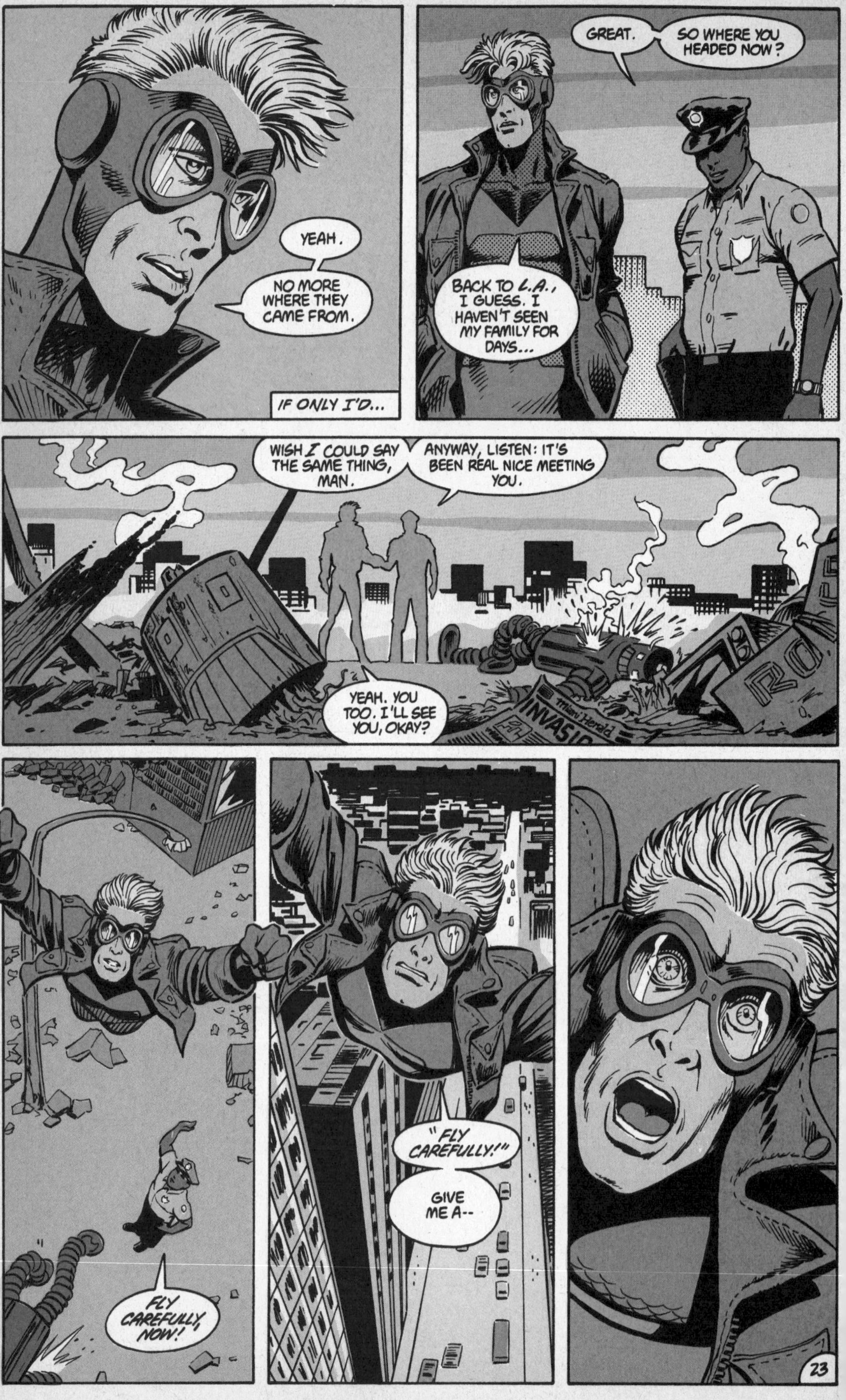
YEAH.
NO MORE WHERE THEY CAME FROM.
IF ONLY I'D...
GREAT.
SO WHERE YOU HEADED NOW?
BACK TO L.A., I GUESS. I HAVEN'T SEEN MY FAMILY FOR DAYS...
WISH I COULD SAY THE SAME THING, MAN.
ANYWAY, LISTEN: IT'S BEEN REAL NICE MEETING YOU.
YEAH. YOU TOO. I'LL SEE YOU, OKAY?
INVASIO
FLY CAREFULLY, NOW!
"FLY CAREFULLY!"
GIVE ME A--

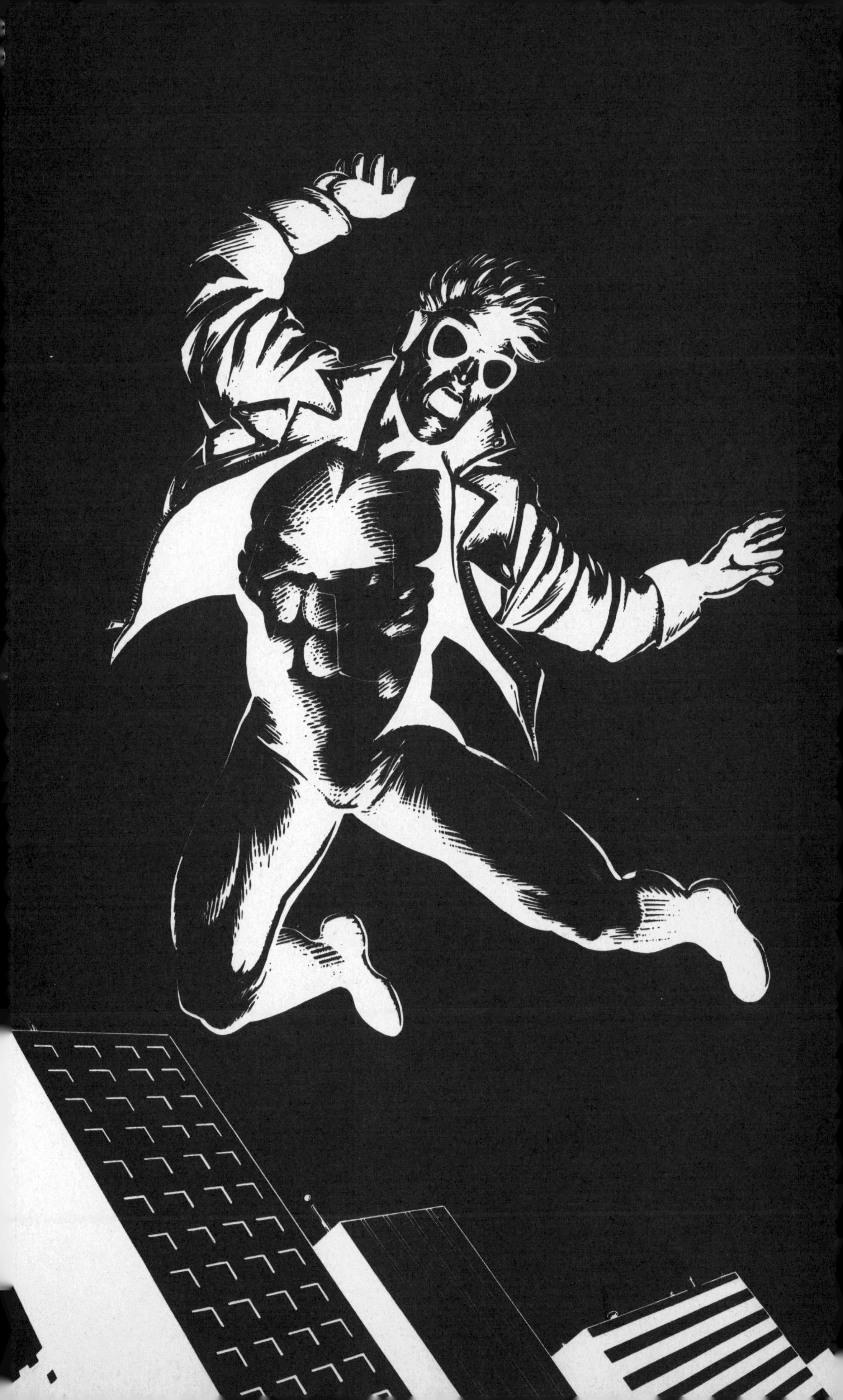

CHAPTER
EIGHT

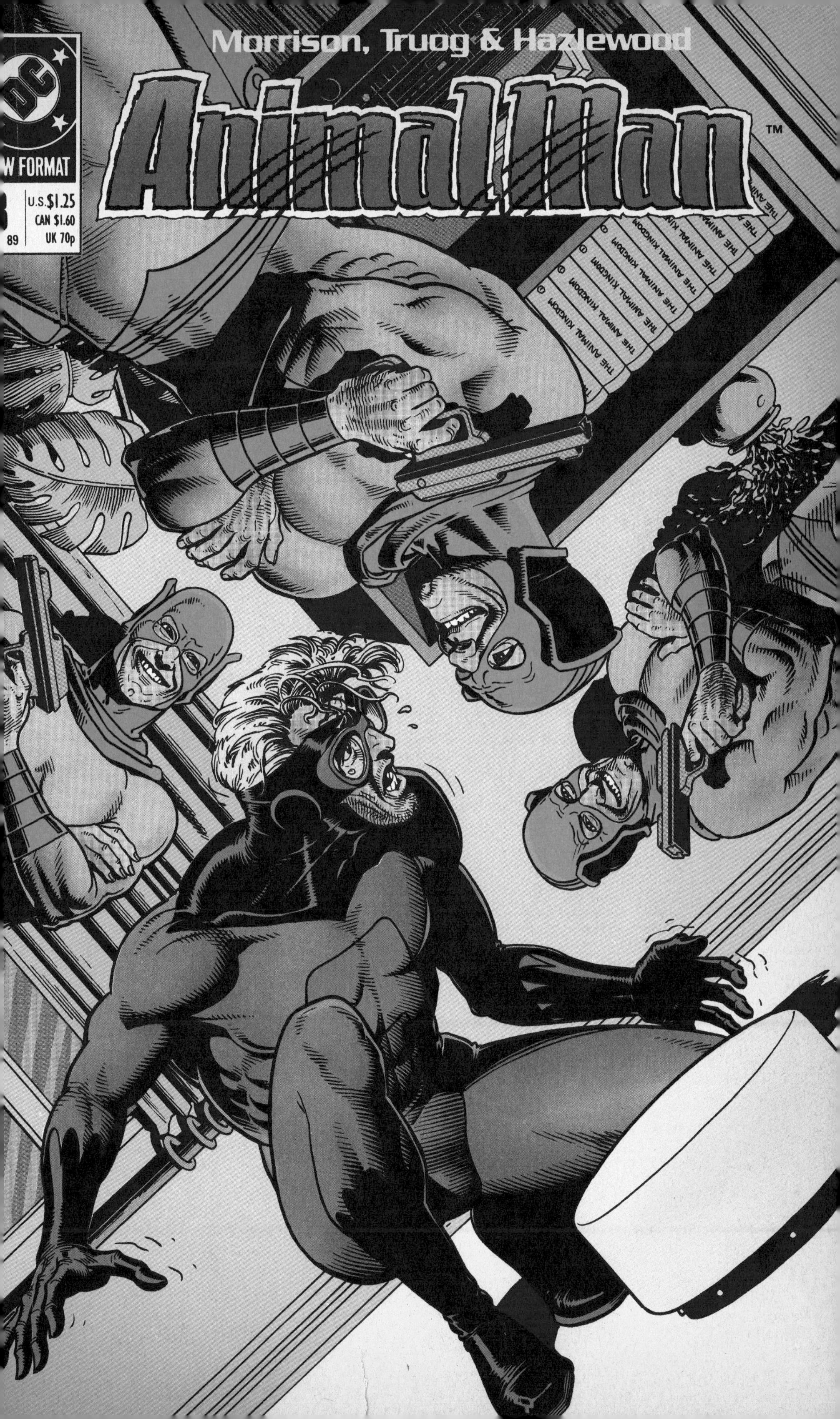
Morrison, Truog & Hazlewood
Animal Man
™
W FORMAT
U.S.$1.25
CAN $1.60
UK 70p
89
THE ANIMAL KINGDOM
THE ANIMAL KINGDOM
THE ANIMAL KINGDOM
THE ANIMAL KINGDOM
THE ANIMAL KINGDOM

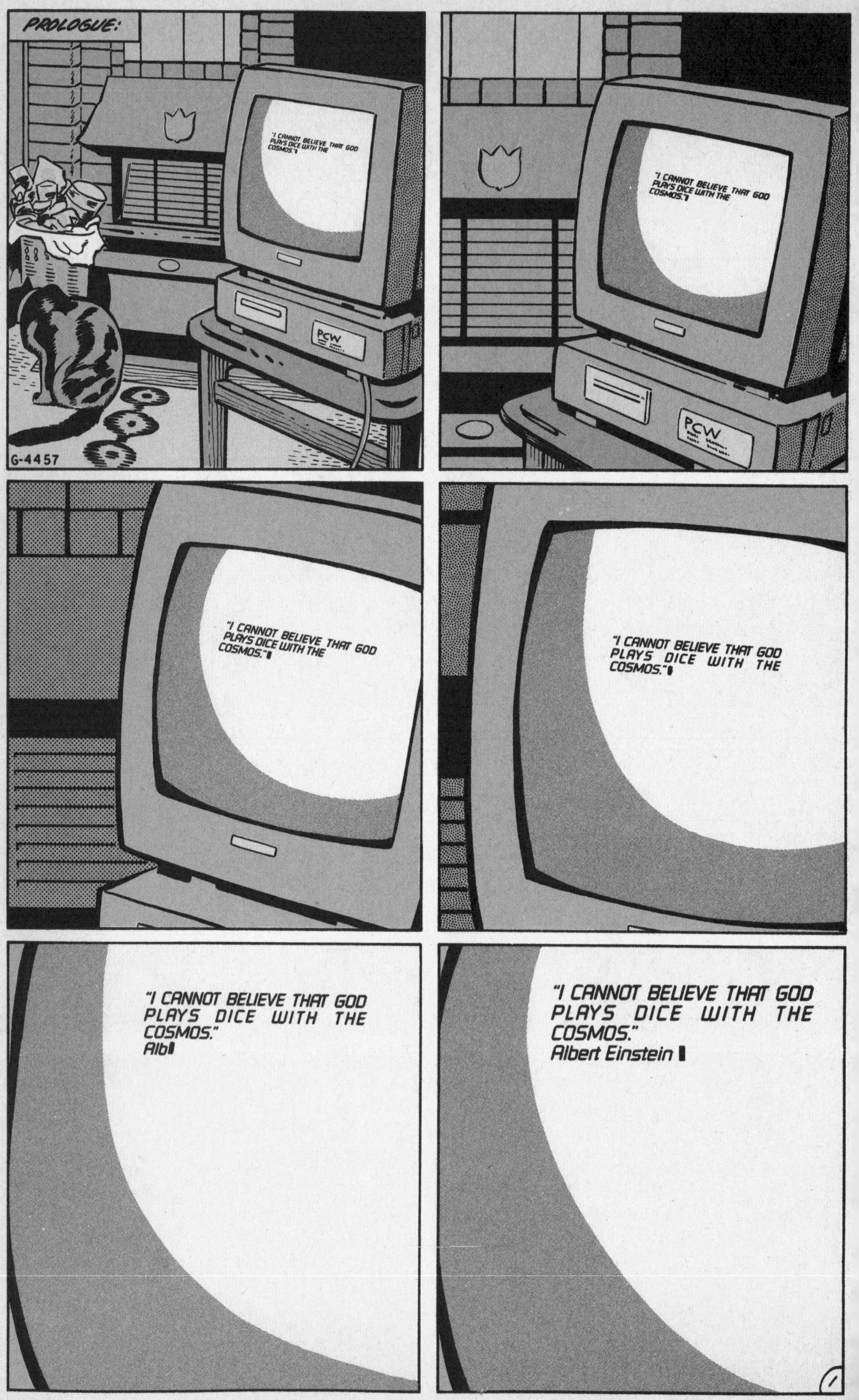
PROLOGUE:
"I CANNOT BELIEVE THAT GOD PLAYS DICE WITH THE COSMOS."
G-4457
PCW
"I CANNOT BELIEVE THAT GOD PLAYS DICE WITH THE COSMOS."
PCW
"I CANNOT BELIEVE THAT GOD PLAYS DICE WITH THE COSMOS."
"I CANNOT BELIEVE THAT GOD PLAYS DICE WITH THE COSMOS."
"I CANNOT BELIEVE THAT GOD PLAYS DICE WITH THE COSMOS."
Alb
"I CANNOT BELIEVE THAT GOD PLAYS DICE WITH THE COSMOS."
Albert Einstein
1

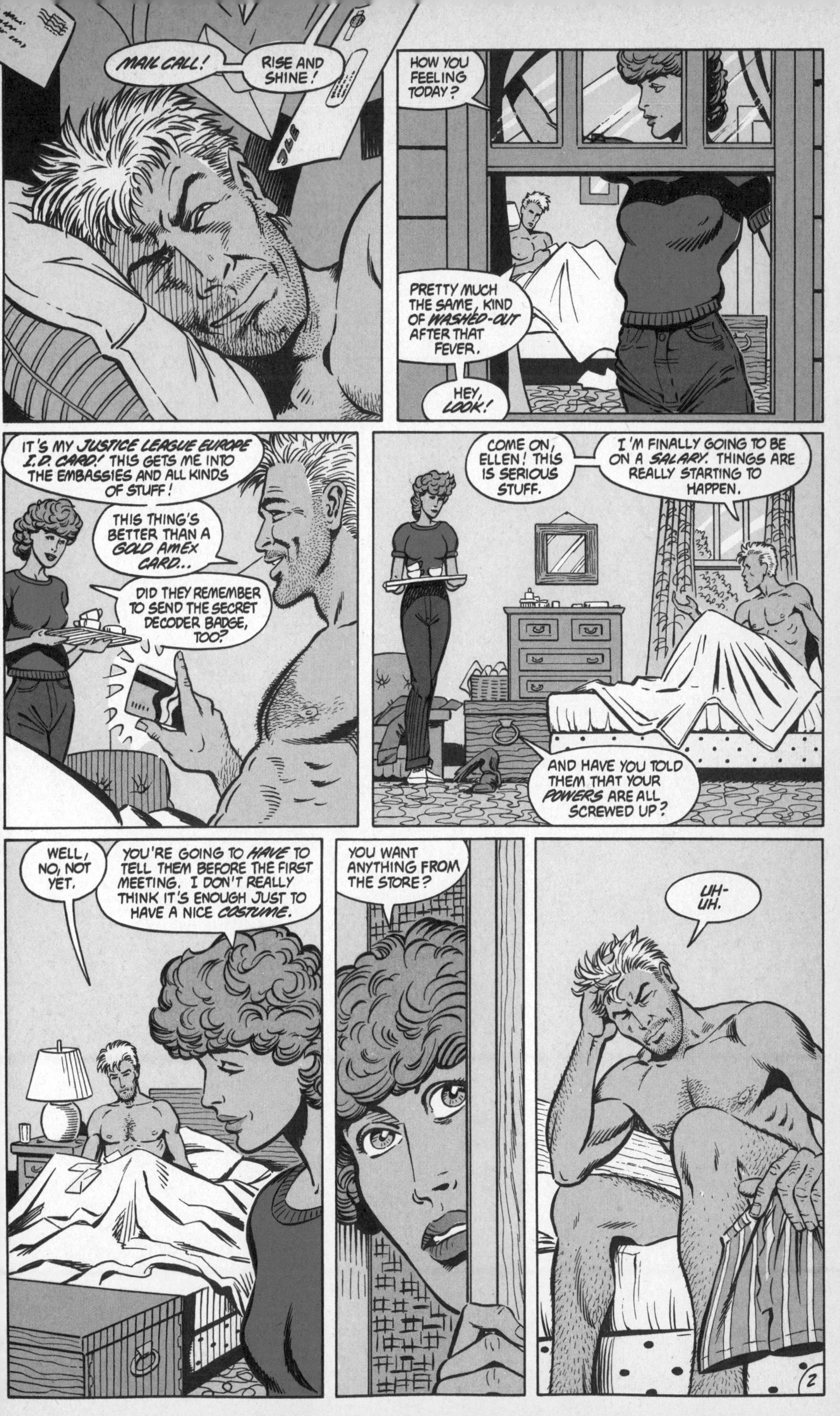
MAIL CALL!
RISE AND SHINE!
HOW YOU FEELING TODAY?
PRETTY MUCH THE SAME, KIND OF WASHED-OUT AFTER THAT FEVER.
HEY, LOOK!
IT'S MY JUSTICE LEAGUE EUROPE I.D. CARD! THIS GETS ME INTO THE EMBASSIES AND ALL KINDS OF STUFF!
THIS THING'S BETTER THAN A GOLD AMEX CARD...
DID THEY REMEMBER TO SEND THE SECRET DECODER BADGE, TOO?
COME ON, ELLEN! THIS IS SERIOUS STUFF.
I'M FINALLY GOING TO BE ON A SALARY. THINGS ARE REALLY STARTING TO HAPPEN.
AND HAVE YOU TOLD THEM THAT YOUR POWERS ARE ALL SCREWED UP?
WELL, NO, NOT YET.
YOU'RE GOING TO HAVE TO TELL THEM BEFORE THE FIRST MEETING. I DON'T REALLY THINK IT'S ENOUGH JUST TO HAVE A NICE COSTUME.
YOU WANT ANYTHING FROM THE STORE?
UH-UH.
2

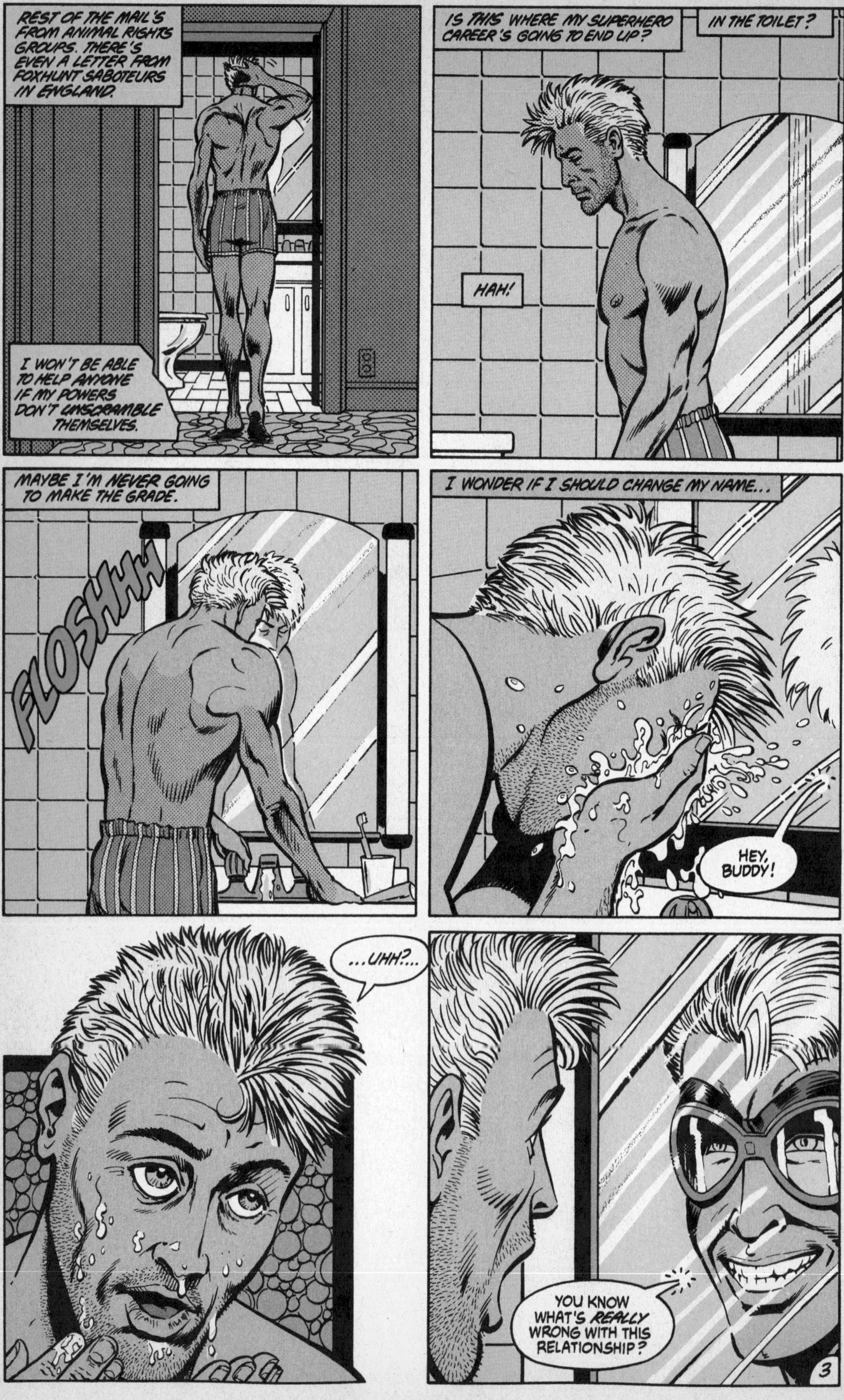
REST OF THE MAIL'S FROM ANIMAL RIGHTS GROUPS. THERE'S EVEN A LETTER FROM FOXHUNT SABOTEURS IN ENGLAND.
I WON'T BE ABLE TO HELP ANYONE IF MY POWERS DON'T UNSCRAMBLE THEMSELVES.
IS THIS WHERE MY SUPERHERO CAREER'S GOING TO END UP?
IN THE TOILET?
HAH!
MAYBE I'M NEVER GOING TO MAKE THE GRADE.
FLOSHHH
I WONDER IF I SHOULD CHANGE MY NAME...
HEY, BUDDY!
...UHH?...
YOU KNOW WHAT'S REALLY WRONG WITH THIS RELATIONSHIP?
3

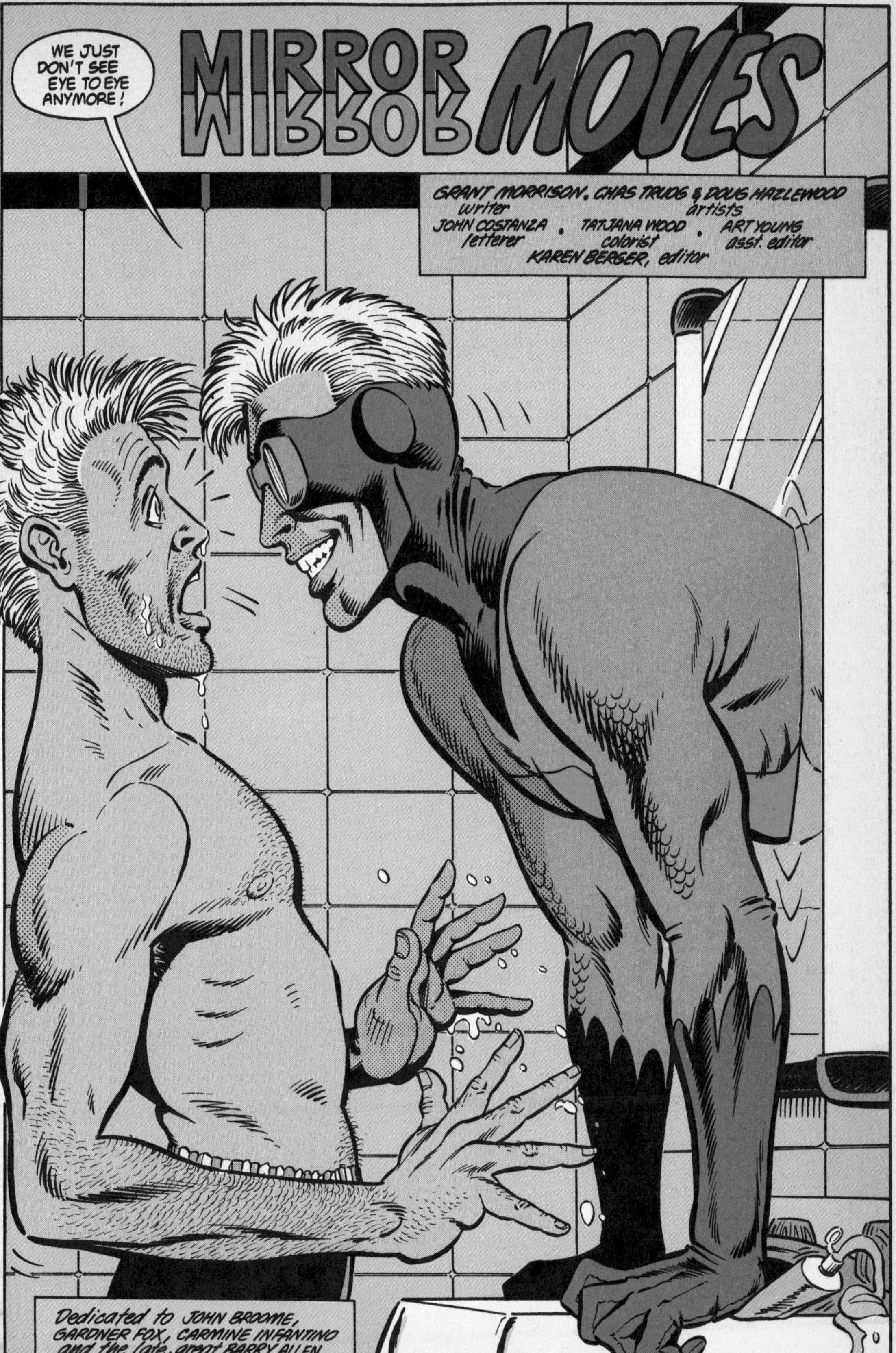

WE JUST DON'T SEE EYE TO EYE ANYMORE!
MIRROR MIRROR MOVES
GRANT MORRISON, writer . CHAS TRUOG & DOUG HAZLEWOOD, artists
JOHN COSTANZA, letterer . TATJANA WOOD, colorist . ART YOUNG, asst. editor
KAREN BERGER, editor
Dedicated to JOHN BROOME, GARDNER FOX, CARMINE INFANTINO and the late, great BARRY ALLEN.
4

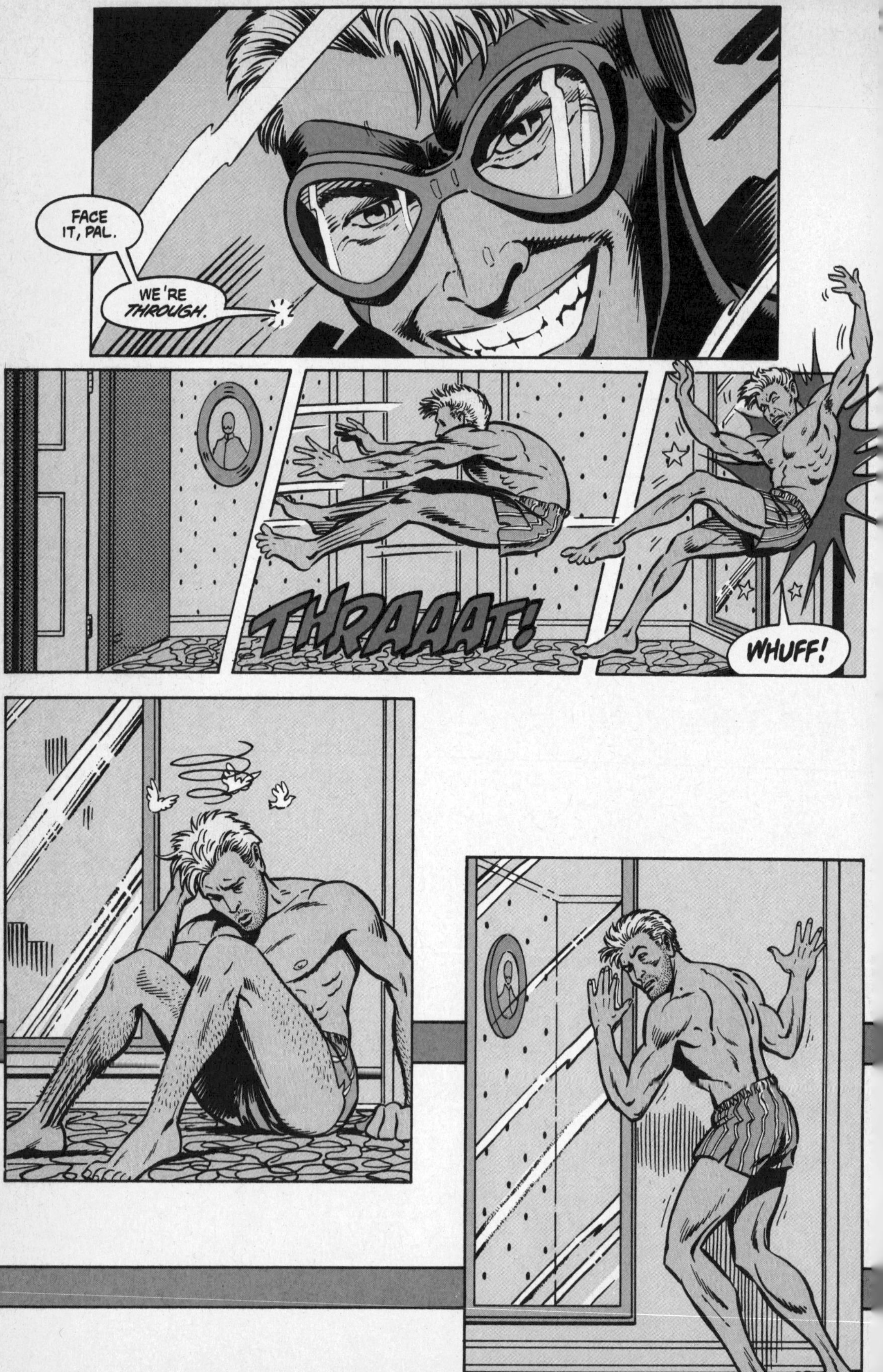
FACE IT, PAL.
WE'RE THROUGH.
THRAAAT!
WHUFF!
5

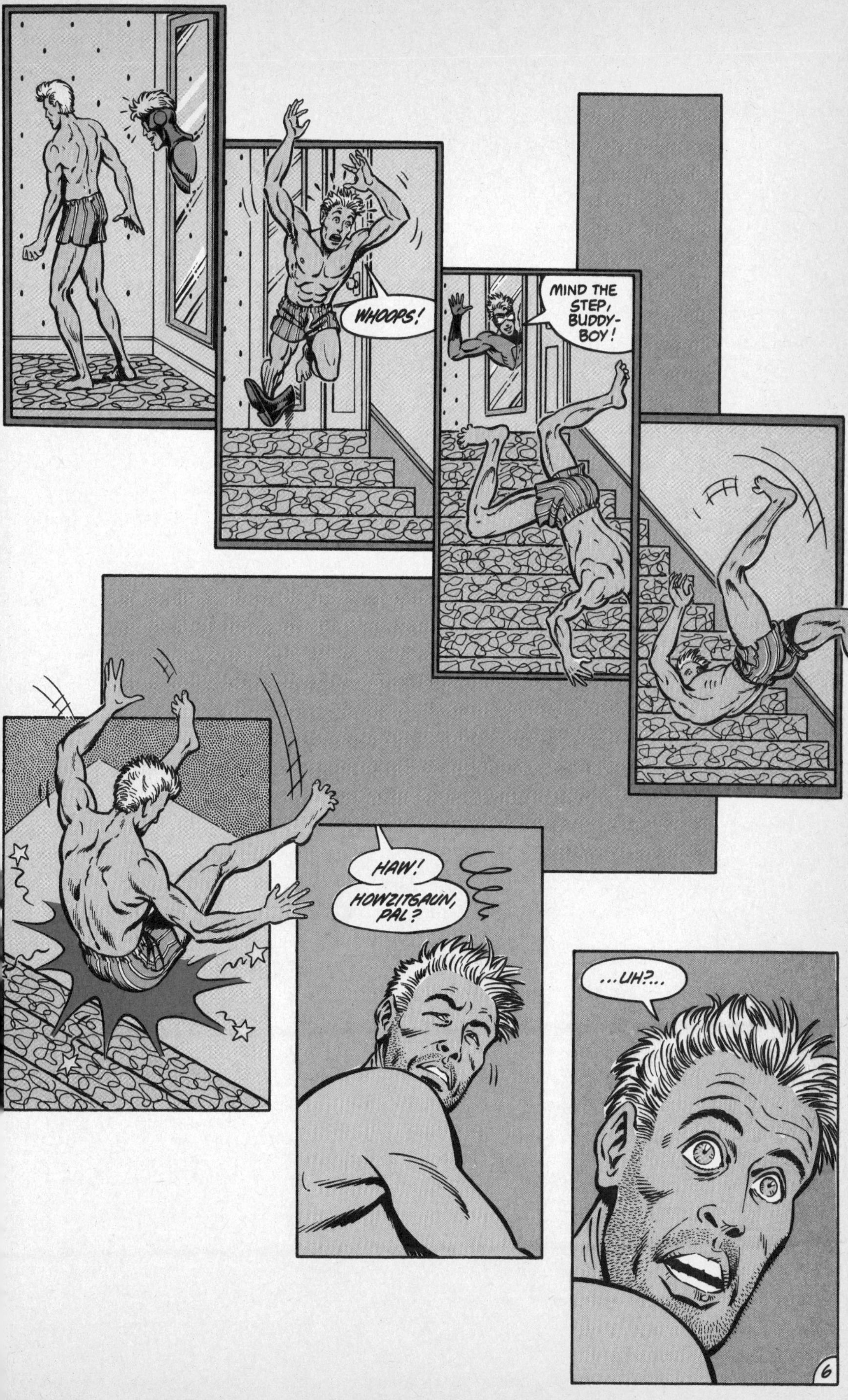
WHOOPS!
MIND THE STEP, BUDDY-BOY!
HAW! HOWZITGAUN, PAL?
...UH?...

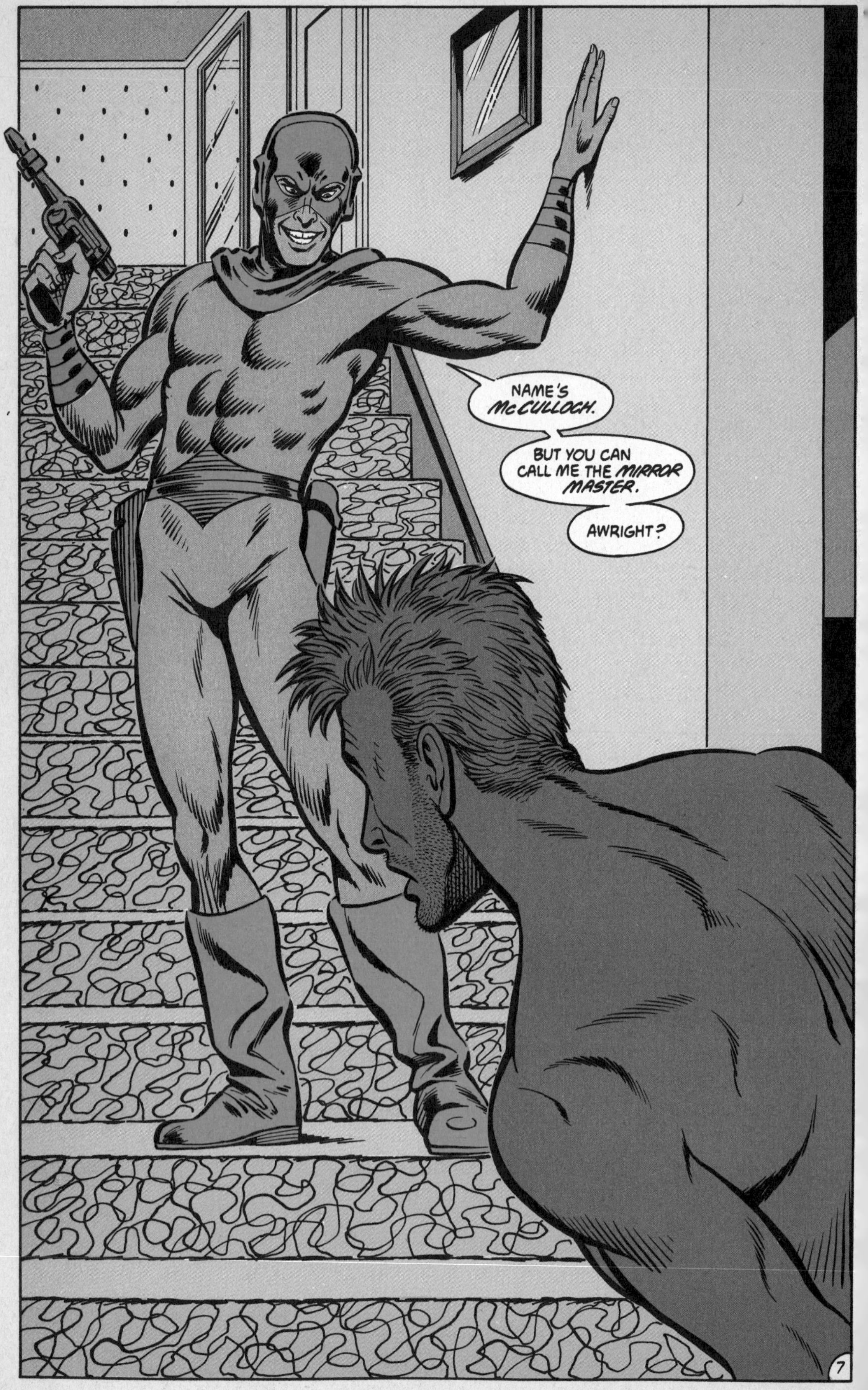
NAME'S McCULLOCH.
BUT YOU CAN CALL ME THE MIRROR MASTER.
AWRIGHT?
7

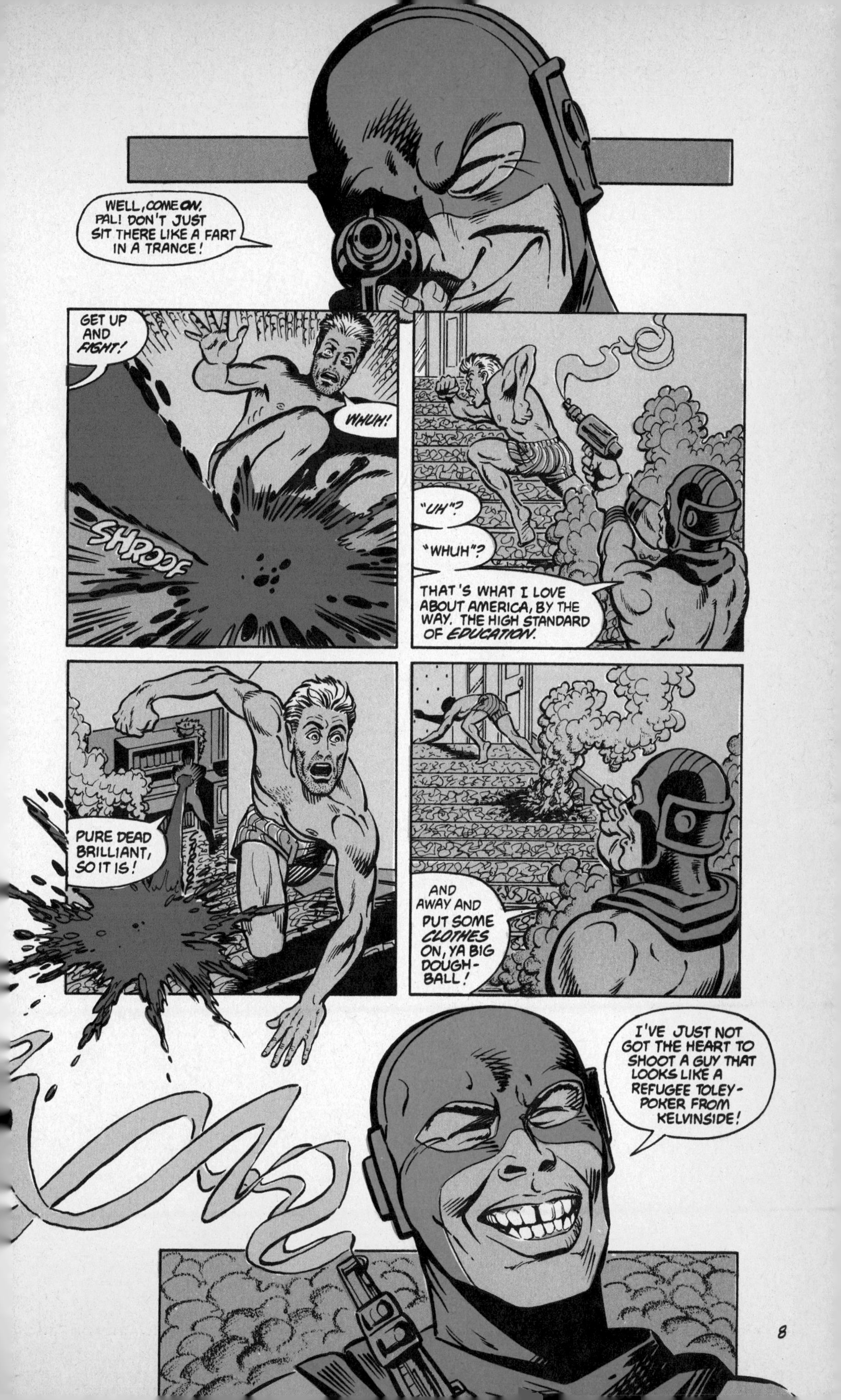
WELL, COME ON, PAL! DON'T JUST SIT THERE LIKE A FART IN A TRANCE!
GET UP AND FIGHT!
WHUH!
SHROOF
"UH"?
"WHUH"?
THAT'S WHAT I LOVE ABOUT AMERICA, BY THE WAY. THE HIGH STANDARD OF EDUCATION.
PURE DEAD BRILLIANT, SO IT IS!
AND AWAY AND PUT SOME CLOTHES ON, YA BIG DOUGH-BALL!
I'VE JUST NOT GOT THE HEART TO SHOOT A GUY THAT LOOKS LIKE A REFUGEE TOLEY-POKER FROM KELVINSIDE!

WHUMMP!

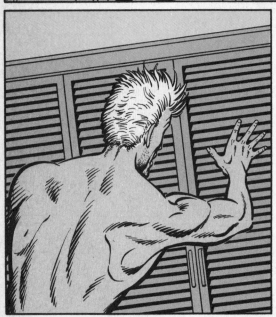

"PUT SOME CLOTHES ON," HUH?

OKAY.

OKAY.

9

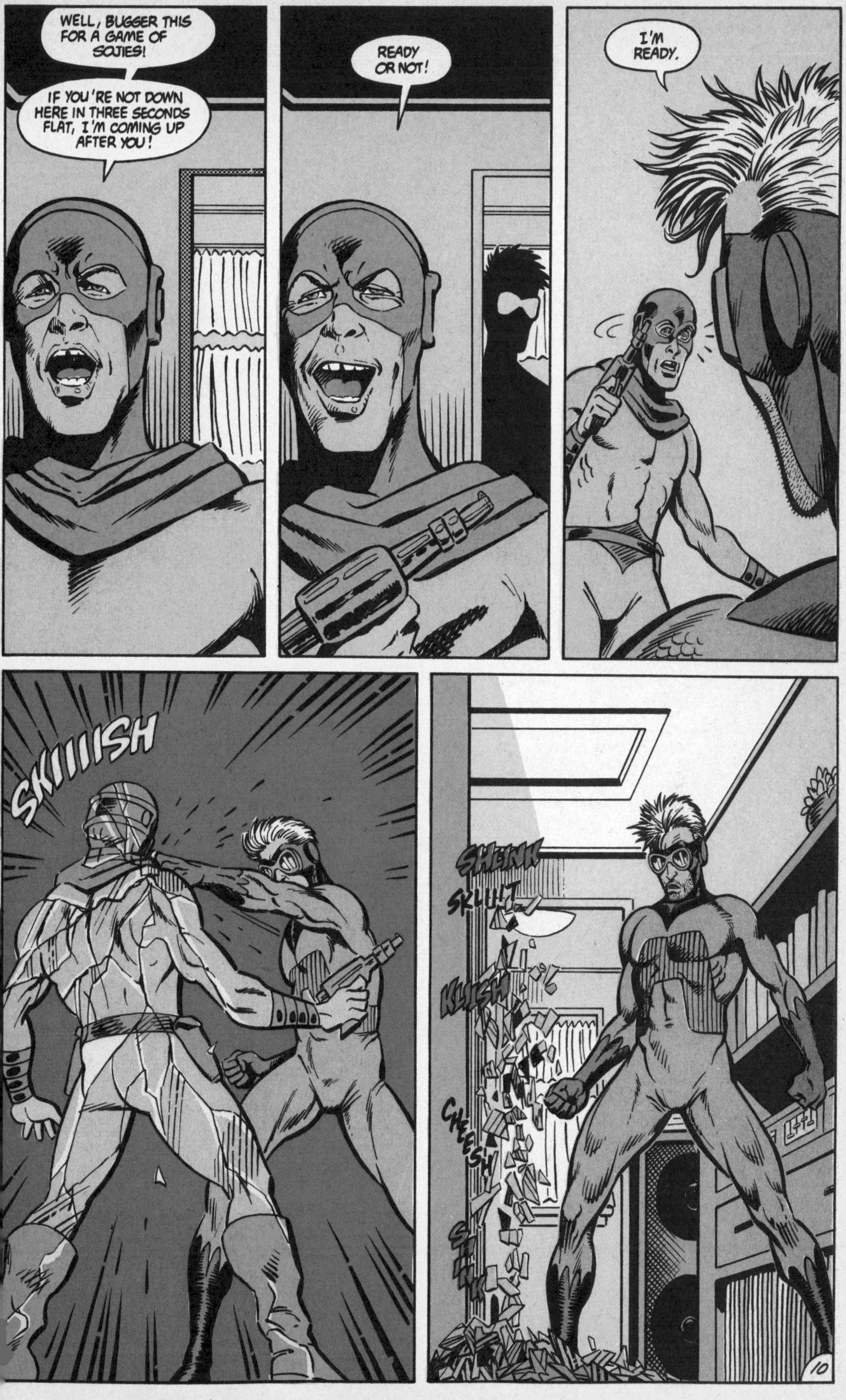
WELL, BUGGER THIS FOR A GAME OF SOJIES!
IF YOU'RE NOT DOWN HERE IN THREE SECONDS FLAT, I'M COMING UP AFTER YOU!
READY OR NOT!
I'M READY.
SKIIIISH
SHLINK
SKLUHT
KLISH
CHEESH
SHINK

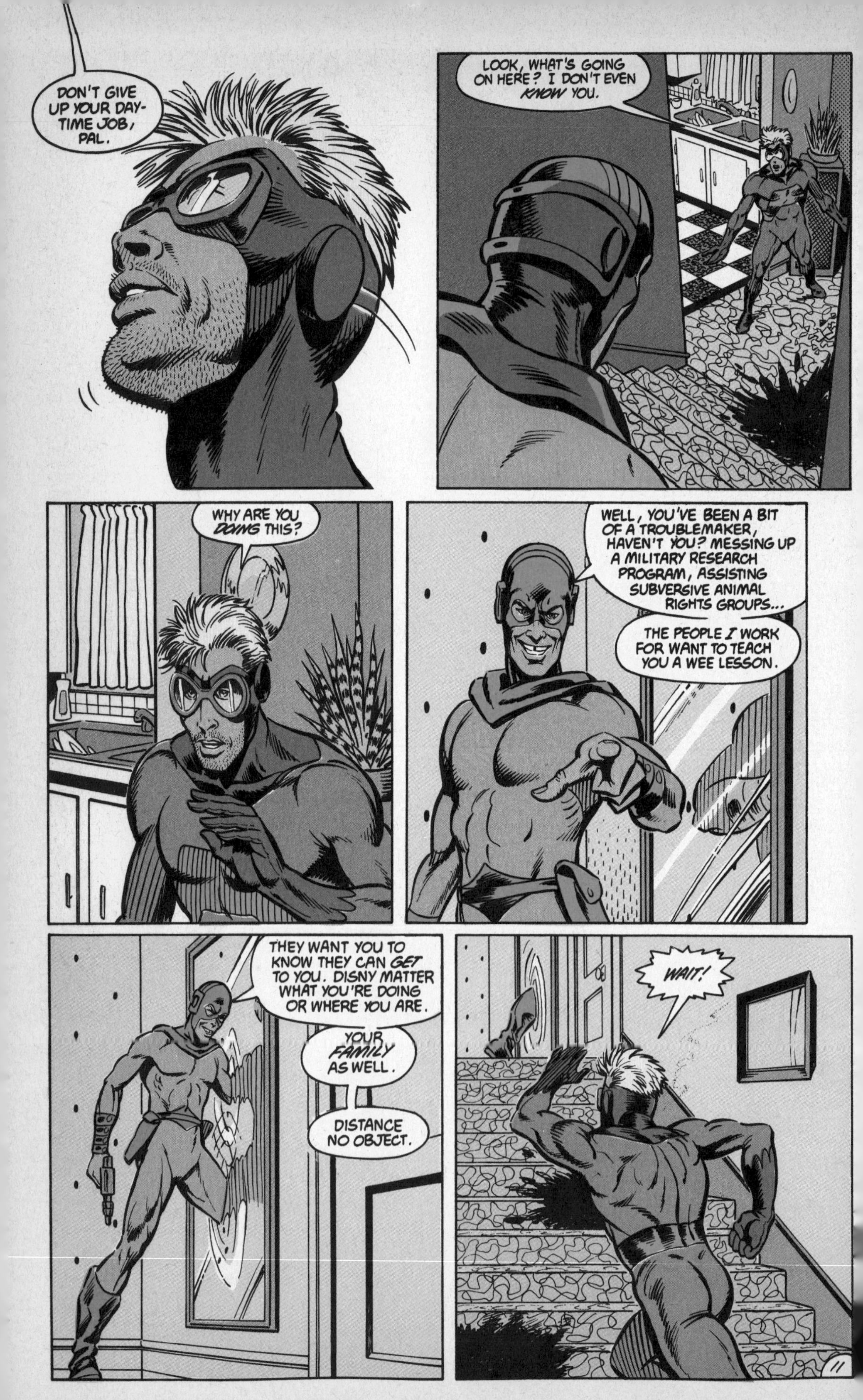
DON'T GIVE UP YOUR DAY-TIME JOB, PAL.
LOOK, WHAT'S GOING ON HERE? I DON'T EVEN KNOW YOU.
WHY ARE YOU DOING THIS?
WELL, YOU'VE BEEN A BIT OF A TROUBLEMAKER, HAVEN'T YOU? MESSING UP A MILITARY RESEARCH PROGRAM, ASSISTING SUBVERSIVE ANIMAL RIGHTS GROUPS...
THE PEOPLE I WORK FOR WANT TO TEACH YOU A WEE LESSON.
THEY WANT YOU TO KNOW THEY CAN GET TO YOU. DISNY MATTER WHAT YOU'RE DOING OR WHERE YOU ARE.
YOUR FAMILY AS WELL.
DISTANCE NO OBJECT.
WAIT!
11

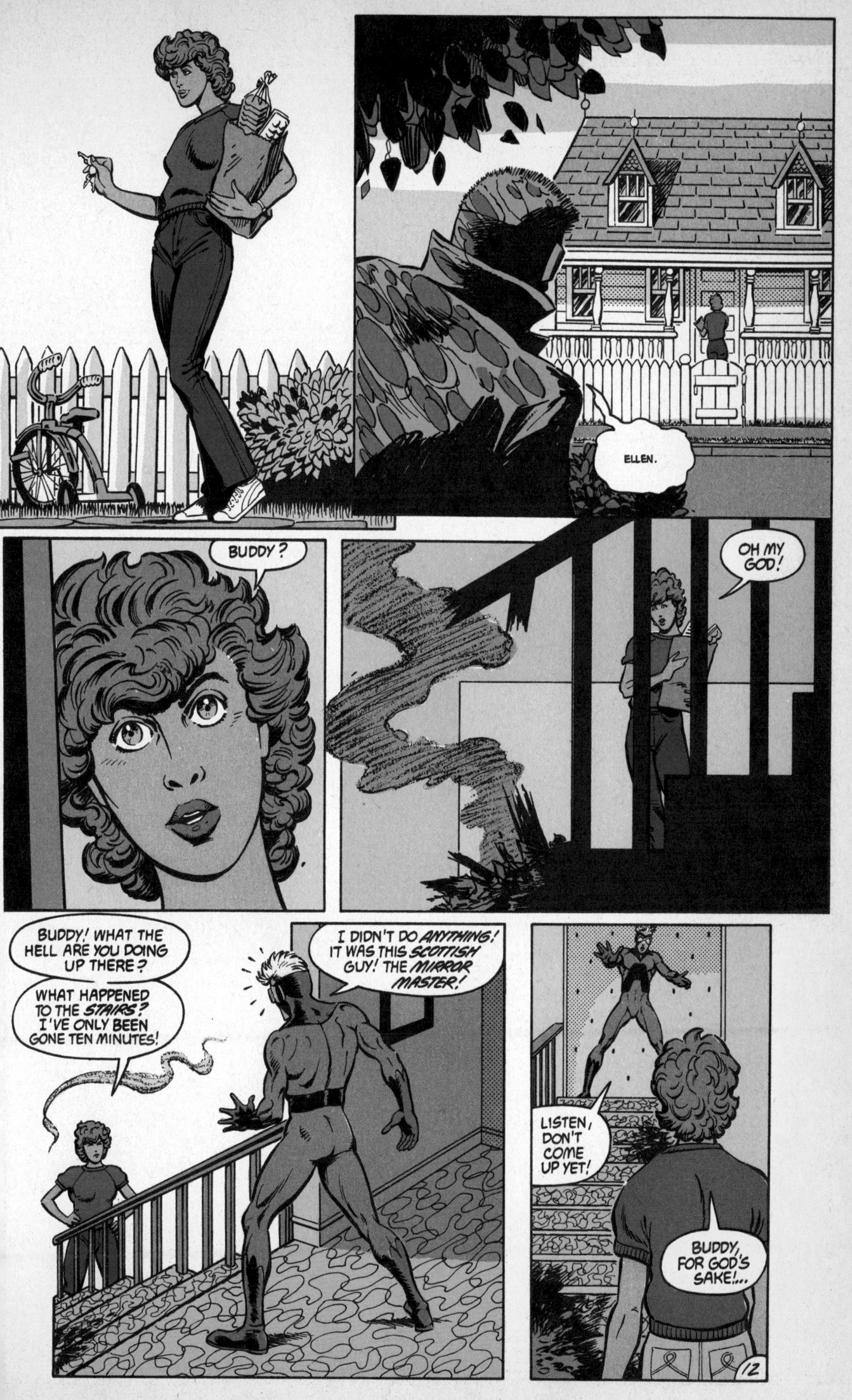
ELLEN.
BUDDY?
OH MY GOD!
BUDDY! WHAT THE HELL ARE YOU DOING UP THERE?
WHAT HAPPENED TO THE STAIRS? I'VE ONLY BEEN GONE TEN MINUTES!
I DIDN'T DO ANYTHING! IT WAS THIS SCOTTISH GUY! THE MIRROR MASTER!
LISTEN, DON'T COME UP YET!
BUDDY, FOR GOD'S SAKE!...
12

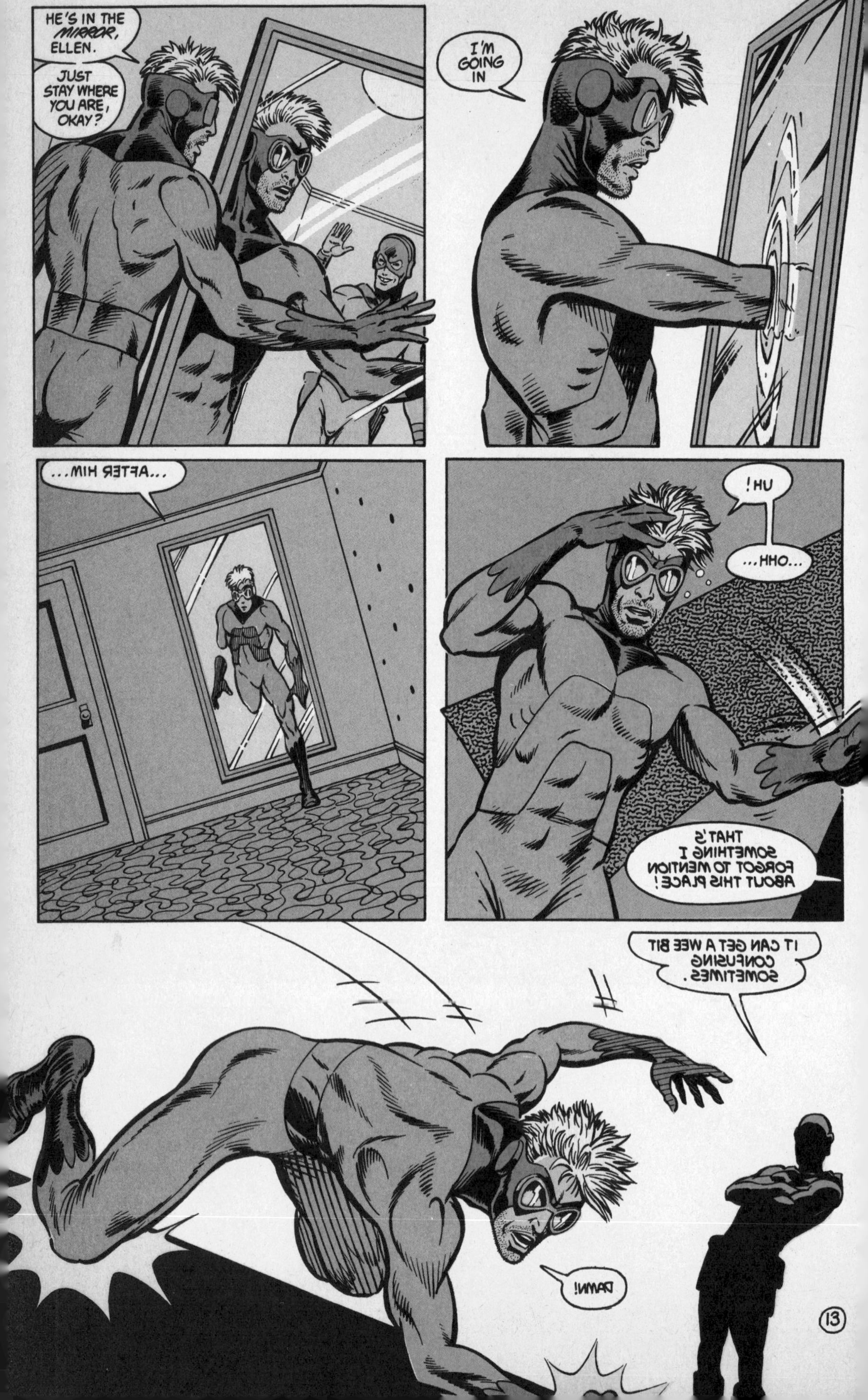
HE'S IN THE MIRROR, ELLEN.
JUST STAY WHERE YOU ARE, OKAY?
I'M GOING IN
...AFTER HIM...
UH!
...OHH...
THAT'S SOMETHING I FORGOT TO MENTION ABOUT THIS PLACE!
IT CAN GET A WEE BIT CONFUSING SOMETIMES.
DAMN!

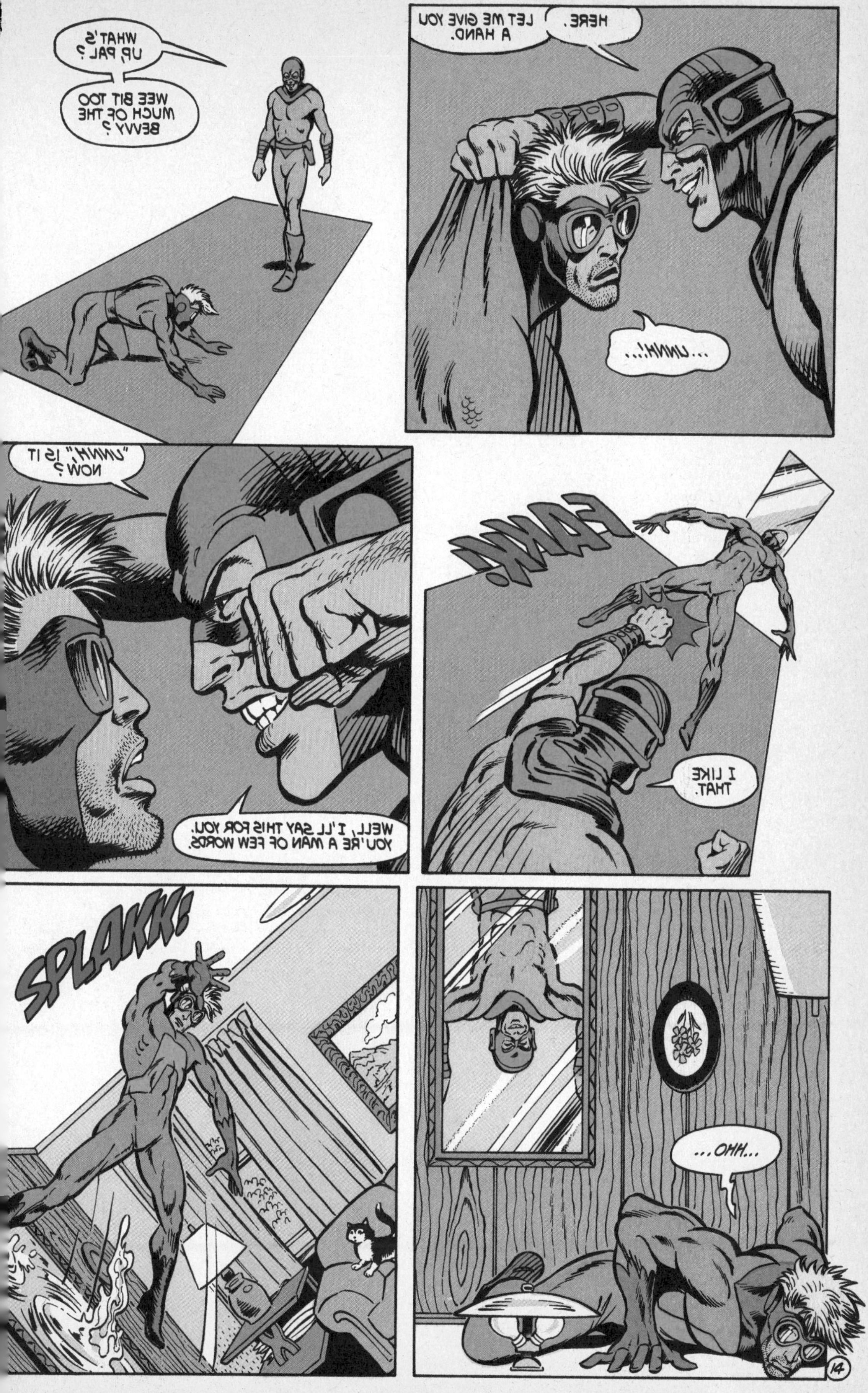
WHAT'S UP, PAL?
WEE BIT TOO MUCH OF THE BEVVY?
HERE. LET ME GIVE YOU A HAND.
...UNNH!...
"UNNH," IS IT NOW?
WELL, I'LL SAY THIS FOR YOU. YOU'RE A MAN OF FEW WORDS.
FAKK!
I LIKE THAT.
SPLAKK!
...OHH...

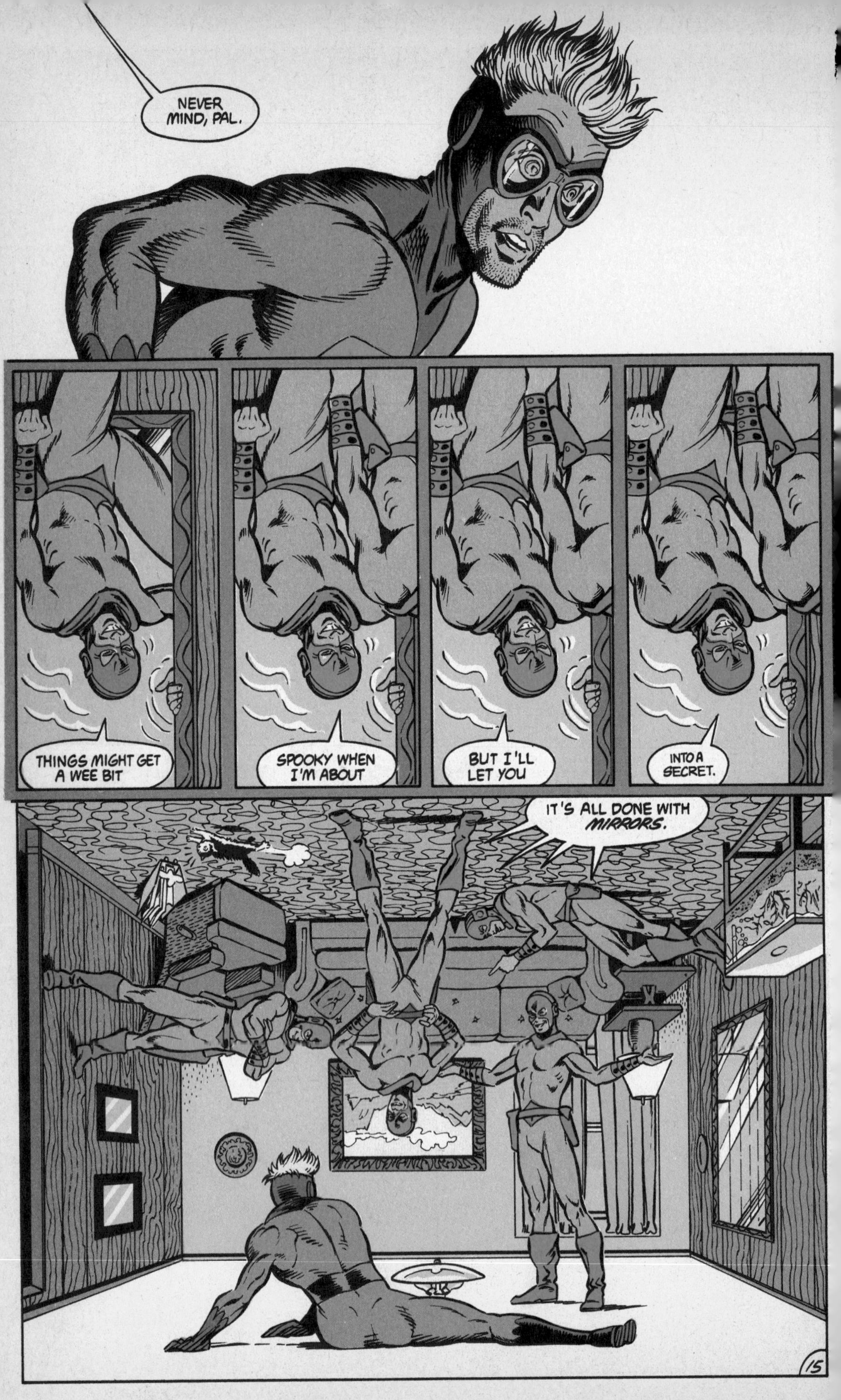
NEVER MIND, PAL.
THINGS MIGHT GET A WEE BIT
SPOOKY WHEN I'M ABOUT
BUT I'LL LET YOU
INTO A SECRET.
IT'S ALL DONE WITH MIRRORS.
15

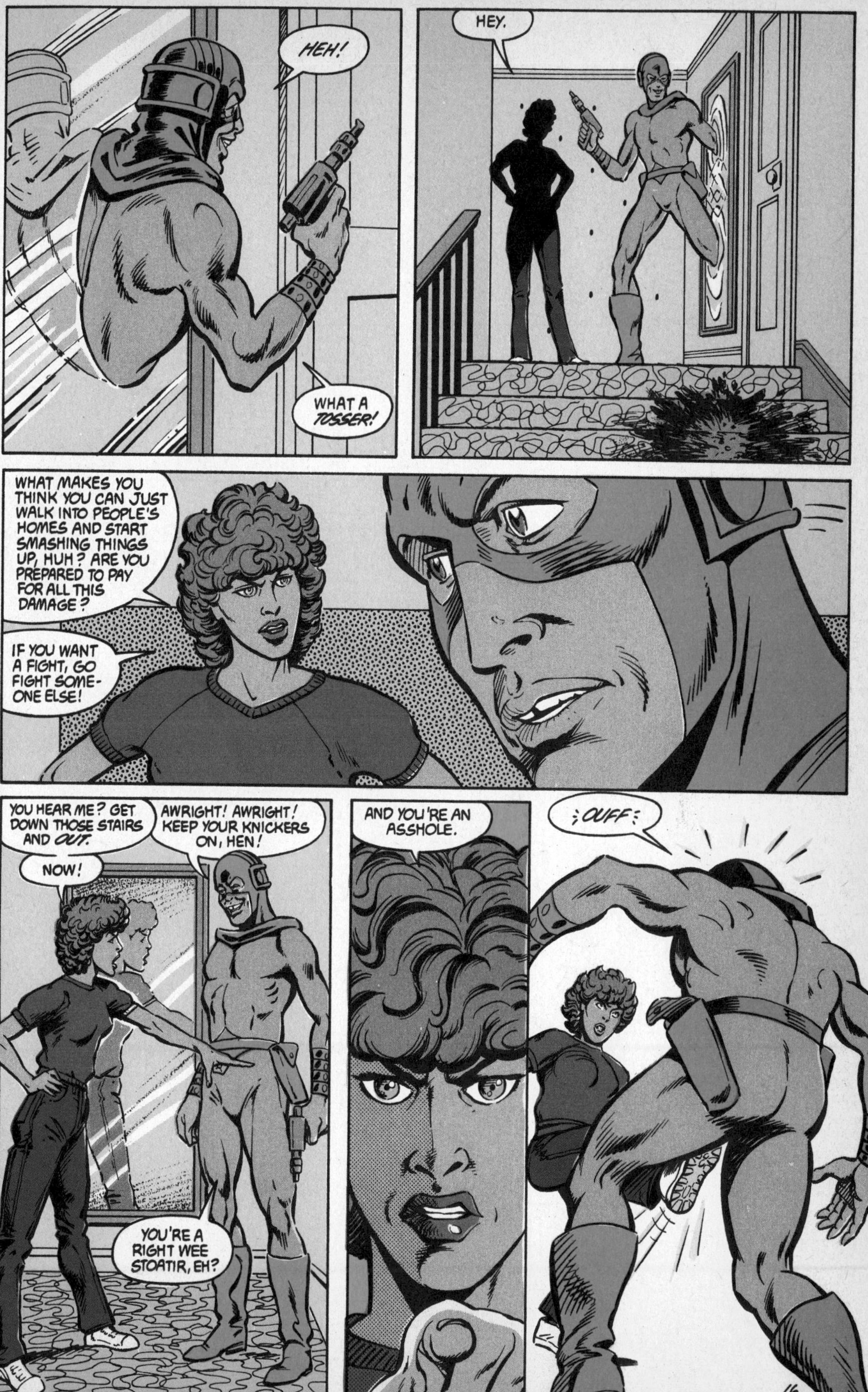
HEH!
WHAT A TOSSER!
HEY.
WHAT MAKES YOU THINK YOU CAN JUST WALK INTO PEOPLE'S HOMES AND START SMASHING THINGS UP, HUH? ARE YOU PREPARED TO PAY FOR ALL THIS DAMAGE?
IF YOU WANT A FIGHT, GO FIGHT SOME-ONE ELSE!
YOU HEAR ME? GET DOWN THOSE STAIRS AND OUT.
NOW!
AWRIGHT! AWRIGHT! KEEP YOUR KNICKERS ON, HEN!
YOU'RE A RIGHT WEE STOATIR, EH?
AND YOU'RE AN ASSHOLE.
OUFF
16

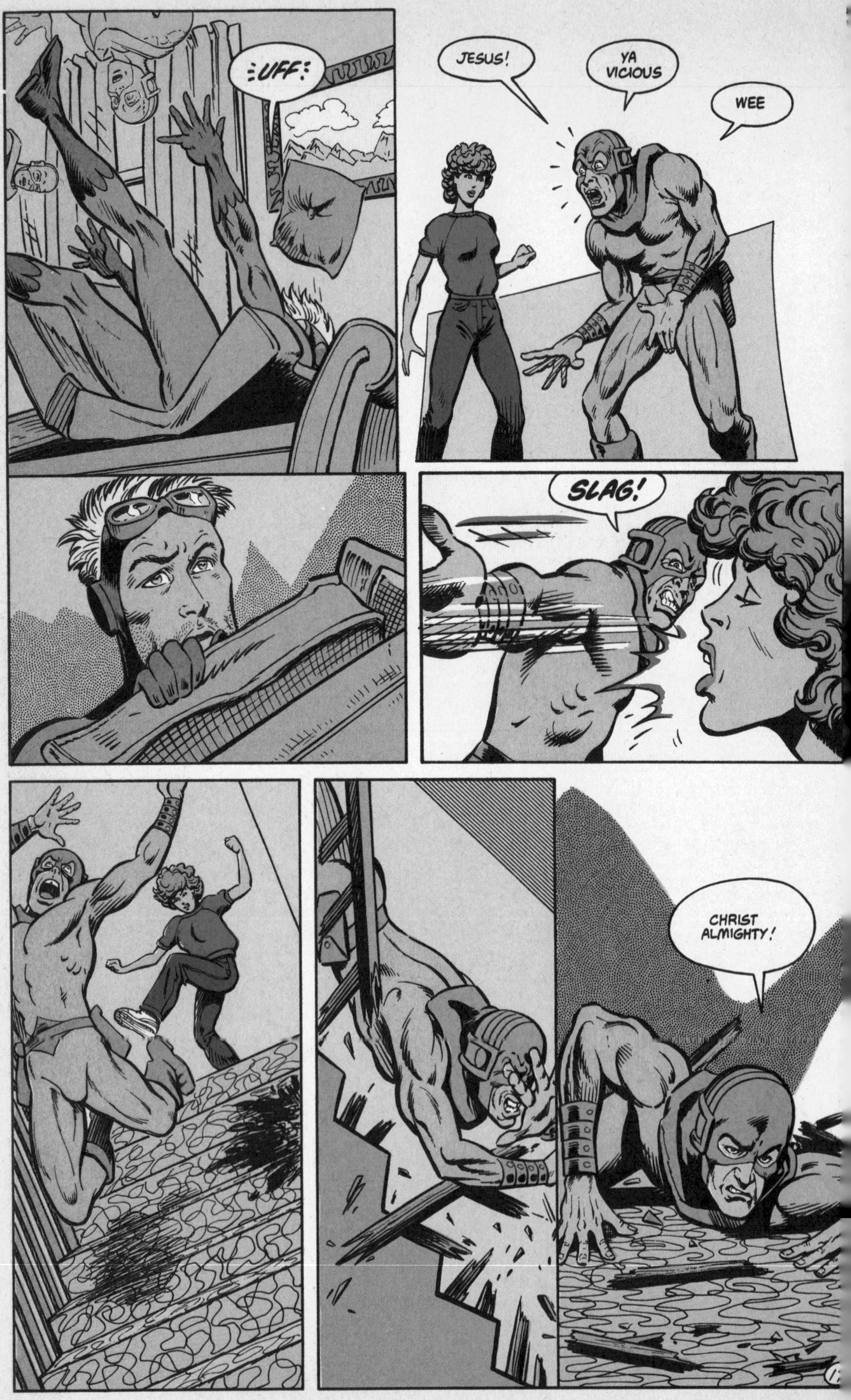
UFF
JESUS!
YA VICIOUS
WEE
SLAG!
CHRIST ALMIGHTY!

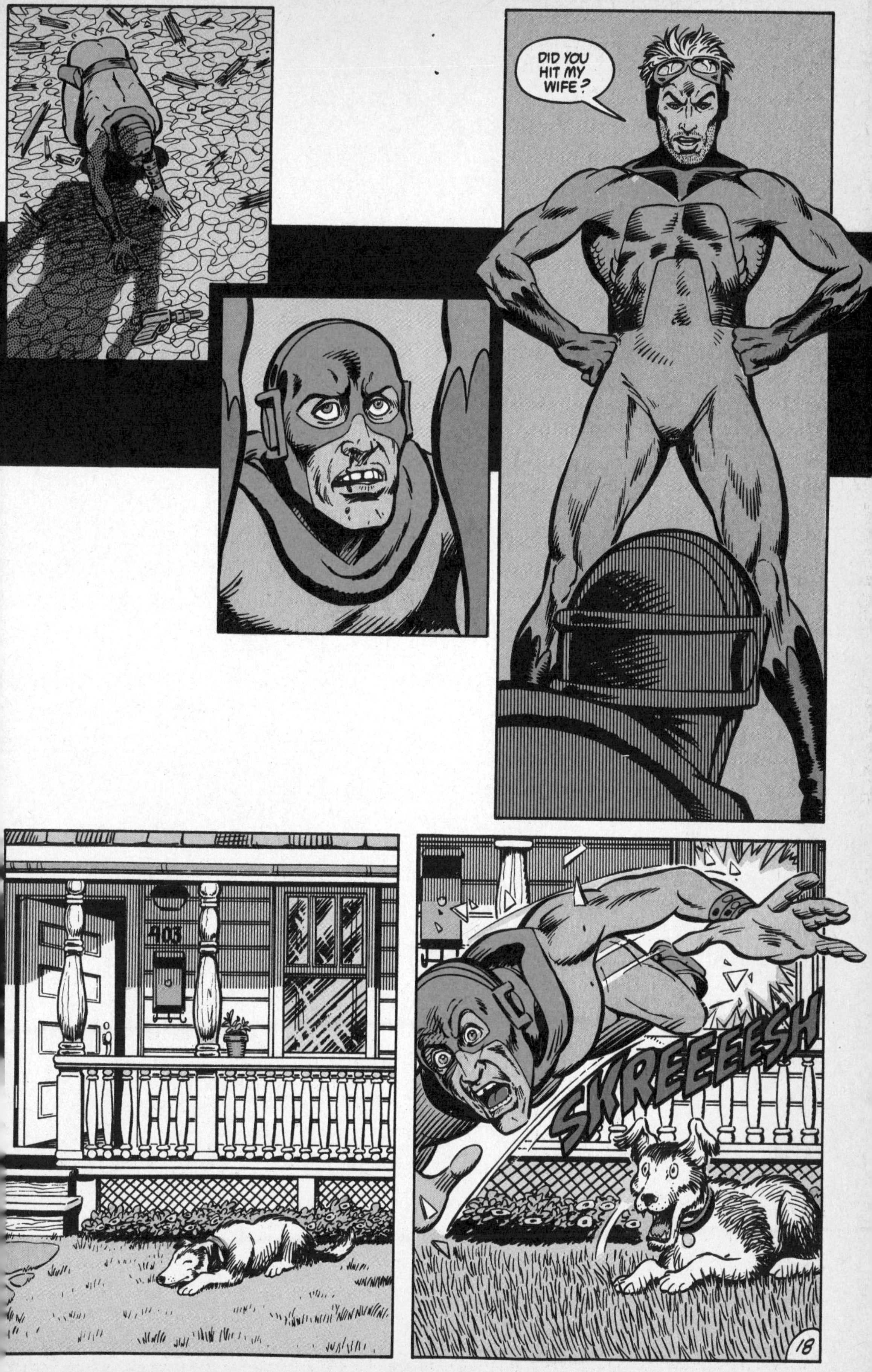
DID YOU HIT MY WIFE?
403
SKREEEEESH
18

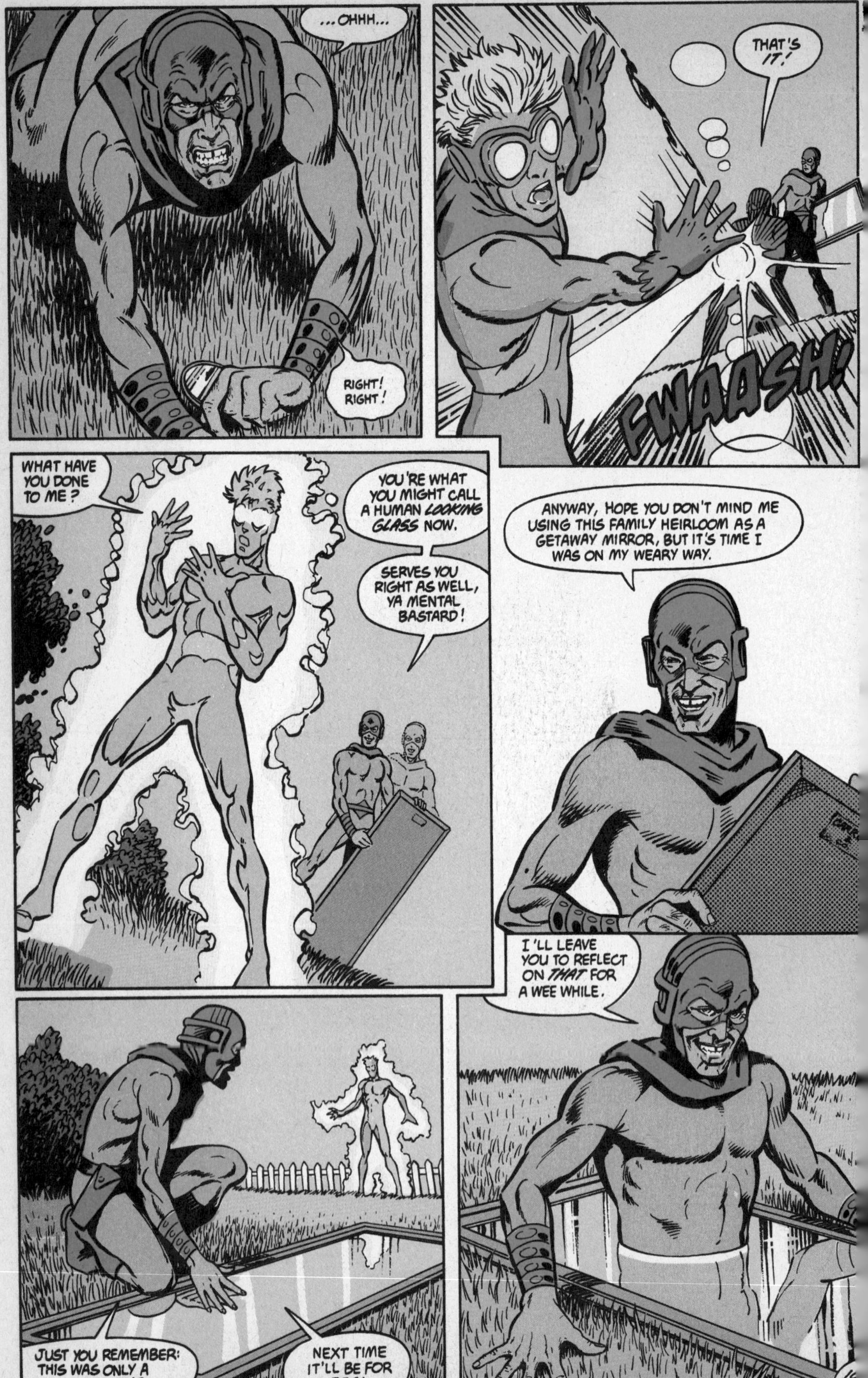
...OHHH...
RIGHT! RIGHT!
THAT'S IT!
FWAASH!
WHAT HAVE YOU DONE TO ME?
YOU'RE WHAT YOU MIGHT CALL A HUMAN LOOKING GLASS NOW.
SERVES YOU RIGHT AS WELL, YA MENTAL BASTARD!
ANYWAY, HOPE YOU DON'T MIND ME USING THIS FAMILY HEIRLOOM AS A GETAWAY MIRROR, BUT IT'S TIME I WAS ON MY WEARY WAY.
I'LL LEAVE YOU TO REFLECT ON THAT FOR A WEE WHILE.
JUST YOU REMEMBER: THIS WAS ONLY A WARNING.
NEXT TIME IT'LL BE FOR REAL.

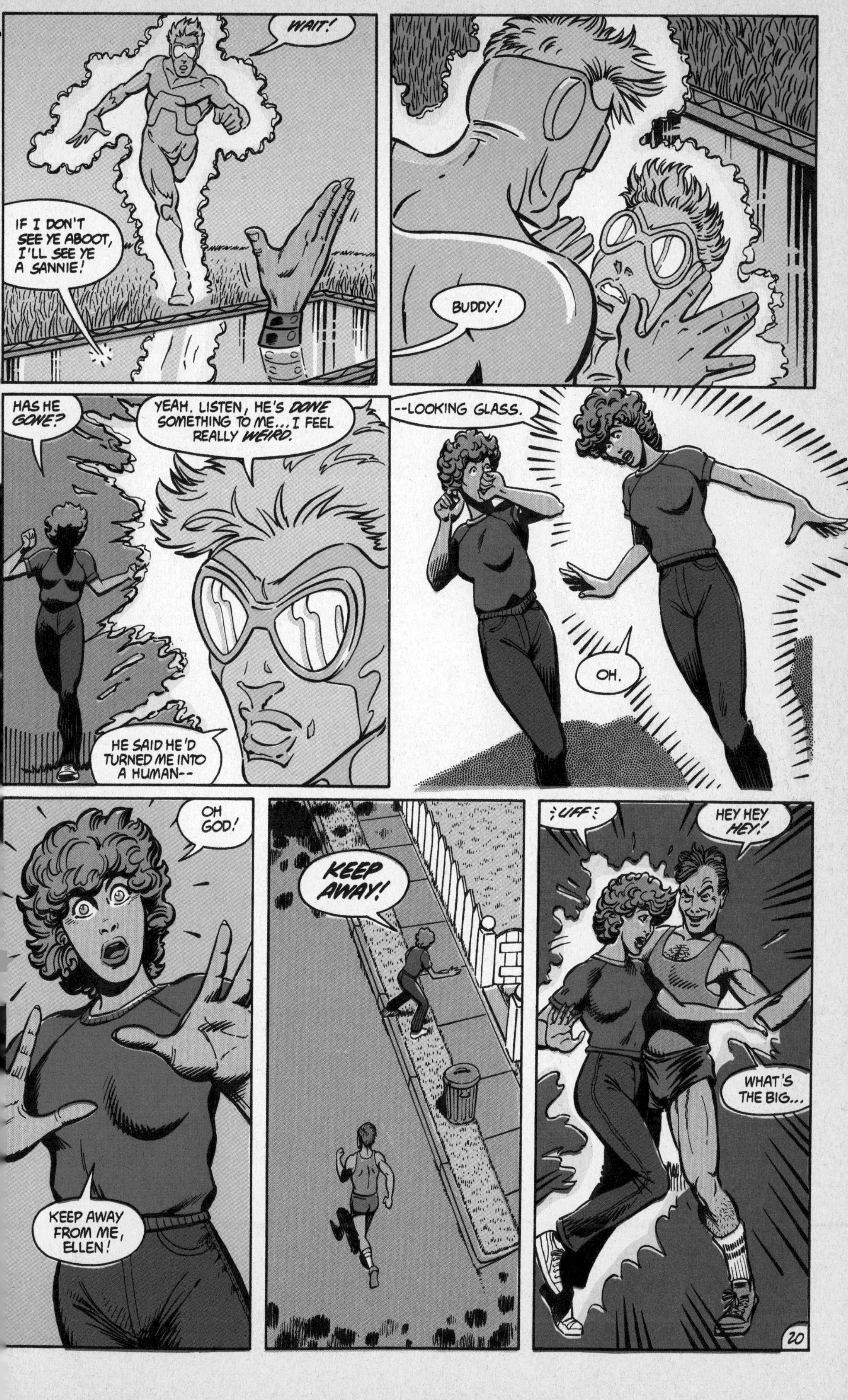
WAIT!
IF I DON'T SEE YE ABOOT, I'LL SEE YE A SANNIE!
BUDDY!
HAS HE GONE?
YEAH. LISTEN, HE'S DONE SOMETHING TO ME... I FEEL REALLY WEIRD.
HE SAID HE'D TURNED ME INTO A HUMAN--
--LOOKING GLASS.
OH.
OH GOD!
KEEP AWAY FROM ME, ELLEN!
KEEP AWAY!
UFF
HEY HEY HEY!
WHAT'S THE BIG...
20

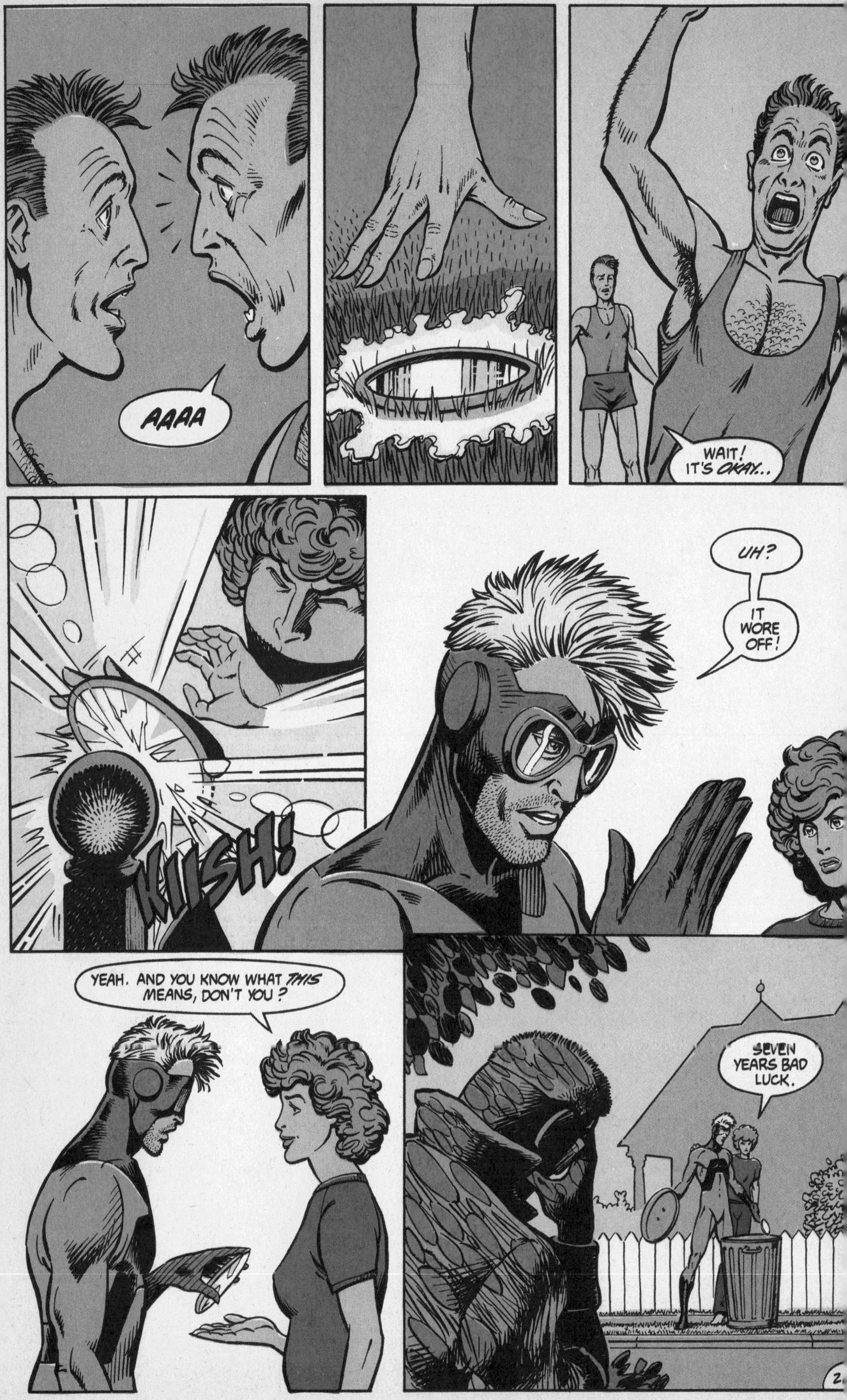
AAAA
WAIT! IT'S *OKAY...*
KIISH!
UH?
IT WORE OFF!
YEAH. AND YOU KNOW WHAT *THIS* MEANS, DON'T YOU?
SEVEN YEARS BAD LUCK.

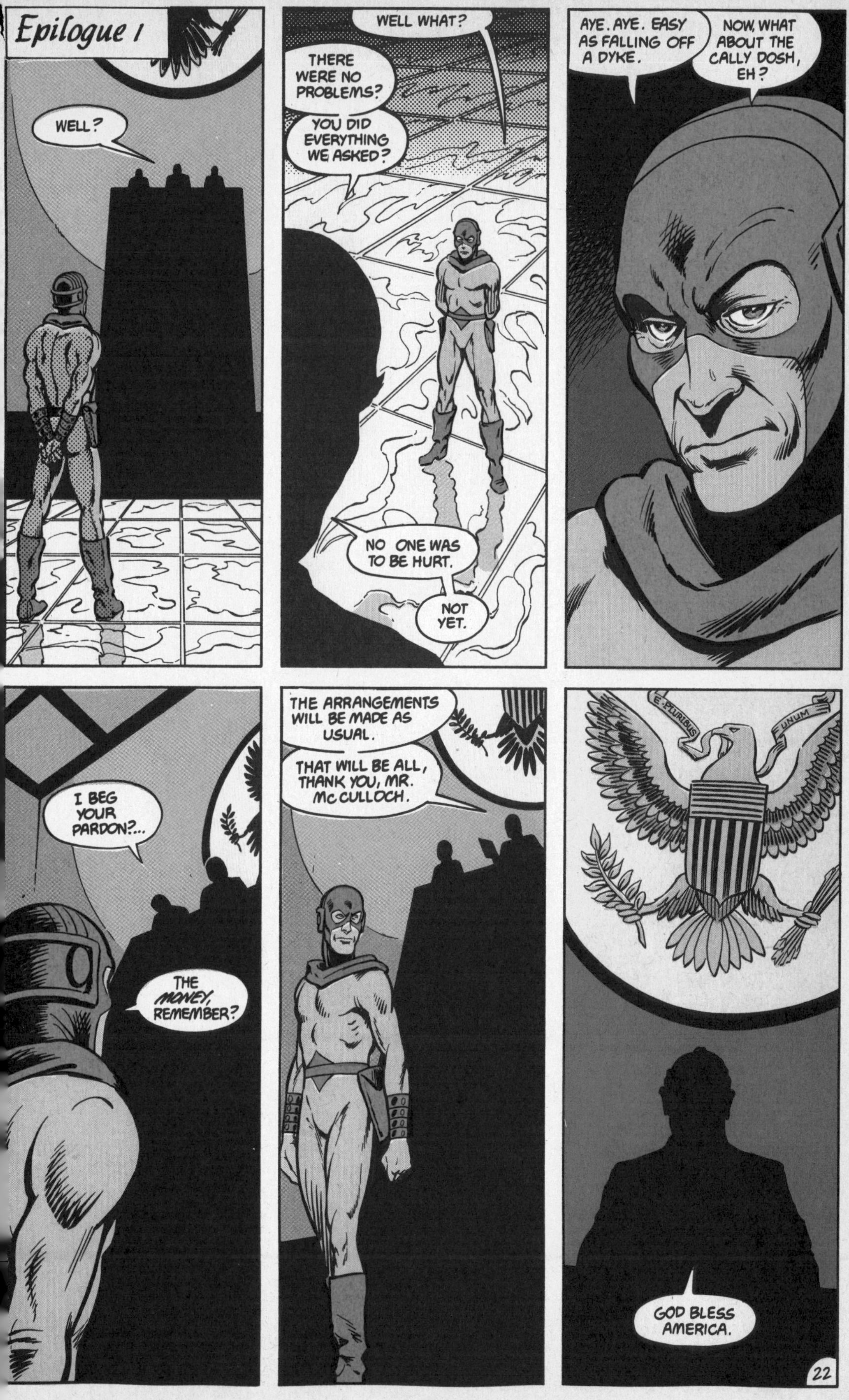
Epilogue 1
WELL?
WELL WHAT?
THERE WERE NO PROBLEMS?
YOU DID EVERYTHING WE ASKED?
NO ONE WAS TO BE HURT.
NOT YET.
AYE. AYE. EASY AS FALLING OFF A DYKE.
NOW, WHAT ABOUT THE CALLY DOSH, EH?
I BEG YOUR PARDON?...
THE MONEY, REMEMBER?
THE ARRANGEMENTS WILL BE MADE AS USUAL.
THAT WILL BE ALL, THANK YOU, MR. McCULLOCH.
E PLURIBUS UNUM
GOD BLESS AMERICA.

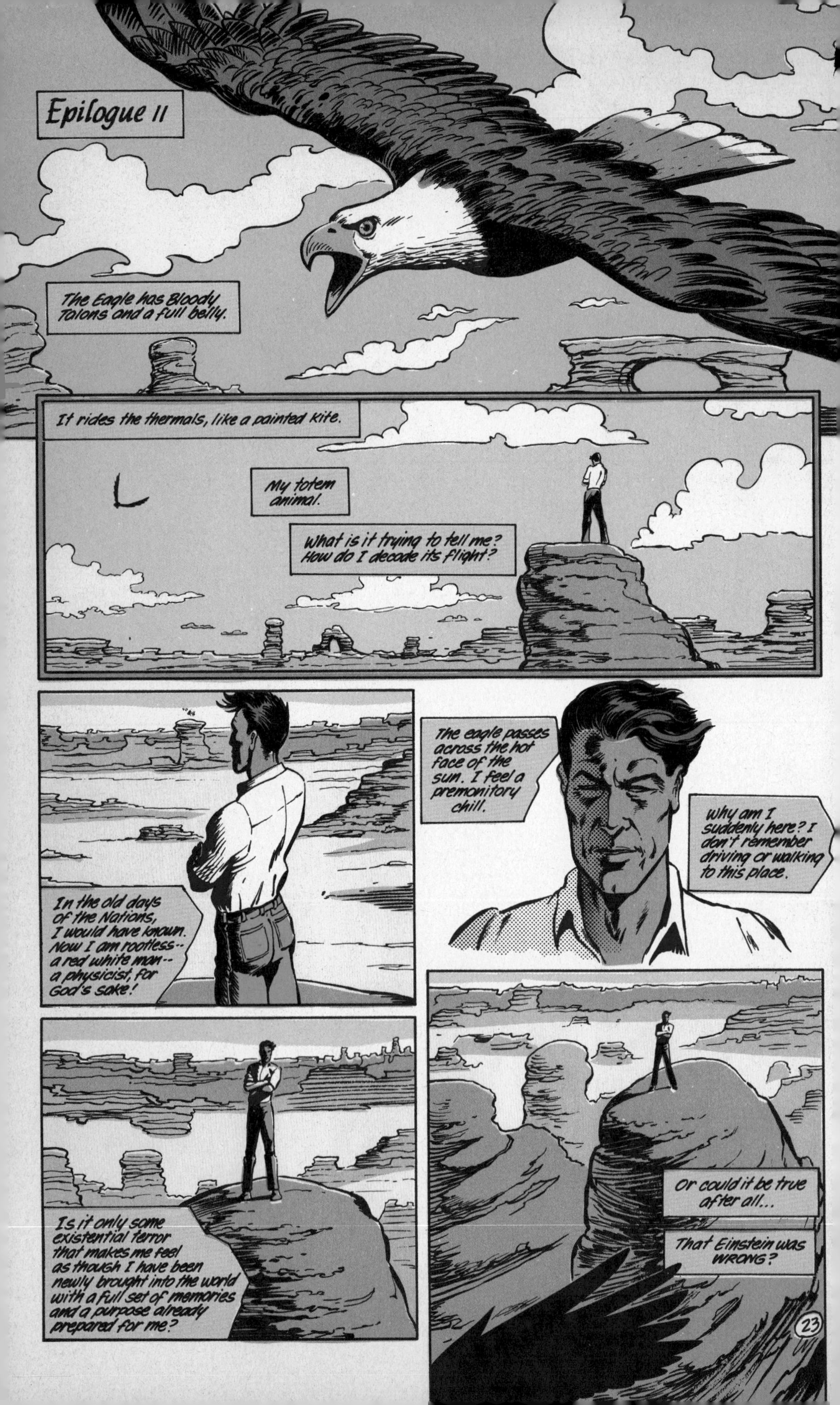
Epilogue II
The Eagle has Bloody Talons and a full belly.
It rides the thermals, like a painted kite.
My totem animal.
What is it trying to tell me? How do I decode its flight?
In the old days of the Nations, I would have known. Now I am rootless-- a red white man-- a physicist, for God's sake!
The eagle passes across the hot face of the sun. I feel a premonitory chill.
Why am I suddenly here? I don't remember driving or walking to this place.
Is it only some existential terror that makes me feel as though I have been newly brought into the world with a full set of memories and a purpose already prepared for me?
Or could it be true after all...
That Einstein was WRONG?
23

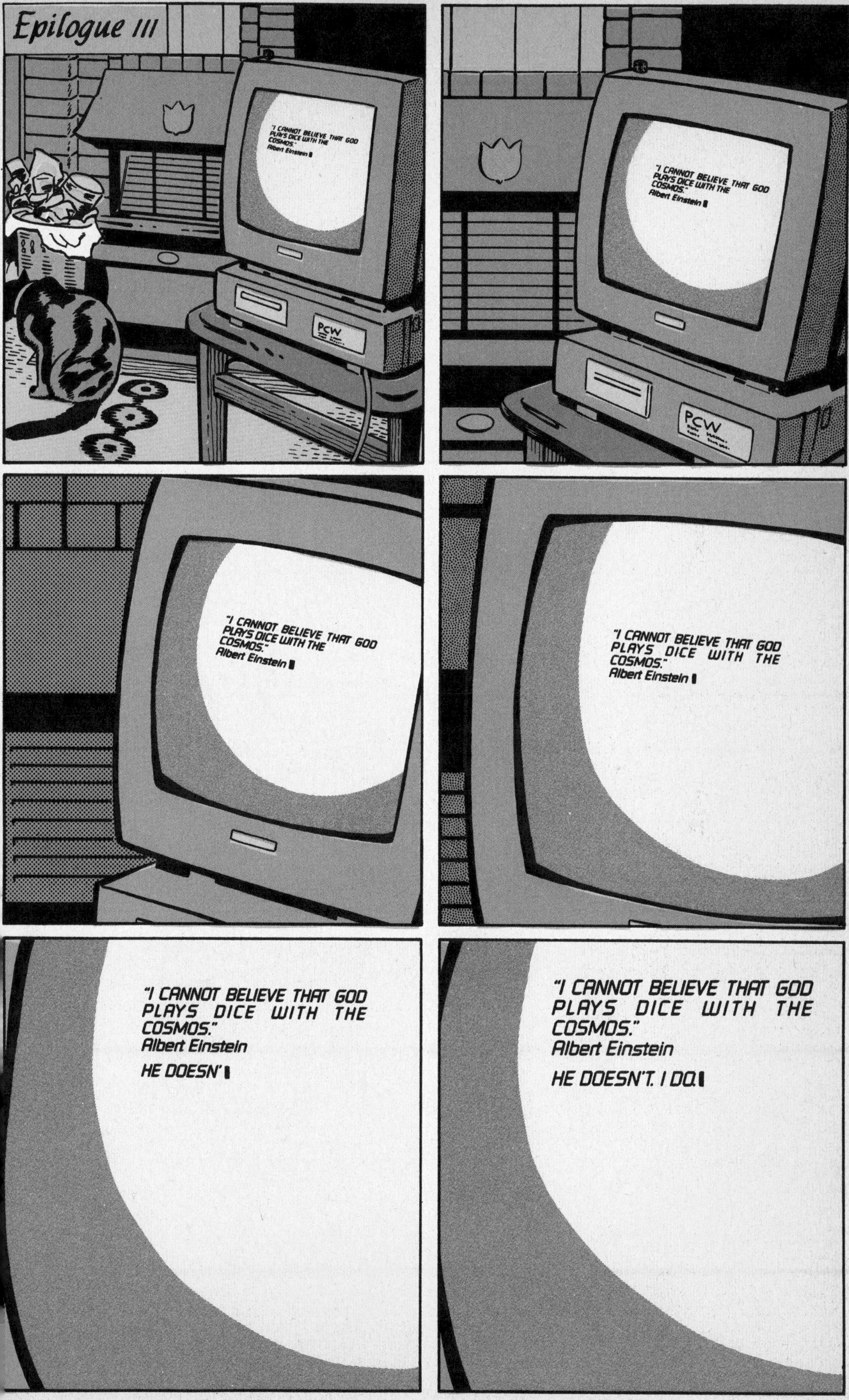
Epilogue III
"I CANNOT BELIEVE THAT GOD PLAYS DICE WITH THE COSMOS."
Albert Einstein
PCW
"I CANNOT BELIEVE THAT GOD PLAYS DICE WITH THE COSMOS."
Albert Einstein
PCW
"I CANNOT BELIEVE THAT GOD PLAYS DICE WITH THE COSMOS."
Albert Einstein
"I CANNOT BELIEVE THAT GOD PLAYS DICE WITH THE COSMOS."
Albert Einstein
"I CANNOT BELIEVE THAT GOD PLAYS DICE WITH THE COSMOS."
Albert Einstein
HE DOESN'
"I CANNOT BELIEVE THAT GOD PLAYS DICE WITH THE COSMOS."
Albert Einstein
HE DOESN'T. I DO.

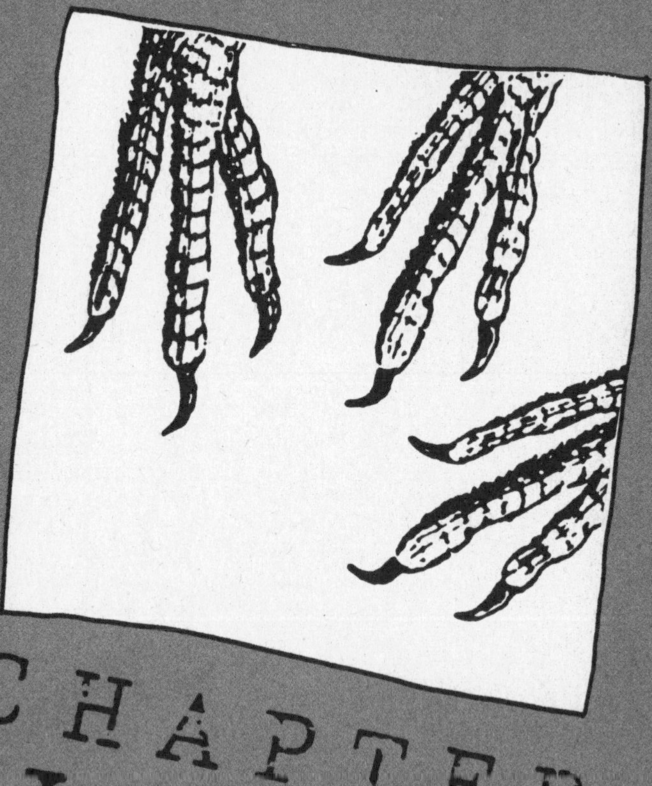

CHAPTER
NINE

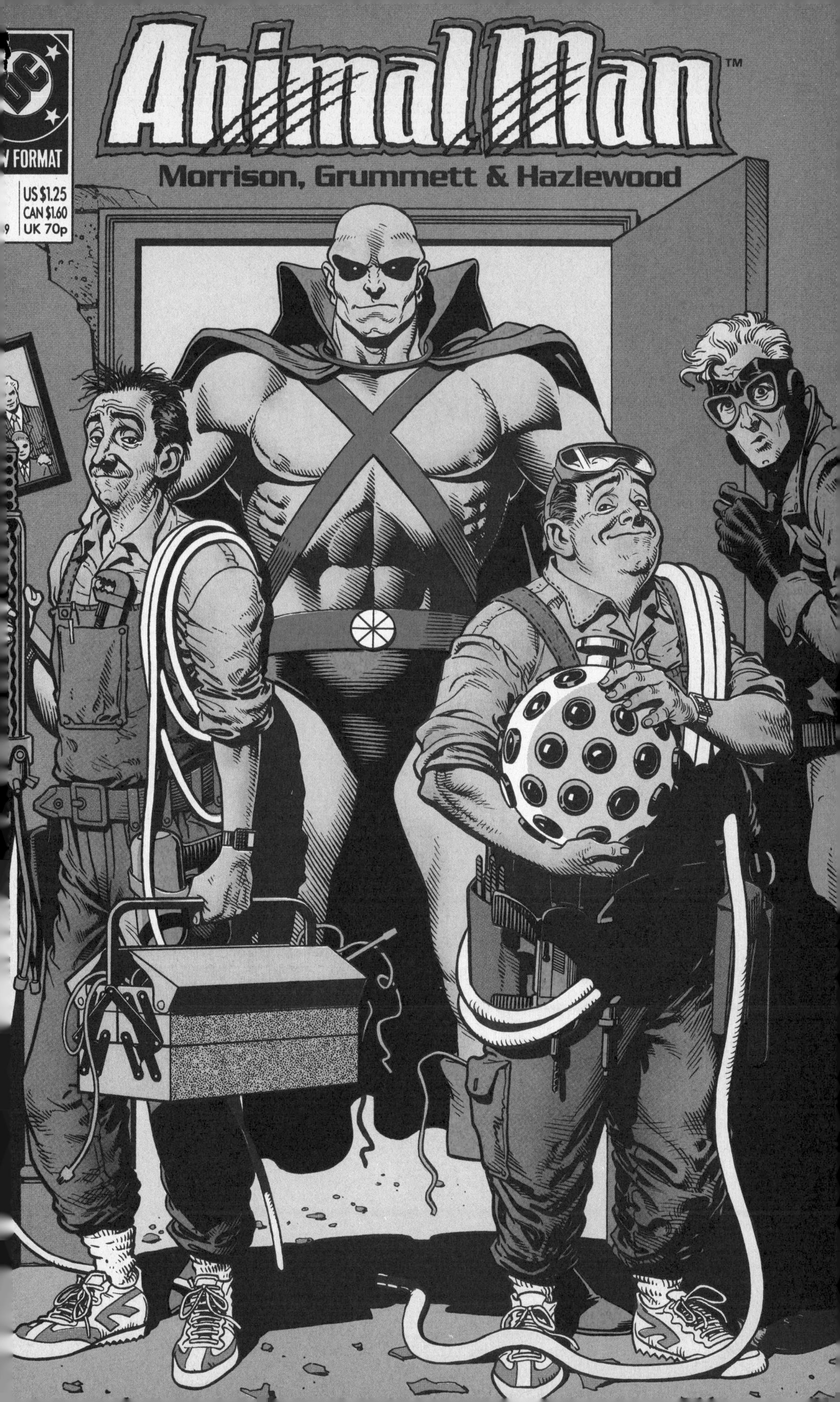

Animal Man
Morrison, Grummett & Hazlewood
US $1.25
CAN $1.60
UK 70p

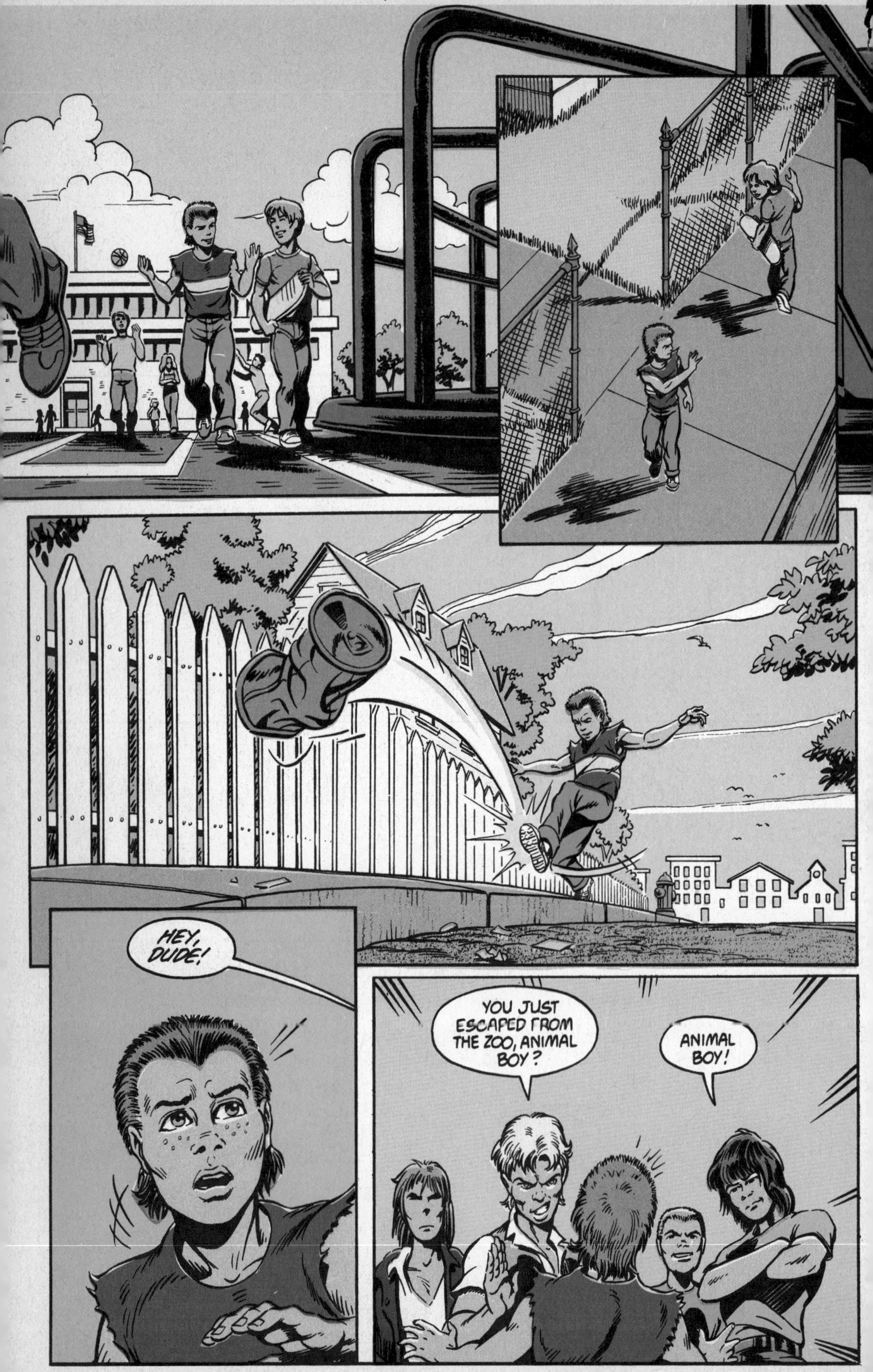
HEY, DUDE!
YOU JUST ESCAPED FROM THE ZOO, ANIMAL BOY?
ANIMAL BOY!

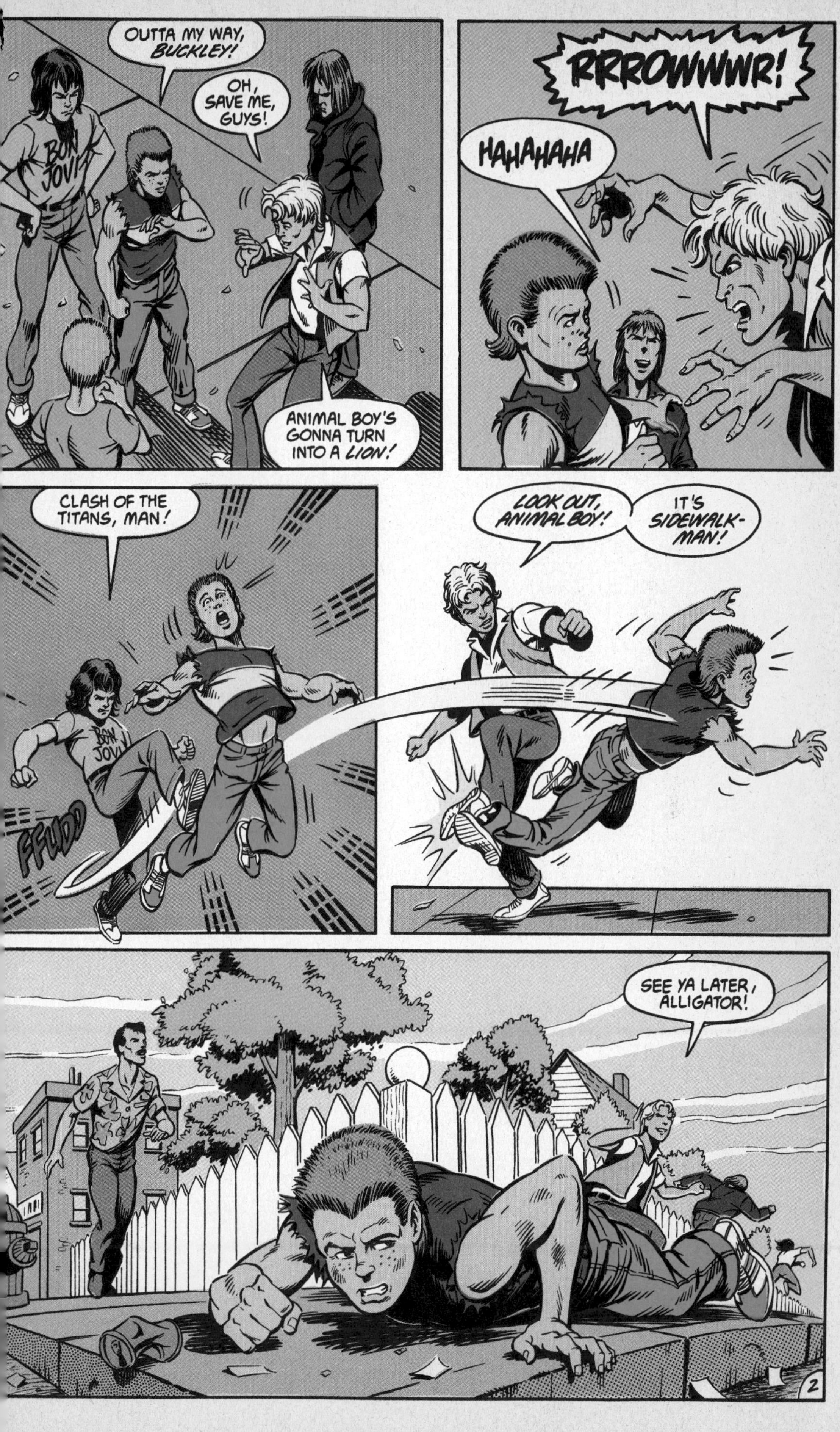
OUTTA MY WAY, BUCKLEY!
OH, SAVE ME, GUYS!
BON JOVI
ANIMAL BOY'S GONNA TURN INTO A LION!
RRROWWWR!
HAHAHAHA
CLASH OF THE TITANS, MAN!
BON JOVI
FFUDD
LOOK OUT, ANIMAL BOY!
IT'S SIDEWALK-MAN!
SEE YA LATER, ALLIGATOR!
2

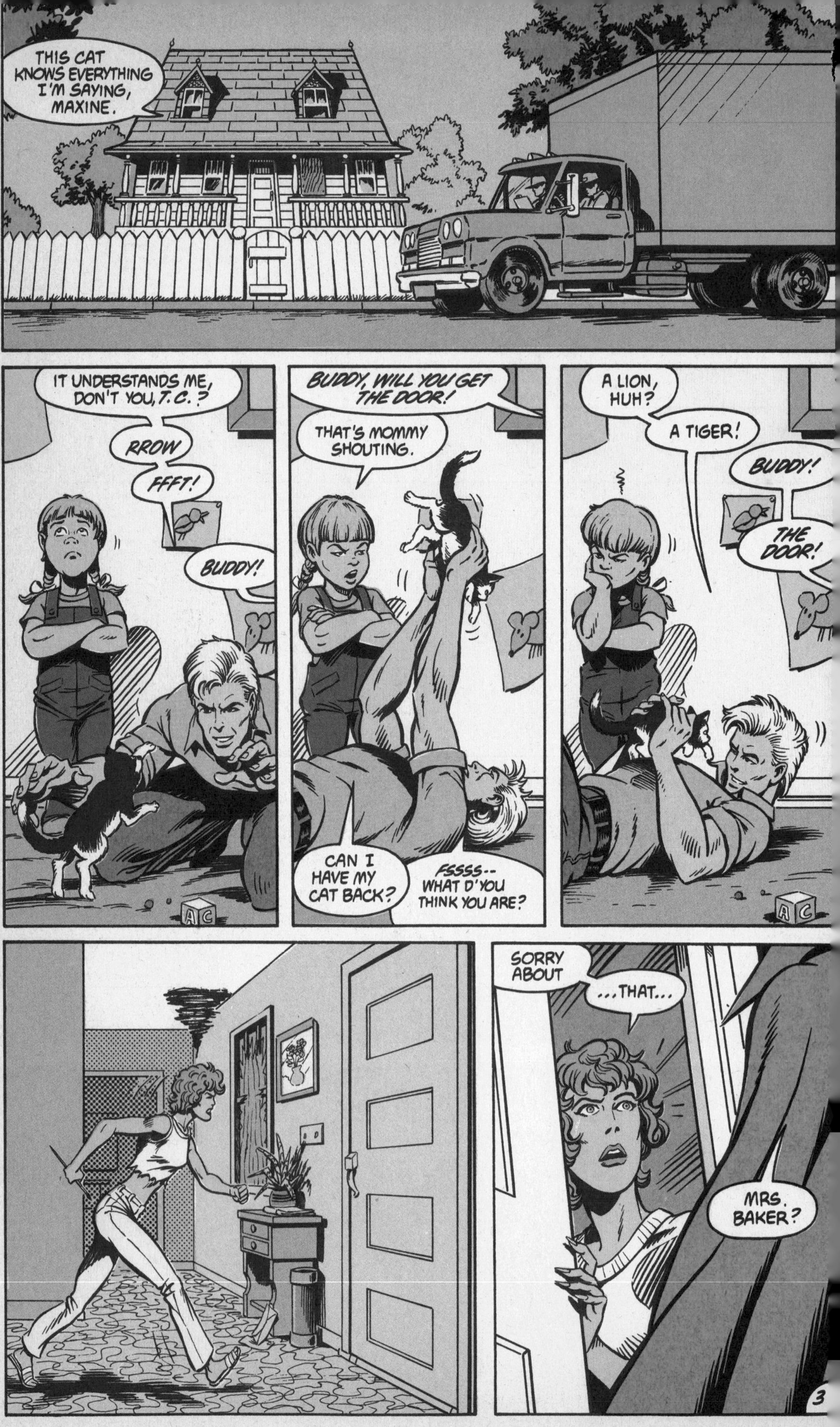
THIS CAT KNOWS EVERYTHING I'M SAYING, MAXINE.
IT UNDERSTANDS ME, DON'T YOU, T.C.?
RROW
FFFT!
BUDDY!
BUDDY, WILL YOU GET THE DOOR!
THAT'S MOMMY SHOUTING.
CAN I HAVE MY CAT BACK?
FSSSS-- WHAT D'YOU THINK YOU ARE?
A LION, HUH?
A TIGER!
BUDDY!
THE DOOR!
SORRY ABOUT
...THAT...
MRS. BAKER?

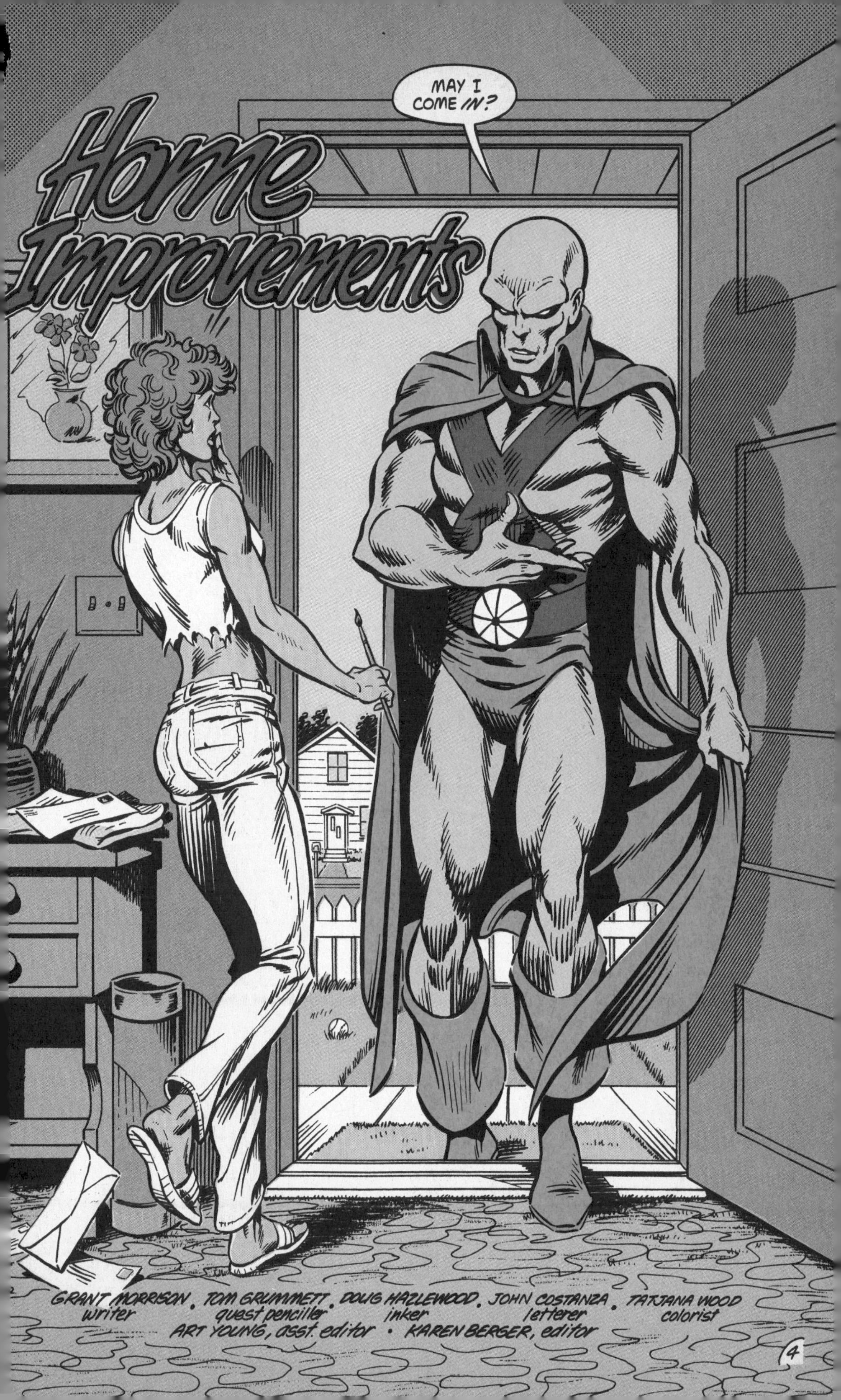
MAY I COME IN?
Home Improvements
GRANT MORRISON . writer
TOM GRUMMETT . guest penciller
DOUG HAZLEWOOD . inker
JOHN COSTANZA . letterer
TATJANA WOOD colorist
ART YOUNG, asst. editor . KAREN BERGER, editor
4

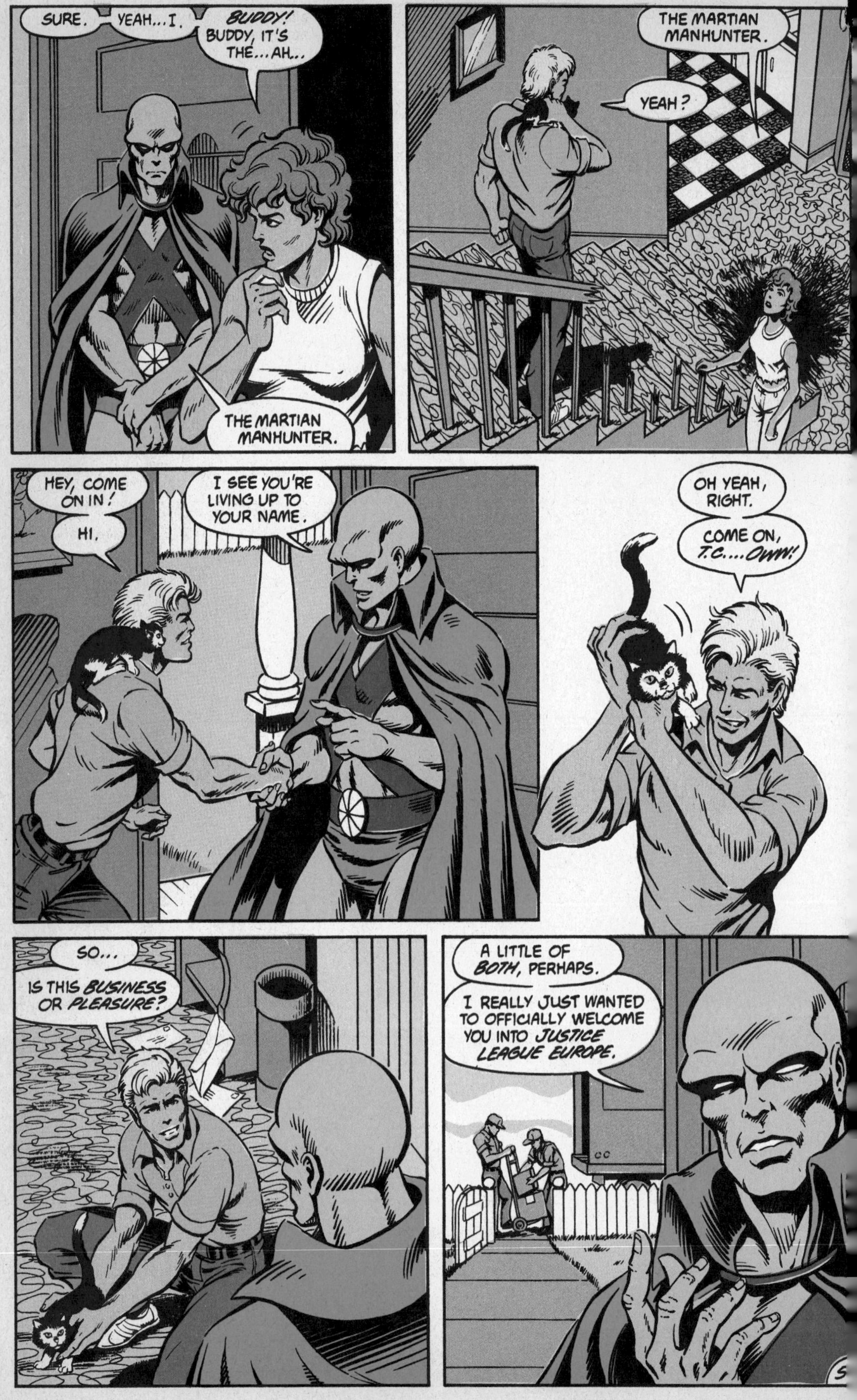
SURE.
YEAH... I.
BUDDY! BUDDY, IT'S THE... AH...
THE MARTIAN MANHUNTER.
THE MARTIAN MANHUNTER.
YEAH?
HEY, COME ON IN!
HI.
I SEE YOU'RE LIVING UP TO YOUR NAME.
OH YEAH, RIGHT.
COME ON, T.C.... OWW!
SO...
IS THIS BUSINESS OR PLEASURE?
A LITTLE OF BOTH, PERHAPS.
I REALLY JUST WANTED TO OFFICIALLY WELCOME YOU INTO JUSTICE LEAGUE EUROPE.

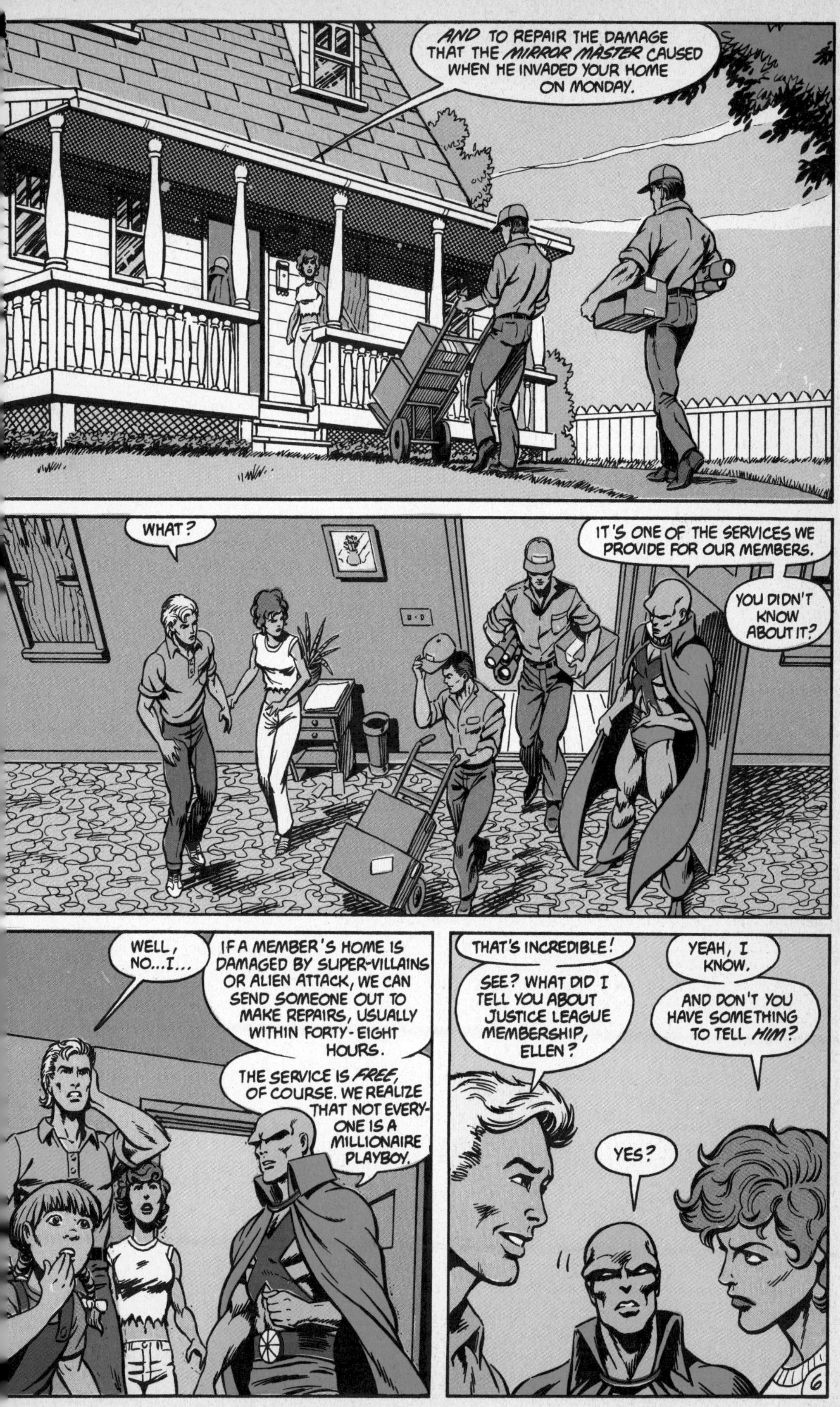

AND TO REPAIR THE DAMAGE THAT THE MIRROR MASTER CAUSED WHEN HE INVADED YOUR HOME ON MONDAY.
WHAT?
IT'S ONE OF THE SERVICES WE PROVIDE FOR OUR MEMBERS.
YOU DIDN'T KNOW ABOUT IT?
WELL, NO...I...
IF A MEMBER'S HOME IS DAMAGED BY SUPER-VILLAINS OR ALIEN ATTACK, WE CAN SEND SOMEONE OUT TO MAKE REPAIRS, USUALLY WITHIN FORTY-EIGHT HOURS.
THE SERVICE IS FREE, OF COURSE. WE REALIZE THAT NOT EVERYONE IS A MILLIONAIRE PLAYBOY.
THAT'S INCREDIBLE!
SEE? WHAT DID I TELL YOU ABOUT JUSTICE LEAGUE MEMBERSHIP, ELLEN?
YEAH, I KNOW.
AND DON'T YOU HAVE SOMETHING TO TELL HIM?
YES?
6

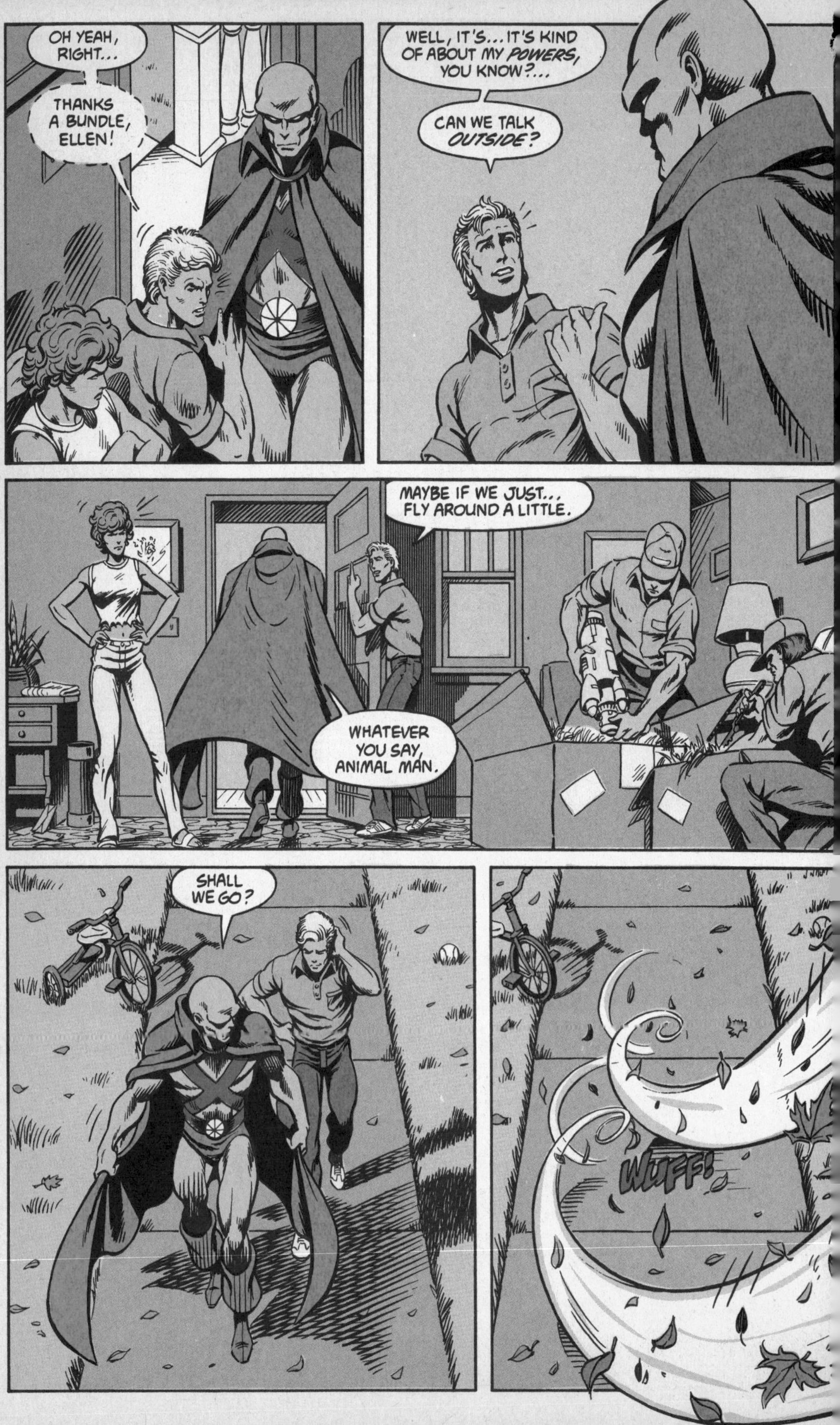
OH YEAH, RIGHT...
THANKS A BUNDLE, ELLEN!
WELL, IT'S... IT'S KIND OF ABOUT MY *POWERS*, YOU KNOW?...
CAN WE TALK *OUTSIDE*?
MAYBE IF WE JUST... FLY AROUND A LITTLE.
WHATEVER YOU SAY, ANIMAL MAN.
SHALL WE GO?
WUFF!

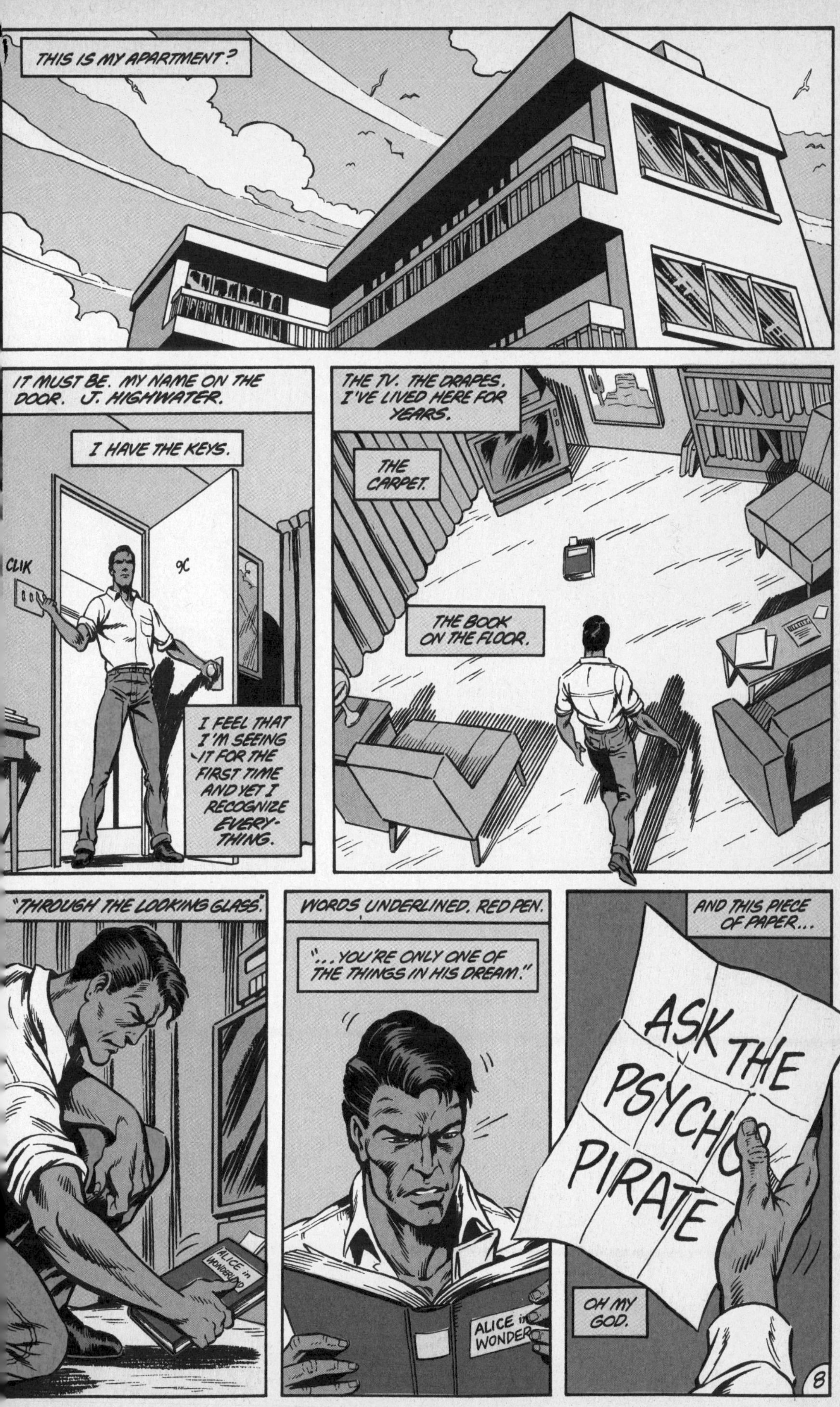

THIS IS MY APARTMENT?
IT MUST BE. MY NAME ON THE DOOR. J. HIGHWATER.
I HAVE THE KEYS.
CLIK
I FEEL THAT I'M SEEING IT FOR THE FIRST TIME AND YET I RECOGNIZE EVERYTHING.
THE TV. THE DRAPES. I'VE LIVED HERE FOR YEARS.
THE CARPET.
THE BOOK ON THE FLOOR.
"THROUGH THE LOOKING GLASS."
ALICE in WONDERLAND
WORDS UNDERLINED. RED PEN.
"...YOU'RE ONLY ONE OF THE THINGS IN HIS DREAM."
AND THIS PIECE OF PAPER...
ASK THE PSYCHO PIRATE
OH MY GOD.
8

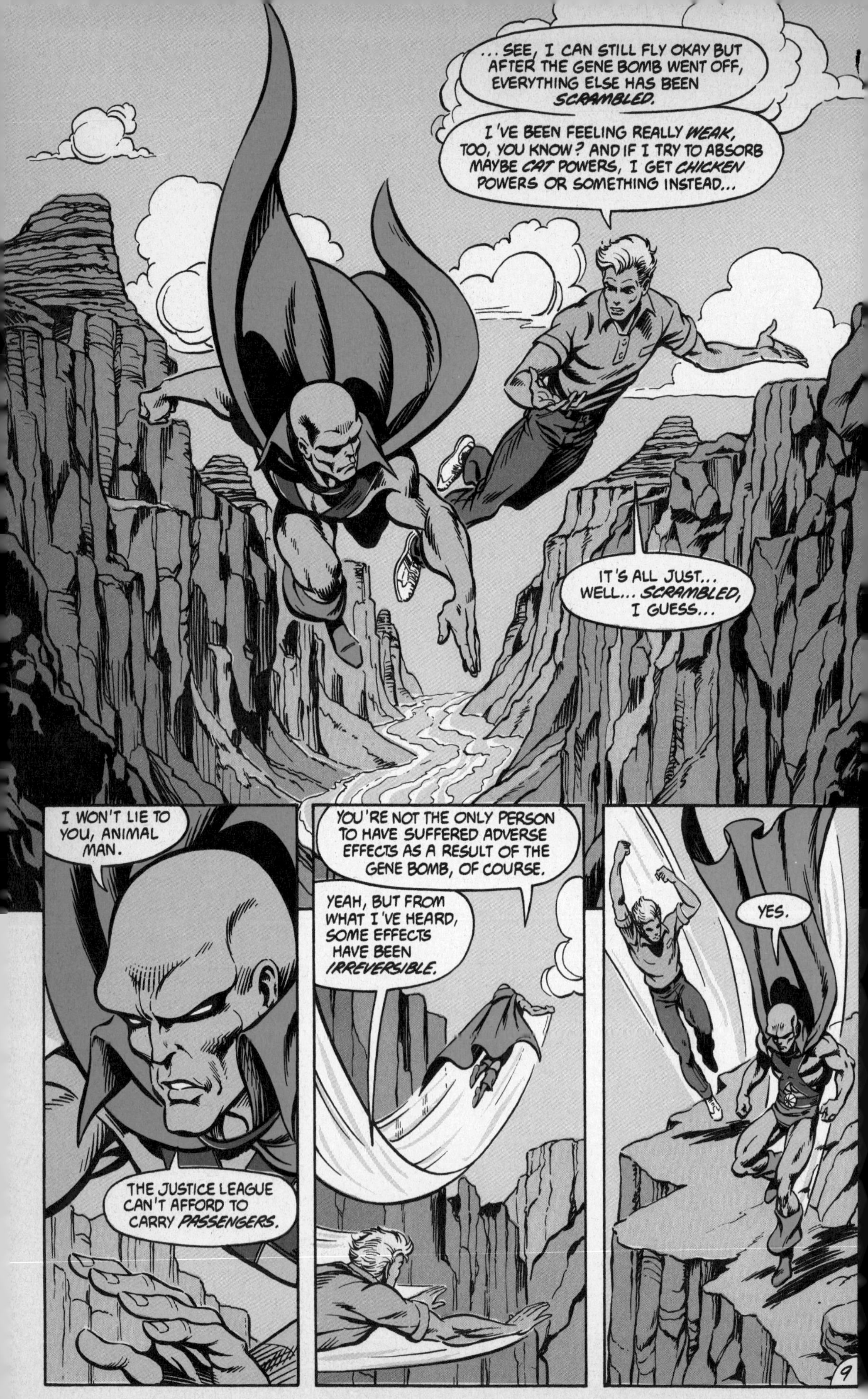
...SEE, I CAN STILL FLY OKAY BUT AFTER THE GENE BOMB WENT OFF, EVERYTHING ELSE HAS BEEN SCRAMBLED.
I'VE BEEN FEELING REALLY WEAK, TOO, YOU KNOW? AND IF I TRY TO ABSORB MAYBE CAT POWERS, I GET CHICKEN POWERS OR SOMETHING INSTEAD...
IT'S ALL JUST... WELL... SCRAMBLED, I GUESS...
I WON'T LIE TO YOU, ANIMAL MAN.
THE JUSTICE LEAGUE CAN'T AFFORD TO CARRY PASSENGERS.
YOU'RE NOT THE ONLY PERSON TO HAVE SUFFERED ADVERSE EFFECTS AS A RESULT OF THE GENE BOMB, OF COURSE.
YEAH, BUT FROM WHAT I'VE HEARD, SOME EFFECTS HAVE BEEN IRREVERSIBLE.
YES.
9

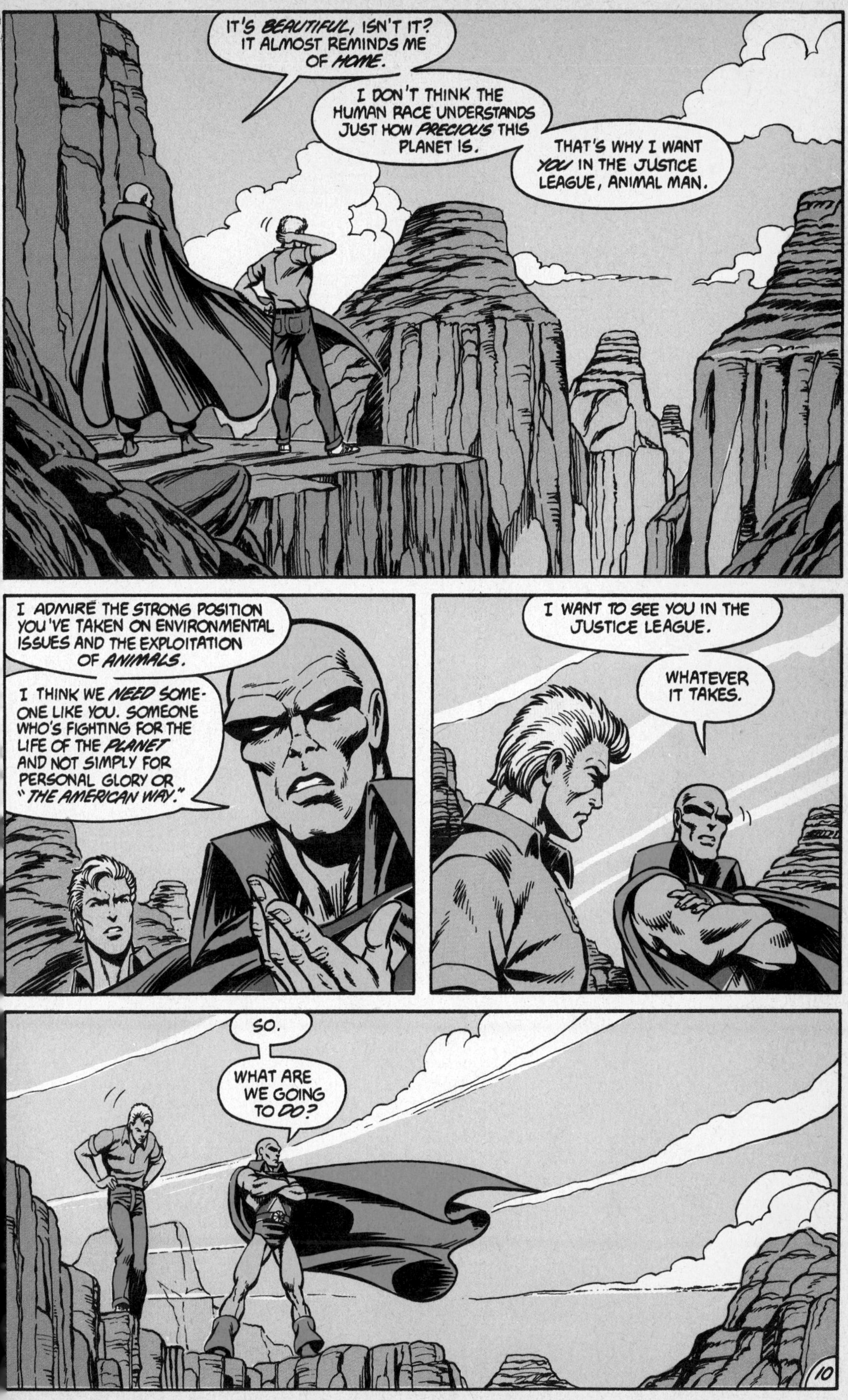

IT'S BEAUTIFUL, ISN'T IT? IT ALMOST REMINDS ME OF HOME.
I DON'T THINK THE HUMAN RACE UNDERSTANDS JUST HOW PRECIOUS THIS PLANET IS.
THAT'S WHY I WANT YOU IN THE JUSTICE LEAGUE, ANIMAL MAN.
I ADMIRE THE STRONG POSITION YOU'VE TAKEN ON ENVIRONMENTAL ISSUES AND THE EXPLOITATION OF ANIMALS.
I THINK WE NEED SOME-ONE LIKE YOU. SOMEONE WHO'S FIGHTING FOR THE LIFE OF THE PLANET AND NOT SIMPLY FOR PERSONAL GLORY OR "THE AMERICAN WAY."
I WANT TO SEE YOU IN THE JUSTICE LEAGUE.
WHATEVER IT TAKES.
SO.
WHAT ARE WE GOING TO DO?
10

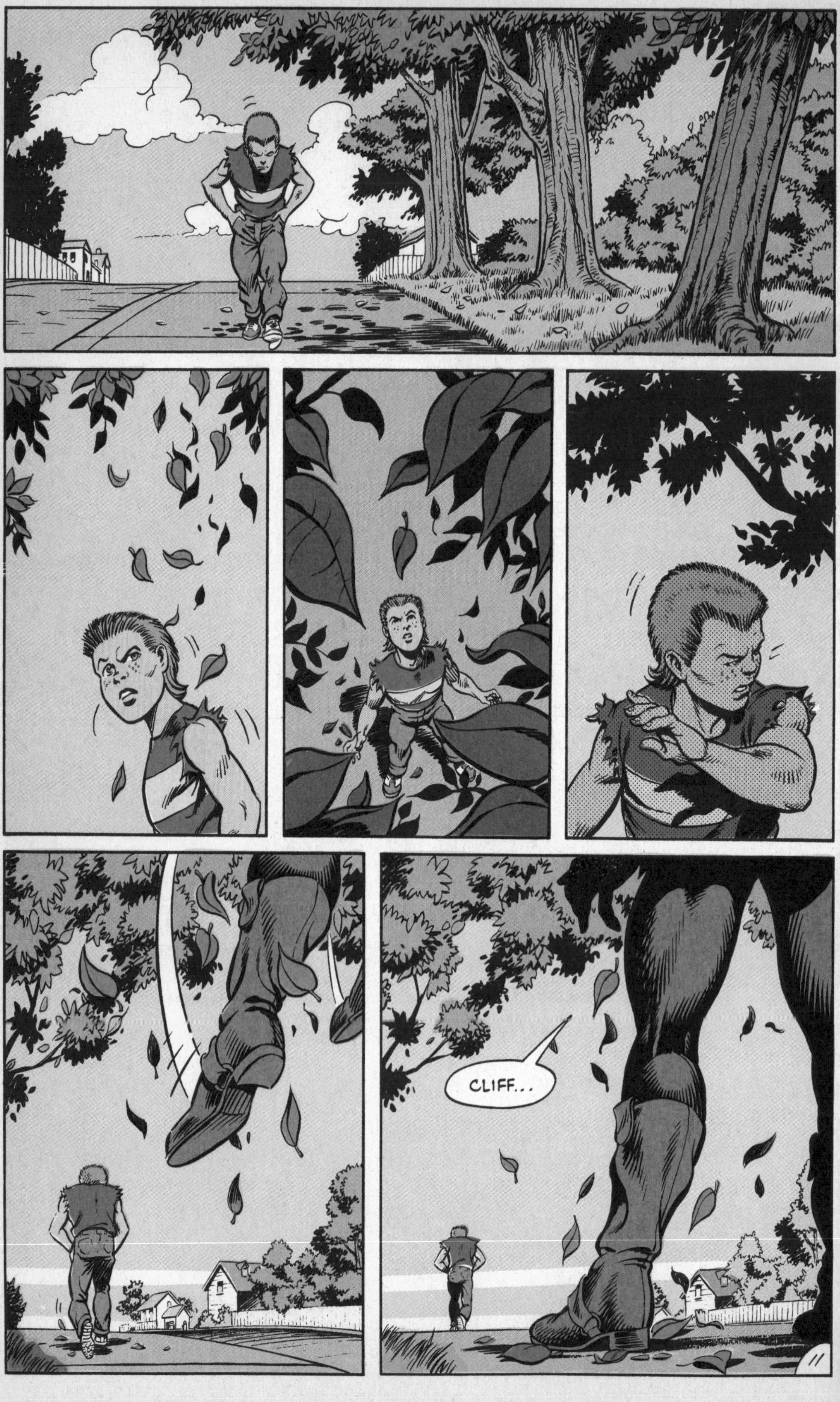
CLIFF...

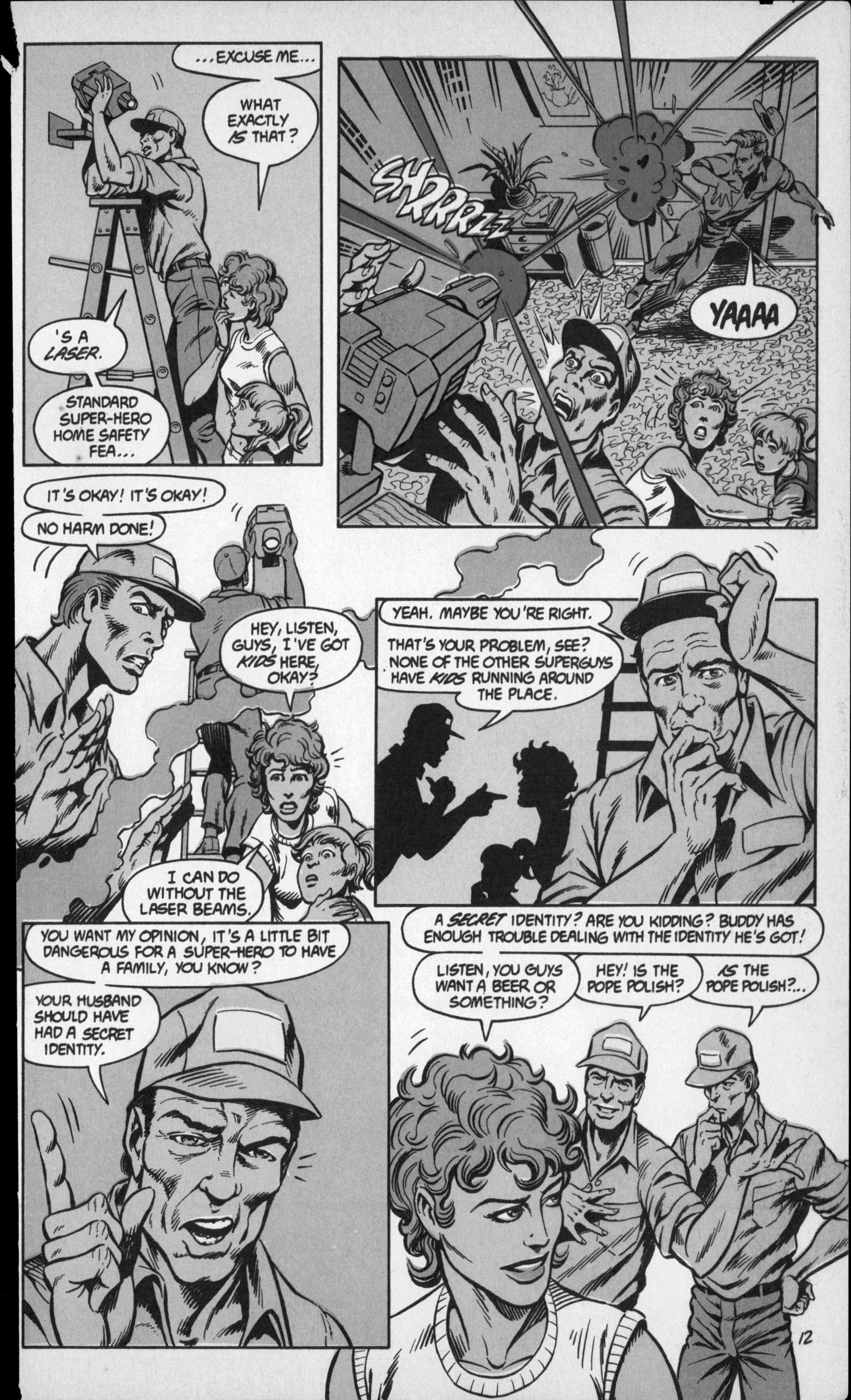
...EXCUSE ME...
WHAT EXACTLY *IS* THAT?
'S A *LASER*.
STANDARD SUPER-HERO HOME SAFETY FEA...
SHRRRZZZ
YAAAA
IT'S OKAY! IT'S OKAY!
NO HARM DONE!
HEY, LISTEN, GUYS, I'VE GOT *KIDS* HERE, OKAY?
I CAN DO WITHOUT THE LASER BEAMS.
YEAH. MAYBE YOU'RE RIGHT.
THAT'S YOUR PROBLEM, SEE? NONE OF THE OTHER SUPERGUYS HAVE *KIDS* RUNNING AROUND THE PLACE.
YOU WANT MY OPINION, IT'S A LITTLE BIT DANGEROUS FOR A SUPER-HERO TO HAVE A FAMILY, YOU KNOW?
YOUR HUSBAND SHOULD HAVE HAD A SECRET IDENTITY.
A *SECRET* IDENTITY? ARE YOU KIDDING? BUDDY HAS ENOUGH TROUBLE DEALING WITH THE IDENTITY HE'S GOT!
LISTEN, YOU GUYS WANT A BEER OR SOMETHING?
HEY! IS THE POPE POLISH?
IS THE POPE POLISH?...
12

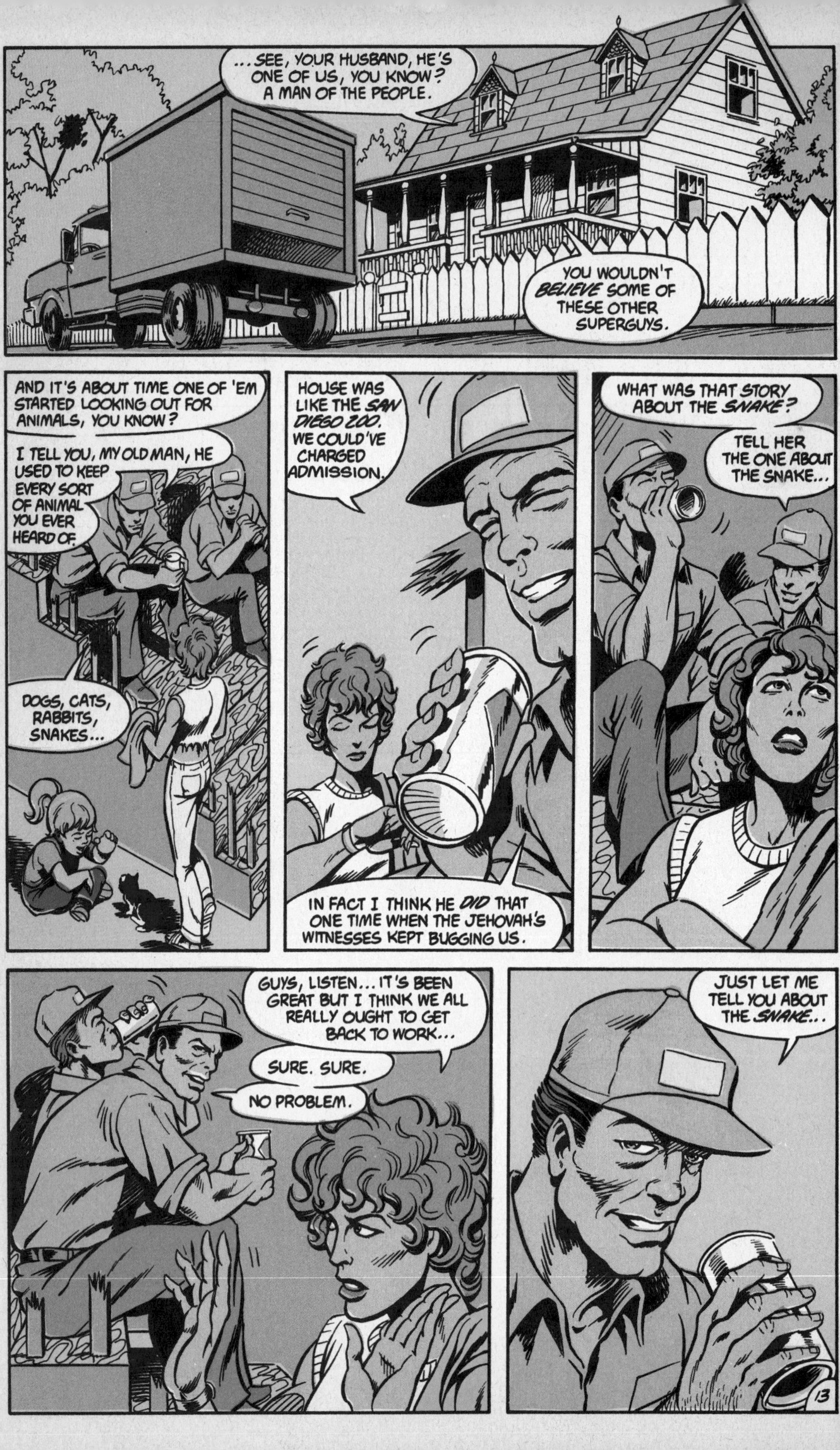
...SEE, YOUR HUSBAND, HE'S ONE OF US, YOU KNOW? A MAN OF THE PEOPLE.
YOU WOULDN'T BELIEVE SOME OF THESE OTHER SUPERGUYS.
AND IT'S ABOUT TIME ONE OF 'EM STARTED LOOKING OUT FOR ANIMALS, YOU KNOW?
I TELL YOU, MY OLD MAN, HE USED TO KEEP EVERY SORT OF ANIMAL YOU EVER HEARD OF.
DOGS, CATS, RABBITS, SNAKES...
HOUSE WAS LIKE THE SAN DIEGO ZOO. WE COULD'VE CHARGED ADMISSION.
IN FACT I THINK HE DID THAT ONE TIME WHEN THE JEHOVAH'S WITNESSES KEPT BUGGING US.
WHAT WAS THAT STORY ABOUT THE SNAKE?
TELL HER THE ONE ABOUT THE SNAKE...
GUYS, LISTEN... IT'S BEEN GREAT BUT I THINK WE ALL REALLY OUGHT TO GET BACK TO WORK...
SURE. SURE.
NO PROBLEM.
JUST LET ME TELL YOU ABOUT THE SNAKE...
13

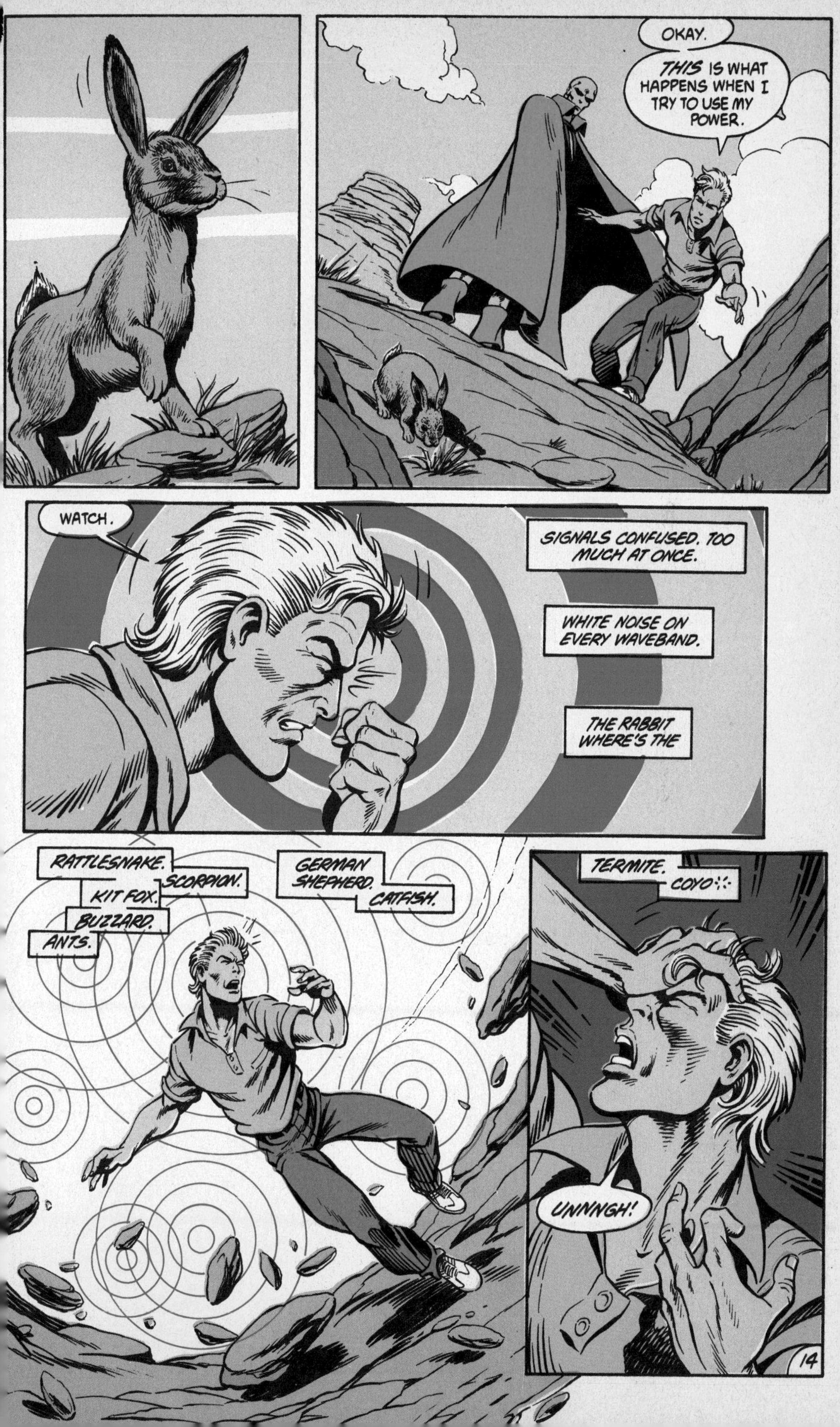
OKAY.
THIS IS WHAT HAPPENS WHEN I TRY TO USE MY POWER.
WATCH.
SIGNALS CONFUSED. TOO MUCH AT ONCE.
WHITE NOISE ON EVERY WAVEBAND.
THE RABBIT WHERE'S THE
RATTLESNAKE.
SCORPION.
KIT FOX.
BUZZARD.
ANTS.
GERMAN SHEPHERD.
CATFISH.
TERMITE.
COYO
UNNNGH!
14

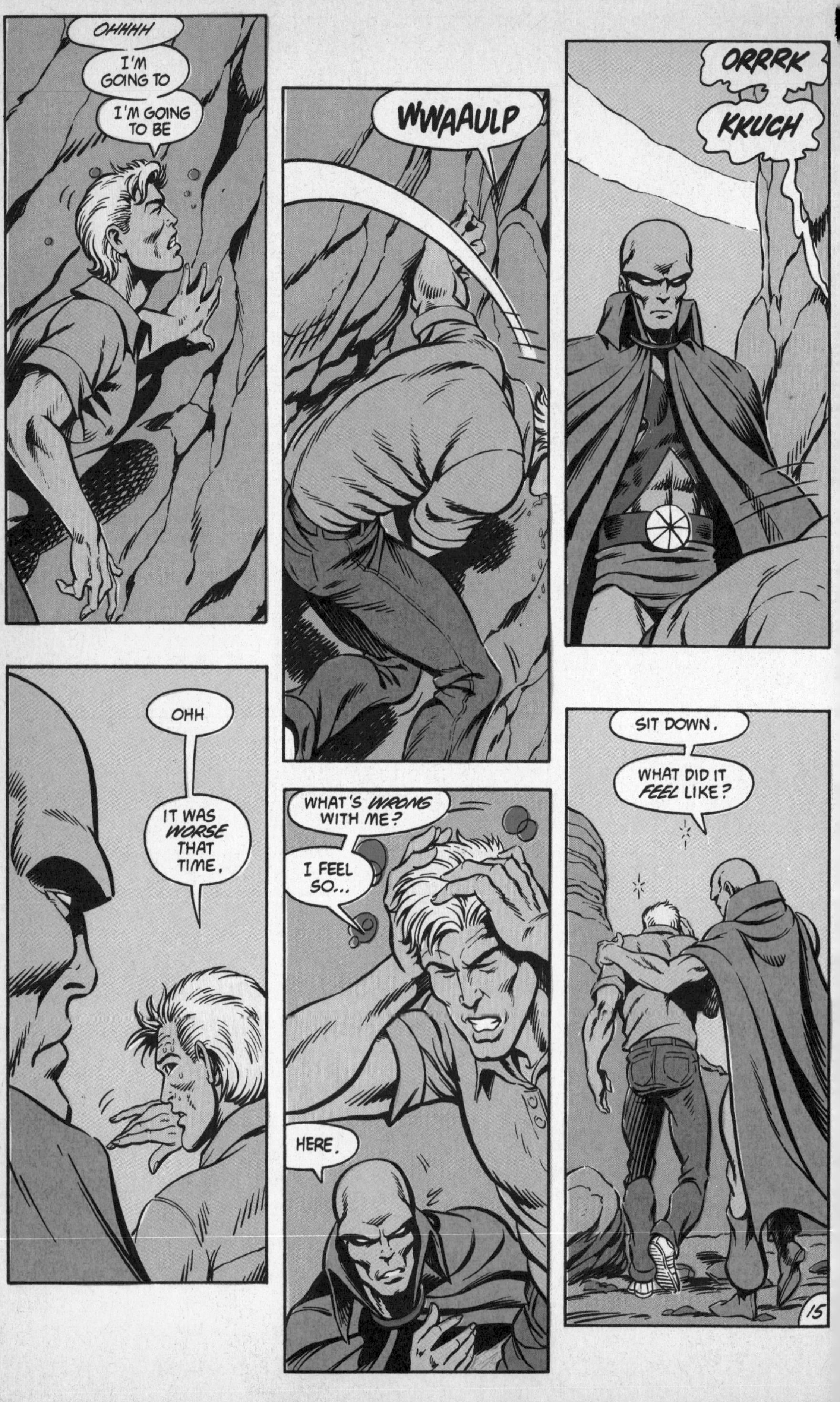
OHHHH
I'M GOING TO
I'M GOING TO BE
WWAAAULP
ORRRK
KKUCH
OHH
IT WAS WORSE THAT TIME.
WHAT'S WRONG WITH ME?
I FEEL SO...
HERE.
SIT DOWN.
WHAT DID IT FEEL LIKE?
15

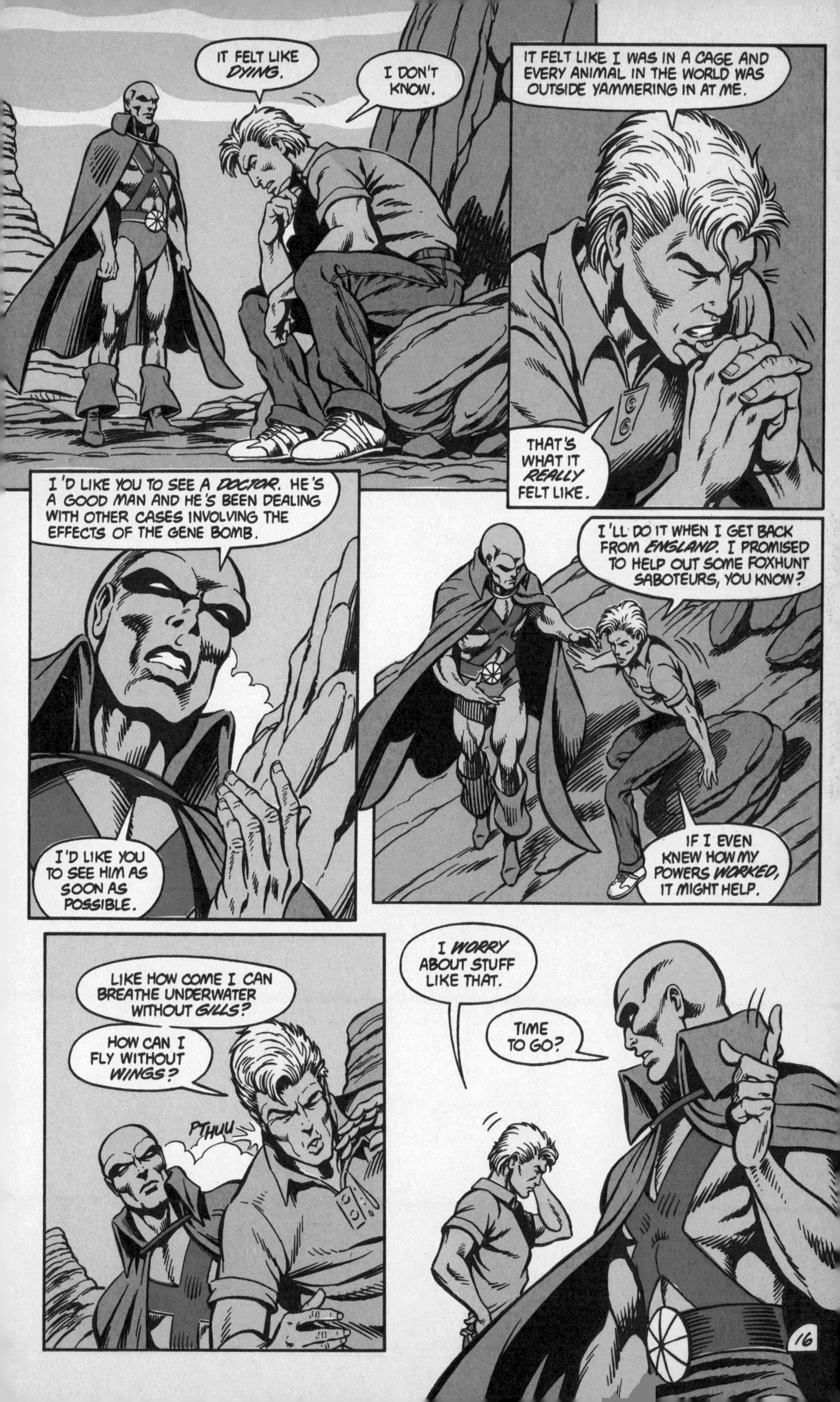
IT FELT LIKE DYING.
I DON'T KNOW.
IT FELT LIKE I WAS IN A CAGE AND EVERY ANIMAL IN THE WORLD WAS OUTSIDE YAMMERING IN AT ME.
THAT'S WHAT IT REALLY FELT LIKE.
I'D LIKE YOU TO SEE A DOCTOR. HE'S A GOOD MAN AND HE'S BEEN DEALING WITH OTHER CASES INVOLVING THE EFFECTS OF THE GENE BOMB.
I'D LIKE YOU TO SEE HIM AS SOON AS POSSIBLE.
I'LL DO IT WHEN I GET BACK FROM ENGLAND. I PROMISED TO HELP OUT SOME FOXHUNT SABOTEURS, YOU KNOW?
IF I EVEN KNEW HOW MY POWERS WORKED, IT MIGHT HELP.
LIKE HOW COME I CAN BREATHE UNDERWATER WITHOUT GILLS?
HOW CAN I FLY WITHOUT WINGS?
PTHUU
I WORRY ABOUT STUFF LIKE THAT.
TIME TO GO?
16

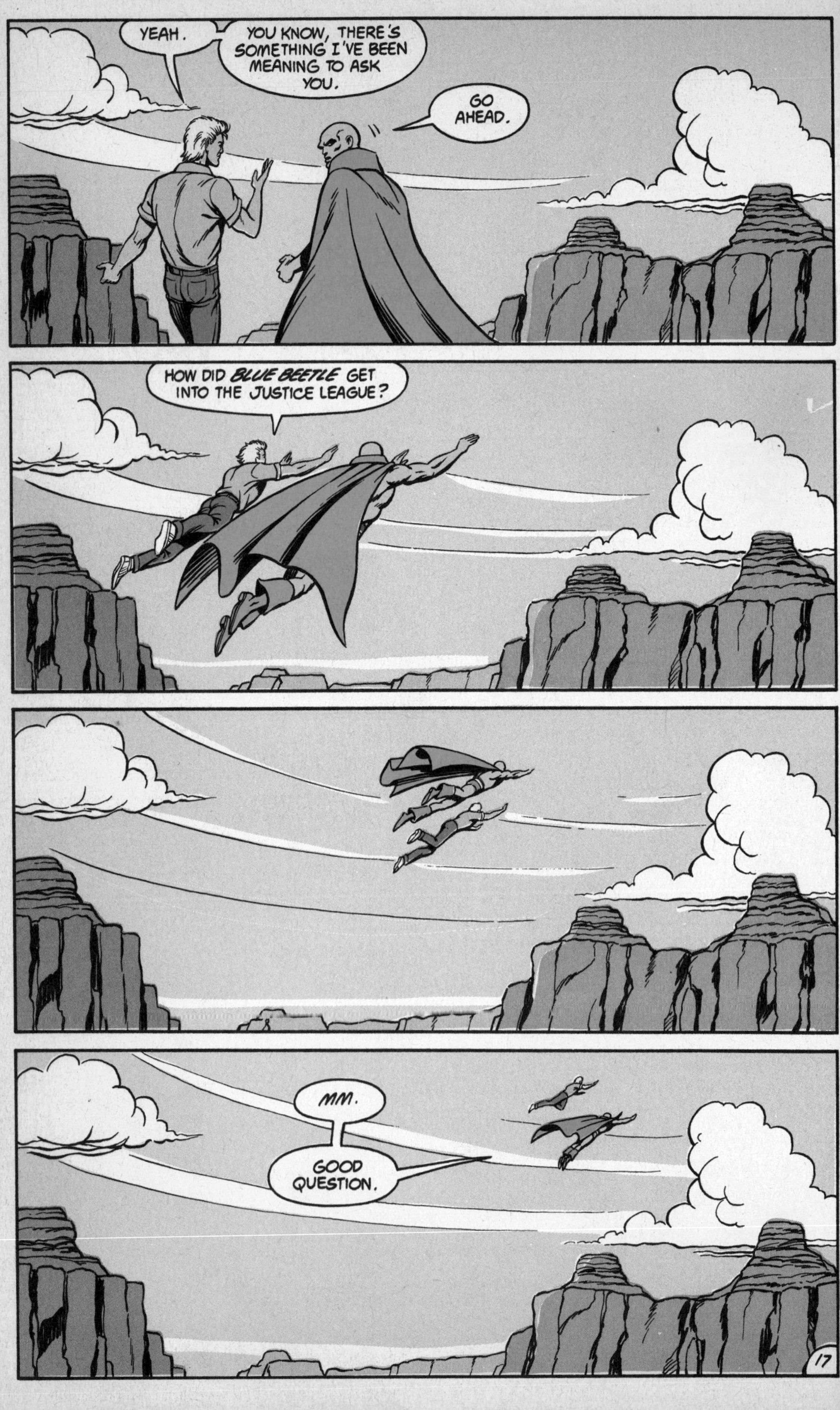

YEAH.
YOU KNOW, THERE'S SOMETHING I'VE BEEN MEANING TO ASK YOU.
GO AHEAD.
HOW DID BLUE BEETLE GET INTO THE JUSTICE LEAGUE?
MM.
GOOD QUESTION.

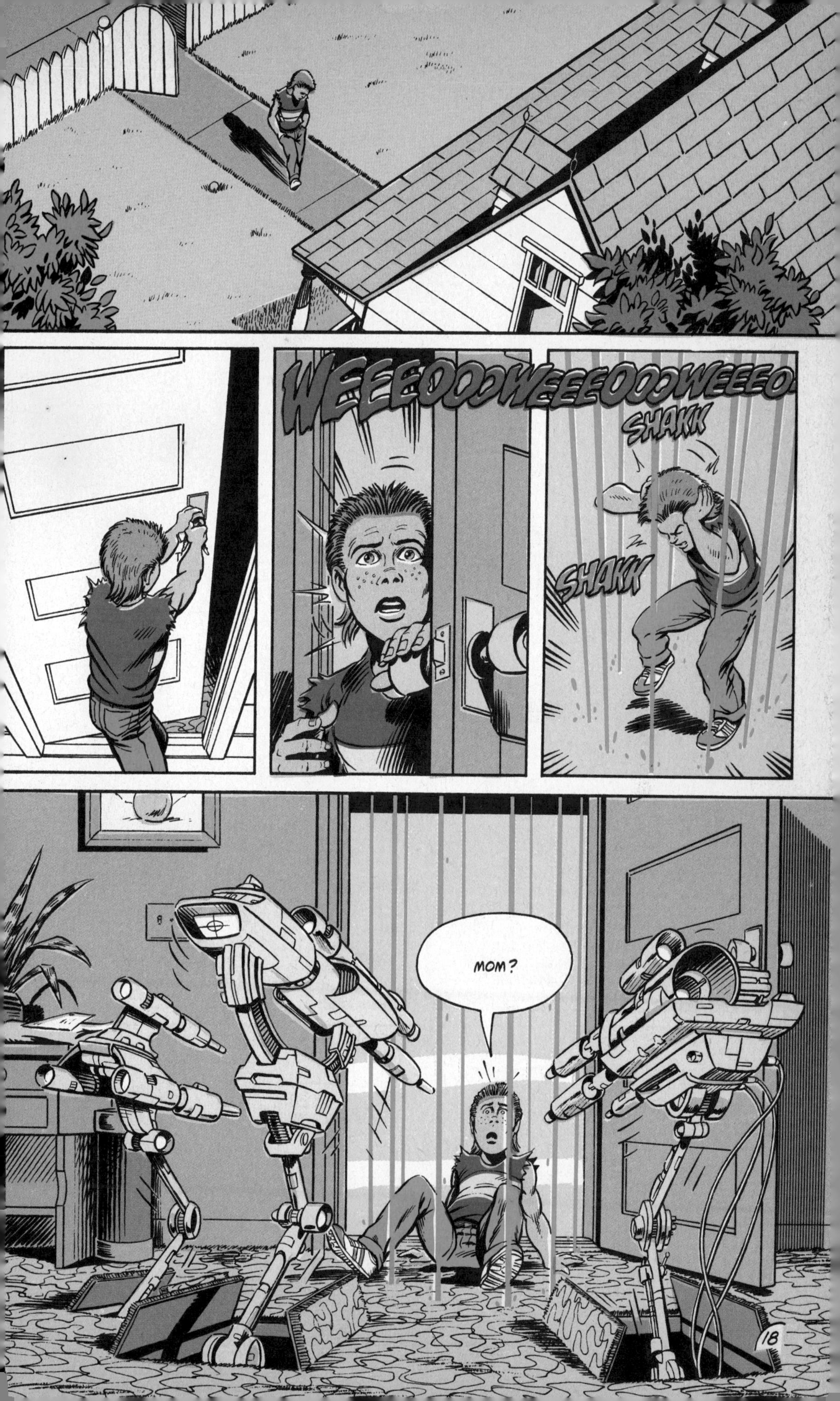
WEEEOOOWEEEOOOWEEEO-
SHAKK
SHAKK
MOM?
18

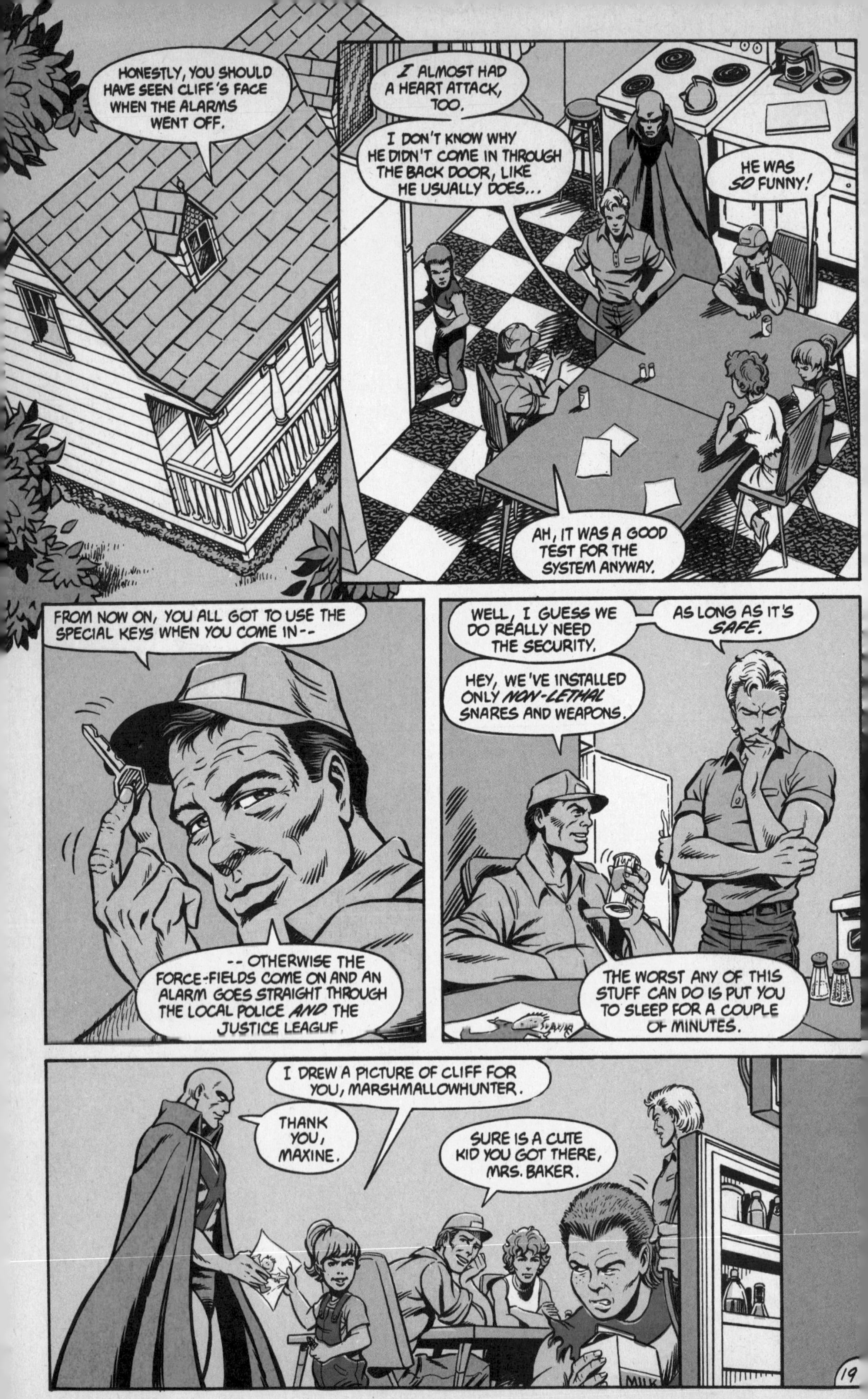

HONESTLY, YOU SHOULD HAVE SEEN CLIFF'S FACE WHEN THE ALARMS WENT OFF.
I ALMOST HAD A HEART ATTACK, TOO.
I DON'T KNOW WHY HE DIDN'T COME IN THROUGH THE BACK DOOR, LIKE HE USUALLY DOES...
HE WAS *SO* FUNNY!
AH, IT WAS A GOOD TEST FOR THE SYSTEM ANYWAY.
FROM NOW ON, YOU ALL GOT TO USE THE SPECIAL KEYS WHEN YOU COME IN--
--OTHERWISE THE FORCE-FIELDS COME ON AND AN ALARM GOES STRAIGHT THROUGH THE LOCAL POLICE *AND* THE JUSTICE LEAGUE.
WELL, I GUESS WE DO REALLY NEED THE SECURITY.
AS LONG AS IT'S *SAFE.*
HEY, WE'VE INSTALLED ONLY *NON-LETHAL* SNARES AND WEAPONS.
THE WORST ANY OF THIS STUFF CAN DO IS PUT YOU TO SLEEP FOR A COUPLE OF MINUTES.
I DREW A PICTURE OF CLIFF FOR YOU, MARSHMALLOWHUNTER.
THANK YOU, MAXINE.
SURE IS A CUTE KID YOU GOT THERE, MRS. BAKER.
MILK

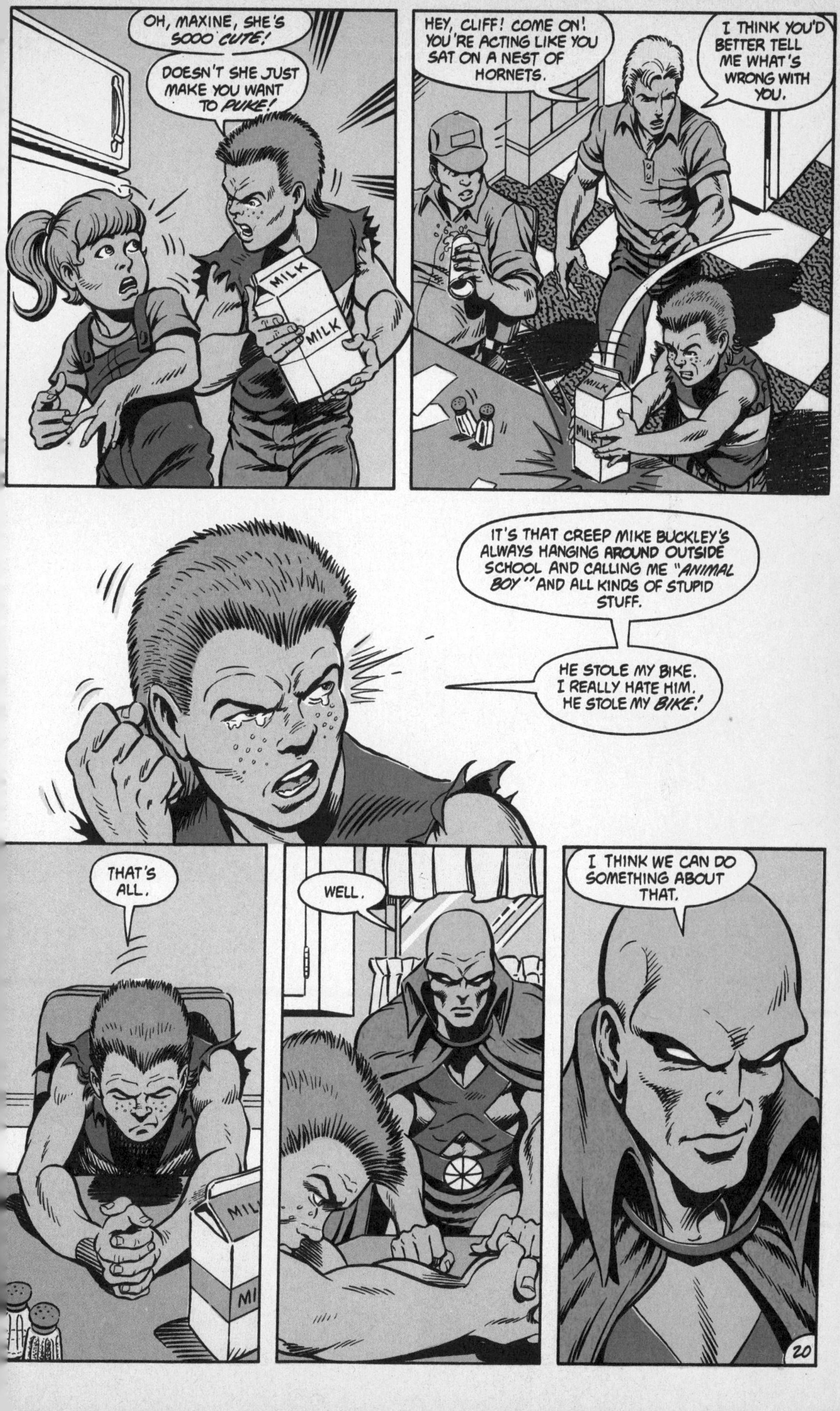
OH, MAXINE, SHE'S SOOO CUTE!
DOESN'T SHE JUST MAKE YOU WANT TO PUKE!
HEY, CLIFF! COME ON! YOU'RE ACTING LIKE YOU SAT ON A NEST OF HORNETS.
I THINK YOU'D BETTER TELL ME WHAT'S WRONG WITH YOU.
MILK
IT'S THAT CREEP MIKE BUCKLEY'S ALWAYS HANGING AROUND OUTSIDE SCHOOL AND CALLING ME "ANIMAL BOY" AND ALL KINDS OF STUPID STUFF.
HE STOLE MY BIKE. I REALLY HATE HIM. HE STOLE MY BIKE!
THAT'S ALL.
WELL.
I THINK WE CAN DO SOMETHING ABOUT THAT.
20

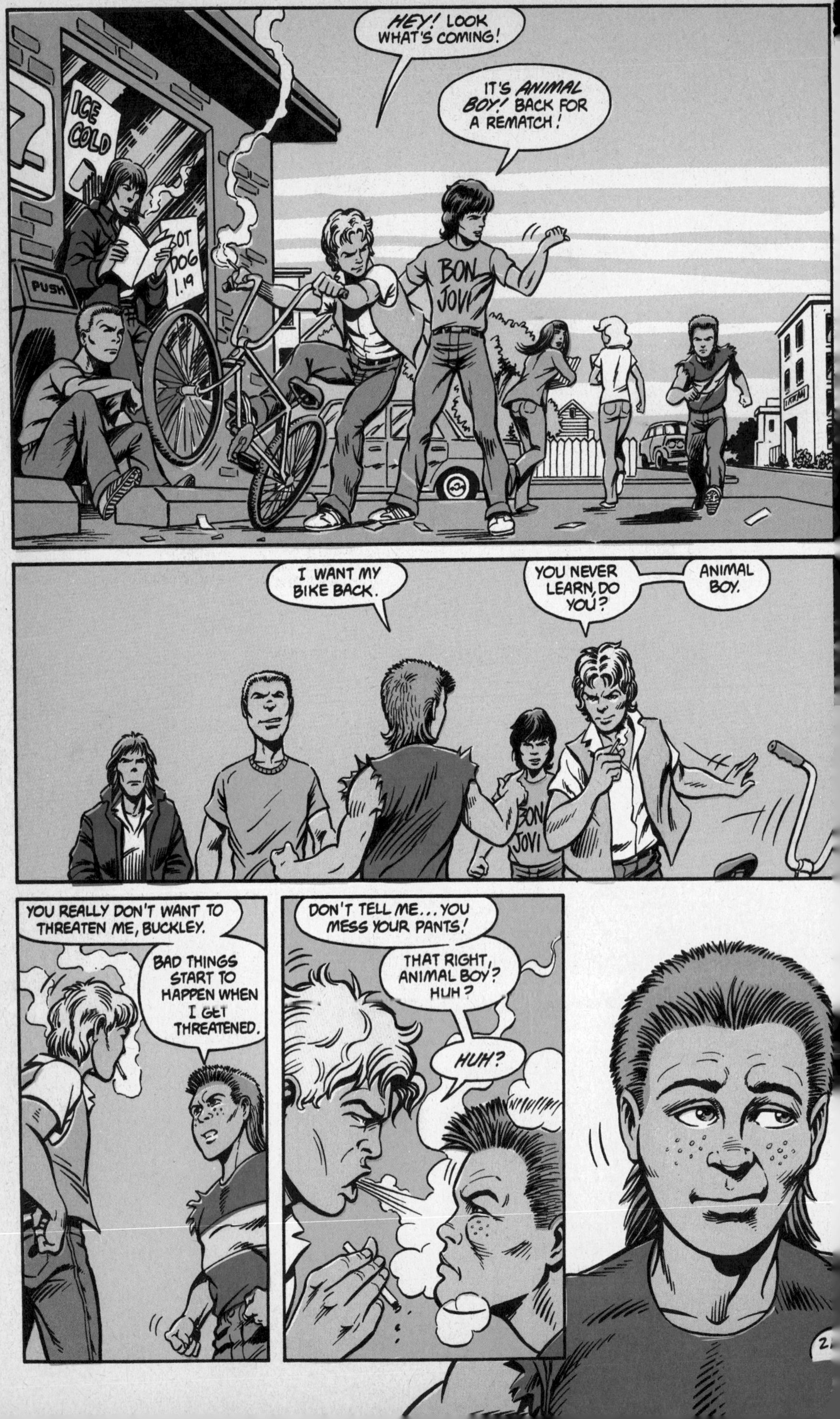
HEY! LOOK WHAT'S COMING!
IT'S ANIMAL BOY! BACK FOR A REMATCH!
ICE COLD
PUSH
BON JOVI
I WANT MY BIKE BACK.
YOU NEVER LEARN, DO YOU?
ANIMAL BOY.
BON JOVI
YOU REALLY DON'T WANT TO THREATEN ME, BUCKLEY.
BAD THINGS START TO HAPPEN WHEN I GET THREATENED.
DON'T TELL ME... YOU MESS YOUR PANTS!
THAT RIGHT, ANIMAL BOY? HUH?
HUH?

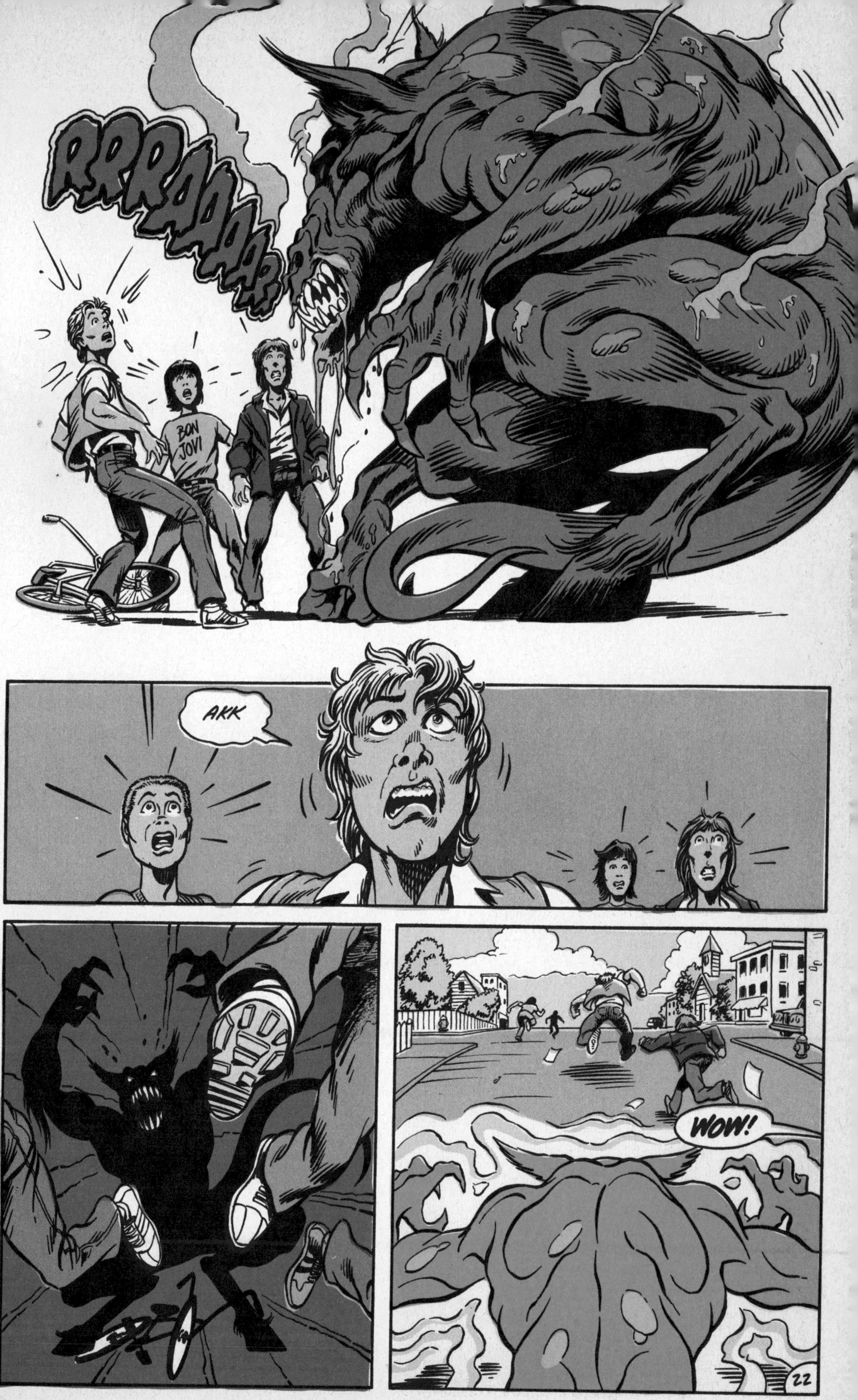
RRRAAAARR
BON JOVI
AKK
WOW!

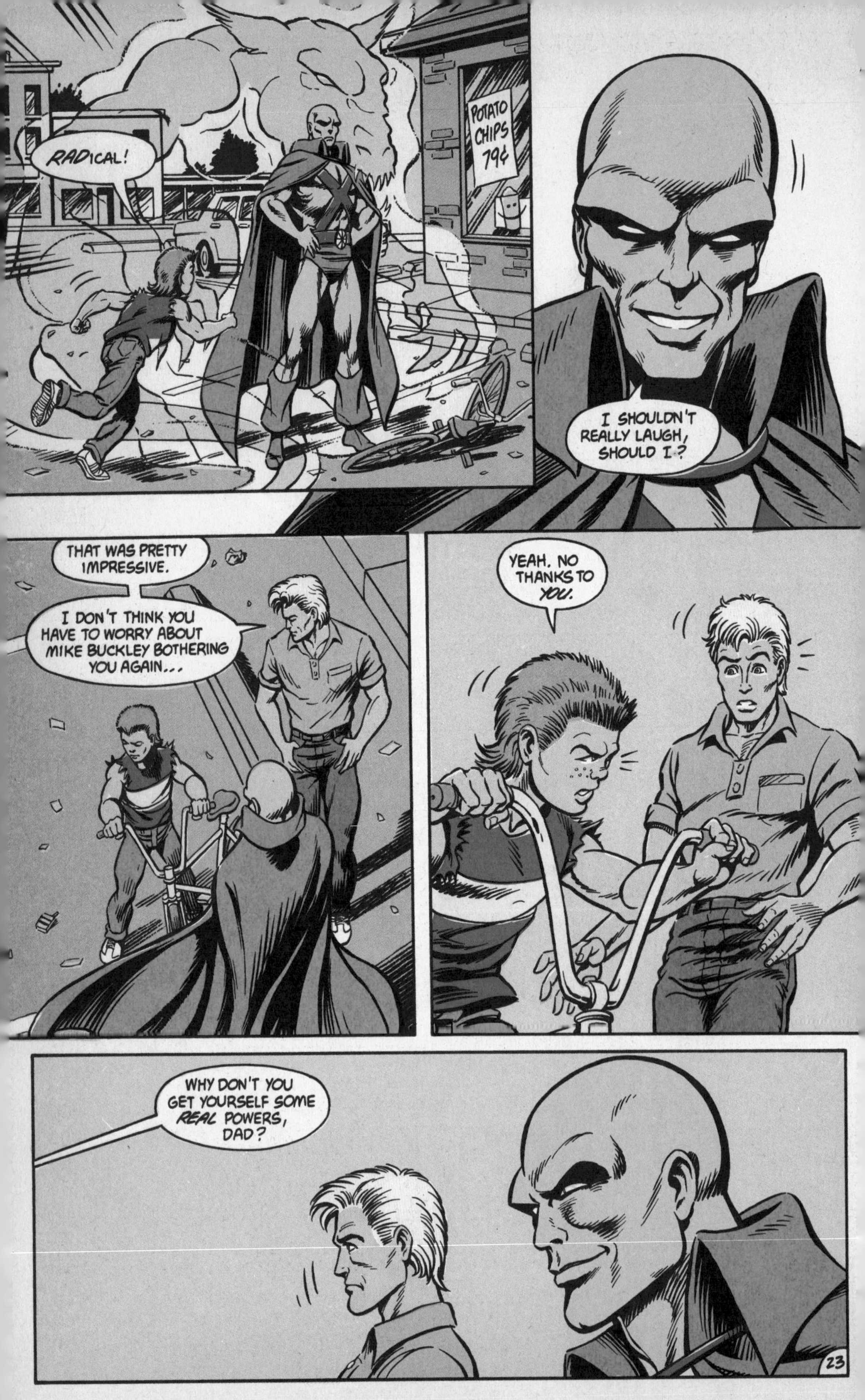
POTATO CHIPS 79¢
RADICAL!
I SHOULDN'T REALLY LAUGH, SHOULD I?
THAT WAS PRETTY IMPRESSIVE.
I DON'T THINK YOU HAVE TO WORRY ABOUT MIKE BUCKLEY BOTHERING YOU AGAIN...
YEAH. NO THANKS TO *YOU*.
WHY DON'T YOU GET YOURSELF SOME *REAL* POWERS, DAD?

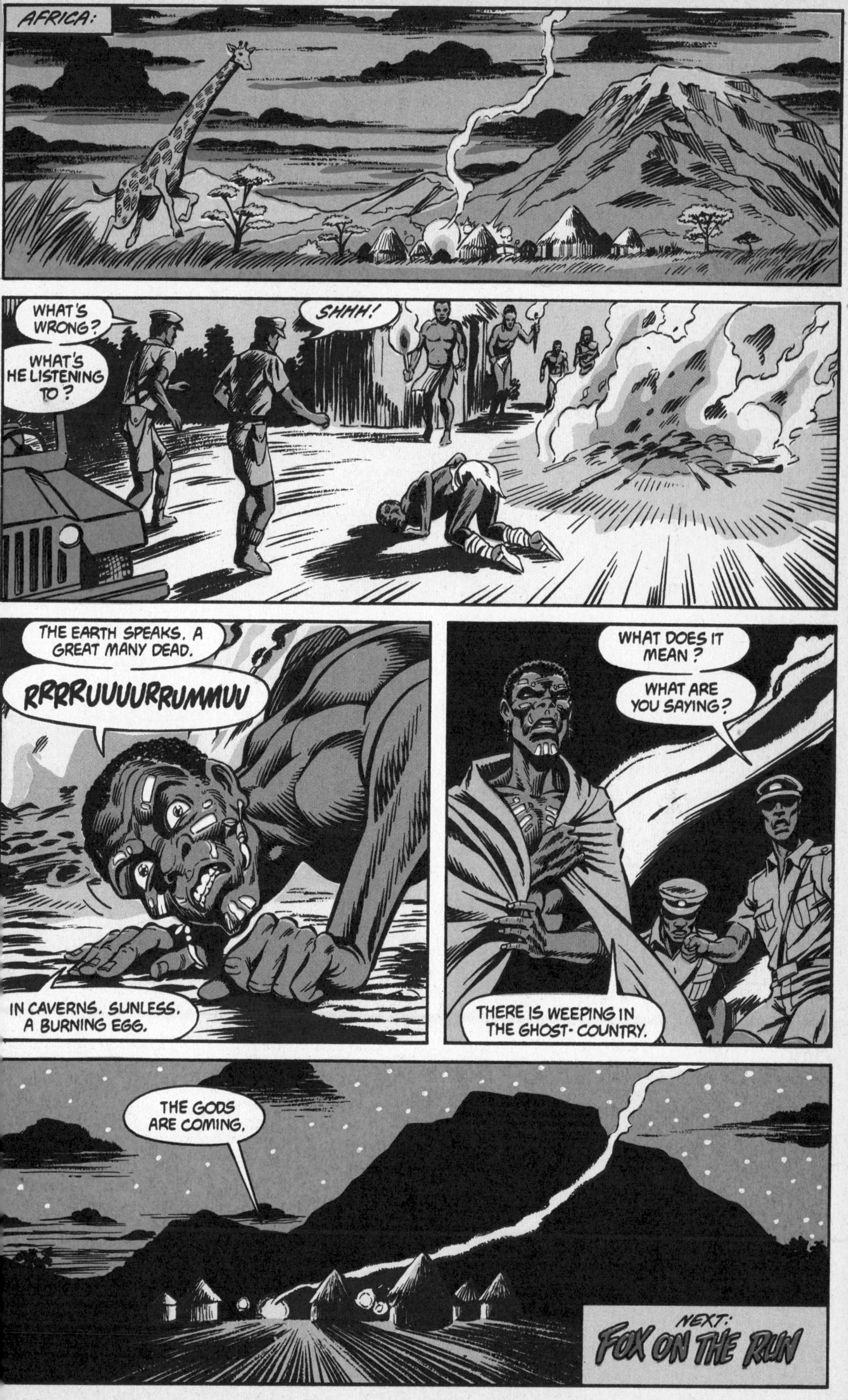
AFRICA:
WHAT'S WRONG?
WHAT'S HE LISTENING TO?
SHHH!
THE EARTH SPEAKS. A GREAT MANY DEAD.
RRRRUUUURRUMMUU
IN CAVERNS. SUNLESS. A BURNING EGG.
WHAT DOES IT MEAN?
WHAT ARE YOU SAYING?
THERE IS WEEPING IN THE GHOST-COUNTRY.
THE GODS ARE COMING.
NEXT:
FOX ON THE RUN

BIOS

GRANT MORRISON'S credits include the groundbreaking
Batman volume ARKHAM ASYLUM; the sort-of-autobiographical *St. Swithin's
Day*; the controversial *New Adventures of Hitler*; two award-winning
plays; and the current, indescribable DOOM PATROL monthly series from
DC. He was born in Scotland in 1778.

CHAS TRUOG pencilled *Coyote* for Epic comics before embark-
ing on his three-year ANIMAL MAN run; his Minnesota farm boyhood
prepared him for an adulthood of drawing animals. Chas holds a BA in
studio art with an emphasis in sculpture. His goal is to produce the
first bas relief comic book.

BRIAN BOLLAND has produced comic art for nearly every
major publisher on both sides of the Atlantic. His previous credits
include CAMELOT 3000 and BATMAN: THE KILLING JOKE for DC, as well as
Judge Dredd and his own creation, *The Bishop and the Actress*. He still
contributes covers to ANIMAL MAN.

DOUG HAZLEWOOD is currently inking ADVENTURES OF SUPER-
MAN. The native Texan's other inking credits include SWAMP THING and
Nick Fury, Agent of S.H.I.E.L.D.

TOM GRUMMETT pencils ADVENTURES OF SUPERMAN and THE NEW
TITANS for DC. He lives in Saskatchewan with his wife, Nancy, and their
two children.

TATJANA WOOD switched careers from dressmaking to comics
coloring and quickly established herself as one of the leading color-
ists in the field. She currently colors ANIMAL MAN and SWAMP THING, as
well as assorted covers.

JOHN COSTANZA entered the comics field in the late '60s,
lettering such groundbreaking series as Denny O'Neil and Neal Adams's
GREEN LANTERN/GREEN ARROW and Jack Kirby's NEW GODS. An accomplished
cartoonist, he is currently developing a line of educational comics
for children.